Access
3613
D1187722

INDO-EUROPEAN SACRED SPACE

TRADITIONS

GENERAL EDITOR

Gregory Nagy
Harvard University

EDITORIAL BOARD

Olga M. Davidson
Wellesley College

Bruce Lincoln
University of Chicago

Alexander Nehamas
Princeton University

A list of books in the series appears at the end of this book.

Indo-European Sacred Space

VEDIC AND ROMAN CULT

ROGER D. WOODARD

LIS - LIBRARY
Date 21.10.10 Fund r
Order No. 2151716
University of Chester

UNIVERSITY OF ILLINOIS PRESS
URBANA AND CHICAGO

© 2006 by the Board of Trustees
of the University of Illinois
All rights reserved
Manufactured in the United States of America
∞ This book is printed on acid-free paper.

C 5 4 3 2 1

Library of Congress Cataloging-in-Publication Data
Woodard, Roger D.
Indo-European sacred space : Vedic and Roman cult / Roger D. Woodard.
p. cm. -- (Traditions)
Includes bibliographical references (p.) and index.
ISBN-13: 978-0-252-02988-2 (isbn 13 cloth : alk. paper)
ISBN-10: 0-252-02988-7 (isbn 10 cloth : alk. paper)
1. Indo-Europeans--Religion. 2. Rome--Religion. 3. India--Religion.
4. Mythology, Roman. 5. Mythology, Indic. 6. Sacred space.
I. Title. II. Series: Traditions (Urbana, Ill.)
BL660.W66 2006
200'.89'09--dc22 2005017055

To the memory of
James Wilson Poultney
Colleague, Mentor, Friend

CONTENTS

PREFACE

Indo-European Sacred Space is a work about two particular bounded spaces—one small, one great—used in the practice of the ancestral Indo-European religion. The focus of the study falls squarely upon the reflexes of those spaces as they survived in two Indo-European descendent cultures, one lying on the western margin of the area of Indo-European expansion in antiquity, the other on the eastern. In the west, the small cultic ground survives as the space of urban Rome, bounded by the pomerium; and the large, as the vast arena which lies between the pomerium and the distal boundary of the Ager Romanus. Comparable spaces, of common origin, are found within the cult of Vedic India; and as on other occasions, the well-attested Vedic structures and usages have much to reveal about Roman cult.

Both in terms of scholarly history and theory, my starting point for this investigation is Georges Dumézil's model of Roman religion, developed vis-à-vis the overarching threefold ideology of Proto-Indo-European society. One of the objectives of the present work is thus to present a clear and concise summary of Dumézil's arguments for the survival of ancient Indo-European ideology in early Roman religion; this is the principal, but not exclusive, focus of chapter 1. A second and more important objective is to jump forward from that Dumézilian platform and to offer a new understanding of Roman and, more generally, primitive Indo-European religious structures and phenomena; one that goes beyond and, in some instances, differs appreciably from Dumézil's own interpretations. The work which is presented herein therefore marks a beginning—certainly not a fait accompli.

Dumézil is not the only eminent twentieth-century scholar of the classical and Indo-European disciplinae with whom this work is connected. Another is my former Johns Hopkins colleague, James Wilson Poultney. It is as a dedication to the memory of his life, his friendship, and his always uncompromising standards of scholarly excellence that I offer this work, and but hope it to be a suitable offering.

ACKNOWLEDGMENTS

Many are those to whom I am indebted for assistance, advice, and support in the preparation of this work. All cannot be named, but I would be remiss not to express special thanks to a few: to Gregory Nagy, editor of this series, for his friendship and support; to Willis Regier and his staff at the University of Illinois Press, for their excellent professionalism and guidance; to Chris Dadian of the Center for Hellenic Studies for his invaluable aid with the manuscript; to N. J. Allen of the Institute of Social and Cultural Anthropology at Oxford University, for his wisdom, expertise, and much more; to my collaborator A. J. Boyle and Penguin Books for their kind permission to utilize translations from our *Ovid: Fasti* (2004). My indebtedness to Katherine and Paul far exceeds what mere words of mortal tongue can convey.

I wish also to express my heartfelt appreciation to the College of Arts and Sciences at the University of Buffalo for generously providing a subsidy to support the publication of this work.

INDO-EUROPEAN SACRED SPACE

CHAPTER 1

The Minor Capitoline Triad

1.1 INTRODUCTION

This first chapter lays a foundation for the rest of the book that follows. Much, therefore, of what appears in chapter 1 is review and restatement, but with some new ideas and interpretations applied. Even among the old ideas, however, some concepts and methods will likely be unfamiliar to a subset of readers. These include basic notions about the tripartition of Proto-Indo-European society—ideas readily associated with, among other scholars, Émile Benveniste and Georges Dumézil. The latter author's interpretation of the survival of a prehistoric tripartite ideology in the attested mythic and religious systems of various Indo-European peoples of antiquity is also fundamental here, and the Romans are the most notable of these ancient peoples for the present chapter. We will examine the evidence for a Pre-Capitoline triad (following Wissowa), Dumézil's interpretation of that triad vis-à-vis Indo-European ideology, and its replacement by the Capitoline triad.

1.2 THE FOUNDING OF THE CAPITOLIUM

That Greek historian of Rome, Dionysius of Halicarnassus, tells us that the monarch Tarquinius Priscus, at war with the Sabines, vowed to Jupiter the building of a great temple (*Ant. Rom.* 3.69.1–2).[1] The vow was not, however, fulfilled in his lifetime; it fell to his eventual successor, Tarquinius Superbus, to lay the foundations and build upon them the opulent temple of Jupiter Optimus Maximus (though Livy [1.38.7] asserts that the foundations had been laid by the elder Tarquinius). Tarquinius Superbus would not himself see the temple finished, continues Dionysius; not until three years after the king's expulsion would the project be brought to completion by the consuls who then held office.[2]

In order to determine the proper location for Jupiter's new temple, Tarquinius[3] summoned Augures, and these divined that the structure was to be built upon the Capitoline hill. That hill, however, was already cluttered with altars dedicated to many other deities; so the Augures took further auspices to determine whether the various divinities concerned would be amenable to having their own altars removed from that space for the construction of Jupiter's temple. All the gods were willing except two: Juventas, goddess of the *iuvenes*, and Terminus, god of boundaries—both refused to budge, in spite of much entreaty on the part of the Augures (*Ant. Rom.* 3.69.3–5).[4] Consequently, altars to each were in the end incorporated with-

[1]The author wishes to express his appreciation to *Arethusa* and the Johns Hopkins University Press for allowing the incorporation of some ideas and elements from Woodard (2002) into the present work.

[2]With regard to Livy's record of a two-stage building program, it is interesting to note Holloway's (1994) remarks concerning the size of the blocks in the temple's foundations. Beginning with the twelfth of the fifteen courses of the foundations, the tuffa blocks become 8 to 10 cm thicker, leading Holloway (p. 8) to suggest the hypothesis of an interrupted construction project. If the foundations themselves were laid in two stages, a reasonable harmonizing of the discrepancy of Dionysius and Livy (and their annalistic sources) on this point becomes possible (the foundation was begun by the elder Tarquin and finished by the younger, who then continued with construction of the temple). Holloway, however, courts the notion of these temple foundations being early fourth century; he notes the existence in the early fourth century of one Marcus Horatius, a military tribune (Livy 6.31.2, 5), and tentatively suggests that some inscriptional record of his name might be the source of the tradition that it was the consul Marcus Horatius Pulvillus (Livy 2. 8.6–8) who dedicated the temple in the early days of the Republic. These foundations would hence be much later than the period of the Tarquins. Concerning this "behemoth among the temples of Etruria and Latium" (p. 8), he writes, "The project for the temple may well belong to the kings of the sixth century. But even so, their resources were not sufficient to carry the work forward" (p. 10). For the present work it matters little how large a temple appeared when.

[3]Dionysius identifies the king at the time as Tarquinius Priscus (*Ant. Rom.* 3.69.3), Livy (1.55.1) as Tarquinius Superbus.

[4]Livy mentions only Terminus in his description of the taking of the auspices; see 1.55.3–5. Later, however, in his presentation of the speech of Camillus, he refers to

in the new temple of Jupiter Optimus Maximus. The obstinacy of the two deities was interpreted as an omen of Rome's longevity, political integrity, and vitality; Dionysius of Halicarnassus (*Ant. Rom.* 3.69.6) records:[5]

> . . . ἐκ δὲ τούτου συνέβαλον οἱ μάντεις ὅτι τῆς Ῥωμαίων πόλεως οὔτε τοὺς ὅρους μετακινήσει καιρὸς οὐθεὶς οὔτε τὴν ἀκμὴν μεταβαλεῖ

> . . . and from this the Augures determined that nothing would ever bring about either the disruption of the boundaries of the Roman city or the loss of its vitality.

Drawing on Varro, St. Augustine (*De Civ. D.* 4.23, 29) preserves the tradition that three deities refused to be ousted: Terminus, Juventas, and Mars. St. Augustine's testimony regarding the inclusion of the war god in this set is important, and we shall return to the significance of this matter in §1.11.

Yet a second omen would reveal itself in conjunction with the preparations for building Jupiter's new temple, one which reinforced the Augures' findings. The account of Dionysius (*Ant. Rom.* 4.59.1–61.4) runs as follows. As the foundations of the temple were being dug, deep in the ground the workmen uncovered a man's head, which appeared to have been freshly severed, with all features intact and warm blood still draining from it. The meaning of the portent escaping the Roman seers, Tarquinius sent a delegation to consult the most skilled of their Etruscan counterparts (see §1.9.1.2). After extended divinatory posturing, the recruited Etruscan seer interpreted the omen to mean that Rome would become the *head* of all Italy (cf. Livy 1.55.5–7). The hill on which the head (*caput*) was found, having formerly been called *Tarpeian*, was now renamed *Capitoline* (Varro, *Ling.* 41).

1.3 TERMINUS AND JUVENTAS

Georges Dumézil has argued that the affiliation of the intractable gods Juventas and Terminus with Capitoline Jupiter is one of deep antiquity (see *ARR*: 200–203). Dumézil proposes that Juventas and Terminus represent the Roman counterparts of those deities known among the Indo-Aryans as Aryaman and Bhaga, close companions of the great god Mitra, who, like

---

the unwillingness of both Terminus and Juventas to move (5.54.7). Livy identifies the condemned sacred structures as *fana sacellaque* vowed by the Sabine ruler Titus Tatius as he fought Romulus (1.55.2).

[5] Dionysius of Halicarnassus, *Ant. Rom.* 3.69.6. See also Livy 1.55.3–4; Florus, *Epit.* 1.7.9; Augustine, *De Civ. D.* 4.29.

Jupiter, is a god of sovereignty. Aryaman is the "spirit of the Arya," the god of Aryan society; Bhaga is the deity who sees that society's goods are rightly divided among society's members. The relationship is one of Pre-Indo-Aryan date; in Dumézil's words: "Zoroastrian transpositions guarantee the antiquity of this structure, the meaning of which is clear: the great sovereign god has two adjuncts, one of whom cares for the persons constituting society, the other for the goods which they share" (*ARR*: 201).[6]

Like Aryaman, Roman Juventas, contends Dumézil, is chiefly concerned with the constituency of society: she "controls the entry of men into society and protects them while they are of the age most important to the state, while they are *iuvenes* . . ." (*ARR*: 202). Like Bhaga, Roman Terminus protects the individual's share of society's holdings—though not portions of the movable property of a pastoralist society, but the parcels of bounded property of a land-owning society. Writes Ovid of Terminus: "Without you all lands would be disputed, . . . You guard entrusted lands with pledge of law" (*Fasti* 2.660, 662).

Dumézil's identification of the Roman triad Jupiter-Juventas-Terminus with Indo-Aryan Mitra-Aryaman-Bhaga is enticing and well argued, and at first blush seems quite natural in light of other Indo-Aryan / Roman cultic parallels.[7] Yet there are unsettling elements in the comparison. To begin with, one aspect of the structure quite readily presents itself as problematic—namely, the character of Terminus.

1.4 THE GODS OF TITUS TATIUS

Dumézil perceived that the hallmark of Proto-Indo-European society was its tripartite nature—a society structuring itself into three *functions*, to utilize his terminology: the first function being that of religion, magic, and sovereignty; the second function that of physical force; the third function that of goods production and fecundity (for a discussion of Dumézil's three functions as evidenced by early Indo-European cultures, see §§1.6–1.7 below). Dumézil also recognized that in the tripartite ideology inherited by the Roman descendants of the Proto-Indo-Europeans, the third function deities manifest themselves as the so-called gods of Titus Tatius, the Sabine

[6] For detailed discussion of the affiliation of Aryaman and Bhaga with Mitra, see Dumézil 1986: 86–114. On the "Zoroastrian transpositions" see ibid., pp. 138–146.

[7] And one which the present author has previously endorsed; see Boyle and Woodard 2000: 201–202.

king who became co-regent with Romulus following the Sabine War.[8] Varro (*Ling.* 5.74) enumerates these for us:

> Ops, Flora, Vediouis, Saturnus, Sol, Luna, Volcanus, Summanus, Larunda, Terminus, Quirinus, Vortumnus, the Lares, Diana, and Lucina.

Dionysius of Halicarnassus (*Ant. Rom.* 2.50.3) provides an abbreviated list, with the names of course Hellenized:

> Helios, Selene, Cronus, Rhea, Hestia, Hephaestus, Artemis, and Enyalius.

He adds that the list could be extended, but the remaining deities have names which are difficult to translate into Greek. Dionysius identifies these as the gods to whom Tatius dedicated ἱερά 'temples' and βωμοί 'altars', having so vowed in battle.[9] A partial list is also offered by St. Augustine (*De Civ. D.* 4.23), who says that among still others, Titus Tatius established as gods:

> Saturn, Ops, Sol, Luna, Volcanus, Lux, and Cluacina.

Augustine prefaces this list with an enumeration of those gods he identifies as introduced by Romulus: Janus, Jupiter, Mars, Picus, Faunus, Tiberinus, Hercules, *et si quos alios*.

Regarding these "gods of Titus Tatius" (and referring specifically to Varro's list, noting it to be "composite" and "in part anachronistic") Dumézil writes: " . . . these gods share among themselves the portions, the dependencies, and the appendages of the domain of prosperity and fertility [that is, the third function], and Quirinus [a member of the Pre-Capitoline triad; see below] is only one member of this great family" (*ARR*: 170).

The problem posed by Terminus is an obvious one. On the one hand, Terminus seems to be closely affiliated with Jupiter, matching Bhaga in his relationship to Mitra, both members of the *first function* of divine society. On the other hand, Terminus is counted among the "gods of Titus Tatius," members of the *third function* of divine society. It seems that nowhere in the great body of his superb scholarship did Professor Dumézil address this problem (let alone attempt a resolution of it). If, however, we begin with

[8]The designation "gods of Titus Tatius" is of course a conventionalization. Dumézil is quick to point out that his use of the term is theological and does not suggest any historical reality linking these deities to a Sabine named Titus Tatius (or to any other person); see *ARR*: 169–170, n. 34.

[9]See note above on Livy's identification of the altars cluttering the Capitoline as vowed by Tatius.

the default position that, as Varro informs us, Terminus is a "god of Titus Tatius"—a deity of the third function—then a solution presents itself, as we shall see in §1.10 and beyond. First, however, we must consider that ancient triad of chief Roman deities to which another of the "gods of Titus Tatius" belongs.

1.5 THE PRE-CAPITOLINE TRIAD

When the temple of Jupiter Optimus Maximus was built (or begun) upon the Capitoline hill in the reign of the Etruscan Tarquins, it was much more than just an ambitious building project. In effect, it marked the occurrence of a religious revolution in which one set of preeminent gods was exchanged for another.

The ancient, or Pre-Capitoline, Roman triad of chief deities consisted of Jupiter, Mars, and Quirinus. Wissowa (1971: 23, 131–134) saw this clearly and Dumézil brought it into sharper focus. There survives a record of various archaic rites and structures revealing the preeminent position of these three deities and of the three priests who served them. The evidence is nicely summarized in *Archaic Roman Religion* (pp. 141–147) and is presented below in modified form.

1.5.1 The ordo sacerdotum

First of all, there is the matter of the identity and hierarchical order of the chief Roman priests. Festus (p. 185M) provides us with a relative ranking (and his interpretation of the reason for the order). At the top is the Rex Sacrorum, followed in descending sequence by the Flamen Dialis (the priest of *Jupiter*), the Flamen Martialis (the priest of *Mars*), the Flamen Quirinalis (the priest of *Quirinus*), and, finally, the Pontifex Maximus. This is also the order of their seating at feasts, and these things are so, in the view of Festus, because the Rex Sacrorum is the most influential; the Flamen Dialis is the priest of the entire *mundus* (the *Dium*); the Flamen Martialis has Mars, the father of Rome's founder, as his god; the Flamen Quirinalis, because Quirinus was acquired from Cures (the Sabine city of Titus Tatius) to be affiliated with the Roman Empire; and the Pontifex Maximus, since he is both judge and arbiter in divine as well as human affairs:

> Maximus videtur Rex, dein Dialis, post hunc Martialis, quarto loco Quirinalis, quinto pontifex maximus. Itaque in soliis Rex supra omnis accumbat licet; Dialis supra Martialem, et Quirinalem; Martialis supra

> proximum; omnes item supra pontificem. Rex, quia potentissimus: Dialis, quia universi mundi sacerdos, qui appellatur Dium; Martialis, quod Mars conditoris urbis parens; Quirinalis, socio imperii Romani Curibus ascito Quirino; pontifex maximus, quod iudex atque arbiter habetur rerum divinarum humanarumque.

As Wissowa observed, the ranking of the various Roman priests departs notably from actual power structures as they existed by the late Republic and so must reflect an archaic hierarchy.

The Flamines are members of an ancient priesthood.[10] In addition to the three Flamines Maiores to whom Festus refers in the above text—those of Jupiter, Mars, and Quirinus—there existed twelve others, the Flamines Minores. The duties of the latter group are obscure, as are indeed some of the gods whom they serve. Festus reports not only the above-noted hierarchy of principal priests, but a hierarchical arrangement of the fifteen Flamines themselves, unfortunately naming only those occupying the top and bottom positions, the Flamen Dialis and the Flamen Pomonalis respectively. The Flamen of Pomona, the Italian goddess of fruits, is the lowest ranking of all Flamines, according to Festus, because his deity presides over the most delicate (*levissimus*) of all produce (Festus p. 155M). Of the twelve Flamines Minores we know the identity of only ten: the Flamines Carmentalis, Ceriales, Portunalis, Volcanalis, Volturnalis, Palatualis, Furrinalis, Floralis, Falacer, and the aforementioned Pomonalis. The last six are cited by Varro (*Ling.* 7.45, after Ennius) with the Flamen Pomonalis again appearing last, perhaps suggesting that Varro's short list also preserves a ranking.[11]

1.5.2 The devotio

The second piece of evidence pointing to the archaic preeminence of the Jupiter-Mars-Quirinus triad is the formula of *devotio*, the Roman practice of a military commander sacrificially offering both himself and the enemy forces which he faces to the goddess Tellus and the infernal di Manes. Livy

[10] If Latin *flamen* is not strictly a linguistic cognate of Sanskrit *brahman*, the two priests, Roman and Indo-Aryan, likely still have a common historical antecedent in early Indo-European times. See Dumézil's comments at *ARR*: 580, n. 7, with references to his earlier work on the relationship between the two priests.

[11] For Dumézil's sensible rebuttal of Latte's (1960) revisionist interpretation of the Flamines, see *ARR*: 102–112. Latte seeks generally and unconvincingly to dismantle the evidence for an archaic divine triad composed of Jupiter, Mars, and Quirinus. For Dumézil's counterarguments see the analysis of *ARR*: 141–147 with references to additional discussion.

(8.9.1–14) records the formula in his account of the suicidal charge of the consul Publius Decius Mus into the ranks of the Latini (340 BC). At the instruction of a Pontifex present on the battlefield, Decius quickly performs the appropriate ritual and recites the following:

> Iane, Iuppiter, Mars pater, Quirine, Bellona, Lares, divi Novensiles, di Indigetes, divi quorum est potestas nostrorum hostiumque, dique Manes, vos precor veneror, veniam peto oroque uti populo Romano Quiritium vim victoriam prosperetis, hostesque populi Romani Quiritium terrore formidine morteque adficiatis. Sicut verbis nuncupavi, ita pro re publica populi Romani Quiritium, exercitu legionibus auxiliis populi Romani Quiritium, legiones auxiliaque hostium mecum deis Manibus Tellurique devoveo.
>
> Janus, *Jupiter*, father *Mars*, *Quirinus*, Bellona, Lares, di Novensiles, di Indigites, gods who hold power over both us and our enemies, and di Manes, you I entreat and worship, your favor I beg and plead, that to the Roman people of the Quirites you would bring strength and victory, and that the enemies of the Roman people of the Quirites you would afflict with terror, horror, and death. As I have spoken these words, so for the Republic of the Roman people of the Quirites, for the army, the legions, the auxiliaries of the Roman people of the Quirites, both the legions and the auxiliaries of the enemy with myself I devote to the di Manes and to Tellus.

As is customary, Janus, god of beginnings, is the first god ritually invoked. The three major deities then called on are those of the three Flamines Maiores—Jupiter, Mars, and Quirinus.[12]

1.5.3 The spolia opima

On rarely attested occasions, beginning with Romulus according to Livy (1.10.4–7) and Plutarch (*Rom.* 16.5–8; see also Propertius 4.10), a Roman commander would make ritual offering of the spoils of an enemy leader whom he had killed in personal combat; such spoils are the *spolia opima*. In the detailed, if fragmented, account of the ritual which Festus (p. 189M) provides, citing Varro and the *Books of the Pontifices*, the *spolia opima* are said to have been offered to three different deities (not just to Jupiter Feretrius,

[12]On the *di Novensiles* (*Novensides*) and *di Indigites*, see Wissowa 1971: 18–23, and the corrective of *ARR*: 14. For a recent brief summary with bibliography of the vexing problem of the identity of these, see also the respective entries in the *Oxford Classical Dictionary*, 3rd ed., pp. 755, 1051. On the formula of the *devotio*, see further *ARR*: 93–96.

who alone is mentioned by Livy and Plutarch). Festus writes of the offering of *prima spolia*, in which an ox is the specified victim; of *secunda spolia*, involving the *solitaurilia* (that is, *suovetaurilia*—from *sus*, *ovis*, and *taurus*—a sacrifice of a boar, a ram, and a bull; see §3.3.3.1); and of *tertia spolia*, with a lamb as the victim. All three are to be made on behalf of the state. Making further reference to a Law of Numa Pompilius,[13] Festus adds that the *prima spolia* are offered to Jupiter Feretrius, the *secunda* to Mars, and the *tertia* to Janus Quirinus; the affiliation of Janus with Quirinus is not uncommon, as in Augustus, *RG* 13.[14]

1.5.4 *The archaic ritual of Fides*

Numa Pompilius, second king of Rome (third if one counts Titus Tatius, Romulus' short-lived co-regent), was a monarch famed for his pious devotion to the gods, for his establishment of Roman priestly offices and holy days, for the order and justice which he brought to Roman society, and for his peaceful reign. Dionysius of Halicarnassus (*Ant. Rom.* 2.75.2–3) records that Numa considered the most sacred of all deities to be Fides (Πίστις, 'Good Faith') and so built for her a temple—her first—and established sacrifices for her. Similarly, Plutarch (*Numa* 16.1) notes that Numa was the first to build temples to Fides and Terminus.

Livy, in his description of Numa's sacred administrations, tells us that the king himself performed many priestly functions, but wisely foreseeing that his sovereign successors would be too occupied with making war to devote ample time to their sacred responsibilities, he founded numerous priestly offices for the performance of those tasks. Livy enumerates these: (i) the Flamen Dialis, who inherited many of Numa's duties (1.20.1–2); (ii) the Flamen Martialis and Flamen Quirinalis (1.20.3); (iii) the Vestal Virgins (1.20.3–4); (iv) the Salii of Mars Gradivus (1.20.4); and (v) the office of the Pontifex (1.20.5–7). After then mentioning Numa's establishment of the altar of Jupiter Elicius and the grove of the Camenae (those nymphs associated with the spring by the Porta Capena from which the Vestal Virgins

[13]Numa, writes Plutarch (*Numa* 22.2–5), had been buried with twelve books of the Pontifices and twelve volumes of Greek philosophy. These were recovered when, in the consulship of Publius Cornelius and Marcus Baebius, heavy rains disturbed the burial. Upon examination of the books and in consultation with the senate, the praetor Q. Petillius Spurinus determined that the information they contained ought not become public, and so they were burned in the Comitium (181 BC).

[14]On Janus Quirinus see *ARR*: 265–266; Boyle and Woodard 2000: 301. For further discussion of the three *spolia opima* vis-à-vis the Pre-Capitoline triad, and interpretation of Festus' remarks, see *ARR*: 166–168.

drew water, and of whom Numa's wife Egeria was said to be one), Livy (1.21.4) goes on to describe the annual ritual that Numa instituted for Fides (see also Servius, *Aen.* 1.292):

> Ad id sacrarium flamines bigis curru arcuato vehi iussit, manuque ad digitos usque involuta rem divinam facere, significantes fidem tutandam sedemque eius etiam in dexteris sacratam esse.
>
> He ordered the Flamines to travel to her shrine in a hooded carriage drawn by a twin team, and to sacrifice with the hand covered right up to the fingers, signifying that Faith must be kept inviolate and that her seat is sacred even [hidden] within the right hand.

The "Flamines" who conduct this archaic ritual are not specified. Livy's silence on their identity, however, comes directly after his attributing to Numa the founding of the offices of the three Flamines Maiores; this concatenation almost certainly reveals the officiating clergy to have been those three major priests—the Flamines of Jupiter, Mars, and Quirinus.

The archaic nature of Fides' ritual is assured by an Umbrian parallel. The Iguvium bronze tablets record a sacrifice offered by the priestly sodality of the *Frater Atiieřiur* (the Atiedian Brothers) to the deity Fisus Sancius (table VIb3–5; text and translation from Poultney 1959: 252):

> Post uerir tesenocir sif filiu trif fetu fiso sansie ocrifer fisiu totaper iiouina poni feitu persae fetu aruio fetu / surur naratu pusi pre uerir treblanir tases persnimu mandraclo difue destre habitu prosesetir ficla / strušla arsueitu.
>
> Behind the Tesenacan Gate he shall sacrifice three suckling pigs to Fisus Sancius for the Fisian Mount, for the state of Iguvium. He shall sacrifice with mead, perform [the sacrifice] upon the ground, offer grain, recite the same formulas as before the Trebulan Gate, pray silently, have a maniple folded double upon his right hand, and add to the parts cut off a *ficla* cake and a *strušla* cake.

The god to whom the Umbrian priest offers this sacrifice, Fisus Sancius, has a name which is clearly etymologically linked to that of Latin Fides and is then transparently "a protector of oaths and solemn pledges" (see Poultney 1959: 252–253; see also Boyle and Woodard 2000: 287–288).

1.5.5 The Salii

As noted above, Livy (1.20.4) places the Salii among those priests ordained by Numa Pompilius. Their name is derived from *salire* 'to dance', and they were famed in antiquity for their dancing promenades around Rome, performed as they sang their ancient songs, the Carmina Saliaria. These hymns are composed in Saturnian verse and preserve a form of Latin so archaic that, writes Quintilian (*Inst.* 1.6.39–41), they were hardly intelligible to the priests themselves by the early first century AD. As they dance the priests carry copies of the *ancile* which had fallen to earth in Numa's reign (the archaic-style shield; see Boyle and Woodard 2000: 215). Dionysius of Halicarnassus describes both their performance and their dress (*Ant. Rom.* 2.70.2–5; cf. Plutarch, *Numa* 13). The priests dance and leap about individually and in unison, and to the accompaniment of a flute they sing their archaic songs. They wear embroidered tunics with wide bronze belts, covered by scarlet-striped robes edged in purple. Tall cone-shaped hats top their heads. A sword hangs from the bronze belt, a spear is held in the right hand, and the *ancile* is fastened to the left arm.

The sodality of the Salii is attested in numerous Italian cities. At Rome the Salii are of two types. Twelve of the priests constitute the Salii Palatini, that body said to have been established by Numa, and are priests of Mars. A second twelve form the Salii Agonales or Salii Collini. These are dedicated to Quirinus and attributed to Numa's successor, Tullus Hostilius (see Dionysius of Halicarnassus, *Ant. Rom.* 2.70.1; 3.32.4; Livy 5.5.2.7; Statius, *Silv.* 5.2.129).

In his commentary on Virgil's *Aeneid*, Servius takes note of the Salii. Concerning these manifestly archaic priests of Rome, Servius writes that they are *in tutela Jovis Martis Quirini*, "in the charge of Jupiter, Mars, and Quirinus" (*Aen.* 8.663), revealing again this threesome as an assemblage in an archaic context.

1.6 THE THREE PROTO-INDO-EUROPEAN FUNCTIONS

By at least the third millennium BC, the peoples of the early Indo-European community—now splintered into daughter cultures—had begun to spread across the European continent and to push deep into Asia.[15] One such group had descended into the Italian peninsula by no later than the early first millennium BC and possibly much earlier (see Mallory 1989: 89–94). With them they brought their age-old ideas about the gods and the

[15] On the Proto-Indo-European community, its early descendent cultures, and their geographic spread, see, inter alia, Mallory 1989; Meier-Brügger 2000: 59–64.

society of the gods. The archaic triad composed of Jupiter, Mars, and Quirinus, Dumézil discerned, is the Roman inheritance of a tripartite division of divine society that characterized Proto-Indo-European theology.

Dumézil's analytic framework for the elucidation of Proto-Indo-European society has already been mentioned (see §1.4). In the course of a long and enormously productive research career, Dumézil developed and refined the notion that the distinctive feature of that society was its tripartite structure and ideology. The three distinct, hierarchically related elements shaping and defining Proto-Indo-European society—the three functions ("les trois fonctions")—are, to use their common shorthand denotations, that of the priests ("prêtres"; the first function), that of the warriors ("guerriers"; second function), and that of the producers ("producteurs"; third function).

Dumézil's first function, the function of sovereign power, itself entails two ideological aspects ("les deux aspects de la première fonction"), one legal, the other magico-religious. These two aspects are embodied, for example, in divine pairs such as Mitra and Varuṇa in the *Rig Veda* (see §1.6.1) and Týr and Óðinn in the Norse *Edda* (see §1.6.3.3), and in the dual juridical and religious roles played by priests in early Indo-European societies, such as Druids in Celtic Europe and Brahmans in India. In his essay, "Les trois fonctions sociales et cosmiques," Dumézil expounds on the first-function nuances:

> . . . le sacré et les rapports soit des hommes avec le sacré (culte, magie), soit des hommes entre eux sous le regard et la garantie des dieux (droit, administration), et aussi le pouvoir souverain exercé par le roi ou ses délégués en conformité avec la volonté ou la faveur des dieux, et enfin, plus généralement, la science et l'intelligence, alors inséparables de la méditation et de la manipulation des choses sacrées . . . .[16]

Dumézil's second function is that of physical power and might:

> . . . la force physique, brutale, et les usages de la force, usages principalement mais non pas uniquement guerriers.[17]

For Dumézil, the second function has a certain solitary character about it, though the great warrior is often accompanied by a warrior band. When interfunctional relationships find mythic expression, the second function typically distances itself from the first function with an attitude of defi-

[16]Dumézil 1992: 96; the essay first appeared in 1958 in the volume entitled *L'Idéologie tripartie des Indo-Européens*.

[17]Dumézil 1992: 96.

ance or disdain. In contrast, Dumézil surmised, the relationship of the second function to the third is one of dependence and a reciprocating, dutiful complicity.[18] Dumézil also came to identify two fundamentally different types of warriors, one savage, monstrous—a kind of "bête humaine"—who kills with his bare hands or with a cudgel, the other a "surhomme," intelligent, civilized, a master of weaponry.[19]

The third function of Indo-European society is for Dumézil the most internally diverse:

> Il est moins aisé de cerner en quelques mots l'essence de la troisième fonction, qui couvre des provinces nombreuses, entre lesquelles des liens évidents apparaissent, mais dont l'unité ne comporte pas de centre net: fécondité certes, humaine, animale et végétale, mais en même temps nourriture et richesse, et santé, et paix—avec les jouissances et les avantages de la paix—et souvent volupté, beauté, et aussi l'importante idée du «grand nombre», appliquée non seulement aux biens (abondance), mais aussi aux hommes qui composent le corps social (masse).[20]

It is a diffuse assemblage in comparison to functions one and two, and this heterogeneity has not gone unnoticed by Dumézil's critics. There are, however, common threads that interlace and draw together these various elements, Dumézil argues; the realm of the third function is that of fecundity—fertility, fruitfulness—its conditions and its consequences:

> Il n'est d'ailleurs pas besoin d'un gros effort de réflexion pour sentir ce qui relie fortement la fécondité (des hommes, des animaux, des plantes) à ses conditions d'une part (la paix tranquille par opposition à la guerre, la sexualité et tout son arsenal physique et psychologique, la santé) et à ses conséquences d'autre part (la richesse sous toutes ses formes, le grand nombre des possesseurs et des choses possédées).[21]

[18]Dumézil 1970: 43–45; ". . . in the circumstances in which he violates the rules of the first function and ignores its gods, the god or king of the second function mobilizes into his service the gods of the third function or some heroes born within it. And it is through these purifiers, healers, and givers of substance that he either hopes to escape, and, in effect, does escape from the grievous consequences of his useful but blameworthy deeds, or to recover the forces he had lost because of a false ally's duplicity. In other words, in these ambiguous situations the third function—itself paying no great attention to the first—is put, or puts itself, at the disposal of the second, in accordance with its rank and nature" (p. 45).

[19]Dumézil 1992: 176–177. These remarks are found in his essay "Les diverses fonctions dans la théologie, la mythologie et l'épopée," originally published in Dumézil 1958.

[20]Dumézil 1992: 96.

[21]Bonnet 1981: 37; see also Dumézil 1982: 50; Allen 1987: 34.

1.6.1 Tripartition and Dumézil

It is important to bear in mind that "Proto-Indo-European tripartition" and "Georges Dumézil" do not constitute identical subsets. This seems to have been overlooked or otherwise misunderstood by many of his critics, especially by classicists who focus on the study of Roman religion. Such a tacit equation is evidenced, for example, by Beard, North, and Price (*BNP*, vol. 1: 14), who write in their survey work on Roman religion:

> Dumézil believed that the mythological structure of the Romans and of other Indo-Europeans was derived ultimately from the social divisions of the original Indo-European people themselves, and that these divisions gave rise to a 'tri-functional ideology'—which caused all deities, myths and related human activities to fall into three distinct categories: 1. Religion and Law; 2. War; 3. Production, especially agricultural production. This was an enormously ambitious claim, and at first Dumézil's theories drew very little acceptance.[22]

Enormously ambitious? Perhaps so, were this a careful statement of Dumézil's research program, which, unfortunately, it is not. At what moment in its history the primitive Indo-European community began to see itself as structured in threes is unknown—possibly unknowable. (And at what point along the continuum of that history would one locate the "original Indo-European people"?) More than that, where does Dumézil claim that it was the social divisions of the Indo-Europeans that gave birth to their "trifunctional ideology"?[23] Dumézil's was an enormously insightful claim, born of erudition and a remarkable breadth of comparative investigation, not confined by the walls of Rome. There is, however, more to Dumézil than tripartition, and tripartition is not unique to Dumézil.

1.6.1.1 TRIPARTITION AND BENVENISTE On the one side, as early as 1932, the French linguist Émile Benveniste had begun independently to explore and develop his own interpretation of Indo-European social classes. The most succinct expression of Benveniste's conclusions is found in his masterly work treating primitive Indo-European economy, society, law, and religion, *Le vocabulaire des institutions indo-européennes* (1969); therein (as earlier) Benveniste argues for a similar hierarchically ordered, three-part social structure:

[22] *BNP*, vol. 1: 14.

[23] This relationship between structure and ideology is a complex matter which has been admirably explored by N. J. Allen (1987: 29–33).

> Par des séries parallèles de termes d'étymologie souvent parlante, mais différents d'une langue à l'autre, l'iranien, l'indien, le grec et l'italique attestent un commun héritage indo-européen: celui d'une société structurée et hiérarchisée selon trois fonctions fondamentales, celles de prêtre, de guerrier, d'agriculteur.[24]

The structure is most readily perceived among the Indo-Iranian peoples, and indeed, in the research path followed by both Benveniste and Dumézil,[25] the reconstruction of an ancestral structure was first projected to Proto-Indo-Iranian society (see Benveniste 1932; Dumézil 1930b). "Cette division qui embrasse la totalité des hommes est-elle limitée à la société indo-iranienne?"—Benveniste asks rhetorically in his great synthetic work of 1969 (vol. 1: 289); the answer: "On peut penser qu'elle est très ancienne et qu'elle remonte au passé indo-européen. De fait, elle a laissé ailleurs des traces." The broader Indo-European evidence that he here invokes for a common ancestral tripartite social structure is that provided by Greek legends of the primitive organization of Ionian society (pp. 289–291) and by the ritual texts of the Atiedian priesthood of ancient Iguvium (pp. 291–292; see below, §3.3.3.2.3).[26] Yet additional evidence could be adduced, he suggests,[27] and he defers to Dumézil regarding matters of religion and mythology generally.[28]

1.6.1.2 MORE THAN TRIPARTITION On the other side, Dumézil's own research program was concerned with much more than simply the tripartition of Indo-European society. In an intriguing article exploring the possibility of a fourth Indo-European function, N. J. Allen (1987) calls attention to various remarks made by Dumézil in which he explicitly addresses this matter; indeed, Dumézil expresses annoyance at the view that his work is narrowly confined to concerns of tripartition. For example, in an interview which Dumézil gave to Jacques Bonnet and Didier Pralon in 1980, the inter-

[24]Benveniste 1969, vol. 1: 279.

[25]This is not to suggest that Dumézil and Benveniste ever undertook anything like a common research effort. On the contrary, and unfortunately, relations between the two appear to have been somewhat distant. Consider, for example, Dumézil's remarks made in an interview with Didier Eribon (Dumézil 1987: 23–29).

[26]On the Atiedian priesthood and other evidence for tripartition provided by (especially) Roman and Greek cult, see Benveniste 1945a.

[27]Consider Benveniste 1945b, in which article he explores Indo-European medical lore and tripartition.

[28]"Au surplus, c'est le domaine auquel M. Georges Dumézil a consacré des travaux fondamentaux, trop connus pour qu'on les rappelle ici" (Benveniste 1969, vol. 1: 292).

viewers ask: "L'idéologie des trois fonctions est-elle la seule composante de l'idéologie indo-européenne?" Dumézil responds:

> Non, et je suis quelquefois agacé de me voir toujours ramené aux trois fonctions. Je me suis occupé d'autres choses: la théorie de l'Aurore par example, et celles du Solstice d'hiver, du calendrier romain, des organisations guerrières. Tout mon travail comparatif n'est pas «accroché» à la tripartition![29]

Volume 3 of Dumézil's magnum opus, *Mythe et épopée*, concludes with three appendixes, the first of which is a study of Roman Mater Matuta, whom Dumézil identifies with the Vedic dawn goddess, Uṣas. Tracking the evolution of his own thought, Dumézil begins:

> Les études sur l'Aurore appartiennent à la seconde période de la nouvelle mythologie comparée. Entre 1935 et 1948, toute l'exploration comparative avait été concentrée sur la conception des trois fonctions, reconnue, en 1938, fondamentale dans l'idéologie des Indo-Européens: on ne s'était occupé que d'en inventorier les expressions, vivantes ou fossiles, dans la religion, dans l'épopée, dans la vie sociale des divers peuples de la famille. C'est ensuite seulement qu'on a pu entreprendre d'appliquer les procédés mis au point sur cette matière centrale à d'autres types de représentation mythologie des commencements, des feux, des saisons, eschatologie.[30]

Allen (1987: 33) summarizes this, quoting from Dumézil's 1958 work, *L'Idéologie tripartite des Indo-Européens*:

> [Dumézil] is perfectly clear that the three functions do not exhaust the ideological heritage from Proto-Indo-European times. "However important, even central, the ideology of the three functions may be, it is far from constituting all the shared Indo-European heritage that comparative analysis can glimpse or reconstruct" (1958: 89).

1.6.2 Tripartition and the present work

For the study at hand, a notion of a primitive Indo-European three-part social structure and ideology—à la Benveniste and Dumézil—constitutes an essential building block. One can hardly see how it could be reasonably denied by the comparativist; the paradigm is fundamental, and elements of such a structure will recur throughout the present work. As the argument develops through the course of this investigation, however, it will

[29] See Bonnet 1981: 34.
[30] *ME* 3.305.

become clear that tripartition is but one plank—and at times, it may seem, not a very central one—in the stage on which our comparative analysis of Indo-European ritual boundaries and spaces is played out. The fundamental "threeness" of ancestral Indo-European self-awareness is, nevertheless, assumed, and crucially so; but to co-opt Dumézil's declaration as a confession: "Tout mon travail comparatif n'est pas «accroché» à la tripartition."

These various clarifications having been made, let us now consider some of the evidence that Dumézil has adduced for Proto-Indo-European tripartition.

1.6.3 Indo-European tripartition: the evidence

Intact reflexes and vestigial remnants of the Proto-Indo-European divine social structure, and of the human structure it mirrors, are preserved across the ancient Indo-European world, but particularly well so at the eastern and western aspects of the Indo-European expansion area in antiquity—in the east, India and Iran; in the west, Scandinavia, but more so Celtic Europe and Italy. After surveying the fundamental evidence from the first several of these (§§1.6.3.1–1.6.3.4), we will turn our attention fully to Italy, specifically to Rome (§1.7).[31]

1.6.3.1 INDIA The picture is clearest in India and Iran. The gods of Vedic India are divided among three classes: (i) the *Ādityas*, gods of sovereignty (first function); (ii) warrior deities, commonly named as the *Rudras* (second function); and (iii), rounding out the tripartite structure, the deities called the *Vasus*—having a corporate denotation meaning literally 'goods, wealth'. In a parallel fashion, Vedic divine society is at times summarized by substituting for these group designations, the names of individual gods: (i) Mitra and Varuṇa; (ii) Indra (along with Vāyu or Agni); and (iii) the Aśvins, also known as the Nāsatyas (see, inter alia, Dumézil 1986: 29–37). The hierarchical prominence of these deities is one of great antiquity, as is

[31]For a convenient overview of Dumézil's interpretations of Indo-European tripartition, see his "Leçon inaugurale," reprinted in Dumézil 1992 (pp. 13–36). For more explicit discussion see the essays collected in part 2 of the same volume: "Les trois fonctions sociales et cosmiques"; "Les théologies triparties"; and "Les diverses fonctions dans la théologie, la mythologie et l'épopée" (pp. 69–193). The fullest single exposition of Dumézil's Indo-European investigations is to be found in Dumézil 1995. A convenient treatment of Dumézilian ideas is found in Puhvel 1987. The development of Dumézil's thought regarding tripartition is traced in Littleton 1982: 43–150. As noted immediately above, N. J. Allen (1987) has argued for expanding Dumézil's tripartite structure by the addition of a fourth Indo-European function; see also Allen 2003.

revealed by their invocation in the treaty made between a king of Syrian Mitanni, Šattiwazza, and the Hittite monarch, Šuppiluliuma, in the fourteenth century BC. The people of Mitanni were predominantly speakers of the non-Indo-European language of Hurrian; however, speakers of an archaic form of Indo-Aryan (or perhaps a form of Indo-Iranian antecedent to the separation of Indo-Aryan and Iranian) entered the region at some early period and for a time gained dynastic control (see Harrak 1997). Called on to witness the treaty are several deities:

mi-it-ra-, u-ru-wa-na-, in-da-ra, and na-ša-at-ti-ia.[32]

Clearly these gods are equivalent to their better-known Indic counterparts:

Mitra, Varuṇa, Indra, and the Nāsatyas.

The same tripartition also characterizes human society in Vedic India. Three Indo-Aryan *varṇas* or classes are identified: the *brāhmaṇa*, the priestly class; the *kṣatriya*, class of the warrior (*rājanya*); and the *vaiśya*, class of cultivators, goods-producers. To these three is appended a fourth, non-Aryan, *varṇa*—that of the *śudras*, the native peoples of India subjugated by the invading Indo-Aryans. We encounter these classes, for example, in *Rig Veda* 10.90.12, in the account of the dismemberment of the primeval giant Puruṣa—from whose body the universe is created—where the relative societal positions of the *varṇas* are clearly revealed:[33]

brāhmaṇo 'sya mukham āsīd bāhū rājaniyaḥ kṛtaḥ
ūrū tad asya yad vaiśyaḥ padbhyām śūdro ajāyata

The Brahman was his mouth,
  arms were made into the Rājanya,
His thighs—they the Vaiśya,
  from feet were born the Śudra.

1.6.3.2 IRAN In spite of the religious reforms undertaken by Zarathuštra, a tripartite division of divine beings can still be found in Iranian theology (see, inter alia, *ME* 1.105–107; Dumézil 1986: 40–51). Zarathuštra elevated his god Ahura Mazdāh to a position of supremacy. The Aməša Spəntas, six abstract beings who embody the attributes of Ahura Mazdāh in the *Avesta* (the Zoroastrian book of scripture), correspond closely to the chief Vedic

[32] In transcription of the syllabic cuneiform script. See Dumézil 1986: 24–26, 213–232.
[33] The text of the *Rig Veda* used herein is that of van Nooten and Holland (1994).

deities as they span the three functions: (i) Aša Vahišta, patron of cattle, and (ii) Vohu Manah, patron of fire, match the sovereign gods Varuṇa and Mitra respectively; (iii) Xšaθra, patron of metal, has a name meaning 'dominion', cognate with Sanskrit *kṣatra-*, from which is derived *kṣatriya*, name of the warrior class (Indra, chief warrior deity in India, has been demonized in Iran); (iv) Spənta Ārmaiti, patron of earth, evokes the Vedic goddess Sarasvatī, the river goddess whose affiliations are with all three functions (one of a set of trifunctional deities attested across the ancient Indo-European world), but who closely aligns herself with the Aśvins; and (v) Haurvatāt̲ and (vi) Amərətāt̲, patrons of waters and plants respectively, corresponding to the Vedic divine twins of the third function, the Aśvins or Nāsatyas.

Iran similarly preserves evidence of a tripartite division of human society. Three classes, or *pištra*, are attested in the *Avesta*: that of the *zaotar*, the priest; the *nar*, the warrior, literally 'man' (cf. Greek ἀνήρ); and the *vāstar*, the herder. Such are their names in the *Gāthās* (the hymns constituting the oldest portion of the *Avesta*); in the later portions of the *Avesta* they are the *āθravan*, the *raθaēštar* 'chariot-rider', and *vāstryō-fšuyant* 'fattening pasturer' respectively (Boyce 1996: 5–6).

1.6.3.3 SCANDINAVIA Among the ancient Germanic peoples, and best attested in Norse records, divine society is again perceived to be of a tripartite nature. Óðinn (Old English Woden, namesake of *Wodnesdæg* 'Wednesday'), king of the gods, belongs to the first function, as does Týr (Old English Tīw, as in *Tīwesdæg*, 'Tuesday'), the god who voluntarily loses a hand to ensure the security of society. The former is a reflex of what Dumézil has identified to be the magico-religious aspect of the first function, and so is a homologue of Vedic Varuṇa; the latter, Týr, belongs to the legal aspect of the first function, making him a homologue of Vedic Mitra (see Dumézil 1973a). Among the Germanic gods, the principal representative of the second function is Þórr (Old English Thunor, eponym of *Thunresdæg*, 'Thursday'). Óðinn, Týr, and Þórr all belong to that group of gods called the Æsir, who in Norse tradition had once been at war with a second family of gods, the Vanir. It is the Vanir who continue the Indo-European divine third function in Scandinavia, chief of whom are Njörðr and his two children, a son Freyr and a daughter Freyja. The war between the Æsir and the Vanir is itself a reflex of a Proto-Indo-European tradition of conflict which pits the third function against the first/second, seen also, for example, in the Indo-Aryan account of a conflict between the Aśvins and Indra.

1.6.3.4 CELTIC EUROPE The tripartite structure of Gaulish society is well known from Caesar's *Bellum Gallicum* 6.13:

> In omni Gallia eorum hominum, qui aliquo sunt numero atque honore, genera sunt duo. Nam plebes paene servorum habetur loco, quae nihil audet per se, nullo adhibetur consilio. Plerique, cum aut aere alieno aut magnitudine tributorum aut iniuria potentiorum premuntur, sese in servitutem dicant nobilibus: in hos eadem omnia sunt iura, quae dominis in servos. Sed de his duobus generibus alterum est druidum, alterum equitum.
>
> In all of Gaul exist two *genera* of people who are of a certain rank and honor. The *plebes* are accounted little more than slaves, who undertake no endeavor on their own and are in no way consulted for advice. The majority of them are weighed down by debt or heavy taxation or by the cruel whims of the more powerful; and so they enslave themselves to the upper classes. The latter classes have the very same authority over them as masters have over slaves. But concerning these other two *genera*, one is that of the Druids, the other that of the *equites*.

Caesar's three Gaulish *genera*—Druid priests, warrior nobles (*equites*), and laboring commoners (*plebes*)—are matched term for term by the three classes of Irish society: *druí*, *flaith*, and *bó-aire* (Rees and Rees 1989: 111–113).[34] Relics of a theological structure of tripartition are also identifiable in medieval (and later) attestations of Irish and Welsh mythic lore (see Dumézil 1988: 153–159; *ME* 1.613–616; Rees and Rees 1989: 141–144).

And so we come to Rome and a principal vestige of Indo-European tripartition in that place, and in so doing begin a new phase of our discussion, one which will begin to move us nearer to the heart of the present investigation. This vestige is of course the Pre-Capitoline triad which we examined in detail above (see §1.5).

1.7 JUPITER, MARS, QUIRINUS

The Pre-Capitoline triad continues this ancient Indo-European tripartition of divine society in Rome. Jupiter, whose name (from **Diove Pater*, 'Jove the Father') is cognate with that of Greek Ζεύς Πατήρ, Vedic *Dyaus Pitar*, and Luvian *(Tatis) Tiwaz,* is god of the first function—the sovereign sky god whose priest, the Flamen Dialis, manifests responsibilities and character-

[34] On a further tripartition within the individual classes of Celtic society, see Rees and Rees 1989: 140–141.

istics aligned with both aspects of the first function, legal and magico-religious (see *ARR*: 176–181).

Mars is the god of the second function, the warrior god whose month, March, opens the season of military campaigns; whose bellicose sacrificial rite, the Equus October, occurs at the end of the campaigning season; whose "wives" in the ancient prayers of the Roman priests (Aulus Gellius 13.23.2) are Moles (the 'masses' of battle) and Nerio, from Proto-Indo-European **ner-*, source of the name of the Iranian warrior class, *nar* (see §1.6.2), Greek ἀνήρ, Armenian *ayr*, Oscan **niir** 'man', Umbrian *nerf* (accusative plural) 'princeps', Old Irish *nert*, Welsh *nerth* 'force', and probably the name of the principal Indo-Aryan warrior god, *Indra* (see *ARR*: 203–213).

Quirinus is catalogued as one of the "gods of Titus Tatius," that set of third-function deities to which Terminus also belongs (see §1.4). Served by one of the three Flamines Maiores, he is clearly the chief member of that group. Quirinus almost certainly owes his name to **co-virio-* 'assemblage of men', and is thus the god of the *curiae*. Reflecting the deity's affiliation with the Roman populace generally, his priest, the Flamen Quirinalis, participates in sacred rites performed on behalf of other gods. An examination of these rites, Dumézil discerned, reveals the god's fundamental affiliation with Roman grain—young grain in the field (the Robigalia), stored grain (the Summer Consualia), and roasted grain (the Fornacalia; see *ARR*: 156–161; Boyle and Woodard 2000: 197–199). Quirinus' Flamen also takes part in the Larentalia—not a festival of grain, but one affiliated with the courtesan Acca Larentia, and so a festival falling squarely within the domain of the third function—realm of fertility and sensuality (see *ARR*: 269; Boyle and Woodard 2000: 206–207).

1.7.1 Response

Among classicists who focus on the study of Roman religion, there are some, chiefly within the Anglo-American tradition, who would casually dismiss Wissowa's and Dumézil's recognition of an archaic triad comprised of the gods served by the three Flamines Maiores, gods who as a set continue the tripartite ideology of the Indo-European ancestors of the Romans, gods who find a "cognate" triad among the Italic deities invoked in the Iguvine ritual of the Atiedian priesthood, as recognized by Benveniste and Dumézil. Such casual dismissiveness could only be maintained by choosing to ignore the great body of comparative evidence amassed by Benveniste and Dumézil, by ignoring the recurring structural patterns attested by widely separated Indo-European peoples within the historical period—in a seeming refusal to look beyond the walls of Rome. This is not to say that some alternative interpretation could not be applied to the data provided by the methodical inquiries of Benveniste and Dumézil; it is to say that the claims of their comparative analyses cannot be dismissed by examining only the evidence internal to Rome, excising it from its cross-cultural Indo-European context.

The necessity of understanding and evaluating Dumézil's work within a comparative framework has of course not gone unrecognized by all classicists presently engaged in the study of Roman religion. In a recent general work on Roman religion, for example, John Scheid writes of Dumézil and his method:

> Dumézil's plan was to reconstruct the Roman religion of archaic times but, despite his brilliant analyses . . . , the religious attitudes reconstructed seem to relate more to the contemporaries of Cato and Augustus than to those of Romulus. But it is only fair to note that, from Dumézil's own point of view, this would not necessarily have made any difference. For, as an Indo-Europeanist rather than a student of Roman religion alone, Dumézil was ultimately more interested in the timeless structures common to all societies which share Indo-European languages than in the precise historical period during which these structures first made their appearance. In the case of Rome, his principal concern was to show how closely the earliest religious structures he could detect matched those of other Indo-European societies . . . .
>
> Despite all the historical problems that they pose, Dumézil's careful analyses of Roman myths, language and institutions provide an incomparable methodological model for the use and interpretation of sources.[35]

Scheid also rightly understands that the vantage point offered by the comparative perspective brings into clearer view what may be blurred in a local view:

> Dumézil's method was always first to examine the evidence within its own context and only then to compare the Roman data to similar structures in the wider Indo-European world (as more recently Walter Burkert has always looked carefully at the evidence before moving on to his own . . . theories). So even if . . . Dumézil's comparison of Roman religious structures with those of other Indo-European societies leads principally to further questions, his careful analysis of the surviving evidence often constitutes a real methodological breakthrough—throwing light, for example, on the *modus operandi* of various shadowy deities and

[35]Scheid 2003: 9–10, 11.

> explaining, as no one had done before, their significance within Roman religion. By combining the philological methods of Wissowa with a more anthropological *savoir faire*, Dumézil effectively invented the religious anthropology of the Romans.[36]

Those scholars of Roman religion who dismiss the Indo-European tripartite heritage of the Pre-Capitoline triad typically do so as part and parcel of a broader Romano-centric rejection of tripartition. Regarding the latter response, consider the comments of Beard, North, and Price:[37]

> If Dumézil were right, that would mean (quite implausibly) that early Roman religion and myth encoded a social organization divided between kings, warriors and producers fundamentally opposed to the "actual" social organization of republican Rome (even probably regal Rome) itself. For everything that we know about early Roman society specifically excludes a division of functions according to Dumézil's model. It was, in fact, one of the defining characteristics of republican Rome (and a principle on which many of its political institutions were based) that the warriors were the peasants, and that the voters were "warrior-peasants"; not that the warriors and the peasant agriculturalists were separate groups with a separate position in society and separate interests as Dumézil's mythic scheme demands. In order to follow Dumézil, one would need to accept not only that the religious and mythic life of a primitive community could be organized differently from its social life, but that the two could be glaringly incompatible.[38]

1.7.1.1 IDEOLOGY (PART 1) Glaringly incompatible? If there is something here which blinds us, it would seem to be reflected from the dazzling prob-

[36]Scheid 2003: 15.

[37]Regarding the Pre-Capitoline triad itself, Beard, North, and Price seem to be somewhat ambivalent. In volume 1 of their *Religions of Rome*, they write (p. 15): "The familiar deities of the Capitoline triad (Jupiter, Juno, and Minerva) failed to fit the [tripartite] model; but [Dumézil] found his three functions in the gods of the 'old triad'—Jupiter, Mars, Quirinus. Although this group was of no particular prominence through most of the history of Roman religion, they were the gods to whom the three most important priests of early Rome . . . were dedicated—and Dumézil found other traces of evidence to suggest that these three had preceded the Capitoline deities as the central gods of the Roman pantheon. They appeared to fit his three functions perfectly . . . . Even supposing Dumézil were right about their very earliest significance, all three soon developed into the supposed domains of at least one and possibly both of the others." The tone appears at least mildly disparaging. However, in volume 2 (pp. 5–6, 9) Beard, North, and Price seem to embrace the concept of the Pre-Capitoline triad.

[38]*BNP*, vol. 1: 15.

lems with such a pronouncement—problems revealing a lack of understanding of Dumézil, Benveniste, their methods, and their conclusions. To begin with, as the authors of this statement must, one would expect, be aware, Dumézil addresses directly the matter of the historical social expression of the prehistoric Indo-European ideology; in *Archaic Roman Religion* he writes:

> In all the ancient Indo-European societies in which this ideological framework exists, it is a problem to know whether, and up to what point, the structure of the three functions is also expressed in an actual structure of society. For there is a difference between making an explicit survey of these three needs and causing a division of social behavior to correspond to them in practice . . . .[39]

Dumézil infers, and reasonably so, that throughout the long travels by which the primitive Indo-Europeans spread themselves from the shores of Ireland to the deserts of central Asia, there survived ipso facto the warrior element that effectuated that successful dissemination and, at least in some regions, the keepers of the sacred and legal traditions. (Consider "the astonishing resemblances . . . . between the Druids and the Brahmans and between the Irish *rí* and the Vedic *rājan*.")[40] He then observes:

> Thus the two higher functions must have been guaranteed by the differentiated groups of the general population, which was often enlarged by the addition of conquered natives, and on which the third function devolved. But it is also certain that at the end of these great travels, after they had settled down, the greater part of the Indo-European-speaking groups sooner or later, often very soon, abandoned this framework in actual practice. It thus remained only ideological and formed a means of analyzing and understanding the world, but with regard to social organization it offered at best only an ideal cherished by the philosophers and a legendary view of the beginnings.[41]

One might profitably ask what precise sense Dumézil assigns to the term "ideology." Allen addresses this point in his study of Indo-European ideology:

> The qualitative question, simpler perhaps, turns on what one expects of an ideology. Dumézil does not spend much time on definitions of the

[39] *ARR*: 162.

[40] Irish *rí* and the Vedic *rājan* are reflexes of the Proto-Indo-European word for king, cognate with Latin *rēx*, all from the root $*h_3r\bar{e}\hat{g}$-. The word survives only at the eastern and western extremities of the Indo-European expansion area; see Benveniste 1969, vol. 2: 9–15.

[41] *ARR*: 163.

> term, but I have collected about a dozen remarks bearing on his use of it. Thus he writes recently (1985: 312): "By analogy with the words 'theology' and 'mythology', which mean respectively the articulated system of deities, and the more or less coherent and finite set of myths, I mean by 'ideology' the inventory of directing ideas that dominate the thinking and behaviour of a society". Elsewhere he talks of realising (towards 1950) that the trifunctional ideology, where one finds it, may only be, and perhaps always have been, "an ideal, and at the same time a means of analysing and interpreting the forces which ensure the course of the world and the life of men" (1981 [=1995, vol. 1]: 15).[42]

Beyond the general case of the social expression of ideology, Dumézil explicitly addresses the situation in Rome:

> The problem must thus arise at Rome as well. But it arises under almost desperate conditions, since too many centuries elapsed between the origins and the account which the annalists gave of them for us to be able to expect authentic information concerning the earliest social organization. If in the eighth century there was any survival of a division of society into three classes, respectively operating the three functions, its last traces quickly disappeared, at any rate before the end of the regal period. It was probably one of the accomplishments of the Etruscan domination to achieve its destruction.

On Dumézil's penultimate point ("If in the eighth century there was any survival of a division of society into three classes . . ."), Beard, North, and Price are thus actually in very close agreement with him. And it is worth noting that on his ultimate point as well ("It was probably one of the accomplishments of the Etruscan domination . . ."), the degree of separation seems not to be great, for Beard, North, and Price write regarding the Etruscans in early Rome:

> Although some particular practices (such as haruspicy) would forever remain linked to Etruscan roots, the "Roman" religious world had become saturated with influences from their Etruscan neighbors which had merged with and transformed the Latin culture of their ancestors. Jupiter was, after all, an ancient Latin deity with an ancient Latin name—and at the same time the focus of what we may choose to classify as (in part at least) Etruscan religious forms (such as the ceremonial of triumph or the Capitoline temple).[43]

[42] Allen 1987: 32.
[43] *BNP*, vol. 1: 60. For a further and fuller consideration of these remarks, see below, §1.9.

We will return shortly to the matter of Etruscan religious influences on Rome.

And what of the above-cited pronouncement of Beard, North, and Price?

> In order to follow Dumézil, one would need to accept not only that the religious and mythic life of a primitive community could be organized differently from its social life, but that the two could be glaringly incompatible.

There are at least two different points to which we should give attention. One concerns the issue of "compatibility" and the other the "social life" of a primitive community vis-à-vis that of its ancestral culture, specifically its linguistic preservations.

1.7.1.2 HETEROGENEITY AND CONTINUITY To begin with, are communities monolithically homogenous? Never. They are striated and heterogeneous. Incompatibility within communities is not an exceptional state of affairs. One must more accurately first determine for what element of this primitive Roman community "the religious and mythic life" might reasonably be construed as "organized differently" and, thus, for whom the invoked incompatibility exists. In his insightful study of Indo-European ideology, N. J. Allen explores the historical continuity of Dumézil's tripartite ideology:

> From this point of view the history of the Indo-Europeans consists in a transition from an early period, when the segmentary [that is, discretely tripartite] ideology was creative and pervasive, to the contemporary period, when it has, to all intents and purposes, given way to non-segmentary ideologies.[44]

Allen then continues, echoing Dumézil's own ponderings on the Indo-European cultural extensions rehearsed above:

> Continua are often difficult to handle, and an ideology can very easily be only partly alive. It may be alive for the masses, dead for the elite, or vice versa. It might be strong enough to effect adaptations, too weak to inspire genuine innovation. It might be alive in narrative, dead so far as institutions were concerned. And so on. I imagine that even the earliest of our sources date from periods when the ideology was no longer alive as it had been when the PIE speakers were beginning to disperse. However it would be arbitrary to assume *that* was the time when the segmentary

[44] Allen 1987: 26.

> ideology was at its strongest. The process of decline could well have begun earlier—one can say nothing about dates.

The Roman ideological remnants of the old Indo-European tripartition, whatever the era of its apogee, survive within the realm of the divine. In Rome that ideology is indeed—in Allen's words—only partly alive. It is kept alive in the domain of ritual and theological structure by the priests, or a subset thereof, guardians of ancient, ancient traditions and knowledge, as elsewhere in the Indo-European world (and beyond). It is at least the priestly element of society that houses the incompatibilities envisioned by Beard, North, and Price. In the modern world, the incompatible differences (one might even say glaring) between the religious ideology embraced by a cleric—Christian minister or priest, rabbi, mullah, and so on—and the actual structures, conventions, and behaviors of society at large, particularly societies fallen under the influence of some "foreign" element, are easily enough perceived; one need only read the headlines.

1.7.1.3 LES QUATRE CERCLES D'APPARTENANCE The second consideration is this. As seems to have been overlooked by Romanist critics of tripartite ideology, Benveniste argued cogently that there were dynamics of early Indo-European social structure quite distinct from tripartition.

> L'organisation tripartite qui vient d'être décrite établit, au sein de la société, des classes de fonction; elle ne revêt pas un caractère politique, sinon du fait que la classe sacerdotale, étant la première, détermine la hiérarchie des pouvoirs. L'organisation proprement sociale repose sur une classification toute différente: la société est considérée non plus dans la nature et la hiérarchie des classes, mais dans son extension en quelque sorte nationale, selon les cercles d'appartenance qui la contiennent.
>
> C'est dans l'ancien Iran que cette structure est la plus apparente. Elle comporte quatre cercles concentriques, quatre divisions sociales et territoriales qui, procédant de l'unité la plus petite, s'élargissent jusqu'à englober l'ensemble de la communauté.[45]

In Iran the innermost circle is that denoted by *dam-* (or *dəmāna-*, *nmāna-*), 'household' or 'family'. The next circle out is that of the *vīs*, 'clan' ("groupant plusieurs familles"), beyond which is the *zantu*, 'tribe' ("proprement «l'ensemble de ceux qui sont de même naissance»"). The outermost circle is that of the *dahyu* 'country'.

It is only in Iran that the structure plainly survives into the histori-

[45] Benveniste 1969, vol. 1: 293–294.

cal period. Even in India it has undergone modification: though Sanskrit cognates of each term are attested, the system no longer remains a living mechanism (". . . nous ne trouvons pas dans l'Inde une liaison organique entre ces quatre dénominations. Elles ne se rejoignent plus"[46]). Much more so elsewhere, though fossils of the system, frozen—sometimes idiomatically—in the lexicon, show themselves scattered across the Indo-European family. For example, each of the social units has its own chief: in Iran they are denoted the *dmāna-paiti*, the *vis-paiti*, the *zantu-paiti*, and the *dahyu-paiti*, respectively; they exist in a hierarchical relationship, still surviving in Middle Iranian. Beside Vedic *dam-pati-* 'master of the home', cognate to Avestan *dmāna-paiti*, Greek preserves δεσ-πότης 'master, despot, lord, owner'; the Avestan *vis-paiti* finds his etymological counterpart not only in Vedic *viś-pati-* 'chief of the settlement, lord of the house', but in Lithuanian *viẽš-pats* 'lord', Albanian *zot* 'lord' (product of obscuring sound change); compare the Old Prussian accusative feminine *waispattin* 'the lady of the house'.[47]

Beyond the core household unit (Iranian *dam-*) with its well-known Greek and Latin linguistic relatives (such as Homeric δῶ, Latin *domus*), there survive, in both Greek and Latin, forms etymologically related to the next two social levels, the Indo-European clan and tribe, though showing semantic distinction. Beside Iranian *vīs*, 'clan', Greek preserves οἶκος (earlier ϝοικος), meaning 'house', and Latin has *vīcus*, 'village; block of houses'; and next to Iranian *zantu*, 'tribe', Greek shows γένος, denoting 'race, offspring, family', and Latin *gens*, meaning 'race, people', as well as identifying a family unit having a shared *nomen* and ancestor. But neither in Greece nor in Rome does the ancient Indo-European social structure in which such linguistic forms have their roots survive:

> La correspondance n'est qu'étymologique. En grec et en latin, ces vocables hérités ne s'ordonnent pas comme en iranien. Ils ne se recouvrent même pas entre le latin et le grec. . . . En latin, nous ne retrouvons pas non plus la structure iranienne: *vīcus* n'est pas le degré supérieur de *domus*; c'est autre chose que la *vīs* iranienne, autre chose aussi que le *(w)oîkos* grec.[48]

The nested ancestral Indo-European social structure with its hierarchically ranked chieftains did not survive the urbanization of the Indo-European peoples who descended into the Italian peninsula and intermingled

[46]Beveniste 1969, vol. 1: 294.
[47]Ibid., p. 295; see also Mallory and Adams 1997: 192–193.
[48]Beveniste 1969, vol. 1: 295.

with the non-Indo-European inhabitants of that place. Vestiges of the archaic nomenclature attached to that structure, however, still dotted the sociolinguistic landscape of spoken Latin.[49]

A parallel process of fossilization was at work on that other distinctive element of Indo-European social structure, tripartition. While a society-wide, living tripartition of functions had long since disappeared, quite possibly before the arrival of the Indo-Europeans in Italy, remnants of the ideology underlying and reflecting that prehistoric social tripartition survived in ancient Rome. Notably, expressions of this ideology were kept alive in ritual and theology by priestly figures—heirs to the yet more ancient first function and the repository of ancestral religious and legal traditions, like their counterparts in other Indo-European places—Brahman, *zaotar*, Druid. Beyond the priests, though assuredly not exclusive of their domain, mythic motifs of Indo-European origin, some of which centrally or incidentally assume notions of a tripartite division of society (as we shall see), were preserved in Roman society at large in the milieu of popular traditions about the gods.

1.7.1.4 IDEOLOGY (PART 2) One of the harsher voices to be raised in recent years against Dumézil from among the ranks of classicists is that of T. J. Cornell—though at the same time, it is a voice of endorsement. In his work on the history of early Italy and Rome—an admirably scholarly work, if at times given to hyperbole and aphorism—Cornell briefly rehearses and dismisses particular elements of Dumézil's trifunctional interpretation of Rome's traditions of its origins. It is important to note, however, that he does not issue a blanket dismissal of Indo-European tripartition à la Dumézil and Benveniste (the latter whom he does not mention); quite to the contrary, he sanctions the notion and its vestigial survival in Rome:

> Although traces of Indo-European myth and functional ideology are undoubtedly present in the stories of early Rome, and in particular in early Roman religion, the problem is to determine the extent and meaning of these traces.[50]

A fair enough assessment with which the present author fully concurs. Cornell later adds:

> The three functions are certainly present in some early Roman religious

[49]For a full treatment of the evidence, see Beveniste 1969, vol. 1: 293–319.
[50]Cornell 1995: 78.

> institutions, most notably the three *flamines maiores*, priests who were specifically attached to the cults of Jupiter, Mars and Quirinus, representing sovereignty, war and production (respectively) . . . .[51]

1.7.1.4.1 The Romulean tribes What Cornell finds dubious in Dumézil's analyses are his interpretations of yet another element of Roman social structure, linked by Dumézil to Indo-European traditions preserved in the accounts of Rome's beginnings. The objection concerns the reported earliest tribal division of Rome—that of the Ramnes, Luceres, and Titienses (see, inter alia, Varro, *Ling.* 5.55; Livy 10.6.7; Ovid, *Fasti* 3.132). Cornell writes, quoting Dumézil (in italics below):

> In his early works Dumézil argued that the three "Romulean" tribes, the Ramnes, Luceres and Tities, were functionally defined castes of priests, warriors and producers (respectively); but later he abandoned this theory (for which there is no supporting evidence in our texts), and argued instead that the framework of the three functions "*remained only ideological and formed a means of analyzing and understanding the world.*"[52]

The quotation that Cornell draws from *Archaic Roman Religion* (p. 163)—and which has a familiar ring to it—would here seem to have been penned by Dumézil as an explicit rejection of some earlier interpretation of the Romulean tribes. In actuality, Dumézil is with these words discussing the general replacement of a living tripartition of functions by a trifunctional ideology as the early Indo-Europeans moved across Europe and Asia and into the pages of history; it is a portion of the very quotation we invoked above (§1.7.1.1) in discussing that replacement.[53] In *Archaic Roman Religion*, Dumézil does, however, have something to say about the Romulean tribes; and in fairness to him, we should examine those remarks, whether or not we are prone to agree:

> . . . . Romulus, the son of a god and the beneficiary of Jupiter's promises, sometimes joined by his Etruscan ally Lucumon, the expert in war, is originally opposed to Titus Tatius, the leader of the wealthy Sabines and the father of the Sabine women, and then forms with him a complete and viable society. Now, this legend, in which each of the three leaders,

[51]Cornell 1995: 80.

[52]Cornell 1995: 77–78.

[53]I.e. "Thus the two higher functions must have been guaranteed by the differentiated groups of the general population, which was often enlarged by the addition of conquered natives, and on which the third function devolved. But it is also certain that at the end of these great travels, after they had settled down, the greater part of the Indo-

> with his respective following, is thoroughly characterized in terms of one of the functions—reread in particular lines 9–32 of the first *Roman Elegy* of Propertius—is intended to justify the oldest known division, the three tribes of which these leaders are the eponyms, the companions of Romulus becoming the *Ramnes*, those of Lucumon the *Luceres*, and those of Titus Tatius the *Titienses*.

Dumézil has set the stage; he now asks a question:

> May we assume from this that the three primitive tribes . . . had in effect a functional definition, with the Ramnes controlling political government and the cult (like the companions of "Remus" in Propertius 4.1.9–26), the Luceres being specialists in war (like Lucumon in the same text of Propertius, 26–29), and the Titienses being defined by their wealth of sheep (like the Tatius of Propertius, 30)?

What is Dumézil's answer to this question in *Archaic Roman Religion*?

> The question remains open. I have offered a number of reasons for an affirmative answer, but none is compelling. In the fourth and third centuries the fabricators of Roman history had only a very vague idea of the pre-Servian tribes, and it is possible that the Ramnes, the Luceres, and the Titienses had received their functional coloration only from the "legend of the origins," which was inherited from the Indo-European tradition and, as such, was faithfully trifunctional. But for the present study, an analysis of tenacious ideas and not a pursuit of inaccessible facts, this uncertainty is not very serious.[54]

From Dumézil's remarks in *Archaic Roman Religion* it would seem clear that to claim that "he abandoned this theory" of an actual functional distinction existing between the three Romulean tribes would be an inaccuracy. We will return to this point below but first must address another portion of Cornell's critique—the parenthetical dependent clause which immediately follows: "for which there is no supporting evidence in our texts."

This is a revealing comment. By the phrase "our texts" Cornell presumably means Roman and Greek texts treating Roman social history. For

European-speaking groups sooner or later, often very soon, abandoned this framework in actual practice. It thus remained only ideological and formed a means of analyzing and understanding the world, but with regard to social organization it offered at best only an ideal cherished by the philosophers and a legendary view of the beginnings." See *ARR*: 165.

[54] *ARR*: 164–165.

Dumézil, "our texts," vis-à-vis the problem of the functional nature of the three so-called Romulean tribes, would encompass a far greater range of textual materials. The difference is that between a Romano-centric dismissal of a particular instantiation of a broad Indo-European phenomenon and a comparative Indo-European affirmation of the same. It is the difference between examining only one part of a system in isolation—a particulate approach—and examining the entire system—a systemic approach to an organic whole.

1.7.1.4.2 The comparative method The methods of Dumézil and Benveniste are modeled on the comparative method of historical linguistics—together with the complementary discovery of the regularity of sound change, one of the preeminent scientific achievements of the nineteenth century.[55] The method is well known, but perhaps a simple illustration would not be out of place. The following phonetically and semantically similar verb forms are attested among the Indo-European languages:

Vedic	*sác-ate*	'(s)he accompanies'
Gathic Avestan	*hac-aitē*	'(s)he follows'
Greek	ἕπ-ομαι	'I follow, accompany'
Latin	*sequ-or*	'I follow'
Lithuanian	*sek-ù*	'I follow'

By setting up correspondence series, isolating and comparing each consonant and vowel sound of the root, the Proto-Indo-European verb root can be easily reconstructed:

Vedic	Gathic Avestan	Greek	Latin	Lithuanian	PIE
s	h	h	s	s	*s
a	a	e	e	e	*e
č	č	p	k^w	k	*k^w

The Proto-Indo-European verb root is thus **sek*^{w}*-*.

With the discovery of the Hittite archives at Bogazköy early in the twentieth century and the subsequent decipherment of the Anatolian Indo-European languages, Hittite and other Anatolian reflexes began to be integrated into such traditional Indo-European correspondence series, fine-tuning reconstructions especially by revealing the presence of the so-

[55] For an excellent and up-to-date discussion of the method, see Ringe 2004.

called laryngeal consonants of the parent language (de Saussure's "sonant coefficients"; see Szemerényi 1996: 121–130; Watkins 1998: 40–44; Hoenigswald, Woodard, and Clackson 2004: 519). Obviously not all Hittite lexemes find a match in such previously identified cognate sets, with many words having been borrowed from non-Indo-European languages prior to the time of earliest attestation (see Watkins 2004: 555–556). A form such as Hittite *ārki* '(s)he cuts up, divides up', for example, is isolated from any previously known set of Indo-European cognates. Yet if the word were of Indo-European origin, it would project back to a Proto-Indo-European root *$*h_1erk$-* (beginning with the number-one laryngeal). From that starting point one could then project forward, by applying independently attested rules of sound change, to Latin *erc-iscī* 'to divide', a word of otherwise unknown origin (see Rix 2001: 240, with further references).

Dumézil's method of identifying individual cultural reflexes of archaic Indo-European institutions and projecting back to the parent culture is methodologically comparable to the process of isolating cognate sets and reconstructing their linguistic antecedent. *Pensée extériorisée*, he called it. Gregory Nagy summarizes beautifully in his foreword to the 1999 English translation of Dumézil's *The Riddle of Nostradamus*:[56]

> In this project, Dumézil applies his theoretical models of "exteriorized thinking" (*pensée extériorisée*) to Nostradamus. . . . Dumézil's empiricism centers on comparing the institutions of societies linked to each other by way of cognate languages that can be traced back to a prototypical common language, known to linguists as *Indo-European*.
>
> The key to this book is the comparative method itself, and how this method can reconstruct a frame of mind by externalizing the traditions that formed that frame. If different minds at different times internalize the same given tradition, then a comparatiste can find a link between these different minds by examining that tradition in its externalized forms. . . .[57]

Benveniste's procedure is fundamentally the same, to the extent that it is likewise an appropriation of the comparative linguistic method. Consider a few remarks from Charles Malamoud's review of Benveniste 1969:

> *Le vocabulaire des institutions indo-européennes*, the book that is the subject of this article, belongs to both the "general linguistic" vein of

[56]First published in 1984 under the title *Le moyne noir en gris dedans Varennes.*

[57]Dumézil 1999: vii. The quotation from Nagy continues: ". . . . that is what Dumézil does in linking a tradition that he finds reflected in the work of the Roman historian

> Benveniste's work and the "comparative grammar vein". To be sure, the lexical material studied in the work is purely Indo-European. And insofar as formal analysis is involved, the methods used are the classical techniques of comparative grammar. Still, both the overall plan of the work and some of its particular arguments illustrate a series of theses set forth in his *Problèmes* [Benveniste 1966: 25]: "Individual and society naturally determine one another in and through language. . . . Society is possible only through language; and through language also the individual . . . . Expression (*langage*) always occurs within a *language* (*langue*), within a specific, defined linguistic structure. Language and society are inconceivable without one another. . . . Through language, man assimilates culture and perpetuates or transforms it. Like each language, moreover, each culture employs a specific symbolic apparatus with which each society identifies."[58]

The comparative method is a powerful theoretical tool which provides the investigator with a synergistic breadth—the capability to discern more of the prehistoric language and community than could be discovered by examining any one of its descendants in isolation. With the ancestral structures delineated, one can then project forward to gain a clearer understanding of the evolutionary products of those structures. Malamoud addresses this back-and-forth procedure, common to both the comparative method in its application to language data as well as social and cultural institutions, and aptly terms it a "complex dialectic":

> What exactly is the book about? Is it about Indo-European society as it must have existed before it fragmented into the many peoples who spoke the various Indo-European languages that have come down to us in written texts? To a certain extent, yes. But can one assign to the initial prehistoric phase everything that can be found in each of the societies that grew out of it, and nothing more? That would amount to very little, and one could not even be certain of the inventory obtained in this way, for there were Indo-European populations that left only fleeting traces, and we cannot be sure that their evidence, if we could only lay our hands on it, would confirm or refute the results obtained elsewhere. And the evidence that we do possess is not all of equal value. In regard to what

Livy, whose life straddles the first centuries BC and AD, with what goes on in the minds of two historical figures who had independently internalized that tradition in the context of their own Classical formation: these two figures are Nostradamus, in the sixteenth century AD, and Louis XVI, in the late eighteenth."

[58]Malamoud 1971; reprinted in Loraux, Nagy, and Slatkin 2001, p. 430. The present author wishes to express his appreciation to Gregory Nagy for bringing Malamoud's review to his attention.

> we believe to be the original state of things, some cultures were more faithful than others, or more faithful in some respects than in others. There is general agreement that the social structures and what Georges Dumézil has called the ideology of the Indo-Europeans were better preserved in Rome and in India than in Greece. But to say this is to imply that we already know what the original state was. In fact, we have filtered the available empirical data in such a way as to construct a model, and then we have used that model to reinterpret and reorganize the same data, thereby, when all is said and done, refining and systematizing our filtering procedure. The result is not, properly speaking, a vicious circle but a complex dialectic, the effect of which is always to make what is most consistent seem most plausible.[59]

This method—this complex dialectic—involves a movement from the known to the unknown; in the words of the great French physiologist and philosopher of the nineteenth century, Claude Bernard, "Man can learn nothing except by going from the known to the unknown."[60] Given the nature of evidence of Indo-European tripartition that otherwise survives in Rome, we would be very much surprised indeed were there found what for Cornell might constitute "supporting evidence" in Latin and Greek texts of "functionally defined castes of priests, warriors and producers" (Cornell, p. 78). In the same way, there is obviously no text which provides supporting details for us of the origin of Latin *erc-iscī*. Nevertheless, we can hypothesize that it is a reflex of the same Indo-European source that gives rise to Hittite *ārki*, having previously reconstructed Proto-Indo-European vocabulary and identified the sound changes giving rise to the individual daughter Indo-European languages.

1.7.1.4.3 The progression of ideas While the above-cited remarks from *Archaic Roman Religion* (see §1.7.1.4.1) suggest that the claim that Dumézil "abandoned" his earlier views on the trifunctional nature of the Romulean tribes overshoots the mark, those views certainly did evolve in the years that elapsed between the publication of *Jupiter Mars Quirinus IV* in 1948 and the appearance of the revised edition of *Mythe et épopée* in 1986, the year of Dumézil's death. Dumézil addresses these developments in, for example, *Mythe et épopée* I (pp. 432–434) and *Idées romaines* (pp. 209–215). In laying out one-by-one his criticisms of Dumézil, Cornell (1955: 78) returns again to his "abandonment" argument:

[59]Malamoud, p. 430.

[60]Bernard 1957: 45. The present author wishes to express his appreciation to Dr. John B. Simpson for bringing Claude Bernard to his attention.

> As we have seen, the idea that early Rome was once divided into three castes of priests, warriors and producers was abandoned even by Dumézil himself; Rome had its three tribes, but nothing links them with a division of functions.

Aside from the problem of the claim itself, already noted, the wording here—"the idea . . . was abandoned even by Dumézil himself"—bespeaks a seeming failure or unwillingness to understand or appreciate the progression of ideas that is common to scientific inquiry. And of course Rome's three tribes can still be linked with a division of functions if we agree, as seems most probable, that what one finds in Rome is a survival of a tripartite ideology, per the conceptualization of society—the internalization of an archaic tradition common to the Indo-European peoples—as evidenced by Propertius, invoked by Dumézil.[61]

1.7.1.4.4 A mythic history A second criticism that Cornell advances concerns Dumézil's interpretation of the annalistic traditions of Rome's origins as a "mythic history"—a transposition of myth into history (see *ME* 1: 281–284). Dumézil finds in that history the Roman reflexes of certain widely attested Indo-European mythic motifs, such as that of a conflict between the functions (first/second versus third), a conflict that is situated at a moment when society begins to take shape (compare §1.6.3.3). In Rome the myth appears in the guise of Rome's first war, that fought between Romulus with his Roman warriors (non–third function) and the Sabines (third function) under the leadership of Titus Tatius (see *ARR*: 66–76; *ME* 1: 290–303). Dumézil also sees in the persons of pre-Tarquin kings of Rome the expression—the embodiment—of Indo-European functions. Romulus and Numa Pompilius, contrasting figures, represent the two distinct aspects of the first function—magical and legal, respectively. The war-making Tullus Hostilius personifies the second function. The wealthy Sabines, providers of fertility to Rome, represent the third function, as already noted.[62]

[61] For additional consideration of the ancient Romulean tribes, see below, §1.9.1.1.

[62] Dumézil also argued for third-function elements residing in the figure of Ancus Marcius (see *ME* 1: 280–281, with references). This is another focal point for Cornell's criticism of Dumézil; citing Dumézil 1947, he states: "The evidence adduced by Dumézil to link Ancus with wealth and production is marginal and the argument is patently unconvincing" (Cornell 1995: 78). The present author would agree that the third-function role of Ancus within the mythic history of Rome is less transparent than that of the Sabines, and less pronounced than the first- and second-function nature of the preceding three kings. This was also, however, the view held, or arrived at, by Dumézil. We, along with Cornell, should give ear to Dumézil's observations on Ancus

Cornell's criticism here is directed at Dumézil's contention that this history is fabricated, a product of the fourth and third centuries BC (see *ARR*: 66, 165; *ME* 1: 269–270): it is "the historicization of myths, . . . the transposition of fables into events" (*ARR*: 75). Cornell (p. 79) asks whether we could not see it the other way around: ". . . even if we allow that the stories of the origins of Rome are expressions of a functional mythology, does it necessarily follow that they are unhistorical?" In other words, could not those stories record actual events that were recast by marrying inherited mythic themes to tellings of those events? Cornell then quotes several phrases from Dumézil's concluding remarks (*ARR*: 73), made after comparing the account of the Sabine War with the North Germanic tradition of the war between the Æsir and the Vanir (see §1.6.3.3); here the quotation is presented in a fuller form, with those portions cited by Cornell placed in italics:

> There is no need to stress the exact parallelism not only of the ideological values which provide the point of departure but also of the intrigues from the beginning to end, including the two episodes[63] which describe

in his work *The Destiny of the Warrior* (1970: 8; trans. of Dumézil 1969): "This functional interpretation of the founding kings has been generally accepted for the first three: the obviously deliberate antithesis between Romulus and Numa, recalling the two opposite yet necessary aspects of the first function, and the wholly warlike character of Tullus, demand little discussion. It has been otherwise for the fourth king, Ancus Marcius. Despite the anachronisms that have long been recognized in the work attributed to him, one cannot help having the impression that it is with Ancus Marcius that historical authenticity begins to carry some appreciable weight in the traditions; that he represents, in the series of kings, the point at which a purely fictitious history, which is intended merely to explain, is welded to a history retouched, reevaluated, to be sure, but in its inception genuine and recorded. This sort of coming to earth of the speculations that a people or a dynasty makes upon its past is always a delicate point for the critic: Upon what ordinal term, for example, in the series of Ynglingar—those descendants of the god Freyr who little by little become the very real kings of the Swedish Uplands, then of southern Norway—must the human mantle first be placed? The matter continues to be debated, and there is considerable divergence of opinion. Mutatis mutandis, it is just the same for Ancus, so that one hesitates—and many evince some reluctance—to recognize, even in one part of his 'history' or a part of his character, a last fragment of a pseudo history of mythical origin only intended to illustrate the successive appearances of the three functions." Cornell has again moved too quickly to judgment.

[63]Succinctly, Dumézil's "two episodes" are those of (i) the treacherous intervention of a gold-desiring woman on the side of the possessors of wealth; and (ii) the battlefield intervention of the god of magic. In each instance there is a less than completely successful outcome. See the discussions in *ARR*: 68–73 and *ME* 1: 295–299.

> the war between the rich gods and the magician gods. It seems hardly imaginable that chance should have twice created this vast structure, especially in view of the fact that other Indo-European peoples have homologous accounts. The simplest and humblest explanation is to admit that the Romans, as well as the Scandinavians, received this scenario from a common earlier tradition and that they *simply modernized its details, adapting them to their own "geography," "history," and customs and introducing the names of the countries, peoples, and heroes suggested by actuality.*

And again Cornell (p. 79) asks, incorporating phraseology from Dumézil's conclusions:

> Would it not be possible . . . to argue that the materials "suggested by actuality" were drawn from an ancient tradition, possibly based on fact, that the original population of the city resulted from a fusion of Latin and Sabine elements?

In the present author's view, the answer to these questions could very well be yes; my own inclination is to suspect just such an intermingling of more ancient Indo-European mythic tradition and less ancient Roman historical tradition. But Dumézil also allowed this possibility, and he states as much in a note on the same page of *Archaic Roman Religion* from which Cornell drew the above citation. Dumézil wrote:

> If it should be possible to demonstrate some day, archaeologically, that there was an ethnic duality in the origins of Rome, the account given by the annalistic tradition would still remain entirely "prefabricated"; the historicized myth would merely be superimposed on history.[64]

We see here, as we saw earlier, that Dumézil's own views are not so far from those of his detractors. It would seem that much of Dumézil—perhaps more of Benveniste—has simply been selectively ignored by those detractors.

1.7.1.4.5 A broader expression From the vantage point of the comparativist, vestiges of a deeply ancient Indo-European ideology are clearly perceptible in Rome, as they are in Iguvium (see Poultney 1951: 19–20; Benveniste 1945a; also see below, §3.3.3.2.3). Indeed, the ideology shows itself to the

[64] *ARR*: 73, n. 17; the passage quoted is reproduced in *Archaic Roman Religion* from Dumézil 1949. Cornell adds (1995: 79): "We could equally suppose that the stereotyped figures of Numa and Tullus were created by imposing functional specialisation upon two kings who were respectively celebrated in tradition for religious reforms and a successful war . . . ." Again, this seems an entirely possible, perhaps probable, scenario.

present day in the annual celebration of the festival for Saints Ubaldo, George, and Anthony in modern Gubbio.[65] Benveniste reminds us of the persistence of the ideology into medieval England:

> Toward the end of the ninth century, Alfred the Great added this observation to his translation of Boethius: "A populated territory: that is the work with which a king concerns himself. He needs men of prayer, men of war, and men of labor." In the fourteenth century, moreover, one could read this in an English sermon . . . "God made clerics, knights, and tillers of the soil, but the Demon made burghers and usurers." With the growth of cities, guilds and commerce, the ancient order in which the preacher saw the natural order came to an end.[66]

Its survival in the *varṇas* of India is self-evident.[67] We leave aside the consideration of its presence in such modern-era social and cultural phenomena as the society of the former Soviet Union and the American governmental system.[68]

1.8 THE CAPITOLINE TRIAD

Our examination of Indo-European tripartition and the comparative method began with a discussion of the archaic Pre-Capitoline triad—Jupiter, Mars, Quirinus (§1.7). The prehistoric threesome, however, would not endure as a synchronic set. With the appearance of the Capitoline temple of Jupiter Optimus Maximus, we find that Mars and Quirinus have been excised from the triad of chief divinities and replaced by two goddesses, Juno and Minerva. How could such a seemingly fundamental shift away from the ancestral Indo-European paradigm have occurred? The question

[65]See Dumézil 1979: 123–143. N. J. Allen (1987: 26) writes: "The legacy of the old ideology may be detectable today in various forms, ranging from straightforward punctate manifestations in folklorist contexts to diffuse attitudes. One thinks of the recent discovery of a trifunctional triad of saints in a festival still performed at Gubbio in Italy . . . , and of the enduring importance of the varṇas in India. But these cannot be recent *inventions*. They are clearly survivals, creations of earlier times. In broad terms, the trifunctional ideology is ancient history, dead and gone, or at most transmuted beyond recognition."

[66]Benveniste 1945a; in Loraux, Nagy, and Slatkin 2001: 447. Benveniste cites Owst 1933: 553 and Moss 1935: 271.

[67]Allen (1987: 26) points to this as well; see note above.

[68]For a discussion of these and other possible modern examples of the persistence of the Indo-European tripartite ideology, see Littleton 1982: 231–232.

is an old one, if not always phrased in quite this manner. Refined revelation has not yet presented itself; but even so, inferences can be made.

1.8.1 An Etruscan source?

In the view of the Romans, the source of the Capitoline temple—within which is ensconced the new triad—is an Etruscan one. Some recent scholarship has attempted to downplay what was previously judged to be an extensive Etruscan cultural impact on the Romans and to emphasize the central-Italian commonality of the two peoples.[69] While the extent to which this reevaluation is viable (as opposed to being merely an expression of academic revisionism) remains to be seen, the "invasionist model" (Cornell 1995: 160) which the new interpretation seeks to eliminate quite likely does stand in need of rehabilitation.

In any event, it appears beyond doubt that Etruria exerted some measure of influence on Latium. The Etruscans acquired the alphabet from the Greeks and passed it on to the Romans in a form indelibly etched with Etruscan intermediacy, hence providing the Romans as a people not only with graphic hardware but with literacy as well. This is surely not to suggest that no one in Rome could read before the creation of the Latin alphabet; the adaptation of the Etruscan alphabet for Roman use was a process almost certainly begun among bilingual speakers of Latin and Etruscan (see Wallace 1989: 125–127; Clackson 2004).[70]

[69]Cornell (1995: 172) surmises: "On the model of a cultural *koinē*, 'Etruscan Rome' is as misleading a description of Rome as 'Roman Etruria' would be of archaic Etruria. Rather, the Etruscan cities, Rome, and other communities in Tyrrhenian central Italy shared the same common culture, formed from an amalgam of Greek, orientalising, and native Italic elements." Presumably, in the last phrase he is using "native Italic" to mean something like 'indigenous to Italy' (as opposed to Greek and Asian/North African); in doing so he fails to recognize the distinct cultural heritage of the Indo-European Italic peoples on the one hand and the non-Indo-European Etruscans on the other. He is, of course, not unaware of the differences (p. 169): "What I am suggesting is that in the archaic period Rome, although different in language, and probably also in self-conscious ethnic identity, from the Etruscan cities, was nevertheless comparable to them in material culture, social structure and institutions." While "comparable" does not mean identical, one is left with the uneasy feeling that the playing field has been overly leveled.

[70]For a view that would minimize the Etruscan role in the Roman acquisition of the alphabet, see Cornell 1995: 103–104. His interpretation is complicated by an overreliance on both the views of Jack Goody and the archaic letters inscribed on a pot recovered from the necropolis at Osteria dell'Osa (early eighth century BC). The letters appear to be Greek, but are unusual; the presence of the inscribed pot likely attests that its owner had affiliations with the south of Italy (see Bietti Sestieri and De Santis 2000: 53). To

It cannot be denied that the Romans present themselves as culturally indebted to the Etruscans; Livy, Dionysius of Halicarnassus, and other ancient authorities[71] detail Etruscan contributions to Rome.[72] Among items the Romans attribute to Etruscan origin are styles of dress, elements of urban architecture, divinatory arts and books, *haruspices* (and eventually a college of these entrails-reading priests), along with yet other elements of cult and religion.[73] Concerning cult and religion, Livy (5.1.6), for example, wrote that the Etruscans were the people who surpassed all others in dedication to religious rites and excelled in the art of their observance. As Beard, North, and Price point out:

> For even if modern archaeology has increasingly come to argue that Etruria and Rome were part of a shared common culture in the sixth century BC and even later, Roman imagination in the centuries that followed did not see it in that way: for them Etruscan religious traditions were different and alien, and sometimes powerful for that very reason.[74]

---

minimize Etruscan cultural impact on Rome generally, it would seem that the Etruscan transmission of the alphabet to the Romans is an obstacle that Cornell must find a way to get around.

[71]For a convenient citation of references, see Cornell 1995: 165, n. 56.

[72]Cornell seeks to turn the recorded Roman view on its head (1995: 169): "In the late Republic Etruscan civilisation seemed to the Romans alien, mysterious, even barbaric [here Cornell notes Cicero, *Nat. D.* 2.11 and Livy 7.17.3]; that there had once been a time when they and the Etruscans had shared the same culture was something of which they were not remotely aware." Perhaps for very good reason, depending on the semantic imprecision one is willing to assign to the phrase "the same culture." Cornell continues (pp. 169–170): "But noting that their archaic temples (for example) were similar in design and decoration to those in Etruria, they assumed that they were 'Etruscan', and explained their presence in Rome as the result of borrowing. The Romans were by no means ashamed of such borrowing; on the contrary, they made a positive virtue of the fact that they owed most of their institutions and customs to other peoples. What made this not only tolerable but even a source of pride was the fact that they had achieved mastery over their erstwhile superiors; and it was ideologically potent because it helped them to come to terms with their complete dependence on Greek culture during the last centuries of the Republic." Summing up, he adds (p. 171): "The paradoxical conclusion is that, so far from attempting to minimise or conceal Etruscan influence on early Rome, our sources are actually guilty of the opposite tendency, and have if anything exaggerated the extent of this influence." One, however, is left with the uneasy feeling that it is the summary claim that may be exaggerated, amounting in effect to an unfalsifiable hypothesis.

[73]On Etruscan religion generally, and its influence on Rome, see, inter alia, *ARR*: 625–696; *BNP*, vol. 1: 20, 54, 59–60; Cornell 1995: 159–172; Burkert 1992: 46–53; Thulin 1968.

[74]*BNP*, vol. 1: 20. Beard, North, and Price offer these remarks in their discussion of the *haruspices*.

As noted immediately above (see also §1.2), the Capitolium project is traditionally attributed to the Etruscan Tarquins, Tarquinius Priscus having vowed a temple to Jupiter, Juno, and Minerva in his final battle with the Sabines (Dionysius of Halicarnassus, *Ant. Rom.* 3.69.1; Livy 1.38.7). The bulk of construction itself fell to his scion Tarquinius Superbus (*Ant. Rom.* 3.69.2; Livy 1. 55.1). Only after the expulsion of the Tarquins and the end of the monarchy, however, was the temple dedicated, the honor falling to the consul Marcus Horatius Pulvillus (*Ant. Rom.* 5.35.3; Livy 2. 8.6–8). The affiliation of the divine trio of Jupiter, Juno, and Minerva with the Etruscans is, of course, otherwise claimed in antiquity. Servius (*Aen.* 1.422) writes of experts in the *Etrusca disciplina* (Etruscan religious practice) who prescribe the requirement that a city have three temples, three streets, and three gates dedicated to Jupiter, Juno, and Minerva (*ARR*: 307–308; 665).[75]

1.8.2 A Greek source?

The traditional Roman view which sees the Etruscan Tarquins as the impetus for the construction of the Capitoline temple obviates not at all the possibility of an ultimate Greek origin of the Capitoline triad (Zeus, Hera, Athena), with—or without—Etruscans serving in some intermediary capacity. As Cornell rightly observes:

> What is absolutely clear is that both Etruscan and Roman ideas of deity were profoundly affected by Greek influences from a very early period. Both Etruscans and Romans adopted Greek gods such as Heracles and Apollo; and they both sought to equate their own gods and goddesses with appropriate figures from the Greek pantheon (thus Greek Hermes = Etruscan *Turms* = Roman *Mercurius*; Greek Aphrodite = Etruscan *Turan* = Roman *Venus*; Greek Hephaestus = Etruscan *Sethlans* = Roman *Vulcanus*, etc.).[76]

He then adds to this two points of emphasis:

[75] Cornell addresses specifically the matter of the Etruscans vis-à-vis the building of the Capitoline temple. His remarks at this point seem particularly revisionist. He writes (1995: 167): "We know, certainly, that the great temple of Capitoline Jupiter at Rome was built by Etruscan craftsmen, and its terracotta sculptures were made by artists from Veii [on which, see below] . . . . But this means only that the Romans were able to call upon the services of the best available craftsmen, and in the late sixth century, as the statues from the Portonaccio temple amply attest, the finest school of terracotta sculpture was situated at Veii . . . ." It means *only* this? As expected, Cornell categorically rejects the notion that the Etruscans were the source of the triad. But, of course, he has no latitude in the matter; rejection is requisite.

[76] Cornell 1995: 161–162.

> First, Etruscan and Roman representations of these deities invariably drew on Greek iconography and mythology; second, evidence of this syncretistic process (sometimes called *interpretatio graeca*) goes back to the very beginning of the archaic period.

This is fine, of course; but he appends yet a third point:

> Greek influence on Roman views of the gods was the result of direct contacts between Rome and the Greek world.[77]

This third is a crucial point for Cornell because he wants to deny that the Etruscans were conduits for the introduction to Rome of Greek ideas about the gods. (Specifically, he is rebutting the claim that the "anthropomorphizing" of Roman gods came about in this way.)

It is certain that the Greeks exerted direct influence on Rome in the realm of the divine, but the picture is a bit more complex than Cornell paints it. That the Etruscans could and did serve as intermediaries in this regard is revealed, for example, by other divine "equations." Thus Greek *Ganymede* (Γανυμήδης) will be introduced to Rome under the name *Catamitus*. The phonological adjustments that have occurred clearly signal that the name, and so Greek tradition in which it figures, was introduced to Latin from the Etruscan language (see Clackson 2004).

This nexus has yet other strands. The list of Greek gods and their Etruscan and Roman counterparts which Cornell presents (cited above) suggests independent Etruscan and Roman processes of *interpretatio*. Other such equivalencies, however, reveal that Etruscans borrowed Italic theonyms associated with Greek deities: thus Latin *Juno* (= Greek Hera) gives Etruscan *Uni*; Latin *Mars* (= Greek Ares) gives Etruscan *Maris*; Umbrian **Nehtuns* (= Greek Poseidon) gives Etruscan *Neθuns*.[78] If one of the newcomers to the great divine triad in Rome (Juno) lends her name to an Etruscan goddess, the other no less shares her name with an Etruscan deity—Latin *Minerva* beside Etruscan *Menerva*—but the direction of borrowing (from Latin into Etruscan or vice versa) is difficult to determine.[79]

That the Greeks, an Indo-European people, could be the source of the nonce triad that replaces an archaic Indo-European configuration (Jupiter, Mars, Quirinus) is not in itself problematic—the Greeks were deeply influ-

[77] Cornell 1995: 162.

[78] On the last-named, see Rix 2004.

[79] A tantalizing example of an Etruscan acquisition of Italic tripartite ideology might possibly be provided by the recent excavation of a sacral complex in Tarquinia (first half of the seventh century: see Bonghi Jovino 2000a). Buried beneath the entrance to

enced themselves by non-Indo-European peoples and traditions, particularly those of the Near East. Direct evidence of a possible Greek cultic template is not good, though such a triad (Zeus, Hera, Athena) is not unknown at a later period (Phocis, second century AD; see *ARR*: 306–307). In *Mythe et épopée*, Dumézil himself conjectures that the source, rather than fully Etruscan, was likely Greek with Etruscan mediation:

> Le nouveau groupement n'est pas latin. Étrusque? Plus probablement grec sous un vêtement étrusque. Peut-être même n'a-t-il été pris par les Tarquins à la Grèce . . . .[80]

Dumézil is of course here referring to the tradition that Demaratus, the patriarch of the Tarquin family, settled in Etruria as a refugee from Corinth. Dumézil's conjecture is not incongruous with current views; thus Cornell writes:

> The migration of Demaratus may well be authentic, at least in a symbolic sense. Our sources use the story to explain the spread of the Greek culture in Etruria. . . . The general picture is borne out by archaeological evidence which confirms the decisive importance of Corinthian influence on Etruscan civilisation during the second half of the seventh century. The story may indeed be literally true, in the sense that Corinthian craftsmen did live and work in the centres of southern Etruria at this time; and in the conditions of the archaic period it is entirely credible that an aristocratic émigré and his retinue could take up residence in a foreign community without loss of social position.[81]

We should make clear, however, that Cornell (1995: 167) "emphatically" rejects the notion that it was Etruscans who introduced the Capitoline triad to Rome.

1.8.3 "How tradition presents it"

In any event, returning to the earlier point, *according to Roman tradition* it was during an Etruscan regime that the temple was built in which a new triad is housed—replacing a triad of canonical Indo-European structure. To

---

the complex were three bronze objects: a ceremonial trumpet, a shield, and an ax head (see Bonghi Jovino 2000b, who writes on p. 270: "Gli oggetti in bronzo, infatti, hanno posto il problema di tre aspetti fondamentali: funzione, simbolo e potere"). Compare the Indo-European talismans described in §2.3.1, especially the Scythian plough and yoke, sword, and votive cup.

[80] *ME* 3: 204.

[81] Cornell 1995: 124.

appropriate Cornell's evaluation regarding the annalistic tradition of the ascension of the Tarquins to the throne of Rome: "Whether any of this is historical does not matter; the question at issue is how tradition presents it" (ibid., 127). For the present work it is of little consequence whether the new Capitoline triad was a common and native Etruscan assemblage of deities; or one acquired by Etruscans, at least Tarquins, from Greeks; or one taken directly from the Greeks by non-Etruscan inhabitants of Rome; or of some yet different origin. This is not to say that this is, in some absolute sense, an inconsequential matter (in other words, perhaps it really does "matter"), only that for the investigation presented in the following chapters it has little immediate relevance. Before leaving the current consideration of the Etruscans vis-à-vis the Capitoline triad and moving on to Mars, with whom this introductory chapter will close, there are a few observations which we should like to offer.

LIBRARY, UNIVERSITY OF CHESTER

1.9 CONTINUITY AND DISSOLUTION

What is fascinating is that, according to the annalistic tradition, a divine reconfiguring occurred during a period of Tarquin rule and that it survived the expulsion of those same Etruscan Tarquins and the collapse of the monarchy. Beard, North, and Price call attention to this continuity:

> The most striking continuity of all concerns Jupiter Capitolinus and his grandiose new temple. The tradition is that the temple was built by the last Tarquin, finished by the time of his fall, dedicated by the very first college of magistrates of the Republic. However unlikely this story may seem to us now, it does at least encapsulate the ambivalent standing of the cult between monarchy and Republic. The position of Jupiter within the triad, the dominant position and scale of the building, the nature of the cult-practice, all suggest that the king had designed the temple as a grandiose expression of his power and that of his régime. It would perhaps have been going too far to expect that the temple would have been razed to the ground when the Tarquins fell; but it is still surprising that what happened was the precise opposite—the cult became central to the new republican era.[82]

Following discussion of the continuance of regal ceremony into the Republic, they add:

> This is not the only example of the survival into the Republic of symbols

[82] *BNP*, vol. 1: 59.

> of power belonging to ancient monarchic practice, though it is perhaps the most dramatic one. It seems comprehensible only on the assumption that what is now thought of as *royal* ceremonial was perceived by the Romans, first and foremost, as *Roman*, certainly not as an arbitrary imposition upon them—whether monarchical or Etruscan. For another factor that might have played a part in the religious conflicts of this period is the apparently "foreign" Etruscan origins of the last kings and the religious institutions associated with them. In fact it was probably as difficult then as it is now to define the boundaries between Etruscan and Roman elements in religion. Although some particular practices (such as haruspicy) would forever remain linked to Etruscan roots, the "Roman" religious world had become saturated with influences from their Etruscan neighbors which had merged with and transformed the Latin culture of their ancestors. Jupiter was, after all, an ancient Latin deity with an ancient Latin name—and at the same time the focus of what we may choose to classify as (in part at least) Etruscan religious forms (such as the ceremonial of triumph or the Capitoline temple). Meanwhile, there was no alternative high culture, or vocabulary of ceremonial to which Romans could turn. It is unlikely that the early republicans ever conceived of isolating, let alone outlawing, the "Etruscan" religion in their midst.[83]

Roman religious practice is conservative. In the words of Cornell (1995: 25): "The Romans were notoriously conservative in the way they maintained ancient cult practices, and were punctilious in the performance of ritual acts in the manner prescribed by tradition." From a comparative Indo-European vantage point, one perceives that Roman religion is manifestly prone to preserve ancestral ideology and structure. This we have examined; only among the Italic peoples and other peoples living along the outer perimeter of the ancient Indo-European speech area—Celts and Indo-Iranians—is the archaic Proto-Indo-European religious ideology well preserved, along with religious and legal vocabulary. That preservation is certainly to be linked to the continuation of age-old priesthoods, of early Indo-European origin, in those same communities.

The events of that process by which the Indo-European Pre-Capitoline triad was supplanted by the triad ensconced in the Tarquin temple on the Capitoline are lost in the depths of unrecorded history. But could we imagine that it was a quick and easy exchange meeting with no priestly

[83] *BNP*, vol. 1: 60. This is a fuller citation of those remarks that we rehearsed above in demonstration of the like-mindedness of Dumézil and Beard, North, and Price; see §1.7.1.1. Presumably Cornell would take issue with the claim, "Meanwhile, there was no alternative high culture, or vocabulary of ceremonial to which Romans could turn," and contend that an "alternative high culture" would be Greek.

resistance? That would certainly appear to be a prima facie implausibility, regardless of how much the boundaries between popular Etruscan and Roman culture may have begun to blur. Sacerdotal conflict is well enough documented in later periods of Roman religious history (see, inter alia, *BNP*, vol. 1: 105–108) and equally well known from the history of religious institutions generally. No one can answer the question of what confliction lies behind the replacement of Pre-Capitoline triad by Capitoline triad. Perhaps we can, however, gain some insight into the nature of the tension and conflict as sustained in Roman memory.

1.9.1 Roman-Etruscan conflicts

Friction and confrontation between Roman priest and Etruscan monarch or priest is recounted plainly in Roman tradition. Let us examine episodes in the Roman memory of such encounters.

1.9.1.1 THE ANCIENT ROMULEAN TRIBES The tradition that Romulus had divided the Roman people into three tribes—the Ramnes, Titienses, and Luceres (Livy 1.13.8)—has already occupied our attention (see §1.7.1.4.1); let us consider that tradition in closer detail. Tarquinius Priscus determined that he would increase the tribal number, naming the new tribes after himself (and his companions, says Dionysius, *Ant. Rom.* 3.71.1). To this tampering with a divinely sanctioned Roman institution, the famed Augur Attus Navius reacted sharply. Romulus had established the tribal structure upon consultation with the Augures, and no change in this structure could be made, contended Navius, unless auspices were first taken and they revealed that the alteration had the approval of the gods (Livy 1.36.3–4). In the account of Dionysius of Halicarnassus, Navius (whom the Greek historian names Attius Nevius) simply refused to allow any meddling with the institutions of Romulus (*Ant. Rom.* 3.71.1–2). Tarquinius schemed to humiliate the Augur publicly and commanded Navius to take auspices concerning some unnamed project which he was contemplating. Favorable omens were observed by Navius and reported to the king, who in response jeered at the Augur and belittled his divining craft, scoffing that the project involved cutting a whetting stone in half with a razor. Tarquinius was silenced as the Augur coolly proceeded to slice the stone with just such a blade (Livy 1.36.4–8; cf. *Ant. Rom.* 3.712–5, where Tarquinius himself does the cutting, severing in addition a portion of an unfortunate hand which happened to be holding the stone). The Romulean tribal structure remained intact.[84]

[84]Notice, however, that the adopted son of Tarquinius Priscus, the Latin-born Servius Tullius, is said to have introduced to Rome and environs the geographic-based tribal

1.9.1.2 THE CAPITOLINE HEAD The annalistic tradition records other Etruscan endeavors to outdo Rome in the realm of the divinely sanctioned. Consider the case of the severed human head found within the Capitoline hill when the foundations of Jupiter's new temple were being dug (see §1.2 for the account). With Roman seers failing to discern the meaning of the discovery, Tarquinius dispatched a Roman delegation to the most skilled of the Etruscan seers, one Olenus Calenus. The Etruscan diviner sketched a map of the Tarpeian hill on the ground at his own home and asked the Roman envoys to point to the place where the portent had appeared. His intention was to trick the Romans into designating Etruscan soil (the ground on which he was drawing) as the point of discovery and in so doing to appropriate the omen for the benefit of his own territory. The Romans refused to be fooled (having been previously alerted to the diviner's likely strategy by his own son) and repeatedly answered that the head had been found in Rome. In the end, the Etruscan seer was thus compelled to answer truthfully and reveal the discovery to be an omen of Rome's coming dominance (see Dionysius of Halicarnassus, *Ant. Rom.* 4.60.1–61.2; Livy 1.55.5–7). Had the Roman envoys been duped, adds Pliny, the *Annals* affirm that Rome's destiny would have been transferred to Etruria (*HN* 28.15).

1.9.1.3 THE CAPITOLINE TERRA COTTA CHARIOT After presenting his account of the preceding event, Pliny (*HN* 28.16–17) immediately invokes his readers' collective memory of another such occurrence, also related to the construction of the Capitoline temple of Jupiter Optimus Maximus:

> Iterum id accidisse tradunt, cum in fastigium eiusdem delubri praeparatae quadrigae fictiles in fornace crevissent, et iterum simili modo retentum augurium.
>
> We're told that it happened also when a four-horse chariot of clay, sculpted for the roof of the same temple, expanded in the kiln, and again, in similar way, the omen was saved.

The incident Pliny mentions is preserved in greater detail by Plutarch (*Pub.* 13.1–4). Tarquinius Superbus had commissioned Etruscan artisans of the city of Veii to craft a clay chariot for the roof of the new temple. When

---

structure, with no apparent opposition; see Livy 1.43.12–13; Dionysius of Halicarnassus, *Ant. Rom.* 4.14.1–2, 15.1–3. The two tribal modifications, one unsuccessful, one successful, differ not only in that the former was initiated by an Etruscan and the latter by the son of Latins but also to the extent that Tarquinius attempted to modify a Romulean institution while Servius superimposed an additional tribal structure.

the piece was fired, rather than shrinking as the clay baked, it expanded, reaching such a size and degree of hardness that even after the kiln had been disassembled it was only with great difficulty that the statue could be removed from it. The Etruscan diviners judged that this marvelous omen marked εὐτυχία 'prosperity' and δύναμις 'power' (*Pub.* 13.3) for those who possessed the statue, and the citizens of Veii refused to deliver it to Rome. Not long afterward, however, at the end of a day of chariot racing in Veii, the victor's team of horses suddenly bolted and ran straight to Rome, refusing to be reined in by the helpless driver. Upon reaching Rome the horses raced to the Capitoline hill, where the driver was thrown from his chariot. The Etruscans deemed this to be a portent and surrendered the clay chariot to Rome. The tradition of this incident is all the more interesting because, though Tarquinius had placed the order for the chariot, the Romans had already driven him from the throne before the Etruscan artists had even begun molding it. Plutarch concedes that he does not know if Tarquinius had the chariot made because he had received a divine directive, or if it was simply his own idea. Either way, the Etruscan-arranged, Etruscan-crafted Capitoline ornament is clearly depicted as destined for Rome, not for Etruria.

1.9.1.4 A GLIMPSE BEHIND THE CURTAIN In each of these three scenarios preserved in Rome's traditions of its own earliest history, Rome is presented as being at odds with Etruria. This is Roman tradition, Roman perception; historical accuracy—or lack thereof—regarding the specific events is secondary. The tension is either internal, expressed between Etruscan monarch and Roman institution, or external, between an Etruscan territory and Rome.

The tension is never far removed from the Tarquin temple of Jupiter Optimus Maximus. Two of the three episodes are associated explicitly with the building of the Capitolium. The incident of the Capitoline head occurs at the very beginning of the temple's construction; that of the terra cotta chariot takes place at the very end. In each case Latins thwart an Etruscan attempt at exploitation. The two events are bookends. They bracket the temple project with tensions between Etruria and Rome—and at each end the Romans gain the upper hand.

The third incident is presented as a confrontation between a Roman priest and the Etruscan monarch who vowed that temple (and who had begun digging its foundations, according to Dionysius of Halicarnassus; see §1.2). It is a confrontation over the Romulean tribes, a division of society which *ideologically* (see §1.7.1.4.1) matches—*function for function*—the Pre-

Capitoline triad which will be supplanted with the completion of Tarquin's temple. Again, historical accuracy is not the concern; Roman ideology and collective memory are. It is improbable that the Romulean tribes ever represented a division of society into "functionally defined castes of priests, warriors and producers" (Cornell 1995: 77). If the population of eighth-century (or otherwise early) Rome was ever divided into three tribal units (as we must allow it may well have been), that division was most probably merely an expression of an inherited Italic idealized conception of society as consisting of three elements: an expression of perceived order and completeness engrained in early Italic culture (surfacing also in Umbria; see §§1.5.4; 3.3.3.2.3). If no such tribal division actually existed, the traditions of such a structure are an ex post facto imprinting on the historical record of the same ideology.

What is important to understand is that the Romulean tribal division of human Latin society is precisely the same division that is applied to the Pre-Capitoline society of the gods: Romulus/Ramnes—Lucumon/Luceres—Titus Tatius/Titienses on the one hand, Jupiter—Mars—Quirinus on the other, each an internalization of the ancestral tripartition of sovereignty, war, fecundity. The tale of the Tarquin disruption of Romulean tribal division, in Roman tradition, is the shadow of the (perceived) Tarquin disruption of the Pre-Capitoline triad—they are avatars of a single legendary event. There is no room for chest-beating in the matter of the triad—historical reality does not allow it; in the shadow account, however, a Latin victory can be trumpeted. When a war is lost, the great stories that are told are those of the battles that were won.

All of these episodes look to point to what was for some Latin element of society in Rome—priestly and élite, perhaps broader—an uncomfortable and confused reality of religious and cultic shift—a tension which seeks relief in the interpretative tradition that Etruscan-directed, Etruscan-manufactured, Etruscan-revealed phenomena are fundamentally a part of the fabric of the divine disposition of Rome. Do these stories not provide a glimpse behind the curtain which hides from view the replacement of the Indo-European Pre-Capitoline triad with the Capitoline triad? Do they not clue us in to a nearly unspoken Roman memory (a perception, whatever the individual historical "facts") that the source of the great divine triad under which Roman prosperity and power would expand was foreign? By the times of the later Republic perhaps we could say with Beard, North, and Price (*BNP*, vol. 1: 60) that "it was probably as difficult then as it is now to define the boundaries between Etruscan and Roman elements in religion." This, however, would probably not be the case among all elements of society as the Republic took shape. The success of the "(in part at least) Etruscan religious forms" (*BNP*, vol. 1: 60) must, however, reveal some measure of broad popular support, and this is very likely grounded in central Italian cultural commonality.

1.10 COMPROMISE AND THE MINOR CAPITOLINE TRIAD

The gods must relocate from the Capitoline so that construction of the Tarquin temple of Jupiter Optimus Maximus may begin. The quaint story (see §1.2) preserved by Dionysius of Halicarnassus and other historians of Rome about Augures consulting the many deities whose altars lay upon that hill and the unwillingness of Juventas and Terminus (setting aside Mars for the moment) to move must conceal a reality of sacerdotal opposition and negotiation. The story of the showdown between Tarquinius and the priest Attus Navius is a symptomatic expression in the annalistic record of such opposition, though concerned only indirectly with the matter of the Capitoline triad. It is impossible to imagine that the Roman priestly establishment—particularly the three major Flamines—already ancient in the era of the monarchy, would simply have buckled in the face of foreign pressure. The public, divine vindication of Navius and humbling of Tarquinius certainly do not point to any Roman memory of such, but to just the opposite. On the other hand, there is certainly no preserved Roman tradition of anything like a martyrdom of Roman priests by the Tarquins. Nevertheless, a fundamental religious change—"Etruscan religious reforms" (*BNP*, vol. 1: 60)—occurred during the Tarquin regime. Should we infer that in the process of this transition some sort of priestly compromise was involved?

The insistence on leaving Juventas and Terminus on the Capitoline and the installation of shrines dedicated to them within the new temple of Jupiter Optimus Maximus must surely be seen as a concession[85] (a well-motivated one as we shall see in chapter 5). Mars and Quirinus, the principal vestiges of the old Indo-European second and third functions are no longer major players; but other members of those ideological realms must remain in their place—Juventas (second function: Goddess of Roman warrior manhood) and Terminus (third function: a "god of Titus Tatius"). Variant expressions of the Pre-Capitoline triad are otherwise known. Thus,

[85]In this regard, Augustine's comment (*De Civ. D.* 4.23; presumably based on Varro) that the installations of Terminus and Juventas within the temple were so obscure as to be practically unknown to even the best informed is, if nothing else, certainly *séduisant*.

for example, the threesome Jupiter, Mars, Ops (with Ops, the goddess of abundant harvest and one of the "gods of Titus Tatius" replacing Quirinus) are joined in the Regia (see *ARR*: 172–174; 267; Boyle and Woodard 2000: 210–211). Jupiter, Mars, and Flora (goddess of flowering crops, and another of the "gods of Titus Tatius") appear as a triad in conjunction with certain ancient chariot races (see *ARR*: 270). Jupiter, Juventas, and Terminus constitute a sort of Pre-Capitoline triad within the Capitolium; we may call them the *Minor Capitoline triad.*

1.10.1 An alternative analysis

There is an alternative to interpreting the installation of the Capitoline triad as simply the consequence of the foreign introduction or imposition of a divine structure—an interpretation which is consistent with the evidence invoked above, and which sensibly accounts for the substitution of Jupiter-Juno-Minerva for Jupiter-Mars-Quirinus, and for the unremarkable aftermath of that replacement following the end of the monarchy (bearing in mind the words of Beard, North, and Price: "It would perhaps have been going too far to expect that the temple would have been razed to the ground when the Tarquins fell; but it is still surprising that what happened was the precise opposite—the cult became central to the new republican era"; *BNP*, vol. 1: 59).

One could imagine that fundamental doctrines and structures which the various Roman priests had inherited from their Indo-European predecessors were—or had come to be—of a heterodox nature. Obviously non-Indo-European influence could have played a role in developing or encouraging heterodoxy; however, by this analysis change would have been initiated from within. Theological variation within a single society is certainly not an unusual phenomenon—in fact, is likely the norm; consider the Hindu sects which would develop in India, the seeds of which can already be detected in the Vedas. The theological shift which is traced to the period of Tarquin rule and survives the downfall of the monarchy, one could imagine, could simply be the result of a realigning of priestly structures of power or interpretation—perhaps the very thing one might expect would happen with the disruption of the structure of political power in a society where priests, or some subset thereof, are never far removed from the political nerve center of society. In this case the Roman affiliation of the Capitoline temple with the Tarquins and the associated stories of Etrusco-Roman conflicts would be best seen as historical reflections of the early annalists who, ignorant of primitive Indo-European theological heterodoxy, naturally attributed the Capitoline shift at the end of the monarchy to Tarquin intentionality. In order to maintain this hypothesis, we would require independent supporting evidence of Indo-European religious heterodoxy along the lines of these two competing Roman triads. An examination and evaluation of the evidence would in itself be a substantial research project and is a line of inquiry which will not be addressed in detail in the present work (though the findings regarding Capitoline Terminus presented in chapter 5 could provide an underpinning for such an interpretation). If a convincing case of such heterodoxy should eventually be constructed, that theory would have no adverse effect on the interpretations and ideas which appear herein. It matters little whether the Minor Capitoline triad arose by Greek or Etruscan influence or ultimately as a consequence of Indo-European heterodoxy.

1.11 MARS

We will bring the first chapter to a close by taking a closer look at St. Augustine's testimony that not only Terminus and Juventas but Mars also was unwilling to vacate the Capitoline hill to make room for Jupiter's resplendent temple. In so doing we will also be looking ahead toward much of what lies before us.

In his disquisition on the goddess Felicitas, St. Augustine turns to the tradition of the ancient deities who refused to be ousted from the Capitoline for the construction of Jupiter's temple (*De Civ. D.* 4.23):

> Nullo modo omnino, si consuleretur, faceret Iuppiter quod ei fecerunt tres dii, Mars, Terminus et Iuventas, qui maiori et regi suo nullo modo cedere loco voluerunt....
> ... atque ipsi inde cedere omnes voluerunt praeter illos quos commemoravi, Martem, Terminum, Iuventatem; atque ideo Capitolium ita constructum est ut etiam isti tres intus essent tam obscuris signis ut hoc vix homines doctissimi scirent.

> Not in anyway at all, if he were consulted, would Jupiter have done what three gods did to him—Mars, Terminus, and Juventas—who by no means were willing to surrender their space to a greater god and king....
> ... And so all [the gods] were willing to yield except those whom I mentioned, Mars, Terminus, and Juventas; and thus for this reason the Capitolium was built so that these very three would be within it, but with images so concealed that the most learned would scarcely know it.

Further along in book 4, St. Augustine returns to the three resolute gods and the vain assurances of the omen of their steadfastness (*De Civ. D.* 4. 29):

> Sic enim, inquiunt, significatum est Martiam gentem, id est Romanam, nemini locum quem teneret daturam, Romanos quoque terminos propter deum Terminum neminem commoturum, iuventutem etiam Romanam propter deam Iuventatem nemini esse cessuram.
>
> Thus, they say, it was portended that the people of Mars—that is, the Roman people—would hand over to no one any place which they held; and that, on account of Terminus, no one would move the Roman boundaries; and again, on account of the goddess Juventas, that the Roman warrior manhood would surrender to no one.

It was a bogus omen, St. Augustine argues. Not only did the Romans surrender to Christ, but long before, they experienced on multiple occasions loss of territory, shrinking of boundaries, and devastation of the army.

What are we to make of St. Augustine's identification of a third immovable god, varying from the accounts of Livy and Dionysius of Halicarnassus? Perhaps we should first remind ourselves that variation exists even in the record of these last two writers. In Livy's telling of the taking of the *auspices* to determine if the *fana* and *sacella* that dotted the Capitoline could be moved, the birds revealed that all indeed could be—save one: *in Termini fano non addixere* (1.55.4; "they were not favorable regarding the shrine of Terminus"). He continues (1.55.4–5):

> idque omen auguriumque ita acceptum est, non motam Termini sedem unumque eum deorum non evocatum sacratis sibi finibus firma stabiliaque cuncta portendere
>
> And this omen and augury was so interpreted: that the seat of Terminus was not moved, and that *he alone* among the gods was not called out beyond the boundary made sacred to him, foreshadowed that all would be steadfast and unfailing.

For Livy it is Terminus "alone among the gods" who cannot be drawn out beyond the sacred boundary. The comparable augural event related by Dionysius (*Ant. Rom.* 3.69.5; so also Florus, *Epit.* 1.7.9) entails the refusal of both Terminus and Juventas to vacate the Capitoline:

> οἱ μὲν οὖν ἄλλοι θεοί τε καὶ δαίμονες ἐπέτρεψαν αὐτοῖς εἰς ἕτερα χωρία τοὺς βωμοὺς σφῶν μεταφέρειν, οἱ δὲ τοῦ Τέρμονος καὶ τῆς Νεότητος πολλὰ παραιτουμένοις τοῖς μάντεσι καὶ λιπαροῦσιν οὐκ ἐπείσθησαν οὐδ' ἠνέσχοντο παραχωρῆσαι τῶν τόπων.
>
> Therefore the other gods and daemons permitted [the Augures] to transfer their own altars to other places, but those of Terminus and

> Juventas were not won over by the Augures—who begged much and persistently—and they refused to be removed from their spaces.

In Livy's account, Juventas only makes an appearance later, in book 5, in the closing words of the speech of Camillus, pleading his case against abandoning Rome following the Gallic devastation (5.54.7):

> Hic Capitolium est, ubi quondam capite humano invento responsum est eo loco caput rerum summamque imperii fore; hic cum augurato liberaretur Capitolium, Iuventas Terminusque maximo gaudio patrum vestrorum moveri se non passi; hic Vestae ignes, hic ancilia caelo demissa, hic omnes propitii manentibus vobis di.

> Here is the Capitoline hill, where once, when a human head was discovered, it was revealed that in this place would be the head of the world and the summit of sovereign rule; here when the Capitoline was cleared out following augural inquiry, Juventas and Terminus, to the greatest joy of your forefathers, refused to be relocated; here the flames of Vesta, here the *ancilia* that dropped down from heaven, here all the propitious gods—upon your remaining.

St. Augustine's polemic purpose is a systematic dismissal of the gods of pagan Rome. The source of St. Augustine's account is undoubtedly Varro and his encyclopedic work on Roman religion (*Antiquitates Rerum Humanarum et Divinarum*), into which St. Augustine dips deeply and repeatedly (see *De Civ. D.* 4.1 and passim). It should come as no surprise that St. Augustine's careful Christian rebuttal of the omen provided by a refusal of certain gods to vacate the Capitoline entails a fuller accounting of the augural event—à la Varro—than that which the historians preserve. Even within Livy's treatment of the subject, as we saw immediately above, there is notable laxity.

The inclusion of Mars in the tradition of the contumacious gods may well be as old as the tradition itself. Regardless, it was a part of the tradition that the antiquarian Varro unwittingly passed on to St. Augustine. That tradition is not likely to have been fabricated by Varro, a scholar revered among Romans for his learning generally and for his refined knowledge of the ancient religion especially (see, inter alia, Cicero, *Acad.* 1.3.9). Let Cornell rehearse Varro's intellectual and scholarly prowess for us:

> The greatest Roman antiquarian (and perhaps the greatest antiquarian of all time) was M. Terentius Varro (116–27 BC), a pupil of Aelius Stilo, a friend of Pompey and Cicero, and a public figure in his own right. This astonishing man is said to have written 490 books by the age of 77 (another tradition gives his total output as 620 works). We know of 55

> titles, but possess only one complete work: the *De Re Rustica*, a work in three books on agriculture, published in 37 BC. Of the twenty-five books of the *De Lingua Latina*, six are partially extant. The rest of Varro's life's work is represented only by fragmentary quotations. Nevertheless, his influence was all-pervasive; in the words of Nicholas Horsfall [1982: 112], he has perished by absorption. His systematic organisation of knowledge provided the foundation for all subsequent Roman scholarship, and he was an indispensable source of factual information for later writes who occupied themselves in any way with the Roman past.[86]

Among some Latinists it is currently fashionable to disparage the ancient knowledge espoused by Varro and to ridicule his reliability. The burden of proof is on those scholars. It was no less so in the twentieth century when Dumézil wrote; in his words:

> We must certainly weigh the testimony of Varro, as of all others, and on the whole it is easy, thanks to the general lines of his system. But we must also be ready to accept his teaching when there is no specific reason to doubt it.[87]

Varro is a remarkably rich source. At what price and to what advantage would we casually dismiss him? Cornell's remarks are balanced and to the point:

> However learned they may have been, the antiquarians were often credulous and facile (as their feeble etymologies so amply attest), and did not possess the kind of skill and expertise that a modern scholar would be able to bring to an ancient inscription or monument. Nevertheless, the materials they were working with were genuine enough. Some modern books give the impression that in the late Republic very little survived from the city's ancient past. This absurd view is the exact opposite of the truth. The amount of evidence available to anyone in the late Republic who wished to investigate the archaic period was simply overwhelming. However poorly they understood what they found, the antiquarians are important because they can put us directly in touch with countless genuine vestiges of a forgotten past that is, almost by definition, missing from the elaborated narratives of the annalists.[88]

For one engaged in scientific inquiry, the casual dismissal of valuable data for reasons of literary fashion would indeed be absurdity. The value of

[86] Cornell 1995: 19.
[87] *ARR*: 100.
[88] Cornell 1995: 23.

Varro's data on Mars is reinforced both by its internal consistencies with Roman tradition, to which we return below, and, more significantly, the external consistencies with comparative Indo-European data, to which we come at the end of this study (see especially §5.2.5).

The presence of Mars in the set Mars-Terminus-Juventas is completely in keeping with the god's profile as revealed in Roman prayer and ritual of the greatest antiquity. There is an asymmetry in the account of *De Civitate Dei*. Even a casual reading of St. Augustine reveals that the auspicious results foreshadowed by the gods' obstinacy is not cleanly distributed across three separate domains. The division in good fortune is fundamentally a bifurcation in its several attestations: preservation of the integrity of Roman lands on the one hand, and a continued flourishing of the vital strength of Rome on the other. Thus, in the account of Dionysius of Halicarnassus (*Ant. Rom.* 3.69.6), the Augures determine the obstinacy of Terminus to mean that the borders of Rome would never be disrupted, and that of Juventas to reveal that Rome would never lose its vitality (ἀκμή). In the terse summary of Florus (*Epit.* 1.7.9), the augural observation is reduced to a promise that all would remain stable and eternal (*firma et aeterna*). The two-way split is plainly evident in St. Augustine's record as well—territorial integrity and vital strength (*De Civ. D.* 4. 29; see above). While the latter is placed within the domain of Juventas (*iuventutem etiam Romanam propter deam Iuventatem nemini esse cessuram*), the former is jointly bound to the two other gods. The boon of Mars is the retention of Roman space (*nemini locum quem teneret daturam*); Terminus retains the encapsulating edges of those spaces (*Romanos quoque terminos propter deum Terminum neminem commoturum*).

St. Augustine's inclusion of Mars in the promises of the stability of Roman space—following Varro—is fully consistent with Mars' role in Roman cultic practice, descended from more archaic Indo-European practice. To this we will turn our attention in chapter 3, and again in chapter 5. First, however, we need to take a closer look at his recalcitrant colleague, Terminus; and this we will do in chapter 2. We must now part company with Juventas and save her story for another occasion.

1.12 CONCLUSION

We have argued that the refusal of Juventas and Terminus to vacate the space of the Capitoline for the building of the temple of Jupiter Optimus Maximus, and their architectural incorporation within that temple, represents a Roman continuation of Indo-European ideology beyond the dismantling of the Pre-Capitoline triad. Juventas and Terminus (like Mars and Quirinus) belong to the warrior and agrarian realms respectively, and are thus not Roman expressions of the assistants of a god of sovereignty, à la Aryaman and Bhaga. Mars himself—a member of the old triad—refuses to go, according to St. Augustine. As we shall see, his continued presence alongside Terminus is completely in keeping with elements of Indo-European myth and the spatial geometry of Indo-European cult as it survives in Rome.

CHAPTER 2

Terminus

2.1 INTRODUCTION

Chapter 2 begins with an examination of the evidence for Indo-European parallels to Roman Terminus. This investigation will take us to Ireland and to India, and we will discover that the Vedic cult of the latter place offers a particularly close match to Terminus. The Vedic comparandum will be examined in detail. The chapter concludes with an examination of the three sacred fires of Vedic India and their Roman counterparts, an initial discussion of Vedic (and, less so, Roman) sacred spaces, and a consideration of the evolutionary development of the Roman *termini sacrificales.*

2.2 TERMINUS AND JUPITER

In the preceding chapter we departed from Dumézil's analysis of Terminus, arguing that the boundary god—one of Varro's "gods of Titus Tatius"—is aligned with the ancient Indo-European third function. Identifying Terminus as a member of that element of society concerned with fertility and growth rather than as a first-function figure such as Indic Bhaga, Mitra's close affiliate (see §§1.3, 1.4), does not, however, obviate a close association of the boundary god and the sovereign deity Jupiter. It is, after all, in the very Capitoline temple of Jupiter Optimus Maximus that the altar of the sacred stone Terminus was installed (Dionysius of Halicarnassus, *Ant. Rom.* 3.69). One curious feature of this altar is that an opening was left above it in the roof; Ovid (*Fast.* 2.669–672) writes:

> Terminus, ut veteres memorant, inventus in aede
> restitit et magno cum Iove templa tenet.
> Nunc quoque, se supra ne quid nisi sidera cernat,
> exiguum templi tecta foramen habent

> Terminus, the ancients tell, was found in the shrine
> And stayed, and shares great Jupiter's temple.
> Even now, so he sees nothing but stars above,
> The temple roof contains a tiny hole.

Festus (p. 368M) amplifies, telling us that Terminus must be worshipped beneath the open sky—this is requisite (see also Servius, *Aen.* 9.446). Dionysius of Halicarnassus (*Ant. Rom.* 2.74.2) can refer to the deity as Ὅριος Ζεύς, 'Jupiter Terminus' (or 'Jupiter Terminalis'), a title also known from Latin inscriptions (see *CIL* 11.351).

2.3 INDO-EUROPEAN PARALLELS

This structure of a sacred stone affiliated with a sovereign figure is not unique to Rome, but is one which recurs on both the eastern and western fringes of the ancient Indo-European world. In India, such a stone was placed on a pyramid in the center of the king's residence. In this stone was believed to reside the essence of sovereignty; the position it occupies was seen as the point where heaven and earth intersect (Gonda 1956: 147). This is a structural assemblage obviously reminiscent of Terminus' position on the Capitoline summit within the temple of Jupiter Optimus Maximus with his altar placed beneath open sky. In India the stone is called a *linga*, a term meaning generally 'mark' or 'token' but in this use specifically denoting a phallus. In Hindu tradition, the sacred stone, the *linga*, is the phallus of the god Śiva.

In ancient Ireland, on the western border of the Indo-European world, the elements of a sacred stone and kingship again co-occur. On the hill of the royal village of Tara, there stood a stone called Fál. According to the *Lebor Gabála Érenn* (*The Book of the Conquests of Ireland*), it had been brought to Ireland by the Tuatha Dé Danann (divine and mortal beings of great knowledge, magic, and skill) from their home in the far north (or, alternatively, by the Sons of Míl, the folk ancestors of the Irish Celts). Ireland is at times referred to as Inis Fáil, "the island of Fál," its king as the "ruler of Fál." This stone is said to be a stone penis, and in time would come to be called the Bod Fhearghais, denoting the member of one Fergus (likely Fergus mac Róich, a great hero of Ulster; see Woodard 2002). This stone reveals the rightful king of Ireland and so is also called the "Stone of Knowledge." The stone is said to announce the rightful king by crying out when that one touches the stone. In the *De Síl Chonari Móir*, we are told that the phallic stone of Fál stands at the end of a chariot course and that when he who is rightful future king of Ireland drives his chariot by the stone, it rubs the axle of his chariot, screeching to announce his royal identity. Access to that chariot course is gained by passage through an opening created when the two great stones, Blocc and Bluigne, normally almost touching, move apart as the legitimate one approaches (Rees and Rees 1989: 29, 146; MacKillop 1998: 181, 264).

2.3.1 Indo-European talismans

In the *Lebor Gabála Érenn*, the Stone of Fál is but one of four talismans said to have been brought to Ireland by the mysterious Tuatha Dé Danann. In addition to the stone, the Tuatha Dé Danann also came with Gáe Assail, the spear of the great god Lug (which ensures victory); the sword of Nuada (from which there is no escape); and the cauldron of the Dagda, a sort of Irish cornucopia that leaves none unsatisfied (Rees and Rees 1989: 29; MacKillop 1998: 366). Dumézil (1992: 103–104; *ARR*: 166) observed that a tradition of such talismans is attested across the ancient Indo-European world—among Scythians in the east, and Greeks, Romans, and Celts in the west—and argued that they reveal a common heritage of Indo-European tripartite ideology.

In the case of Scythian (Iranian), Greek, and Roman traditions, the talismans all fall from the sky. Herodotus (4.5) preserves the Scythian account in his stories of the origins of those Iranian peoples, relating how in the beginning three bothers ruled (Lipoxaïs, Arpoxaïs, and Colaxaïs) who saw three talismans fall from the sky:

> ἐπὶ τούτων ἀρχόντων ἐκ τοῦ οὐρανοῦ φερόμενα χρύσεα ποιήματα, ἄροτρόν τε καὶ ζυγὸν καὶ σάγαριν καὶ φιάλην, πεσεῖν ἐς τὴν Σκυθικήν
>
> At the time of their reign, there reportedly fell from the sky into Scythia objects of gold—a plough and a yoke, a sword, and a cup.

The Scythian talismans readily lend themselves to an interpretation of tripartite ideology: plough and a yoke, third function; sword, second function; votive φιάλη, first function.

The Greek talismans fallen from the sky are the stones of Orchomenos, identified with the Graces (αἱ Χάριτες). Pausanias writes that the Boeotians claim Eteocles to have been the first to offer sacrifice to the three Graces (9.35.1) and that in the temple of the Graces in Orchomenus (the oldest temple of that Boeotian city) are worshipped the stones which fell from heaven in the time of Eteocles (9.37.1). A vestige of their affiliation with the three functions is seen in Pindar's invocation of the λιπαρᾶς ἀοίδιμοι βασίλειαι Χάριτες Ἐρχομενοῦ ("the Graces, well-sung queens of shining Orchomenus") and prescription that they are well sought by the wise (first function), beautiful (third function), and famed (for courage [second function]; *Olympian Odes* 14.1–7 with scholia; see Vian 1960: 218–219).

In Rome, the tradition is preserved in the account of the *ancile* which Jupiter dropped to earth during the reign of Numa. The implement is one, not three; but the Salii, those priests who bear the original shield and its eleven copies as they leap about Rome during the month of March, provide evidence that a tripartite ideology is bound to the tradition of the *ancile*. As discussed in chapter 1 (see §1.5.5), these Salii are linked to each of the three deities of the Pre-Capitoline triad, being identified as *in tutela Jovis Martis Quirini* (see *ARR*: 166, 591; Boyle and Woodard 2000: 215).

The Irish tradition of the tripartite talismans, unlike the three preceding, does not present the implements as plummeting to earth. The element of airborne arrival is, however, still to be found. The Tuatha De Danann, unlike the "invaders" of Ireland who preceded them, came not through the sea by ship, but were transported through the sky on dark clouds. They descend onto a mountain in the west of Ireland and their arrival is marked by an eclipse which lasts three days (Rees and Rees 1989: 29–30; MacKillop 1998: 366). As we have seen, among those talismans which they bring in their journey through the sky is the stone of Fál, the first-function talisman, affiliated with Irish sovereignty.

2.4 AN INDO-EUROPEAN MATRIX

In the three ancient Indo-European cultures most faithfully preserving the Proto-Indo-European religious language and institutions—Indo-Iranian, Celtic, and Italic—we find the recurring tradition of a sacred stone. In Rome it is the boundary stone identified with Terminus, the god installed within the temple of Jupiter Optimus Maximus after he refused to abandon the Capitoline hill. In India, it is the *linga* of the god Śiva, a phallus, housed in the king's residence. In Ireland it is the stone of Fál, stationed on the hill of Tara, announcing the identity of the legitimate king, woven into the tradition of the tripartite talismans. In each of these primitive Indo-European cultures the stone is drawn into the realm of the first function, being affiliated with a figure of sovereignty. The stones share a common spatial feature—each occupies a particular elevated sovereign space. In each culture the stone is also explicitly identified with the domain of fertility or sexuality. Thus, the Roman sacred stone, Terminus, is one of the Sabine deities, Varro's "gods of Titus Tatius," who continue the Indo-European third function. In both India and Ireland the stone is a phallus. These elements constitute a recurring structural matrix:

	Sacred Stone	Fertility/ Sexuality	Figure of Sovereignty	Sovereign Space
India	*linga*	phallus	human king	pyramid within the royal residence
Ireland	*Fál*	phallus	human king	hill of the royal village of Tara
Rome	*Terminus*	gods of Titus Tatius	Jupiter	Capitoline hill

FIGURE 2.1. *An Indo-European structural matrix*

This recurring set of matrix features, clustering remarkably at both the eastern and western fringes of the ancient Indo-European world, brings into sharper focus the common Indo-European antecedent which must lie behind the matrix.

There is, however, one coordinate within the matrix at which the Roman stone shows a small but notable departure. In both the Indic and Irish configurations the stone is identified with the phallic member of a warrior figure. In India that warrior is Śiva (who lends his name through his Vedic equivalent to the class of warrior gods, the Rudras; see §1.6.1). In Ireland the stone is the penis of Fergus, probably Fergus mac Róich, who was famed for the size of his genitals (MacKillop 1998: 191). The Romans have their deified phallus; he, however, is not Terminus but the god Mutinus Titinus (see Palmer 1974: 187–206). Otherwise Terminus fits quite neatly into the matrix.

The probable reason for this slight variation—as will become clear further along in our study—is that the three daughter traditions attesting the matrix—Indic, Roman, and Celtic—project to different stages in the history of the parent Indo-European tradition. Roman Terminus continues what may well be a more primitive stage of the tradition, born of primitive Indo-European worship practice—one which is also preserved in Vedic cult. The two phallic reflexes—the Indic Śiva *linga* and the Celtic penis of Fergus—would then ipso facto appear to be secondary developments. Whether that development occurred in a common Indo-European period or took place independently among the Celts and Indo-Aryans is unclear at present.

Terminus does, nevertheless, also have an affiliation with a warrior deity—with two in fact. On the Capitoline summit he is coupled with Juventas, the warrior representative of the Minor Capitoline triad. More than that, as we discovered in §1.11, St. Augustine—following Varro—notes that even the old chief warrior deity Mars is retained, if inconspicuously, on the Capitoline alongside Terminus, following the introduction of the Capitoline triad.

An additional observation therefore presents itself. Like the Pre-Capitoline and Minor Capitoline triads of Rome, the Indo-European matrix of the sacred stone is a consummate expression of the totality of Indo-European society. Using Dumézilian terminology, we could call the matrix *trifunctional*. In each of the cultures evidencing the matrix, the stone itself is representative of the Indo-European third function—the domain of fecundity and sensuality. The stone is linked to a member of the second function, a warrior. The stone is affiliated with the realm of sovereignty—the first function—and resides in an elevated sovereign space. And this observation will prove important in identifying Proto-Indo-European cultic structures of which the matrix is an analytic abstraction.

2.5 THE BOUNDARY QUESTION

Why was Terminus, god of boundaries, present on the Capitoline prior to the construction of Jupiter's great temple? What boundary was he marking? For Dumézil, Terminus' presence in the Capitolium is not a matter of the presence or absence of any boundary on the Capitoline hill, or of any previously existing altar dedicated to Terminus on the Capitoline; it follows instead from the ancient nature of Terminus' affiliation with Jupiter. Here we again part company with Dumézil and will affirm that Terminus' presence on the Capitoline marks a quite particular boundary—one of paramount importance for Roman theology and cult. At the same time, nevertheless, we would agree that the boundary god's affiliation with Jupiter is one of great antiquity. That ancient affiliation, however, connects the "sacred stone of fertility" with the divine sovereign; it is not a relationship of two first-function figures paralleling that between Indic Bhaga and Mitra.

This observation immediately raises the question why a sacred stone of fertility should be associated with boundaries at all. One could imagine that the development would be entirely secondary. One might expect that the nomadic Proto-Indo-European pastoralists had no need for boundary stones. In the sedentary Indo-European daughter cultures, such as that of Rome, stones provide an effective means for marking boundaries, and the archaic sacred stone might naturally be assimilated to such markers. Indeed, Terminus is not always a stone but at times is identified with a stump that serves to demarcate adjacent properties (see Ovid, *Fast.* 2.641–642; Tibullus 1.1.11). Terminus can even be a tree. Prudentius writes (*C. Symm.* 2.1006–1011):

> .... et lapis illic
> si stetit, antiquus quem cingere sueverat error
> fasceolis vel gallinae pulmone rogare,
> frangitur et nullis violatur Terminus extis,
> et quae fumificas arbor vittata lucernas
> servabat, cadit ultrici succisa bipenni.

> .... and if there a stone
> stood, which ancient delusion use to ring
> with ribbons or supplicate with a hen's lung,
> it is crushed and Terminus is defamed, gutless,
> and the streamered tree that sheltered smoking
> lamps is laid low by the avenging ax.

Compare Horace (*Epist.* 2.2.170), who refers to poplar trees used to mark boundaries. Ovid (*Fast.* 2.641) writes that sacrifices to Terminus are made at stone and stump alike. Siculus Flaccus discusses in detail the use of trees for marking boundaries (see Campbell 2000: 110.1–112.8) and states that in some places wooden stakes are considered to be *termini* (*in quibusdam vero regionibus palos pro terminis obseruant*), stakes made of holm oak, olive, or juniper (see Campbell 2000: 104.34–6). The use of wooden sacrificial stakes and their eventual replacement by stone boundary markers are attested for both Latium and Campania (see Campbell 2000: 172.27–174.14).[1] One

[1] On the use of the stakes called *pali sacrificales* along the boundaries of colonial territories, see Gargola 1995: 38.

could argue that these boundary markers would have been particularly common in rural areas and that this prominence in agrarian settings would have then promoted the identification of Terminus, an agrarian deity (that is, a third-function "god of Titus Tatius"), with such markers of stone and of wood.

Even the divine name itself, *Terminus*, one might imagine, could be wholly secondary and have more to do with the boundary stone than with the god's ultimate third-function nature. The etymology of the name is reasonably clear, having a good Indo-European pedigree with close cognates found in both Hittite and Greek. Hittite *tarma-* means 'nail' or 'peg', and is also attested in various derived forms. Greek τέρμα and τέρμων offer semantic matches to Latin *terminus*, meaning 'boundary, end'; τέρμα is also used specifically for the post at the end of a chariot course—a use which brings to mind images of the Irish stone of Fál. These cognates are to be traced to either Proto-Indo-European **terh*$_1$- 'to rub, to bore through' or **terh*$_2$- 'to pass through'. The former root is ancestor of words such as Greek τερηδών, naming various kinds of boring worms, and English *drill*; the latter provides, for example, Old English *thyrl* 'hole', as in modern English *nostril* 'nose hole'.

Etymological inquiry does not, however, clarify the relationship between the name of the god (*Terminus*) and the denotation of the boundary stone (*terminus*). Roots meaning 'to bore through' or 'to pass through' could obviously be associated immediately with either male fertility and sexuality, or with boundaries and boundary markers. Thus, while the etymological origin of Latin *Terminus* is fairly transparent, the Proto-Indo-European etyma in themselves do not obviate the possibility that the ancestor of Latin *terminus* was primarily linked to male fertility (and the phallus), and that the 'boundary marker' sense is of secondary origin.

2.6 INDO-EUROPEAN CULTIC BOUNDARIES

Yet this historical-semantic line of inquiry may not only be ambiguous and generally unrevealing, but perhaps moot as well. Though the Proto-Indo-European pastoralists probably had little or no use for boundary stones that divided separately owned plots of land, boundary markers must have certainly served a function in early Indo-European cultic practice. Vedic India provides the evidence. The Śiva *linga* has an antecedent form used in the Vedic cult. It is the post called the *yūpa*. The sacrificial victim is tied to this post, and it serves to mark the *boundary* of the sacrificial space, the border between the ordered realm of the sacrificial cult and the disordered and menacing domain of the wilderness (see Biardeau 1991a: 811–812). Like the *linga* of Śiva, the *yūpa* stands as an *axis mundi*, as Gonda terms it, and appropriately so, "being an intermediary between the divine world and earthly life" (Gonda 1993: 81). To avoid any confusion, however, which might arise through the use of this ancient phrase and notion, owing to various nuances it may carry for some, we will coin a more neutral term to use in its place, *columna mundi*. Also like Śiva's *linga*, the *yūpa* of the Vedic cult may already have phallic symbolism (see Gonda 1993: 173). The Vedic *yūpa* is associated with Indra (*AV* 4.24.4), the god whose weapon is the thunderbolt (and who is eventually identified as king of the gods), but belongs especially to Viṣṇu (*ŚB* 3.6.4.1, 9), the three-stepping creator of space. Both gods, like Śiva, are warriors. Let us examine the *yūpa*, its production, erection, and function in some detail.

2.6.1 The Yajur Veda and Brāhmaṇas

The use of one or more *yūpas* is required for the offering of an animal sacrifice, whether it be conducted as a stand-alone rite or as a part of the various Soma sacrifices, the basic form of which is called the Agniṣṭoma (all other forms of the Soma sacrifice being a variant thereof; see §3.3.6.3). The *Yajur Veda* (*YV* 5.41–43; 6.1–6; *TS* 1.3.5–6; 6.3.3–4) preserves the ritual for preparing the *yūpa*; amplification is provided by the *Śatapatha-Brāhmaṇa*. First, an Adhvaryu (the Vedic priest who performs the sacrificial rites, including establishment of the sacrificial space, and whose prayers comprise the *Yajur Veda*) makes an offering to Viṣṇu, the god who brings order and prosperity (see Biardeau 1991a: 811). The *yūpa* is proclaimed to belong to Viṣṇu, and Viṣṇu himself is said to be the sacrifice (*ŚB* 3.6.4.1–2, 9). The priest, accompanied by a woodcutter, then goes into the forest to select a tree (such as a *palāśa*, *khadira*, or *bilva*; see *AB* 2.1.1; *ŚB* 13.4.4.5). Addressed as Vanaspati, 'Lord of the Forest', the tree is anointed with the ritual butter called *ghee*, verses are recited, and the tree is felled, either to the east, north, or west, but never to the south, the direction of the Pitaras (the Manes). The stump must be left sufficiently low so as not to obstruct the axle of a cart (*ŚB* 3.6.4.11–12; according to *TS* 6.3.3.4, this is necessary for the well-being of the sacrificer's cattle). As the tree falls, the priest prays that it will neither graze the sky nor injure the air, but that it will be united with the earth—invocations required as the tree is said to be a thunderbolt (as is the ax; *ŚB* 3.6.4.10, 13–14). The stump is then anointed with *ghee* (which is also said to be a thunderbolt) so that evil will not come from it and the stump will be endowed with seed and experience further growth (*ŚB* 3.6.4.15–16). Next the trunk is trimmed so as to produce a *yūpa* having eight corners, and a length of no less than five cubits if it is to be used in a Soma sacrifice (according to *ŚB* 3.6.4.17–27; in contrast, *ŚB* 11.7.4.1 states that the common length of the *yūpa* for the independent animal sacrifice is three to four cubits).

The *Śatapatha-Brāhmaṇa* describes in detail the elaborate ritual of preparing and erecting the *yūpa* on the eastern border of the great sacrificial area, the space called the Mahāvedi. First, using a spade (addressed as "a woman" in *ŚB* 3.7.1.1), the priest outlines the hole that will be dug for the post at the eastern boundary of the sacrificial space, traced half within and half without the area of the altar according to *Kātyāyana Śrauta Sūtra* 6.2.8, declaring that he has thereby cut off the heads of the demonic Rākṣasas (the spade also being "a thunderbolt"). He then digs the hole, throwing the dirt to the east and laying the pole in front of the hole, with its top also pointed eastward ("the highest place of Viṣṇu"; Gonda 1993: 94). On the pole he places blades of ritual grass along with the first chip that had been cut from the tree when it was felled for the making of the *yūpa*. He mixes barley (*yava*) with water and sprinkles the *yūpa* with this sacred water solution (thereby purifying the post), doing so in three sections, and so providing protection for the sky, the air, and the earth. The remainder of the water is then poured into the hole, purifying the world of the Pitaras. The priest then arranges in the hole blades of *barhis* grass, throws in the chip, and spoons in *ghee* (*ŚB* 3.7.1.1–10). According to the *Taittirīya Saṃhitā* (6.3.4.2), the depositing of *barhis* grass in the hole is required since whatever is "dug in" belongs to the Pitaras; thus, were the *barhis* not added, the Pitaras would be the deity of the *yūpa*.

The priest next turns his attention to the pole and to the top-piece[2] which is to be affixed to it. He anoints both with milk and then crowns the post with the top-piece (which in the description of the ritual is likened to a berry). After more anointing with *ghee*, the priest grabs the pole by an encircling cinch strap and raises it aloft while another officiant, a Hotar (the priest responsible for chanting verses from the *Rig Veda*), recites a verse to the post, declaring that its top touches heaven, its mid portion fills the air, and its base ("foot") stabilizes the earth. The priest then sets the *yūpa* upright in the prepared hole as he himself recites another verse, one dedicated to the wide-striding god Viṣṇu. The sacrificer then touches the *yūpa* and recites *Rig Veda* 1.22.19–20, in praise of Viṣṇu, Indra's close ally—

[2] A wooden cap, sometimes described as a top-ring. The cap can also be made of a wheat dough; see *ŚB* 5.2.1.6.

the stated reason for the recitation is that "Indra is the god of the sacrifice and the *yūpa* belongs to Viṣṇu" (*ŚB* 3.7.1.11–18; see also *VS* 6.4–5).

That procession of ritual acts which begins with preparations to select and fell a tree for the sacrificial post and ends with the sacrificer approaching and touching the dedicated and erected *yūpa* is thus bracketed by affirmations that the post belongs to Viṣṇu. The same affirmation recurs in other texts; for example, *Taittirīya Saṃhitā* (1.3.5.c); and according to *Taittirīya Saṃhitā* (6.3.3.1), "the *yūpa* has Viṣṇu for its deity." More than that, in the *Viṣṇu Purāna* (1.8.19) we are told that Viṣṇu *is* the *yūpa* (see Gonda 1993: 81).

More decorating of the *yūpa* follows. The priest wraps a triple rope made of grass around the pole, and underneath the rope he slips a chip left over from the carving of the post (*ŚB* 3.7.1.19–24). The height at which the grass rope is attached correlates with the quantity of rain desired by the sacrificer: higher than the navel, more rain; lower than the navel, less rain.[3] Notice that a somewhat different binding is described for the *yūpa* of the Vājapeya Soma sacrifice (see §2.6.1.1); here the post, seventeen cubits long (*KB* 10.1), may be wrapped in seventeen cloths (*ŚB* 5.2.1.5–7) for the seventeen victims to be offered (*KŚS* 14.1.20–21).

Like its descendant, the Śiva *linga*, fixed atop a pyramid at the king's residence, the Vedic *yūpa* so erected and arrayed is clearly an *axis mundi*—or *columna mundi* (see §2.6)—providing access to the entire cosmos—the portion underground to the world of the Pitaras, the portion between the ground and the grass rope to the world of humankind, the portion above the rope to the world of the gods (*ŚB* 3.7.1.25). Consider the remarks of Gonda (1993: 83):

> It seems to be in perfect harmony with the character of Viṣṇu as it appears to have been under other circumstances, that the *yūpa* should belong to him. Traversing the parts of the universe and linking these, and especially the sun and the earth, forming the mythic centre of the cosmos, being the path which leads to the upper regions, the sacrificial stake and the other objects equivalent to it . . . belong to the god who pervades the universe . . . .

This *yūpa* cum *columna mundi* is a delight to all the gods (*TS* 6.3.4.7).

To the *yūpa* is tied the sacrificial victim. After various anointings and oblations and a ritual of carrying fire around the sacrificial animal, the victim is untethered from the *yūpa* and taken to a designated slaughter-

[3]See Keith 1998a: 325. Thus *TS* 6.3.4.5–6, in which the distance above or below the navel is also correlated with imparting and taking away strength.

ing place for immolation outside of the delimited sacrificial space (the *Mahāvedi*), being led by a fire-carrying priest, an Agnīdh (see, inter alia, *ŚB* 3.7.3.1 - 3.8.1.16). For the animal sacrifice of the Agniṣṭoma as described in *Śatapatha-Brāhmaṇa* 3.7.2.1–2, eleven posts are erected at the eastern boundary of the sacrificial space,[4] and a twelfth is left rough-cut, lying on the ground on the south side of the altar as a threatening thunderbolt, designed to protect against attack from the Rākṣasas.[5] The eleven upright *yūpas* are said to stand as brandished thunderbolts, by means of which the sacrificer takes possession of the earth and prevents his enemies from having a part of it. This earth is equated with the altar beside which the *yūpas* are erected, and the size of that earth is determined by the size of the altar (*ŚB* 3.7.2.1).

Following immolation of the victim,[6] several things happen. The priest called the Neṣṭar leads the sacrificer's wife to the victim. Carrying a vessel of water, she pours a portion of the water over the sacrificed victim, now stretched out on the ground. The remainder of the water is then sprinkled onto the sacrifice by the Adhvaryu and the sacrificer (*ŚB* 3.8.2.1–11). With a ritually purified knife (called a "thunderbolt") the Adhvaryu draws blood from the victim and dabs both ends of a stalk of grass in the blood. The bloodied grass is then thrown down as an offering to the Rākṣasas, designed to drive them away and hold them in the darkness of the underworld (*ŚB* 3.8.2.12–15). It should be noted that after the victim has been butchered (see below), the blood, as well as stomach and excrement, will be offered to the Rākṣasas, being poured into a pit outside of the great sacrificial space (see Keith 1998a: 326). It is the Rākṣasas who are the regular recipients of blood (see Keith 1998a: 281 with references), and who are thereby kept away from the sacrifice (*AB* 2.7).[7] On this offering as one made to chthonic powers, see below (§2.7.2).

Much attention is given to the victim's omentum (the fatty fold of tissue covering various visceral organs). With two spits it is removed and cooked,

[4]In the Sutyā days ritual of the Aśvamedha (the Vedic horse sacrifice), described at *ŚB* 13.4.4.5 and 13.5.1.14, twenty-one sacrificial posts are set up.

[5]On such attacks on the sacrifice, see Keith 1998a: 238.

[6]The common method of sacrifice appears to have been strangulation; on this and the offerings made from the victim's body, see Keith 1998a: 280–281.

[7]The ritual called the *Śūlagava* entails an offering of a bull to Rudra in spring or autumn for the purpose of bringing prosperity to the herds. In the rite as described in the *Śāṅkhāyana Śrauta Sūtra* (4.19.7–8), excrement and blood are placed on six *palāśa* leaves for the "host of Rudra." For description of the ritual, see Keith 1998a: 364 (with additional textual references); Renou 1957: 113–114. On the affiliation of snakes with Rudra, see *AGS* 4.8.28.

coated in clarified butter and roasted over fire. As drops of fat and butter drip into the altar flames, verses from the *Rig Veda* addressed to Agni are recited to the drops—the result will be the securing of rain. The cooked omentum is covered with pieces of gold and *ghee* and placed on the altar (*ŚB* 3.8.2.16–30; also see *AB* 2.12–14; *ŚŚS* 5.18.1–5.19.11).[8]

Following the preparation of a sacrificial cake of rice and barley, the sacrificed animal is then cut up into parts. Offerings are made of particular portions, and others are eaten by the priests and sacrificer (*ŚB* 3.8.3.1–37). Next, still additional offerings are presented, concluding with offerings made from the victim's tail (*ŚB* 3.8.4.1–3.8.5.7). The chip of the *yūpa* is burned (see Keith 1998a: 326), and the spit on which the heart was roasted is then ceremonially buried at a place where "dry land and wet land meet," with an invocation made to Varuṇa.

2.6.1.1 THE VĀJAPEYA The form of the Soma sacrifice called the *Vājapeya* (perhaps meaning 'Drink of Strength'), with its *yūpa* of seventeen cubits and seventeen coverings (the number seventeen recurs throughout the ritual), was mentioned above. The Vājapeya is interesting in several respects, displaying unusual features which commence with the midday Soma pressing (Keith 1998a: 339).[9] This ceremony, conducted for the purpose of bringing the sacrificer gain (especially food) and preeminence over rivals, has been described as preserving particularly primitive ("folk") elements; it is clearly of great antiquity (see Keith 1967: cx). Renou (1957: 107–108) writes: "The 'drink of victory' is also no doubt one of those rites which are secondarily associated with the Soma observances . . . . It is a fertility rite." Keith (1998a: 340) surmises: "The nature of the rites is clearly on the one hand that of the attainment of victory and power by the symbolic acts of winning, of being hailed as a victor, and anointing [see below]: references to fertility are obvious also . . . ." The Vājapeya is commonly identified as an autumn festival, and, according to the *Śatapatha-Brāhmaṇa* (5.1.1.11–14) belongs to the *brāḥmana* and *kṣatriya* classes, though the *Kātyāyana Śrauta Sūtra* (16.17.4) indicates that the rite is also open to the *vaiśya* class (see the remarks in Keith 1998a: 340; 1967: cix-cxi).

One of the characteristic features of the Vājapeya is the running of a chariot race at the time of the midday Soma pressing (see *ŚB* 5.1.4.1–

[8]Strabo (*Geography* 15.3.13) records that the Persian Magi (according to some sources), after dividing up the meat of the sacrificial animal among the people, offer a portion of the omentum in the flames.

[9]For additional discussion of the description which follows, and for further textual references, see Keith 1998a: 339–340; Renou 1957: 107–108.

5.1.5.28). A Rājanya (Kṣatriya), stands within the Mahāvedi, aims his bow northward between the Cātvāla and the Utkara (a pit and rubbish mound situated north of the great sacred space; Eggeling 1995, pt. 3: 25, n.1), and shoots seventeen arrows in sequence. He then marks the spot where the seventeenth arrow falls by planting a stake of *udumbara* wood to serve as the course marker around which the racing chariots will turn (*ŚB* 5.1.5.13–14; *KŚS* 14.3.16–17). The sacrificer—predetermined victor of the event—races with a chariot drawn by three horses. Against him run sixteen "competitors" in four-horse chariots. While the race is being run, seventeen drums are beaten and a Brahman sits atop a chariot wheel, mounted horizontally on a navel-high post, and is rotated sunward (that is, clockwise) while he sings a *sāman* for the racehorses (*ŚB* 5.1.5.1–2; Eggeling 1995, pt. 3: 23, n.1). An Adhvaryu likewise hymns the horses as the chariots run (*ŚB* 5.1.5.18–24). Following the "victory" of the sacrificer, the horses are made to smell the Bārhaspatya pap (an offering to the god Bṛhaspati), as they had before the race as well (*ŚB* 5.1.5.25–27).

Not only is Soma offered in this rite, but offerings are also made of *surā*, a popular fermented beverage (a kind of spiced rice wine; see Eggeling 1995, pt. 5: 223, n. 2) that only rarely receives ritual use—otherwise principally used in the Sautrāmaṇī[10] (on which see §3.3.3.1). The Vājapeya is characterized by seventeen *stotras* and *śastras* (hymns and praise-songs), being a Ṣoḍaśin ceremony (having sixteen *stotras* and *śastras*; see §4.8.3) extended by one *stotra* and *śastra*—we have already noted the significance of the number seventeen for this ritual. Thus, in addition to seventeen cups of Soma, seventeen cups of *surā* are offered (see *ŚB* 5.1.2.10–14; Keith 1998a: 339). A further ritual accoutrement present in the Vājapeya is a cup of honey; following the completion of the chariot race, the sacrificer and an Adhvaryu walk out of the front door of the Soma-cart shed (on this and other structures constructed within the great sacred space, the Mahāvedi, see §4.3), and carrying the cup, they place it into the hand of a Vaiśya or a Rājanya who has competed in the race. A Neṣṭar then processes out of the back door and around the back side of the shed carrying cups of *surā*, one of which is likewise placed in the hand of the Vaiśya or Rājanya. The cup of honey is then presented to a Brahman (see *ŚB* 5.1.5.28).

After the chariot race, the ritual turns to the seventeen-cubit *yūpa* wrapped in its seventeen cloths, with which both the sacrificer and his wife will interact with great immediacy. This *yūpa* is capped not with the

[10]See Keith 1998a: 255. On the *Sautrāmaṇī*, a complex ritual performed for various purposes, including an overindulgence of Soma, see Keith 1998a: 352–354; Renou 1957: 110.

typical wooden top-piece (see above) but with a disk made of wheat dough. At the appropriate moment, a Neṣṭar brings up the sacrificer's wife to the *yūpa*, after first seeing that she has cloaked herself in a special ritual covering of *kuśa* grass, or of some other material (see *KŚS* 14.5.3–4), worn above her normal ceremonial garment. According to the *Taittirīya Brāhmaṇa* (I.3.7.1), the sacrificer likewise wears a special garment, the one called a *tārpya*—also to be worn by a king in the celebration of the *Rājasūya* (the rite of inauguration; see *ŚB* 5.3.5.20). A ladder is propped against the *yūpa*, the sacrificer calls to his wife to ascend to the sky with him, and together they (as specified in *KŚS* 14.5.7), or he alone on their joint behalf, climbs the ladder, bound for the top of the *yūpa* and its wheel of dough. Touching the wheel, the sacrificer exclaims, "We have gone to the light, O gods." Then climbing still higher so that his head extends beyond the top of the *yūpa*, he declares, "We are become immortal"; the sacrificer and his wife are said thus to have gained the world of the gods (*ŚB* 5.2.1.10–14; cf. *ŚB* 3.7.1.25). Looking in all directions, the sacrificer utters mantras designed to instill in him all those advantages provided by the Vājapeya. Seventeen bundles of salt wrapped in *aśvattha* leaves are then thrown up to him (by Vaiśyas, according to *ŚB* 5.2.1.17), whereby the sacrificer is said to obtain food. From the *yūpa*, the sacrificer looks down on the earth, paying homage to mother earth and entering into an auspicious relationship with her, whereupon he descends to be seated on a throne of *udumbara* wood (see *ŚB* 5.2.1.5–25).

According to the *Śatapatha-Brāhmaṇa* (5.1.5.1), in offering the Vājapeya, the sacrificer secures gains which span the breadth of the cosmos. By the running of the chariot race he gains the earth. By the singing Brahman sitting atop the revolving wheel he gains the world of the air. By the climb up the *yūpa* he gains the world of the gods.

2.6.2 The Rig Veda

The most ancient of the Vedas is the *Rig Veda*. The picture of the *yūpa* which takes shape in this work, as one would expect, is consistent with that fuller image which emerges from the *Yajur Veda* and its *brāhmaṇas*. Particularly precious in revealing the primitive nature of the sacrificial column is *Rig Veda* 3.8, the hymn dedicated to the *yūpa*. Addressed to the Vanaspati, 'Lord of the Forest', the hymn begins (*RV* 3.8.1–3):

> yad ūrdhvas tiṣṭhā draviṇeha dhattād yad vā kṣayo mātur asyā upasthe
> samiddhasya śrayamāṇaḥ purastād brahma vanvāno ajaraṃ suvīram
> āre asmad amatim bādhamāna uc chrayasva mahate saubhagāya
> uc chrayasva vanaspate varṣman pṛthiviyā adhi

When standing erect, grant us wealth,
    as when lying in this mother's caress.
Positioned east of the kindled flame, hearing
    prayer that staves off old age, mighty,
Driving poverty far away from us,
    rise up for great blessings.
Rise up, Lord of the Forest,
    on the highest place on earth.

The commentator of the *Aitareya Brāhmaṇa* (2.1.2), the oldest of the Vedic commentaries, tells us that the "enemy" driven away is hunger, and describes the *yūpa*, as a "giver of food," adding that the sacrificial post provides grain to humankind. The affiliation of the cultic boundary marker with provision for fecundity and fertility is fundamental to this cultic apparatus, as we saw in the *Yajur Veda* and its commentaries. The theme recurs in lines 6–7 of the Rig Vedic hymn 3.8:

te devāsaḥ svaravas tasthivāṃsaḥ prajāvad asme didhiṣantu ratnam
ye vṛkṇāso adhi kṣami nimitāso yatasrucaḥ
te no viyantu vāriyaṃ devatrā kṣetrasādhasaḥ

Let those divine posts standing here
    give us riches and abundance of children,
Which having been felled upon the earth
    and set upright, receiving the offering ladles
May they gain wealth for us
    among the gods, endowing the fields with blessings.

Śatapatha-Brāhmaṇa 11.7.3 (compare *Aitareya Brāhmaṇa* 2.1.1) describes the type and shape of tree which should be chosen for the *yūpa* in order to effect the acquisition (i) of cattle, (ii) of long life, or (iii) of prosperity and absence of hunger.

The Vedic hymn continues, revealing that provision is being made for the sacrificer across the span of divine society (Ādityas, Rudras, Vasus; on the three classes of gods, see §1.6.1), and likening the colorfully decorated *yūpas*[11] to gods (*RV* 3.8.8–9):

ādityā rudrā vasavaḥ sunīthā dyāvākṣāmā pṛthivī antarikṣam
sajoṣaso yajñam avantu devā ūrdhvaṃ kṛṇvantu adhvarasya ketum
haṃsā iva śrayaṇiśo yatānāḥ śukrā vasānāḥ svaravo na āguḥ
unnīyamānāḥ kavibhiḥ purastād devā devānām api yanti pāthaḥ

[11] On the ornamentation of the sacrificial columns see also *Rig Veda* 1.92.5; 4.51.2; *Aitareya Brāhmaṇa* 2.1.2.

Ādityas, Rudras, Vasus, wise guides
heaven and earth, Pṛthivī and atmosphere,
May the gods in unison bless the rites,
and lift high the sacrificial banner.
Like swans flying in a row,
swathed in color, the posts have come to us.
Lifted high by sages, to the east
they go—gods to the place of the gods.

As in the *Yajur Veda* and the *Śatapatha Brāhmaṇa*, so in the *Aitareya Brāhmaṇa*, the protective function of the *yūpa* is noted, and is indeed quite pronounced in the last-named. This ancient commentary on the *Rig Veda* identifies the *yūpa* as an eight-edged weapon, protecting the sacrificer (*AB* 2.1.1). This protective function is further emphasized by the appropriation to the *yūpa* of verses that invoke the assistance and protection of the fire deity Agni (*RV* 1.36.13–14), identifying the *yūpa* as the destroyer of the demonic Rākṣasas (*AB* 2.1.2).

The *yūpa*, situated on the "highest spot on earth" (*RV* 3.8.3) links together the entire cosmos: the world of the Pitaras, the world of humankind, the world of the gods (*ŚB* 3.7.1.25). It gives the sacrificer and his wife a state of immortality and access to the world of the gods (*ŚB* 5.2.1.10–14). As we have observed and as Gonda (1993: 81–82) and other earlier investigators (see Auboyer 1949: 74–104) perceived, like the *linga* atop the pyramid in the king's residence, the *yūpa* represents the *columna mundi.*

2.6.3 Related structures

In addition to the *linga*, yet other by-forms of the *yūpa* exist. Each equally embodies the *columna mundi*. These we will consider in turn.

2.6.3.1 THE SKAMBHA The sacrificial post—boundary marker of the Vedic great sacrificial space—finds a cosmic equivalent in the pillar called the *skambha* 'prop, support' in the *Atharva Veda* (10.7; 10.8). The *skambha* is presented as the very centerpiece and frame of the universe. Gonda (1993: 81–82)[12] writes:

> This fulcrum or pillar likewise represents the vertical axis which forms the centre of the universe linking heaven and earth (cf. e.g. *AV* 10.7.35 etc.); it sustains the components of the universe; all existence has entered it; being the frame of creation, it enters the thousandfold aspects and

[12] On the *skambha*, see also Auboyer 1949: 77–78.

> components of the universe (cf. st. 9), sun and moon stand fixed in it (12), all the gods are set together in it (13).

Unlike the *yūpa*, the *skambha* is not explicitly identified with Viṣṇu, though, as Gonda (1996: 28) suggests, such a link is perhaps forged indirectly. Thus, in *AV* 10.7.7–8, the creator deity Prajāpati is linked with the frame of the *skambha* in his creative activities. Consider then that in the *Śatapatha-Brāhmaṇa* (6.7.2.10–12), Prajāpati is said to have created offspring by taking the "Viṣṇu-steps"—the three steps of Viṣṇu associated with his own creative acts. And again, in *Śatapatha-Brāhmaṇa* 6.7.4.7, we read that "by the Viṣṇu-steps, Prajāpati created this world." On the other hand, in the *skambha* hymn *Atharva Veda* 10.7, the cosmic pillar is explicitly identified with Indra in parallel verses (10.7.29–30).

2.6.3.2 THE LIṄGODBHAVA To this set can be added the post that appears in the geographically widely attested Hindu myth of the *liṅgodbhava* ('born from a *linga*'), the bejeweled *linga* form of Śiva. This *linga* is presented as a great, flaming cosmic pillar; the other two members of the Hindu divine threesome (the *Trimūrti*)—Brahmā, and Viṣṇu—are unable to reach its end points. Brahmā in the form of a *haṃsa* (perhaps a swan, the word is cognate with English *goose*) tries to fly to its top; Viṣṇu in the form of a boar tries to dig to its foundation. Both are unsuccessful and in consequence worship Śiva.[13]

2.6.3.3 THE INDRADHVAJA Yet another member of the set is that vertical projection called the *Indradhvaja*, 'Indra's banner'. As Gonda notes (1993: 81), in *Rig Veda* 3.8.8, the *yūpa* is itself explicitly referred to as the "banner" (*ketu-*) of the sacrifice (for the hymn see §2.6.2)—a denotation that certainly draws the *Indradhvaja* and the *yūpa* together within the same sphere. The banner of Indra is described in the *Bṛhatsaṃhitā of Varāhamihira* 43 and the *Bhaviṣya Purāṇa* (summarized in Gonda 1993: 255–259; Kramrisch 1947). Fearing the demons, the gods took counsel with Brahmā, who instructed them to obtain from Viṣṇu a banner which would protect them from the demons (*VarāhBS* 43.1–2). The banner that Viṣṇu provided was created from his own radiant energy (*tejas*), shining like the sun. With the raising of this banner, decorated with garlands, bells, and other small objects, Indra defeated the enemy (*VarāhBS* 43.5–6). Indra subsequently presented its

[13] On the *liṅgodbhava* see Gonda 1993: 143–144; Biardeau 1991a: 812–813; Filliozat 1961: 46–56.

bamboo staff to Vasu Uparicara, a heroic figure turned ascetic whom Indra had assisted in acquiring the kingship of Cedi (see *Mahābhārata* 1.63). Vasu Uparicara venerates Indra by celebrating a festival that entails the setting up and decorating of Indra's staff. Thereafter, by Indra's own pronouncement, kings desiring victory and power for themselves and prosperity and fecundity for their kingdoms should do likewise (*VarāhBS* 43.9–10, where it is also stated that the banner will augur good and ill).

The ritual manufacture of an *Indradhvaja* involves first selecting and cutting the appropriate material for the staff. On an auspicious day and at an auspicious hour, a tree is to be selected—nothing weak or defective; only a strong tree such as an *arjuna*,[14] *ajakarṇa*, *priyaka*, *dhava*, or *udumbara*. It is to be worshipped by a Brahman during the night before it is felled at dawn. The tree is only to be used if it falls in an auspicious manner and, after being trimmed, can be conducted to the town gate without a carriage mishap. On a specified calendrical day the trunk is to be draped with cloth and garlands, perfumed, and carried into the town with much fanfare. On the third day following, after the trunk has been planed, a royal priest clothed in white offers oblations to Agni and verses to Indra and Viṣṇu (*VarāhBS* 43.12–30). On the next day the *Indradhvaja* is erected and decorated with various ornaments (like ornaments said to have been given by the gods in a more ancient time; *VarāhBS* 43.38–51), bringing greater power to the banner. The king recites verses to the *Indradhvaja*, calling it "unborn, imperishable, eternal, of unchanging form"; addressing it as "Viṣṇu, the wild boar" as well as "Indra" (Gonda 1993: 256). Invoking Agni and Indra, destroyer of the monster Vṛtra, the king prays that his warriors will achieve victory (*VarāhBS* 43.52–55).

The upright banner stands decorated with a potpourri of objects: parasols, flags, mirrors, fruits, crescents, garlands, sugar canes, images of snakes and lions, ornaments, and more (*VarāhBS* 43.57–58). Alongside it stand smaller banners called *Indra's daughters* (five or seven; *VarāhBS* 43.39–40, 57–58). It is said to be raised "for the destruction of the king's enemies" and the top is to be pointed in the direction of the city of that enemy. Four days only it remains standing (being dismantled on the fifth), during which time it is susceptible to portentous occurrences, omens of ill for the king, his family, and his subjects requiring expiation (*VarāhBS* 43.60–68).

Regarding the pronounced affiliation of Viṣṇu with Indra's banner, Gonda's interpretative remarks are worth reciting in full; after placing the

[14] A tree said to presage good rains; see *VarāhBS* 29.11.

Indradhvaja in the context of widely attested tree-cults and noting that the ornaments which decorate Indra's banner were said to be gifts of various gods,[15] he observes (Gonda 1993: 259):

> That Viṣṇu's share could be so important that he was considered the originator of this "tree-cult" . . . can in my opinion only be accounted for by realizing his old and intensive relations with prosperity in general and fertility in particular. In the mythical account of the origin of the Indra banner Viṣṇu is, again, the divine power in the background who assists Indra in conquering the demons by introducing the standard festival. And although this cult remained, in general, associated with the ancient representative of the vital energy in nature [that is, Indra], Viṣṇu even here succeeded in incidentally taking over this function, or playing his part.

2.6.3.4 THE SADAS POST With the Sadas post we return to the Vedic cultic space of the Soma sacrifice. The ceremony described in §2.6.1 for the digging and preparation of the hole for the *yūpa* and the anointing of the post prior to its erection at the eastern edge of the great sacrificial space, the Mahāvedi, is—rather remarkably—not unique to this occasion. A similar, if less elaborate, procedure had been followed earlier in the Soma ritual for the planting of the post which stands in the shelter called the Sadas, said to be "Viṣṇu's stomach" and sacred to Indra (*ŚB* 3.6.1.1). The Sadas is located east of the fire called the Āhavanīya (see §2.8.1) and at the western edge of the Mahāvedi; beneath it are positioned the Dhiṣṇya-hearths of the several priests who play a role in the Soma sacrifice (see §4.3.2). The pit for the post is marked off with a spade. The post is laid down with its top pointed eastward. Water is mixed with barley and sprinkled on the post in three sections; the remainder is poured into the hole, purifying it—an excursion into the world of the Pitaras. *Barhis* grass is placed in the hole and the post is sunk therein; as the column drops into the pit, the priest invokes Dyutāna, the son of the Maruts (warrior gods of the storm; see §4.8.2), to plant the Sadas post and calls on Mitra and Varuṇa for support. Dirt is heaped around the post and tamped down. Water is poured on the surrounding earth, the sacrificer is made to touch the post, and the top of the post is anointed with *ghee*. This is all familiar ritual territory.

The Sadas post is no less a *columna mundi* than the *yūpa*. It is anointed in three sections in order to bring strength to the sky, the air, and the earth

[15] On the identification of these various ornaments and their significance, see Kramrisch 1947: 198–199.

(*ŚB* 3.6.1.12, 15). It is sunk into the world of the Pitaras (*ŚB* 3.6.1.13–14). As dirt is heaped around the base of the post, the priest addresses it as "winner" of the *brāhmaṇa* and *kṣatriya* and of increase in wealth and abundance (*ŚB* 3.6.1.17–18)—making provision across the three-fold ideological realm of Vedic society (see §1.6.1). The sacrificer prays to the post for stoutness, offspring, and cattle (*ŚB* 3.6.1.20).

Functionally, the Sadas post is very close to the *yūpa* (excepting that the latter is used for tethering the sacrificial victim). Structurally, the Sadas post and the *yūpa* are quite distinct, though complementary. Each stands at the edge of the great sacrificial arena, the Mahāvedi—the Sadas post on the west, the *yūpa* on the east. Both columns lie approximately along the east-west axis that runs through that space and the smaller space located west of the Mahāvedi (the Sadas post is positioned one step to the south of center; *ŚB* 3.6.1.3). Both stand by altars—the *yūpa* to the east of the altar called the Uttaravedi (the Āhavanīya shifted eastward; see §4.3), the Sadas post to the west of the Dhiṣṇya-hearths of the priests. Each a *columna mundi*, the proximal Sadas post and the distal *yūpa* bracket the great sacrificial space.

2.7 TERMINUS AND THE YŪPA

Let us begin this section by recapitulating some salient points. Terminus forms a constituent of the Indo-European structural matrix of §2.4, closely paralleling the *linga* of Śiva. The *yūpa*, marking the eastern boundary of the Vedic sacrificial space and antecedent of the *linga* in Vedic cult, embodies the *columna mundi*, like the *linga*. Within the context of the sacrificial arena, the *Rig Veda* (3.8.3) proclaims that the *yūpa* occupies the "highest spot on earth."

The idea of a column representing "the vertical axis which forms the centre of the universe linking heaven and earth" (Gonda 1993: 82) is clearly well developed among the early Indo-Aryans. On the one hand, that the notion is so well developed must be linked to the seminal presence among the gods of India of the "three-stepping," "wide-striding" Viṣṇu[16]—the god who creates and transcends space, and who is closely identified with the *yūpa* and with the sacrifice. To cite but one of many pertinent references—in *Rig Veda* 1.154 Viṣṇu is presented as separating and propping apart the spaces of earth and heaven, of supporting the threefold uni-

[16]On the manifold significance of Viṣṇu's three strides see Gonda 1993: 55–72.

verse, where the verb meaning 'prop' is built from the same Sanskrit root as *skambha*, denoting the cosmic axis of the *Atharva Veda* discussed above (see §2.6.3.1).[17] On the other hand, the affiliation of this warrior deity with the boundary marker of the great sacred space may well have a prehistory in Proto-Indo-European theology and cult in light of the structural matrix of the "sacred stone" which recurs on the eastern and western edges of the ancient Indo-European world (see §2.4; we shall return to this in chapter 5). Given this structural relationship which exists between Roman Terminus and the Indic *linga*, and the latter's affiliation with the Vedic *yūpa* and the *columna mundi*, the question which next presents itself is naturally the following. Can we identify Terminus as a Roman reflex of those early Indo-European ideas and traditions which manifest themselves in the Vedic *yūpa* as the *columna mundi*?

2.7.1 Penes Iovem sunt summa

Citing Varro and his categorizing of the pagan gods, St. Augustine writes in his polemical exposition of Janus and Jupiter (*De Civ. D.* 7.9):

> Sed cur ei praeponitur Ianus? . . . "Quoniam penes Ianum," inquit, "sunt prima, penes Iovem summa. Merito ergo rex omnium Iuppiter habetur. Prima enim vincuntur a summis quia, licet prima praecedant tempore, summa superant dignitate."

> But why is Janus put before [Jupiter]? . . . "Because," says [Varro], "beginnings (*prima*) are in the power of Janus and the heights (*summa*) in the power of Jupiter. Therefore, Jupiter is rightly held to be king of all. Indeed, beginnings are subservient to heights because, though beginnings come first in time, heights supersede in dignity."

Dumézil (*ARR*: 181) is certainly right in seeing that same formulaic characterization of Janus (*prima*) and Jupiter (*summa*) offered by Varro also reverberating in Ovid's description of the Kalends and Ides of January. *Primus* occurs often in Ovid's verses dedicated to January's Kalends, the first day of the month. The Kalends is a day on which Janus, god of beginnings, is invoked each month (see Macrobius, *Sat.* 1.9.16) and is particularly significant in his own month of January. The Ides (the fifteenth day in months having thirty-one days; the thirteenth in shorter months) is sacred to Jupiter.[18] In his entry for the Ides of January, Ovid, in a crescendo

[17] See the note in O'Flaherty 1981: 127 with further references.

[18] On the Ides the Flamen Dialis sacrifices a white lamb to Jupiter. On the Ides of January the Flamen also offers a gelded ram to his god.

of adjectives, recalls the deeds of *Magnus* (that is, Pompey; l. 603), of one whose name is yet *maior* (Julius Caesar; l. 604), and of *Maximus* (Quintus Fabius; l. 606). This process reaches its climax with a reference to Augustus, whose name is shared by Jupiter Summus (*socium summo cum Jove*; l. 608) 'highest Jupiter'. Janus' day, the Kalends, is a day of *prima*; Jupiter's day, the Ides, is affiliated with *summa*. In the old lunar calendar on which the Roman calendar is based, the day of the Ides corresponded generally to the day of the full moon. As such it represented the pinnacle, the height, of the lunar cycle and the month, and it must be for this reason that the Ides belong to Jupiter.

If there is any semblance of a Roman cultic "cognate" of the *columna mundi* which in India takes the form of the Vedic *yūpa*—as well as the Sadas post and the several other *yūpa* variants—it is certainly to be located in the altar of the sacred stone as it stands on the mount of the Capitoline. On that summit, on the border of earth and sky, Terminus is housed within the temple of the god who possesses the *summa*, much as the spot on which the *yūpa* stands on the border of the Vedic sacrificial space is declared to be the highest point on earth (*RV* 3.8.3). There Terminus' altar stands beneath a skylight (it is required; Festus p. 368M—see §2.2) in open communication with the sun, moon, and all other celestial bodies, bathed both in sunlight and full moonlight on the Ides, that pinnacle day which belongs to Jupiter, who shares his temple with Terminus.

2.7.2 Fecundity

Terminus and the *yūpa* share in common another vital trait. Both are boundary markers prominently linked, idiosyncratically, to the realm of productivity and fertility. Chief among those blessings which the sacrificer obtains from the *yūpa* are cattle, sustenance, and prosperity—including longevity (see §2.6.2)—all fundamental elements of the Indo-European third function. This is certainly not to say that in Vedic India the *yūpa* was in some way perceived as belonging to the class of the *vaiśya* (the third function of human society) or particularly linked to the Vasus (the divine third function), but simply that the principal blessings bound to the *yūpa* belong conceptually to the third function. In Rome Terminus is counted among the "gods of Titus Tatius," deities who embody elements of the archaic third function. Behind the Roman sacred boundary stone, deified as Terminus, and the Vedic column erected on the boundary of the great sacrificial space lies a common Indo-European cultic antecedent intimately linked to the realm of productivity and fecundity.

2.8 SPACE AND FIRE

There is an additional common cultic element that draws together Roman Terminus and the *yūpa* of Vedic India. That element is sacred space. In the remainder of this chapter we will turn our attention first to the three canonical flames of the small sacred space, and then to some preliminary and general considerations of the positioning of Terminus along the boundary of cultic space.

2.8.1 The three fires

A fundamental component of Vedic rite is the presence of three distinct fires. These are required for all *śrauta* rituals (the non-household rites, requiring the participation of priests), which can be essentially divided into (i) Iṣṭis (of several types, the basic forms of which are the new-moon and full-moon sacrifices; Keith 1998a: 319–321) and (ii) the Soma sacrifices (again, having various forms, based on the Agniṣṭoma; Keith 1998a: 326–332). The sacrificer must set up the three fires[19] within a delimited space; in the case of the Soma sacrifices there are two distinct spaces: the smaller space of the Iṣṭi containing the three canonical fires, and the larger sacrificial space lying to its east, the Mahāvedi. In the present discussion we will be concerned chiefly (though not exclusively) with the smaller space, that of the Iṣṭi,—which henceforth we will denote by the term "Devayajana," and turn to the larger space of the Mahāvedi in chapter 3.

The three Vedic fires conform to a constant geometry. Two lie along an east–west axis running through the sacrificial space. To the west burns the Gārhapatya, the fire of the "master of the house"; its shape is round; it is referred to as "the earth" ("this world," "the world of men"; *ŚB* 12.4.1.3; 7.3.1.8, 10, 12); and the sacrificer's wife is positioned by it. It is from this flame that the two other fires must be lit; the flame of the Gārhapatya itself can have three possible sources: (i) it can be generated by a fire drill; (ii) it can be preserved from a previous sacrificial fire; or (iii) it can be brought from the hearth of a *vaiśya* (the class of herders and cultivators), regardless of the *varṇa* (social class; see §1.6.1) to which the sacrificer belongs (*ARR*: 313). East of the Gārhapatya burns the fire named the Āhavanīya, having the shape of a quadrangle and called "the sky" ("the other world," "the world of the gods"; *ŚB* 12.4.1.3; 7.3.1.9–10, 12). By this fire are positioned the Brahman (the priest who sees that the rite is conducted properly) and

[19] For general discussion of the three fires, see Keith 1998: 288–289; Renou 1957: 97–98.

the sacrificer; in its flames the offering is consumed. At the southern edge of the enclosure is the third fire, the Dakṣiṇāgni, standing guard against a possible attack by evil forces; its shape is a semicircle and it is identified as "the atmosphere" (being positioned south of and at about the midpoint of the east-west axis that passes through the other two fires, it stands between earth and heaven; *ŚB* 12.4.1.3).

Dumézil perceived that these three principal fires of the Vedic sacrificial area have remarkable correspondences at Rome, both in terms of the altars and sacrificial practices affiliated with individual temples (see *ARR*: 314–315; 1954: 31–33), but also—and more significantly—in terms of the sacred architecture of Rome. The Gārhapatya, he argued, has a counterpart in the Roman "temple" of Vesta, identified with Earth, round in shape, tended by priestesses (the Vestals; compare the sacrificer's wife and her position by the Gārhapatya), in which burns the sacred flame of Rome that must be generated by friction. The Āhavanīya corresponds to quadrangular temples of Rome, each with its associated altar in which offerings are burned. Finally, the Dakṣiṇāgni matches the flame of the temple of Volcanus, situated beyond the city walls (on this requirement see Plutarch, *Quaest. Rom.* 47; Vitruvius 1.7.1). Dumézil (*ARR*: 320–321), apparently referring to the ancient Palatine *pomerium* (a sacred boundary beyond which the urban auspices, *auspicia urbana*, could not be taken; see §4.4) notes in addition another liminal and primitive area dedicated to Volcanus:

> . . . there was a still more ancient place of worship, and, before the incorporation of the Capitol into the city, this place had been located, if not outside the city limits, at least at them. At the foot of the southeast flank of the Capitol, between the Comitium and the Forum, there was a small open space, called the Volcanal, with an altar open to the sky, the *area Volcani*. Here the devouring fire mounted guard at one of the extremities of the Forum, and to it were entrusted the duties of mystical cleansing, particularly in connection with the misdeeds of its celestial brother, the *fulmen*.[20]

2.8.2 *Termini sacrificales*

Within the context of the shared Indo-European cultic apparatus of the three fires and the sacrificial space, an additional strand connecting Terminus and the *yūpa* comes to light. Ritual treatment of the two markers of the sacred boundary—Vedic and Roman—shows remarkable similarity.

[20]For additional discussion of the three flames, see *ARR*: 312–326; Dumézil 1954: 27–43; Boyle and Woodard 2000: 278–279; 291–293.

Just as in India the *yūpa* functions as a cultic implement in the observance of sacrificial rite, so does Terminus, the sacred boundary marker, in Rome. Though this is not so of just any *terminus*, but of those boundary markers that were explicitly designated for ritual use, the *termini sacrificales*, as we learn from the writings of the *gromatici*, the land surveyors of ancient Rome.[21] Often these *termini sacrificales* were not actually situated on the boundary lines with which they were associated, but only in their general vicinity, being placed in a spot suitable for making sacrifice. Frontinus writes that the *termini sacrificales* frequently stood beneath lush trees, accounting for this by noting that roads frequently pass along boundary lines and trees tend to flourish by the roadside (see Campbell 2000: 30–31). Yet again, he adds, many landowners will place these *termini* right on the boundary, *propter quod adimi fides sacrificalibus palis in totum non debet* (on another conjunction of Fides and Terminus, see below).

In his *De Condicionibus Agrorum*, Siculus Flaccus (see Campbell 2000: 106–107) can write of an ancient ritual to which there is no longer strict adherence in his own day. It was once the custom, he observes, that before boundary stones were sunk into the earth, they were set out close by the holes prepared for them and were anointed and decorated with coverings (*velamina*) and with wreathes. When a sacrifice had been offered, a victim immolated and burned, the celebrants dripped blood into the hole and tossed in frankincense and grain (*fruges*). They also added in honeycombs and wine and other materials customarily offered to Terminus. All of the ritual materials were then incinerated, and while they were still hot, the boundary marker was lowered into place on top of the burned relics. The celebrants are somewhat cryptically described as *cooperti*. Apparently they are completely covered over—but in what sense exactly? This particular occurrence of the participle receives its very own sense entry in the *Oxford Latin Dictionary* (p. 442, *cooperio*, 1.c.), where it is glossed as "(app.) with the head covered, veiled."

This ancient, neglected rite is intriguing in light of the prima facie parallels between Terminus and the *yūpa* which have already begun to emerge. Here again, in the ritual of preparing and raising the sacred boundary markers—the Roman *terminus* and the Vedic *yūpa* (and Sadas post)—striking similarities present themselves:

[21]See *Agrim.*, pp. 43.3; 73.34; 127.4; 221.17; 227.6; 401.19; Campbell 2000: 30.5, 11; 92.24; 170.24; 174.9; 176.25; 188.25, 33; 192.1; 194.28; 198.4; 254.3. In several of these passages the objects described are "sacrificial stakes" (*pali sacrificales*), commonly further specified as wooden.

1 The *yūpa* is laid out on the ground in front of the hole which has been dug to receive it, pointing eastward. The *terminus* is positioned straight (or vertically?) on the ground next to the prepared hole (*ipsos quidem lapides in solidam terram rectos conlocabant proxime ea loca in quibus fossis factis defixuri eos erant*).

2 The *yūpa* is anointed with sacred barley water and decorated with blades of ritual grass; a cinch strap encircles the post, and after the *yūpa* has been erected, a grass cord will be tied around it. The *terminus* is anointed and decorated with wreathes.

3 In that particularly primitive Soma ritual of the Vājapeya, the *yūpa* is wrapped in seventeen cloths. The *terminus* is wrapped with coverings (*velaminibus*).

4 Before the *yūpa* is set upright, sacred barley-water, blades of *barhis* grass, a chip from the *yūpa*, and *ghee* are deposited in the hole which was dug to receive the post. Before the *terminus* is set upright, into its hole the celebrants deposit frankincense, grain, honeycombs, wine, and other sacred materials appropriate for Terminus (*aliaque quibus consuetudo est Termini sacrum fieri*). Blood from a sacrificial victim is also poured in the hole; to this we shall return immediately below (see §2.8.2.1).

5 In the archaic Vājapeya, the sacrificer's wife wraps around herself a cloth, worn on top of the customary ceremonial garment, as she approaches the *yūpa*; the sacrificer wears a special garment, a *tārpya*. At the sacrifice of the victim for the *terminus*, the celebrants are described as *cooperti*. The typical meaning of the term, 'completely covered' (with *con-* lending to the verb its common sense of 'completeness'), must surely obtain in the present instance, and not the exceptional sense of the *OLD*'s 'veiled'. Veiling would be the expected attitude at sacrifice; a more complete covering—as at the Vājapeya—is intended here, in the proximity of the *terminus*.

2.8.2.1 BLOOD, FERTILITY, AND CHTHONIC BEINGS The pouring of the victim's blood into the hole dug for the *terminus* is particularly intriguing, if for no other reason, because of the rarity of the use of blood in Roman ritual. Warde Fowler drew attention to this long ago, when in a general discussion of the immolation of sacrificial victims and inspection of the viscera, he noted: "What became of the blood we are not told; I have already remarked that blood has curiously little part in Roman ritual and custom" (1911: 180–181), adding in a footnote: "I cannot find that any one of the many utensils used in sacrifice were for pouring out blood" (p. 196, n. 36).

When blood does make an appearance as an element of Roman ritual it occurs conspicuously within the context of rites promoting Roman fertility. During the festival of the goddess Dea Dia, her priests, the Fratres Arvales, share together several ritual meals. One of these, a *gustatio* taken within the grove of the goddess, consists of the meat of pigs sacrificed earlier in the day and a dish prepared with the blood of those pigs, *sangunculus* («fricassée de sang»; see Scheid 1990: 566–567). The Arvals are priests who bring fertility to the Roman fields; the ritual use of pigs' blood in their archaic ceremony is made the more interesting because of the priests' affiliation with sacred space and sacred boundary, as we shall see below (§4.7).

Plutarch preserves the record of a strange rite observed annually as a component of the Lupercalia, festival of the rustic god Faunus, celebrated on February 15. Dumézil's interpretative synopsis of the day is worth quoting (*ARR*: 346): "Once a year, for one day, the balance between the ordered, explored, compartmented world and the savage, untamed world was upset, when Faunus took possession of everything." On this day, the Luperci, members of a priestly sodality, ran naked around the Palatine, carrying strips of goat hide with which they struck bystanders. The lashes were intended to impart fertility to Roman women (see Ovid, *Fast.* 2.425–448) and to Roman fields (see Lydus, *Mens.* 4.25). Plutarch describes certain preparations for the race (*Rom.* 21.4–5):

> σφάττουσι γὰρ αἶγας, εἶτα μειρακίων δυοῖν ἀπὸ γένους προσαχθέντων αὐτοῖς, οἱ μὲν ᾑμαγμένῃ μαχαίρᾳ τοῦ μετώπου θιγγάνουσιν, ἕτεροι δ' ἀπομάττουσιν εὐθύς, ἔριον βεβρεγμένον γάλακτι προσφέροντες. γελᾶν δὲ δεῖ τὰ μειράκια μετὰ τὴν ἀπόμαξιν.
>
> For they slaughter goats, and then two boys of noble family having been brought to them, some touch them on the forehead with a blood-stained knife and others immediately wipe it off, applying wool soaked in milk. Then the boys must laugh after the wiping off.

The specific symbolic and theological significance of the curious rite has been long lost in the crevices of time, but it is undoubtedly linked to the imbuing of fertility with which the day's activities are manifestly concerned.

In Ovid's description of the private rites of the Terminalia (*Fast.* 2.655–656), festival of Terminus (to which we shall come shortly; see §2.8.5), the poet writes of the boundary stone that separates neighboring lands and how on this day it is splattered with the blood of a suckling pig and a lamb. The likely intent of his poetic description is, however, that the animals were sacrificed on the stone, rather than that the blood of the victims was ritually washed over it (compare Lucretius 5.1201–1202).

Blood also appears notably in quite a different ritual context. Whatever his source and inspiration for the ritual acts described, Virgil (*Aen.* 6.236–254) recounts the sacrifices that were required in order for Aeneas to gain access to the world of Dis. The description of one of the sacrifices—the Sibyl's offering of four black cows to Hecate deep within a cave—makes conspicuous mention of the victims' throats being slashed and their blood collected in a vessel. In addition, Aeneas himself offers a black lamb to Night, mother of the chthonic Eumenides, and to Terra (Gaea); he sacrifices a sterile cow to Proserpina; and he burns bulls for Pluto. While we should be cautious in turning to rites addressed to Greek deities in search of evidence for deeply archaic Roman practices, Aeneas is probably leading us down a right path.

Vedic evidence casts light on the Roman practice. In the observance of the Soma sacrifice (see §2.6.1), after the sacrificial victim has been untied from the *yūpa*, led to the place of sacrifice (outside of the Mahāvedi), and killed (by suffocation), the Adhvaryu lacerates the victim, and touching each end of a stalk of grass to the bloody wound, he exclaims, "You [the blood, that is] are the share of the Rākṣasas." The priest throws the bloodied grass down onto the Utkara, a rubbish mound located north of the sacred space, and stomps on it. He thus treads underfoot the demonic Rākṣasas and holds them in darkness (*ŚB* 3.8.2.12–15). Beyond this, the blood from the butchered victim will be poured into a pit for the Rākṣasas (see Keith 1998a: 281). Keith suggests that blood so poured into a cavity in the earth should likely be interpreted as an offering made to chthonic powers, as evidenced by the pouring out of blood for snakes (1998a: 194, 281; see also *AGS* 4.8.27).

Blood is not poured into the hole dug for the *yūpa*, but protection is indeed offered from chthonic beings. Into that hole, the priest pours *ghee*, the melted butter identified as a "thunderbolt," and the "life-sap of the universe" (see *ŚB* 7.2.3.4). *Ghee* belongs especially to the fire god Agni (see *ŚB* 9.2.2.2–3), who is himself the principal protector of the offering from the Rākṣasas (see *ŚB* 1.6.1.11–15; Keith 1998a: 238). The *ghee* ladled into the hole prevents evil spirits from rising from below (*ŚB* 3.7.1.10).

The barley water which the priest pours into holes dug for the *yūpa* and for the Sadas post purifies the world of the Pitaras (equivalent to the Manes), for whom also *barhis* grass is added to the holes—pits being sacred to the Pitaras (*ŚB* 3.6.1.13–14; 3.7.1.6–7). These venerated spirits of the dead may not be commonly perceived as menacing chthonic figures, but they clearly have earth affiliations—as we have just witnessed—and are at times set over against the gods (see Renou 1957: 80–81). The southern reaches of the larger sacred space, the Mahāvedi, belong to the Pitaras, the northern region belongs to the gods (see *ŚB* 9.3.4.11–13; the northeastern region belongs to gods and men; *ŚB* 12.7.3.7). According to *Śatapatha Brāhmaṇa* 12.8.1.17, those who perform the Sautrāmaṇī at the southern fire established for the rite go down to the Pitaras. To the Pitaras belongs the world of plants, and the Pitaras hide among the roots of plants (*ŚB* 13.8.1.20).

Vedic comparanda and independent Roman evidence clarify the picture. The blood which is poured into a hole dug for a *terminus* must certainly be an offering made to beings of the earth, into whose realm the post or stone is being sunk. Indeed, some or all of the other materials deposited in the hole—frankincense, grain, honeycombs, wine, and so forth—may serve a similar purpose.[22] The Roman use of blood in the *gustatio* of the Fratres Arvales and especially its presence in the rites of the Lupercalia may suggest that the offerings of blood serve a second function, to bring fertility to the ground in which the *termini* are installed. If this is so, this is perhaps a secondary Roman development, but one linked to the provisions of fertility otherwise associated with the ancestral Indo-European sacred boundary marker.

2.8.3 Analogy and homology

A helpful distinction that can be introduced into our analysis of the two boundary markers—one Vedic, the other Roman—is that of analogy versus homology. The contrastive notion of analogous and homologous relations constitutes a fundamental principle of the disciplines of comparative anatomy and evolutionary biology, first developed in a systematic fashion by the nineteenth-century British anatomist, Sir Richard Owen. Among related species, anatomic structures that have their origin in an ancestral organism common to the species are said to be *homologous*. This is so even if the related structures no longer serve the same function. In contrast, structures that do perform similar functions but which are not of common origin are called *analogous*. For example, the arms of a kangaroo and the front legs of a horse share a similar anatomy and are of common evolutionary descent, and are thus identified as homologous, even though they function in quite different ways. On the other hand, the wings of a hummingbird and those of a bumblebee serve a similar function, holding aloft

[22] And why are they incinerated? Is this fire, like that of Agni, further protection from the infernal?

their possessor by rapid movement, but have no common origin in a single ancestral creature; the two sets of wings are thus analogous structures.[23]

The Roman *terminus sacrificalis* and the Vedic *yūpa* are clearly homologous structures, by the analysis proposed herein: they have a common origin in the early Indo-European cult, in which their ancestral structure stood as a marker along the boundary of a delineated sacred space (which likewise gave rise to homologous structures in Roman and Vedic cult, as will be discussed at length in the ensuing chapters). The relationship of those materials placed within the holes prepared for the *terminus* and the *yūpa* is perhaps of a more complex nature. Like the boundary markers, these substances must also have a common ancestral form—ritual materials used by early Indo-European priests and worshippers to protect the sacrifice from deities and powers that inhabit the earth, where the boundary marker is an intrusion. While functionally equivalent, the Roman and Vedic materials consist, however, of quite distinct ingredients; in one or both of the daughter cultures, the ritual materials have been replaced. Between parent and daughter rituals, there is ideological continuity, but not strict structural continuity. As evolutionary biologists and comparative anatomists do not ordinarily concern themselves with ideology (or the mind of God), our own methodology at this point necessarily veers somewhat from its biologic inspiration. The principle is, however, fundamentally the same.

Yet some may ask, "Why could the *terminus sacrificalis* and the *yūpa* not be identified as analogous structures which have developed independently in the two sibling Indo-European cultures, Italic and Indic?" The answer is straightforward: for the same reason, mutatis mutandis, that the comparative anatomist assigns the similarities in the front limb structures of the mammalian kangaroo and horse to the category of homology. From a purely pragmatic perspective, the redundancy entailed in mounting the argument that closely related, idiosyncratic ritual structures arose completely independently and accidentally in two related cultures otherwise showing common ritual and religious structures, having a common origin in a single parent-culture, and so descended from a common ritual tradition, strains the limits of credulity in the face of the elegantly simple and naturally obvious solution of homology. From the perspective of theoretical economy, analogy is immediately eliminated in favor of homology;

[23]For a general discussion of homology and analogy, the reader is directed to the *Encyclopaedia Britannica*, 15th ed., vol. 6, p. 29.

Occam's Razor demands it: the evaluation metric for choosing between two competing analyses dictates the selection of the simpler (that is, less redundant). The only recourse left to the diehard cynic is to disparage the genetic relatedness of the Italic and Indo-Aryan languages and cultures—that is, to deny the existence of the Indo-European language family and the parent Proto-Indo-European language and culture. Taking that step is not unheard of; it is, however, without any rational defense in the real world.

2.8.4 Termini Romani

In examining the *termini Romani* we surely get a clean look at an evolutionary bifurcation—at the distinction which developed between a cultic boundary marker of great antiquity and its more utilitarian, benchmark alloform. The evolutionary split obviously may have been pre-Roman, may have been pre-Italic, but the presence and use of the marker outside of the sacrificial cult certainly multiplied with the rise of landed Indo-European societies in Italy. Thus, the Indo-Europeans arrived in Italy equipped with a cult that used a sacrificial space delimited by a sacred marker; as society became sedentary and individual ownership of land was claimed, the use of the marker was automatically extended to, or expanded in, nonritual, proprietary use. There is, in fact, a Roman memory of the initiation of this practice, and in this memory it is Numa Pompilius, the successor of Rome's founding king, who is credited with establishing the practice of marking property boundaries (both private and public) by *termini* as one element of his campaign to bring order and justice to Roman society.

Yet even in their land-marking capacity the *termini* are not completely removed from the realm of the sacred. Numa declared—writes Dionysius of Halicarnassus (*Ant. Rom.* 2.74.3–4)—that whoever destroys or tampers with one of these boundary markers would be deemed "devoted to the god" and could be killed without the homicide incurring blood guilt. Festus (p. 368M) concurs.[24]

On the subject of Numa and Terminus, consider what Plutarch has to say. In his *Life of Numa*, Plutarch writes that the good king was the first to dedicate temples to Terminus as well as to the goddess Fides. Plutarch goes on to claim that while in his own time sacrifices to Terminus involve the spilling of blood, in early days, offerings to the god were not bloodstained—Numa having speculated that as the boundary god is guardian of peace and witness of justice, his worship should not be tainted by slaughter (*Numa* 16.1). The point is made again in *Roman Questions* 15, where Numa is contrasted with the aggressor Romulus, always eager to expand his borders.

[24] On legislation prohibiting removal of boundary stones, see Campbell 2000: 471.

Dionysius of Halicarnassus, on the other hand, says that even in his day the sacrifices made to Terminus were not of living creatures, as it was not lawful to bloody the boundary stones. Instead, offerings were made of "cakes of Demeter" (πέλανοι Δημήτριοι) and of certain other firstfruits. Dionysius' affirmation is curious. Plutarch has on his side (i) Ovid, who writes of a lamb and suckling pig as sacrifices meet for Terminus (see immediately below, §2.8.5); (ii) Horace, who alludes to the "lamb slain at the feast of the Terminalia" (*Epodes* 2.59); and (iii) Prudentius (*C. Symm.* 2.1008) with his "hen's lung" presented to the stone (see §2.5).

Terminus had not been free from blood rites for at least as long as the ancient custom of dribbling blood into his pit had been practiced. But memories of a mythic past in which the stone was venerated only with vegetable offerings may not be completely without grounding. The Vedic homologue of Terminus, the *yūpa* that marks the boundary of the great sacred space, is intimately acquainted with the sacrificial victim of the Soma rituals—that victim being tethered to the post. Although the *yūpa* is referred to as the "sacrificial stake," the victim is not in actuality killed at the post. As we have seen (§2.6.1), after the victim is anointed and fire passed around it, the priest unties the animal and leads it to an area designated for immolation, outside of the great sacred space. This well-documented Vedic practice, on the one hand, and the collective Roman memory of a past when Terminus was unsullied by blood, on the other, may share a common origin in early Indo-European cult. If so, the sacred boundary marker which is ancestor both to Terminus and to the *yūpa* was kept free from the stain of blood. As the *termini* in Italy shifted from being solely markers of the boundary of a space delineated for the performance of sacred ritual to markers segregating bounded plots of land at which sacred rites were performed, those rites were assimilated, by this scenario, to rites of immolation. The process of assimilation may have been facilitated by a Roman—or more generally Mediterranean—belief in the efficacy of blood in promoting land fertility. The incorporation of bloodshed into the ritual of setting up *termini* would then likewise find an origin in this Mediterranean practice, or perhaps it would hark back to a primitive Indo-European rite of making blood offerings to chthonic beings that had previously not formed an element of the ritual of the setting up of the sacred boundary marker. These matters are, however, presently beyond our reach.

2.8.5 The private rites of the Terminalia

Yet another of Numa Pompilius' religious institutions, according to Dionysius of Halicarnassus (*Ant. Rom.* 2.74.2–3), was the festival of Terminus.

The Terminalia, annual rites of the boundary god, are celebrated on February 23, very close to the boundary of the Roman year. Thus Varro (*Ling.* 6.13) can write in discussing the etymologies of various festival days:

> Terminalia, quod is dies anni extremus constitutus . . . .
>
> The Terminalia [are so named] because the day is set at the year's end . . . .

While perhaps *extremus*, the Terminalia are not celebrated on the last day—not even the last festival day—of the year; on the importance of which, see Woodard 2002.

Both private and public rites were observed, and both are noted by Ovid in his *Fasti* entry for February 23 (2.639–684). For the present investigation, the private rites of the Terminalia are less important than those of the public observance—the former being further removed from comparable Vedic ritual practices involving the homologue of Terminus, the *yūpa* (used only in the great Soma sacrifices, *śrautas*, not in domestic ritual), and so further removed from ancestral Indo-European cultic convention (as will become clearer). This removal is consequent to the shift in use of the ancient boundary marker, to which we have already alluded. No longer is the marker simply erected along the perimeter of a space explicitly delineated for ritual activity; now in the landed society of Rome, it is a permanent fixture of *boundary*. The private rites of the Terminalia are the celebration of this fixture. While we are in the neighborhood, however, the private rites are worth a quick look.

In his *Fasti* accounts of the events of February 23, Ovid provides more precise information about the ritual components of the celebration of the Terminalia in the private cult than in the public (ll. 639–658):

> Nox ubi transierit, solito celebretur honore
> separat indicio qui deus arva suo.
> Termine, sive lapis sive es defossus in agro
> stipes, ab antiquis tu quoque numen habes.
> te duo diversa domini de parte coronant,
> binaque serta tibi binaque liba ferunt.
> ara fit: huc ignem curto fert rustica testo
> sumptum de tepidis ipsa colona focis.
> ligna senex minuit concisaque construit arte,
> et solida ramos figere pugnat humo;
> tum sicco primas inritat cortice flammas;
> stat puer et manibus lata canistra tenet.
> inde ubi ter fruges medios immisit in ignes,
> porrigit incisos filia parva favos.

vina tenent alii: libantur singula flammis;
    spectant, et linguis candida turba favet.
spargitur et caeso communis Terminus agno,
    nec queritur lactans cum sibi porca datur.
conveniunt celebrantque dapes vicinia simplex
    et cantat laudes, Termine sancte, tuas.
When night has passed, honour with traditional rites
    The god whose mark partitions the fields.

Terminus, whether you are a stone or a stump buried
    In earth, your worship, too, is ancient.
Two landowners from opposite sides crown you,
    And offer you two garlands and two cakes.
An altar is built. The rustic farm-wife lugs there
    A cracked pot blazing with her warm hearth-fire.
The old man chops wood, assembles the pieces with skill,
    And battles to stick branches in the stiff ground.
Then he arouses the first flames with dry bark.
    A boy stands by, clutching wide baskets.
When the corn has been hurled three times into the fire,
    A small daughter presents cut honeycombs.
Others clasp wine for separate libations to the flame;
    A crowd in white watches with silent tongues.
Communal Terminus is doused with a slain lamb,
    And does not whine when offered suckling pig.
The simple neighborhood meets and celebrates the feast.

Regarding the private rites, and their institution by Numa, Dionysius of Halicarnassus (*Ant. Rom.* 2.74.2–3) writes:

> κελεύσας γὰρ ἑκάστῳ περιγράψαι τὴν ἑαυτοῦ κτῆσιν καὶ στῆσαι λίθους ἐπὶ τοῖς ὅροις ἱεροὺς ἀπέδειξεν Ὁρίου Διὸς τοὺς λίθους, καὶ θυσίας ἔταξεν αὐτοῖς ἐπιτελεῖν ἅπαντας ἡμέρᾳ τακτῇ καθ' ἕκαστον ἐνιαυτὸν ἐπὶ τὸν τόπον συνερχομένους, ἑορτὴν ἐν τοῖς πάνυ τιμίαν τὴν τῶν ὁρίων θεῶν καταστησάμενος. ταύτην Ῥωμαῖοι Τερμινάλια καλοῦσιν ἐπὶ τῶν τερμόνων ....
>
> For having ordered everyone to delineate their own property and to set stones on the boundaries, he pronounced the stones sacred to Jupiter Terminus; and he commanded all that they were to gather at the place each year on a designated day and to make sacrifices to the stones, having established among them a high holy festival of the boundary gods. The Romans call it the *Terminalia* after the *termini* ....

At least one aspect of the private rites found in Ovid's description catches our eye, given the Indo-European context in which we have been examining Terminus. In his portrayal of the festival as an affair of family and community, the poet makes salient reference to the presence of both the "rustic farm-wife" and "the old man," and of their particular duties in the celebration of the rites of Terminus—bringing flame from the hearth and preparing the sacrificial fire. Given the archaic heritage of Terminus and his connections with the Vedic *yūpa*, the reference is *séduisant*. The early Indic sacrificer and his wife must jointly participate in the sacrifice—this is a sine qua non. Jamison (1996: 30–31) writes:

> One of the main technical requirements for being a Sacrificer is that he must be a householder (*gṛhastha*); he must be married. Not only that but the presence and participation of his wife is required at all the solemn rituals. Sacrificer's Wife (*patnī* in Sanskrit) is a *structural role* in ritual with particular duties and activities that cannot ordinarily be performed by anyone else. . . . A ritual without a wife is not a ritual at all according to the *Taittirīya Brāhmaṇa* (II.2.2.6). The first major duty of a wife is to serve as ritual partner, and this requirement is so strong that, according to some legal authorities, a wife may not be repudiated once the couple has jointly kindled the fires that establish them as Sacrificers.

More than this, in Ovid's description the country wife brings flame for the altar from the domestic hearth; in Vedic ritual, the position of the sacrificer's wife is beside the Gārhapatya, the fire of the "master of the house" (see §2.7.1).[25] We must leave this as only a tantalizing tidbit.

2.9 CONCLUSION

The boundary stone, Terminus, is situated within a matrix of features which recurs along the eastern and western fringes of the ancient Indo-European world—a sacred stone associated with fertility occupies an elevated space which is conspicuously bound to the realm of sovereignty. Unlike the corresponding Celtic and Indic stones, Terminus is not identified as the phallus of a warrior figure. The Indic equivalent to Terminus within this matrix is the Śiva *linga*. This stone, however, has an ancestral Vedic form, the *yūpa*—standing on the distal boundary of the great sacred space, the Mahāvedi—which is yet far more valuable for comparison to Terminus, the Roman boundary marker.

The *yūpa*, like Terminus (a "god of Titus Tatius"), is also conspicuously

[25] Moreover, that fire can be lit from the hearth of a Vaiśya (the Vedic social class to which agricultural workers belong).

affiliated with the realm of fertility and fecundity—as a cultic implement standing on the sacred boundary it brings wealth, an abundance of offspring, and blessings to the fields (*RV* 3.8.6–7).

Like the later *linga* of Śiva, the *yūpa* represents the *columna mundi*; it spans the cosmos from the world of the Pitaras beneath ground to the world of the gods above. Terminus, housed on the summit of Jupiter and standing beneath a hole in the temple roof, a marker typically planted within earth, must also continue a primitive Indo-European icon of the *columna mundi*.

The *yūpa* has several by-forms, each of which likewise represents a *columna mundi*—the *skambha*; the flaming *liṅgodbhava*; the richly ornamented *Indradhvaja*; the Sadas post located at the opposite (western) boundary of the large sacred space. Likewise, the sacred boundary stone Terminus has its variant forms—markers of wood, stumps, even trees decorated with streamers and lamps.

Identifying Terminus as a cultic cognate of the Vedic *yūpa* reveals an evolutionary bifurcation whereby the ancient marker of the boundary of sacred space is generalized as a marker of the boundary of possessed space in the land-owning society of Rome. The rites of erecting the structurally homologous Vedic *yūpa* and Roman *terminus sacrificalis* are notably similar, with the well-attested Vedic procedures providing certain insights into the process described by the Roman *gromatici*. The archaic *Vājapeya* proves to be especially relevant in this regard. The inherently contradictory Vedic practice of removing the sacrificial victim from the vicinity of the "sacrificial stake"—the *yūpa*—to which it is tethered prior to sacrifice may provide a diachronic rationale for the synchronically conflicting accounts among Roman authors regarding the bloodying of the sacred boundary stones.

Like the *linga* of Śiva—and the Irish stone of Fál—the Vedic *yūpa* is also possessed by a warrior deity. The *yūpa* belongs to Viṣṇu, affiliated with the warrior element of divine society, and is also associated with Indra (compare its alloform, the *Indradhvaja*, 'Indra's banner'). That the *yūpa* should share this trait with the later *linga* and the Irish stone is particularly intriguing. As we have seen, the *yūpa*, a sacred boundary marker, provides a closer and more significant match to Roman Terminus than does even the *linga*—we have argued that the *yūpa* and the *terminus sacrificalis* are homologous structures having a common origin in Proto-Indo-European cult. But we have not yet seen a comparably close affiliation of the Roman boundary marker with a warrior—divine or otherwise (which is not to say we have seen no affiliation). Bearing this in mind, we press ahead to chapter 3.

CHAPTER 3

Into the Teacup

3.1 INTRODUCTION

The public rites of the Terminalia, the Ambarvalia, the Arval celebration of the goddess Dea Dia, ancient rituals of lustration preserved in the writings of Cato, Virgil, and Tibullus—these are the things which will occupy our attention in chapter 3. We will examine these rituals and their component parts comparatively, holding them up to the light side by side, and shining the illuminating brilliance of Vedic ritual and cult on them. We begin where we left off in the preceding chapter.

3.2 THE PUBLIC RITES OF THE TERMINALIA

In chapter 2, we examined the private festival of the Terminalia; the public observance, as will become clear, is of greater interest and significance for our study. It is at the sixth milestone of the Via Laurentina that the public rite of the boundary god is celebrated on February 23. Of the sacrifice and road, Ovid writes (*Fast.* 2.679–684):

> Est via quae populum Laurentes ducit in agros,
> quondam Dardanio regna petita duci:

Illa lanigeri pecoris tibi, Termine, fibris
 sacra videt fieri sextus ab Urbe lapis.
Gentibus est aliis tellus data limite certo:
 Romanae spatium est Urbis et orbis idem.

There is a road which leads folk to Laurentine fields,
 The realm once sought by the Dardan leader;
Its sixth stone from the city sees a woolly sheep's guts
 Being sacrificed, Terminus, to you.
For other nations the earth has fixed boundaries;
 Rome's city and the world are the same space.

In lines 683–684, the poet echoes an ideology to which he had given expression in his description of the events of January's Kalends (1.85–88):

Iuppiter arce sua totum cum spectet in orbem,
 nil nisi Romanum quod tueatur habet.
Salve, laeta dies, meliorque revertere semper,
 a populo rerum digna potente coli.

Jupiter, viewing all the world from his citadel,
 Observes nothing un-Roman to protect.
Hail, joyful day, and happier returns always,
 Worthy festival of a master people.

To these words, we shall return (see §4.5).

The reason for the locale where the public ritual is observed is not given. The common and certainly accurate interpretation has been that the sixth milestone coincides with an old boundary between the Roman and Laurentine territories (see Alföldi 1965: 296–304; Frazer 1929, vol. 2: 486; Warde Fowler 1899: 327). In other words, the mile marker occurred at the site of an ancient *terminus*, erected by a roadway (the Via Laurentina; compare Frontinus' remarks in §2.8.2 about the placement of *termini* close to roads) passing through the Ager Romanus—a *terminus* which at a certain moment in Rome's history marked the frontier boundary.

Dionysius of Halicarnassus makes oblique reference to the observance of the public rites but provides us with little additional information. After relating how Numa had declared that the removal or destruction of a *terminus* was a sacrilege, and that a person who consequently murdered the perpetrator of such an act was not guilty of homicide (this crime being the referent of τοῦτο . . . τὸ δίκαιον in the passage below; see §2.8.2), the historian adds (*Ant. Rom.* 2.74.4–5):

τοῦτο δ' οὐκ ἐπὶ τῶν ἰδιωτικῶν κατεστήσατο μόνον κτήσεων τὸ δίκαιον, ἀλλὰ καὶ ἐπὶ τῶν δημοσίων, ὅροις κἀκείνας περιλαβών, ἵνα καὶ τὴν Ῥωμαίων γῆν ἀπὸ τῆς ἀστυγείτονος ὅριοι διαιρῶσαι θεοὶ καὶ τὴν κοινὴν ἀπὸ τῆς ἰδίας. τοῦτο μέχρι τῶν καθ' ἡμᾶς χρόνων φυλάττουσι Ῥωμαῖοι μνημεῖα τῆς ὁσίας αὐτῆς ἕνεκα. θεούς τε γὰρ ἡγοῦνται τοὺς τέρμονας καὶ θύουσιν αὐτοῖς ὁσέτη, τῶν μὲν ἐμψύχων οὐδέν (οὐ γὰρ ὅσιον αἱμάττειν τοὺς λίθους), πελάνους δὲ δημητρίους καὶ ἄλλας τινὰς καρπῶν ἀπαρχάς.

And he established this right not with regard to private property only, but indeed to public property as well—having circumscribed these with boundary-stones also, so that the boundary gods might both separate Roman land from that of neighboring peoples, as well as common land from private. To the present day, the Romans preserve this practice as a remembrance of an earlier time—for the sake of ritual itself. For they consider the *termini* gods and year by year they make offerings to them, but not of living things (for it is not lawful to bloody the stones), rather of cakes of grain and certain other firstfruits.

Does Dionysius suggest that the observance of the public ritual took place at more locales than one? So it would seem.

3.3 THE AMBARVALIA

In his commentary on the *Fasti* (2: 497), a paradigm of scholarship from the early part of the last century, Sir James Frazer could segue naturally from his discussion of the public observance of the Terminalia to remarks on the Ambarvalia, one festival being sufficiently reminiscent of the other in flavor and in particulars. Both are celebrations fundamentally concerned with boundaries and bounded spaces; both belong to the ritual sphere of the earth and its protection; both are celebrated publicly along roadways leading from Rome, at about the same distance from the city; both must have their origin in a rustic, distant past.

3.3.1 Strabo

The Greek geographer Strabo (5.3.2), describing the site where Romulus and Remus would establish their city and the towns which then surrounded that place, writes:

μεταξὺ γοῦν τοῦ πέμπτου καὶ τοῦ ἕκτου λίθου τῶν τὰ μίλια διασημαινόντων τῆς Ῥώμης καλεῖται τόπος Φῆστοι. τοῦτον δ' ὅριον ἀποφαίνουσι τῆς τότε Ῥωμαίων γῆς, οἵ θ' ἱερομνήμονες θυσίαν ἐπιτελοῦσιν ἐνταῦθά τε καὶ ἐν ἄλλοις τόποις πλείοσιν ὡς ὁρίοις αὐθημερόν, ἣν καλοῦσιν Ἀμβαρουίαν.

In any event, between the fifth and sixth stones marking the miles from Rome is a place called Festi. And this was then, they claim, the boundary of Roman territory; the Pontifices celebrate a sacred festival both there and, on the same day, at still other places—these being boundaries. They call the festival the Ambarvia.

Strabo's *Festi* (Φῆστοι)—the only one of those boundary-places that he identifies at which are celebrated the Ambarvalia, or Ambarvia (Ἀμβαρουία) as he names the rite—is not otherwise known, and its geographic identification has provided fuel for speculation over the years. Since the mid-nineteenth-century work of De Rossi,[1] many scholars have assumed that this Festi ought to be equated with the *lucus* 'grove' of the Fratres Arvales, those priests whom we encountered in chapter 2 in our discussion of the Roman ritual use of blood (see §2.7.2). But this could only be so were the Ambarvalia and the rites of Dea Dia, the goddess served by the Fratres Arvales, one and the same (see Scheid 1990: 99–100). They are undeniably similar, but probably not a single ritual. (We shall return to this problem immediately below.) Beyond this general equation, other—more idiosyncratic—conjectures have been made concerning the presumed toponym Festi. Thus, Münzer (*RE* 4: 1832) suggested that there might be an etymological link with the name of P. Curiatius Fistus Trigeminus. Schulze (1904: 564, n.3) proposed that Festi might be related to an Oscan place name Fistlus, from a conjectured earlier *Fisti.

Norden (1939: 175–176), accepting none of the aforementioned suggestions, tentatively offers a potential connection between Festi and the verbal phrase *f(inis)esto*, which is conjectured to occur in the archaic and quite problematic augural formula preserved by Varro (*Ling.* 7.8):[2]

> [i]tem<pla> tescaque † me ita sunto quoad ego † eas te lingua[m] nuncupavero.
>
> ullaber arbos quirquir est quam me sentio dixisse templum tescumque[m] † festo in sinistrum.
>
> ollaner arbos quirquir est quod me sentio dixisse te<m>plum tescumque[m] † festo dextrum.

[1]De Rossi 1858; on the history of the problem see Alföldi 1965: 298.

[2]For the restoration of Varro's text, see Norden 1939: 3–106; for *f(inis)esto*, see especially pp. 31–45.

inter ea conregione conspicione cortumione utique ea erectissime sensi.

Norden arrives at a possible explanation of the place name by drawing on a matrix of connections involving the following: (i) the Pontifices; (ii) augural space; (iii) the Ager Romanus; and (iv) the *pomerium*. Remarking that it falls to the Pontifices—the priests (ἱερομνήμονες) of Strabo's Ambarvia—to consecrate the sacred spaces delimited by the Augures, he invokes the affinities of the augural boundaries and those of the Ager Romanus, citing Varro *Ling.* 5.33:

> Ut nostri augures publici disserunt, agrorum sunt genera quinque: Romanus, Gabinus, peregrinus, hosticus, incertus. Romanus dictus unde Roma ab Rom<ul>o; Gabinus ab oppido Gabi<i>s; peregrinus ager pacatus, qui extra Romanum et Gabinum, quod uno modo in his serv<a>ntur auspicia; dictus peregrinus a peregendo, id est a progrediendo: eo enim ex agro Romano primum progrediebantur: quocirca Gabinus quoque peregrinus, sed quod auspicia habet singularia, ab reliquo discretus; hosticus dictus ab hostibus; incertus is, qui de his quattuor qui sit ignoratur.
>
> As our public Augures detail, there are five types of *agri*: the Ager Romanus, Gabinus, Peregrinus, Hosticus, and Incertus. The Ager Romanus is so named after Romulus [Romus?], as is Rome; the Ager Gabinus from the town of Gabii. The Ager Peregrinus is land subdued, which is outside the Ager Romanus and Gabinus, because in these two, auspices are observed in a single way; Peregrinus takes its name from a 'going onward', from an 'advancing': indeed, into this *ager* they were first making advances from the Ager Romanus. In this way of course the Ager Gabinus is likewise Peregrinus, but because it has its particular form of auspices, it is kept distinct from the rest. The Ager Hosticus is named after *hostes* 'enemies'; Ager Incertus is that which is uncertain in its affiliation to these four.

Norden additionally, and parenthetically, draws attention to the role of the Augures in fixing the boundaries of the urban sacred space, the *pomerium*, as described by Aulus Gellius (*NA* 13.14.1):

> Pomerium quid esset augures populi Romani qui libros De Auspiciis scripserunt istiusmodi sententia definierunt: Pomerium est locus intra agrum effatum per totius urbis circuitum pone muros regionibus certeis determinatus, qui facit finem urbani auspicii.
>
> The Augures of the Roman people who wrote the books *De Auspiciis* defined *pomerium* as having this meaning: "The *pomerium* is that space

> within the *ager* that the Augures delineate along the circuit of the entire city, lying beyond the walls, fixed by firm bounding-lines and constituting the boundary of the urban auspices."

The pontifical-augural-sacred boundaries connection being made, Norden—with much caution clearly intended—asks whether the place name Festi might not be a fictive plural (the rite is celebrated at several places) based on the *f(inis)esto* of Varro's augural formula.[3] As Scheid (1990: 100) observes, the interpretation is certainly ingenious, but no more satisfying than those which Norden dismisses. We walk away empty-handed, wondering whether the place name has any significance at all.

3.3.2 Festus

In the Latin literary record, the name of Strabo's festival, Ambarvalia (or Ambarvia, as the Greek writer actually calls it), occurs only in the work of two writers, though rituals are elsewhere described that have been commonly identified as celebrations of the Ambarvalia, if not so named. To Strabo's remarks can be added Festus' brief identification of the adjective *Ambarvales* (p. 5M):

> Ambarvales hostiae appellabantur, quae pro arvis a duobus fratribus sacrificabantur.
>
> Ambarvales is the name they gave to the victims which were sacrificed on behalf of the lands (*arva*) by the two Brothers.

And in his note on the meaning of the word *amptermini*, Festus adds this (p. 17M):

> Amptermini, qui circa terminos provinciae manent. Unde amiciri, amburbium, ambarvalia, amplexus dicta sunt.
>
> *Amptermini*—in that they are situated around (*circa*) the extremities (*termini*) of a *provincia*; whence *amiciri, amburbium, ambarvalia, amplexus* have been so named.

Whatever it is that is being defined, one clearly perceives Festus, to the extent his record has been preserved, to have understood that the term *ambarvalia* means 'around the lands' or 'fields' (*arva*). One could assume that such a meaning is trivially self-evident, and records of land-lustra-

[3]"Macht nun ΦΗΣΤΟΙ nicht den Eindruck einer fiktiven Pluralbildung von FESTO?" (Norden 1939: 176).

tion rites have survived which explicitly describe the circumambulating of land-boundaries, though without naming the rites as "Ambarvalia." To this also we return below.

3.3.3 Cato

In an early treatise on agriculture and estate management (c. 160 BC), Cato (*Agr.* 141) preserves for us the description of a rite of land lustration. Among the liturgical elements that Cato records is a prayer offered up to Mars—an invocation of great antiquity. In his analysis of the structure of the prayer, Watkins (1995: 197) writes: "This prayer to Mars has been justly qualified by Risch 1979 as the 'oldest Latin text preserved,' 'actually older than Early Latin literature,' the monuments of authors of the third and second centuries BC." He continues (p. 199): "This prayer . . . is indeed not only the most ancient piece of Latin literature but the oldest Latin poem that we possess." Here are Cato's words:

> Agrum lustrare sic oportet. Impera suovitaurilia circumagi:
>
> "Cum divis volentibus quodque bene eveniat, mando tibi, Mani, uti illace suovitaurilia fundum agrum terramque meam quota ex parte sive circumagi sive circumferenda censeas, uti cures lustrare."
>
> Ianum Iovemque vino praefamino, sic dicito: "Mars pater, te precor quaesoque uti sies volens propitius mihi domo familiaeque nostrae, quoius re ergo agrum terram fundumque meum suovitaurilia circumagi iussi, uti tu morbos visos invisosque, viduertatem vastitudinemque, calamitates intemperiasque prohibessis defendas averruncesque; utique tu fruges, frumenta, vineta virgultaque grandire beneque evenire siris, pastores pecuaque salva servassis duisque bonam salutem valetudinemque mihi domo familiaeque nostrae; harumce rerum ergo, fundi terrae agrique mei lustrandi lustrique faciendi ergo, sicuti dixi, macte hisce suovitaurilibus lactentibus inmolandis esto; Mars pater, eiusdem rei ergo macte hisce suovitaurilibus lactentibus esto."
>
> Item cultro facito struem et fertum uti adsiet, inde obmoveto. Ubi porcum inmolabis, agnum vitulumque, sic oportet: "Eiusque rei ergo macte suovitaurilibus inmolandis esto." Nominare vetat Martem neque agnum vitulumque. Si minus in omnis litabit, sic verba concipito: "Mars pater, siquid tibi in illisce suovitaurilibus lactentibus neque satisfactum est, te hisce suovitaurilibus piaculo." Si in uno duobusve dubitabit, sic verba concipito: "Mars pater, quod tibi illoc porco neque satisfactum est, te hoc porco piaculo."

Following is how one should perform a lustration of a field:

Undertake the preparations for the *suovitaurilia* to be driven about: "So that each [victim][4] may be allotted propitiously to the good-willed gods, I bid you, Manius, that you determine in which part that *suovitaurilia* is to be driven or carried around my farm, land (*ager*) and earth—that you take care to purify."[5]

First invoke Janus and Jupiter with wine and recite this: "Mars Pater, I beseech and implore you, that you might be gracious and propitious to me, my house and my household, and on this account I have directed the *suovitaurilia* to be driven around my land, earth and farm; that you might avert, keep away, and ward off sickness, seen and unseen, scarcity and desolation, disaster and extremes of nature; and that you might allow crops, grains, vines and bushes to grow large and to bear well, that you might keep safe herders and herds and give well-being and good health to me, my house and my household. On account of these things, on account of purifying my farm, earth and land and performing a lustration, just as I have declared, be honored with these suckling victims, the *suovitaurilia*; Mars Pater, on account of this same thing, be honored with this suckling *suovitaurilia*."

In addition, with the sacrificial knife prepare the *strues*-cake and the *fertum*-cake,[6] that it be at hand, and then make the offering. When you immolate the pig, lamb and calf, you should do so with: "On account of this, be honored with the immolated *suovitaurilia*." It is forbidden to name Mars and the lamb and calf. And if you obtain less than favorable omens in all three, utter these words: "Mars Pater, if anything in that suckling *suovitaurilia* has not satisfied you, I make atonement to you with this *suovitaurilia*." If there is uncertainty over one or two, utter these words: "Mars Pater, because something of that pig has not satisfied you, I make atonement to you with this pig."

3.3.3.1 SUOVETAURILIA The *suovetaurilia* (sometimes *suovitaurilia*, as here in Cato's text) or *solitaurilia* is a sacrifice which consists of three victims: a boar, a bull, and a ram—hence the name, being derived from *sus*, *ovis* plus, *taurus* (see Benveniste 1969, vol. 1: 28–36, vol. 2: 156–157; 1945a). As dis-

[4]The "each," i.e. the neuter adjective *quodque*, must surely be construed as referring to each of the component elements of the *suovitaurilia*, just as neuter *quid* is so used below (*siquid tibi in illisce suovitaurilibus lactentibus . . . .*). For the common use of *evenio* in the sense 'be allotted to', see *OLD*.

[5]Or perhaps the sense is "you take charge of the lustration."

[6]The cake called *strues* is said by Festus (p. 310M) to look something like joined fingers, encased within overlying 'strips of dough' (? *panicula*). As here, *strues* is commonly mentioned in conjunction with the cake called *fertum* (or *ferctum*); indeed, Festus (p.

cussed above (see §1.5.3), the *suovetaurilia* is the sacrifice of the *secunda spolia*, offered to Mars (Festus, p. 189M). The *suovetaurilia* is offered in conjunction with various rites of purification; Mars is again characteristically the recipient. In the case of the field lustration as described by Cato, the animals are young (*lactentia suovetaurilia*); in other instances, adult animals are offered (*suovetaurilia maiora*; see *CIL* 6.2099.2.8). In an episode dated to the reign of Servius Tullius, Livy (1.44.2–3) records an offering of the *suovetaurilia* on the Campus Martius at the time of the first census, undertaken for the purification of the army. Valerius Maximus (4.1.10) makes passing reference to Scipio Africanus conducting the census and emending the prayer recited by a scribe as a *suovetaurilia* was being offered. Varro (*Rust.* 2.1.10) states that when the *populus Romanus* is purified, a *suovetaurilia* is driven about. In an instance of *devotio* (see §1.5.2), writes Livy (8.10.14), if the spear on which a consul has stood in making the prayer of *devotio* should fall into enemy hands, then atonement must be made by the offering of a *suovetaurilia* to Mars. Tacitus (*Hist.* 4.53) records how when the Capitoline temple was restored under Vespasian, the area of the temple was purified by the offering of a *suovetaurilia* by the praetor Helvidius Priscus, under the supervision of the Pontifex Plautius Aelianus.

The census and lustration of the army during the rule of Servius Tullius that Livy describes, to which we alluded above, is similarly preserved by Dionysius of Halicarnassus (*Ant. Rom.* 4.22.1–3); but the Greek historian gives his fuller account a curious twist:

> Τότε δ' οὖν ὁ Τύλλιος ἐπειδὴ διέταξε τὸ περὶ τὰς τιμήσεις, κελεύσας τοὺς πολίτας ἅπαντας συνελθεῖν εἰς τὸ μέγιστον τῶν πρὸ τῆς πόλεως πεδίων ἔχοντας τὰ ὅπλα, καὶ τάξας τούς θ' ἱππεῖς κατὰ τέλη καὶ τοὺς πεζοὺς ἐν φάλαγγι καὶ τοὺς ἐσταλμένους τὸν ψιλικὸν ὁπλισμὸν ἐν τοῖς ἰδίοις ἑκάστους λόχοις, καθαρμὸν αὐτῶν ἐποιήσατο ταύρῳ καὶ κριῷ καὶ κάπρῳ. τὰ δ' ἱερεῖα ταῦτα τρὶς περιαχθῆναι περὶ τὸ στρατόπεδον κελεύσας ἔθυσε τῷ κατέχοντι τὸ πεδίον Ἄρει. τοῦτον τὸν καθαρμὸν ἕως τῶν κατ' ἐμὲ χρόνων Ῥωμαῖοι καθαίρονται μετὰ τὴν συντέλειαν τῶν τιμήσεων ὑπὸ τῶν ἐχόντων τὴν ἱερωτάτην ἀρχήν, λοῦστρον ὀνομάζοντες.
>
> Then Tullius, when he had completed the census, after ordering all the citizens to assemble with their arms in the largest of the fields before the city, and after marshaling the cavalry according to their units, and the

85M) makes explicit reference to their joint use at sacrifices (*ferctum genus libi dictum, quod crebrius ad sacra ferebatur, nec sine strue . . .*). Aulus Gellius (*NA* 10.15.14) reports that among those many, peculiar proscriptions to which the Flamen Dialis must adhere is the requirement that a box containing both *strues* and *fertum* be kept at the foot of his bed.

infantry in battle order, and the light-armed soldiers in their individual *centuriae*, he offered for them a purificatory sacrifice of a bull, a ram, and a goat [*sic*]. Having ordered these victims to be led around the army three times, he sacrificed them to Mars, who possesses that field. To my own day, the Romans are purified with this sacrifice after the completion of the census by those holding the most sacred office, calling it a *lustrum*.

That the Roman *suovetaurilia* consisted of a bull, a ram, and a boar—not a goat—is completely beyond doubt. Why does Dionysius' record miss this? Some error of scribal transmission seems most probable—and not inexplicable in the light of Greek sacrificial tradition. The Greeks have their own threefold sacrifice of a bull, ram, and boar, the τριττύς. However, the Greek set shows variation, such as a bull, a boar, and a goat; and a boar, a ram, and a goat.

The Indo-European antiquity of the threefold sacrificial set is demonstrated by the existence of a Vedic counterpart as well. The three animals sacrificed in the Indic rite are a bull, a sheep, and a goat (identical to Dionysius' set), pigs not being used for sacrifice in Vedic India (along with wild beasts, fish, birds, and dogs; see Keith 1998: 279). The Vedic sacrifice occurs as a part of that ritual called the Sautrāmaṇī. As noted above (§2.6.1.1), the Sautrāmaṇī is one of two rituals which are characterized by the use of the intoxicating liquid called *surā*, the other being the Vājapeya. This unique linkage of the Sautrāmaṇī to the Vājapeya with its primitive flavor is intriguing and not likely to be of a purely coincidental nature, further suggesting the deeply archaic heritage of the triple sacrifice. The Sautrāmaṇī is of two types, occurring as an independent rite (the Kaukiḷī), on the one hand, and as a component of the Rajāsūya, on the other. The Rajāsūya is the ceremony in which the king is consecrated and is itself functionally linked to the Vājapeya (see Keith 1998a: 340). Just as the Roman *suovetaurilia* is a sacrifice offered to the warrior god Mars, so the Vedic Sautrāmaṇī belongs chiefly to Indra, taking its name from his epithet Sutrāman, 'good protector'.

The Vedic rite is, however, rather complex; while Indra is the principal recipient, deities of the realm of fertility and fecundity figure prominently. Both the Aśvins, the divine twins of the third function, and the goddess Sarasvatī (see §1.6.2), also receive a share of the triple sacrifice—the former the goat, the latter the sheep. In light of this comparandum, the clearly distributive sense of Cato's rationale—"So that each [victim] may be allotted propitiously to the good-willed gods, I bid you, Manius, that you determine in which part that *suovetaurilia* is to be driven or carried around my farm, land (*ager*) and earth . . . ."—comes more sharply into focus. The evidence for the distributive quality of the threefold offering is, however, not only comparative. On the basis of internal Roman evidence (following Krause 1931), Émile Benveniste (1945a) long ago contended similarly with regard to *suovetaurilia* recipients: the pig is the sacrifice typically offered to the earth, Tellus (though also to other earth and agricultural deities; see §3.3.4); the sheep or lamb is the victim of Jupiter; the bull characteristically goes to Mars. Both the Roman and Vedic rights of the triple sacrifice, while performed for the warrior god, have their own distributive sets of constituent recipients.

There is, in addition, another set of offering recipients that are conspicuously present in the Vedic Sautrāmaṇī. Libations are poured not only to the Aśvins, to Sarasvatī, and to Indra (the same three recipients of the triple animal sacrifice) but also to the spirits of the departed, the Pitaras (equivalent to the Roman Manes). Thereby the Pitaras find enjoyment, are satisfied, are purified, "for the Sautrāmaṇī is a means of purification" (*ŚB* 12.8.1.8). As we shall see, chthonic elements are also conspicuously present in Cato's rite.[7]

3.3.3.2 MANIUS A second important element of Cato's lustration rite that needs to be addressed is the identity of "Manius." It has been conjectured that this one who plays a vital role in the driving around of the *suovetaurilia* might be a slave; or that the name essentially functions to identify "person X" (whose identity is of no particular importance);[8] or that he is perhaps some sort of land manager or "soothsayer" (Scullard 1981: 124). A close reading of the initial invocation of the ritual coupled with general considerations of context suggest a rather different identification for Manius. The name itself is simply too suggestive for us to default to the interpretation that it is nothing more than an arbitrary appellation that Cato has pulled out of his hat and placed in the mouth of his ideal worshipper in order to fill out the liturgy.

3.3.3.2.1 The Lares As is well known, the Lares, those divine protectors of Roman households and guardians of crossroads (places of intersecting boundaries, where images of Lares were commonly erected), beings that

[7]For discussion of the Sautrāmaṇī, see Keith 1998a: 352–354; Renou 1957: 110. Dumézil's views are presented in Dumézil 1947: 117–158; 1996: 237–240.

[8]Thus, for example: ". . . . In any case, Cato envisages here (as in the public ritual) that the officiant at the sacrifice recites the prayer, while a man of lower status actually conducts (and kills) the animals." *BNP*, vol. 2: 153, n. 1.

exist in all geophysical spaces, also play an agrarian role, protecting fields and imbuing fertility. In *Fasti* 5.129–132, verses describing the dedication of an altar to the *Lares Praestites* on the Kalends of May (the third day of the *ludi* 'games' of Flora, goddess of flowering crops), Ovid appears to allude to the tradition that the Lares were introduced into Rome by the Sabine king Titus Tatius (l. 131; see Boyle and Woodard 2000: 259–260). Varro (*Ling.* 5.74) makes it explicit, as we have seen already (§1.4), listing the Lares among the "gods of Titus Tatius":

> Ops, Flora, Vediouis, Saturnus, Sol, Luna, Volcanus, Summanus, Larunda, Terminus, Quirinus, Vortumnus, the Lares, Diana, and Lucina

—deities whose affiliation is generally with the realm of fecundity and goods production.

Tibullus writes of the Lares, invoking them in company with other agrarian deities (1.1.7–24):

> ipse seram teneras maturo tempore vites
> rusticus et facili grandia poma manu:
> nec spes destituat sed frugum semper acervos
> praebeat et pleno pinguia musta lacu.
> nam veneror, seu stipes habet desertus in agris
> seu vetus in trivio florida serta lapis;
> et quodcumque mihi pomum novus educat annus,
> libatum agricolae ponitur ante deo.
> flava Ceres, tibi fit nostro de rure corona
> spicea, quae templi pendeat ante fores;
> pomosisque ruber custos donatur in hortis
> terreat ut saeva falce Priapus aves.
> vos quoque, felicis quondam, nunc pauperis agri
> custodes, fertis munera vestra, Lares.
> tunc vitula innumeros lustrabat caesa iuvencos:
> nunc agna exigui est hostia parva soli.
> agna cadet vobis, quam circum rustica pubes
> clamet "io, messes et bona vina date."

> On just the right days, let this rustic plant the tender vines
> and the sturdy fruit-trees with a nimble hand.
> And let hope not fail, but mounds of grain always
> supply and lush new wines for a full vat.
> For I pay homage, whether a lonely stump in the fields wears
> flowered garlands, or an aged stone at crossroads;
> and whatever fruit the new season furnishes for me,
> an offering is placed before the farmer's god.

For you, yellow-haired Ceres, a crown of grain from my estate
  comes to hang at the doors of your temple;
and the red sentry is stationed in the fruit-filled gardens,
  Priapus, scaring the birds with his savage sickle.
And you too, protectors of a once prosperous farm—
  now poor—receive your tributes, Lares.
Then, a slaughtered calf used to purify countless bullocks;
  now, a lamb is the paltry victim for a desolate patch.
A lamb will fall for you, and around it country folk will cry,
  "Please—give us bountiful harvests and wine."

Bracketed by expressions of hope and supplication for harvests of much grain and wine, the Lares join Terminus (whether "stump" or "stone"; see §2.5) and Ceres as recipients of the country folk's offerings.

The Fratres Arvales, whom we have already encountered on two occasions, celebrate rites which resemble those of the Ambarvalia (to be equated with the Ambarvalia, say some: see §3.3.6), rites designed to make the fields fertile (Varro, *Ling.* 5.85). In the archaic and somewhat obscure hymn which they sing, the Carmen Arvale, the priests invoke the Lares, as well as the Semones (see §4.9.2.1) and Mars (the translation that follows is based on that of Schilling 1991: 604):

Enos Lases iuvate, | [e]nos Lases iuvate, enos Lases iuvate!
Neve Luae Rue Marma sins incurrere in pleores, neve Luae Rue Marmar | [si]ns incurrere in pleoris, neve Lue Rue Marmar sers incurrere in pleores!
Satur fu, fere Mars, limen | [sal]i, sta berber, satur fu, fere Mars, limen sali sta berber, satur fu, fere Mars, limen sa[l]i s[t]a berber!
[Sem]unis alternei advocapit conctos, Semunis alternei advocapit conctos, Simunis altern[ei] advocapit | [conct]tos!
Enos Marmor iuvato, enos Marmor iuvato, enos Marmor iuvato!
Triumpe, triumpe, triumpe, trium[pe, tri]umpe!

Help us, O Lares; help us, O Lares; help us, O Lares!
Mars, O Mars, don't let Dissolution, Destruction pounce upon the people (?)! Mars, O Mars, don't let Dissolution, Destruction pounce upon the people (?)! Mars, O Mars, don't let Dissolution, Destruction pounce upon the people (?)!
Be surfeited, savage Mars; leap to the border, take your position! Be surfeited, savage Mars; leap to the border, take your position! Be surfeited, savage Mars; leap to the border, take your position!
You will invoke the Semones one by one, all together! You will invoke the Semones one by one, all together! You will invoke the Semones one by one, all together!

Help us Mars, O Mars! Help us Mars, O Mars! Help us Mars, O Mars!
Victory, victory, victory, victory, victory!

3.3.3.2.2 The Mater Larum The Acta of the Fratres Arvales record the offering of sacrifices made to the Lares, two male sheep, and also sacrifices to their mother, the Mater Larum, who receives two ewes (see Scheid 1990: 589–590, and n. 70). Moreover, from the heights of the temple of their goddess Dea Dia, the Fratres Arvales offer a meal to the Mater Larum. Vessels of clay (*ollae*) filled with *puls* are consecrated within the temple. *Puls* is a type of boiled porridge made from *far*, said by Varro (*Ling.* 5.105) to have been the most ancient of Roman foods. This common meal of early Romans remained in ritual use. In addition to its presentation to the Mater Larum, it was fed, for example, to sacred chickens used in the taking of auspices (see Festus, p. 285M; Valerius Maximus 2.5), and employed in the performance of various other ancient rites (see Pliny, *HN* 18.85). Wagenvoort (1956: 113) notes the comparison of Roman *puls* and Greek πέλανος, a mixture of meal and honey offered to gods and to the dead.

Following the consecration of the vessels, certain members of the brotherhood, those holding the offices of Magister and Flamen, along with the public slaves (*publici*) who served the Fratres, and two priests,[9] carry the *ollae* to the temple doors and pitch them down the slope leading up to the temple as a dinner for the Mater Larum (*cena Matri Larum*).[10] Since Eitrem 1910, this rite has been commonly, though not universally,[11] interpreted as an offering typical of those made to the dead (see, inter alia, Radke 1972: 434–435; Wagenvoort 1956: 113–114;[12] Taylor 1925: 299–300), with comparison made to, inter alia, the following:

1 The Greek custom of presenting offerings to Hermes, god of the dead, in clay pots called χύτροι.
2 The Lemuria, festival of the *lemures* (ancestral ghosts who leave their

[9]On the roles of these various officiants within this rite, see Scheid 1990: 588, n. 67.

[10]*Et (pro)magister et flamen et publici, duo sacerdotes, ollas acceperunt et ianuis apertis per clivum matri Larum cenam iactaverunt*; Scheid 1990: 585.

[11]See Wissowa 1917. Compare the remarks of Scheid 1990: 589–592.

[12]Wagenvoort (p. 114) writes: "To our mind Eitrem comes nearer to the right solution when he presumes: 'The Romans too buried the dead in earthen vessels and this gives us an indication how to explain the worship of the *ollae* in the rites of the Arvales, which *ollae* were thrown out of the temple door down the slope, which will certainly have meant sending them after the souls (cf. θύραζε κᾶρες and *manes exite paterni*)'. It is indeed not quite clear how the *ollae* full of porridge could have had anything to do with the earthen vessels used for funerals. But that they were sent after the souls of the dead must however be correct."

tombs and return to their former earthly dwelling places), who are dispelled by the casting down of black beans (see Boyle and Woodard 2000: 267–268).

3 The account of the origin of the Lacus Curtius, which tells how a great abyss opened in the Roman forum and how one Marcus Curtius, a courageous young warrior, rightly interpreting an augury, plunged in, having dedicated himself to the gods above and to the abyss and to the Manes. Bystanders threw offerings and grain in after him (Livy 7.6.4–5; Valerius Maximus 5.6.2). According to Varro (*Ling.* 5.148), Haruspices determined that the sacrifice was demanded by the god Manius (*deus Manius*), requiring that the bravest citizen be sent down to him (*id est civem fortissimum eo demitti*). Compare the annual tossing of coins into the Lacus Curtius for the well-being of Augustus (Suetonius, *Aug.* 57.1).

The Mater Larum is named by Varro (*Ling.* 9.61) as Mania (compare Arnobius, *Adv. Nat.* 3.41). Macrobius (*Sat.* 1.7.34–35) likewise identifies her and writes that in the time of Tarquinius Superbus, during the celebration of the Compitalia (see below), games were held at crossroads in honor of the Lares and their mother Mania, and that boys were sacrificed to the latter for the well-being of a family; after the expulsion of the Tarquins, the consul Junius Brutus substituted heads of garlic and of poppies for those of boys (cf. Ovid, *Fast.* 3.327–348). The abbreviation *MA* appearing in the entry for May 11, middle day of the Lemuria, in the only surviving Republican calendar, the Fasti Antiates Maiores, is very likely a reference to a sacrifice made to Mania (see Scullard 1981: 119).

The above-mentioned Compitalia is a winter festival of moveable date, celebrated between the Saturnalia of December 17 and the Nones of January.[13] Its name is derived from the place of celebration, the *compita* 'crossroads'; at these loci of intersecting boundaries were worshipped the Lares Compitales, along with their mother Mania, as we have noted. Dionysius of Halicarnassus (*Ant. Rom.* 4.14.3–4) attributes the institution of the Compitalia to Servius Tullius and writes that slaves play a leading role in the performing of the rites, doing so with their slave-status (τὸ δοῦλον) temporarily suspended. Dionysius adds that each individual household contributes cakes to the celebration, while Festus (p. 121M) describes a further rite:

> Laneae effigies Conpitalibus noctu dabantur in conpita, quod lares, quorum is erat dies festus, animae putabantur esse hominum redactae in numerum deorum.

[13] On the movable date and, by the fourth century AD, its reported restriction to early January, see Scullard 1981: 58; 244, n.47.; Frazer 1929, vol. 2: 454; Warde Fowler 1899: 279.

> During the Compitalia, woolen effigies were placed at night at crossroads, because the Lares, to whom the festival belongs, were considered to be the souls of men brought into the body of the gods.

And more specifically, Festus (p. 239M) writes:

> Pilae et effigies viriles et muliebres ex lana Conpitalibus suspendebantur in conpitis, quod hunc diem festum esse deorum inferorum, quos vocant Lares, putarent, quibus tot pilae, quot capita servorum; tot effigies, quot essent liberi, ponebantur, ut vivis parcerent et essent his pilis et simulacris contenti.
>
> Balls and effigies of men and women, made of wool, were suspended at crossroads during the Compitalia, because they considered this festival to belong to infernal gods, whom they call Lares. For these they hung up as many balls as there were heads of slaves and as many effigies as free people, so that the Lares might leave the living alone and be satisfied with these balls and images.

Following his remarks concerning Brutus' substitution of garlic and poppy heads for human heads in the Compitalia sacrifice to Mania, Macrobius (*Sat.* 1.7.35) similarly notes that effigies were hung up for Mania before the doorways of each house to avert any harm that might threaten the families living within.[14]

3.3.3.2.3 Mania and Manius Mania, the Mater Larum, thus revealed, plainly appears to be an infernal or chthonic deity. Her nature is, however, almost automatically complicated by the scholarly uncertainty which has characterized interpretations of the original nature of her sons, the Lares.[15] Are they in origin spirits of the dead or are they guardians of crossroads, of the agrarian home, and other spaces? For Dumézil, she is a "difficult question," quickly addressed (see *ARR*: 341 n. 20). He doubts that the idea of a "mother of the Lares" is an ancient one, "if we grant that the mythology of Rome's historical times had eliminated filiations and that they were reintroduced only under Greek influence." Here he alludes, inter alia, to the apparent absence in Rome of genealogical connections among the gods such as those so well known in Greek tradition (see *ARR*: 47–50); thus, he remarks (*ARR*: 49):

[14] For cross-cultural, typological parallels of this Roman practice of presenting effigies to infernal beings as substitutes for human life, see Frazer 1929, vol. 2: 456–458.

[15] On the complexity of the evidence revealing the Mater Larum which is provided by the rites of the Fratres Arvales, see Scheid 1990: 587–598.

> At the end of the Etruscan period, when the three Capitoline gods were united in a single temple with three *cellae*, it is not certain that Juno Regina was Jupiter's "wife," even though an indirect Greek influence was probable about this time. Ops and Consus form a theological and ritual couple, not a married pair.

But could not one equally imagine the relationship of the Mater Larum and the Lares—mother and sons—as chiefly of a theological and ritual nature? Such a relationship would certainly seem to be suggested by the few contexts in which record of the Mater Larum is preserved.

There are other filiations sanctioned by Dumézil. He allows the ritual preservation of an Indo-European divine sister relationship in the Matralia (June 11), festival of the dawn goddess Mater Matuta, though in its Roman expression the sibling relationship is transferred to the human domain (see Boyle and Woodard 2000: 301–302). Compare also Nerio and Moles, presented by Aulus Gellius (*NA* 13.23.2) as the "wives" of Mars.[16] Nerio appears to have been supplanted by Minerva, under the influence of Greek Athena; hence, it is Minerva and Mars, along with Volcanus and Lua Mater (compare "Luae" in the Carmen Arvale, above) to whom the battlefield spoils are presented.[17] Dumézil sees the Roman affiliation in the threesome Mars, Nerio, Moles recurring in the Norse triad Thor, Mothi, Magni (*ARR*: 207–208). Regardless of the ultimate antiquity of the relationship of the Mater Larum and the Lares, synchronically our Roman sources portray her as their mother (cf. Scheid 1990: 592–593), and it is this which is of most importance presently.

Dumézil's second misgiving regarding the Mater Larum is that even if she "were a goddess of the underworld, . . . this would not affect the Lares themselves . . . . In short, the Mater Larum cannot serve as a point of departure for an exegesis of the Lares" (*ARR*: 341 n. 20). This may be true enough regarding some "original" nature of the Lares, but again, from a synchronic perspective, her character likely does reflect what the Lares were perceived to be. This is essentially the point that Scheid (1990: 592) makes when he writes: "Il n'en demeure pas moins qu'à l'époque de César et d'Auguste, l'interprétation démoniaque, infernale, des *Lares* et de leur mère avait

[16]The names occur in a listing of goddesses (divine personifications of abstract qualities) affiliated with other deities which Aulus Gellius reports to have encountered in priestly books and prayers: Lua-Saturn, Salacia-Neptune, Hora-Quirinus, Virites-Quirinus, Maia-Vulcan, Heries-Juno, Moles-Mars, Nerio-Mars. Nerio as wife of Mars is discussed at length in 13.23.3–19. On the tradition of Nerio as wife of Mars, see Boyle and Woodard 2000: 222–223.

[17]See *ARR*: 209, 272, 305; Boyle and Woodard 2000: 222–223.

bien cours: on la trouve chez Varron et Festus, elle est aussi attestée par la traduction grecque de Lares (ἥρωες, parfois δαίμονες), notamment dans les *Res gestae* d'Auguste" (*RG* 4.19). Though, as already observed, the synchronic picture of the Lares is a complex one: "Nous savons également que d'autres explications encore circulaient, souvent sous la plume des mêmes auteurs" (Scheid 1990: 592).[18]

We have already noted the Roman priestly propensity for pairing female deities—deified abstractions—with (usually) male gods. When Aulus Gellius couples Mars with Nerio and Moles, he also writes (*NA* 13.23.1–3):

> Conprecationes deum inmortalium, quae ritu Romano fiunt, expositae sunt in libris sacerdotum populi Romani et in plerisque antiquis orationibus. In his scriptum est: "Luam Saturni, Salaciam Neptuni, Horam Quirini, Virites Quirini, Maiam Volcani, Heriem Iunonis, Moles Martis Nereienemque Martis."

> Prayers to the immortal gods, which are made according to the Roman rite, have been set out in the Books of the Priests of the Roman people and in many ancient treatises. In these is written: "Lua of Saturn, Salacia of Neptune, Hora of Quirinus, Virites of Quirinus, Maia of Volcanus, Heries of Juno, Moles of Mars, and Nerio of Mars."

Whatever the greater syntactic context of the prayers might have been, an affiliation of the various female divinities (in the accusative) with their coupled gods (in the genitive)[19] is certainly denoted. In some instances these divine pairings are independently attested. For example, in addition to traditions about Mars and his wife Nerio noted above, Macrobius (*Sat.* 1.12.18) writes that Maia (*Maia Volcani*) was wife of Vulcan and that his ancient priest, the Flamen Vulcanalis, sacrificed to Maia on the Kalends of May. Ovid (*Met.* 14.829–851) recounts how Hersilia, the Sabine wife of Romulus, was transformed into Hora (*Hora Quirini*) after Romulus was deified as Quirinus. Salacia (*Salacia Neptulni*) is a sea goddess, whom Varro (*Ling.* 5.72) calls wife of Neptune (etymologizing her name as a derivative of *salum* 'billow, sea'); and the learned grammarian makes passing reference to "Lua of Saturn" (*Lua Saturni*) at *De Lingua Latina* 8.36 in a discussion of homonymy.

[18]For an overview of the alleged similarities between the Mater Larum and Acca Larentia, see Scheid 1990: 590–592. According to Ausonius (*Technop.* 8.9), the mother of the Lares is Larunda, one of those deities whom Varro includes in his list of the "gods of Titus Tatius" (see §1.4). On Acca Larentia and Larunda, see Boyle and Woodard 2000: 206–207.

[19]*Heriem Iunonis* is the exception.

Such pairings are well established among agrarian deities. The most obvious example is provided by the ancient Italic pair Liber and Libera, god and goddess of fertility, both agricultural and human. Together with Ceres, Liber and Libera formed an Aventine triad; perhaps a plebeian response, in effect, to the Capitoline triad (see *ARR*: 378–380; Boyle and Woodard 2000: 223–226).

Ceres herself has a male counterpart, Cerus, whether or not he should be viewed as her "spouse."[20] For an Italic cognate compare the Iguvine deity Çerfus Martius, a chthonic god to whom dark-colored victims are sacrificed (Poultney 1959: 283), and the masculine and feminine epithets Çerfius and Çerfia used of the deities Prestota, Tursa, and Hondus. In the lustration ritual of the city of Iguvium, as described in the bronze tables of the Atiedian priesthood, a triad of deities plays a central role—a triad which receives no other mention in the tables (Poultney 1951: 277): the male deity Çerfus Martius, and the female deities named as "Prestota Çerfia of Çerfus Martius" (Prestota Çerfia Çerfer Matier), and "Tursa Çerfia of Çerfus Martius" (Tursa Çerfia Çerfer Matier). This formulaic denotation of the goddesses compares precisely to Aulus Gellius' "Moles of Mars," "Nerio of Mars," and so forth.

Roman Cerus is invoked in the Carmen Saliorum, the song of Mars' priests, the Salii. Thus Festus (p. 122M), writing of the goddess Mater Matuta and etymologically related forms, records:

> Matrem Matutam antiqui ob bonitatem appellabant, et maturum idoneum usui, et mane principium diei, et inferi di Manes, ut subpliciter appellati bono essent, et in Carmine Saliari Cerus Manus intellegitur creator bonus.
>
> The ancients coined *Mater Matuta* from her 'goodness', and *maturus* ['ripe, mature, timely'] from being 'proper in use', and *mane* ['morning'] from the 'beginning of the day'; and the infernal gods are dubbed *Manes*, as they were humbly invoked for 'good'; and in the *Carmen Saliorum*, *Cerus Manus* means 'good creator'.

And among the lines of the hymn of the Salii preserved by Varro (*Ling.* 7.26), we read, as a god of procreation—Consivius—is addressed:

[20]Frazer (1929, vol. 3: 263) writes, "In her original form [Ceres] seems to have had a male partner or husband named Cerus . . . . This coupling of the goddess with a god of the same name is evidence of the native antiquity of the pair; and a further proof of it is furnished by the assignment of a flamen, with the title flamen Cerialis, to their worship at Rome, for none but genuine old Italian deities were served by flamens . . . ." For Wagenvoort (1956: 160), in contrast, the two form "not a pair but a doublet."

Ianeus iam es, duonus Cerus es, duonus Ianus

Now you are the Gatekeeper, you are good Cerus, you are good Janus.

For Macrobius (*Sat.* 1.15–16), *Consivius* is an epithet of Janus, derived from *consero* 'to sow'. It may well be the case that the antiquarian has conflated two archaic deities, originally distinct. In the same breath, Macrobius also speaks of Janus Quirinus, where conflation has undeniably occurred (on Janus Quirinus, see Boyle and Woodard 2000: 301, with references). With the masculine Consivius, compare feminine Consiva, a name used for Ops, goddess of abundant harvest, according to Festus (p. 186M). A similar female-male pairing appears to be provided by Tellus, goddess of earth, closely associated with Ceres, and Tellurus, mentioned by Martianus Capella (1.49). Compare with Tellurus the god Tellumo, whom St. Augustine, citing Varro, identifies as the male counterpart of Tellus (*De Civ. D.* 7. 23).

Festus' etymological set composed of Mater *Matuta*, *maturus*, *mane*, *Manes*, and Cerus *Manus* is a legitimate one. All are ultimately descended from a root **meh$_2$-* meaning 'good' (see Watkins 2000: 50; *DELL*: 383–384, 386, 391); compare Old Irish *maith*, Welsh *mad* 'good' (see *WP* 2: 220–221). Regardless of the particular derivational pathway involved, *Mania*, the name of the mother of the Lares, is certainly also to be included in this set (see Tabeling 1975: 90–92). As a common noun, *mania* is used to denote certain effigies: Macrobius (*Sat.* 1.7.35) uses it to name the woolen images suspended at the doorway during the Compitalia (see above; cf. Varro, *Sat. Men.* 463); Festus (p. 129M) records that the word denotes grotesque figures made of flour and says that it is the name nurses give to ghosts when frightening small children. Besides Mania, Mother of the Lares, and undoubtedly a by-form of her (see Tabeling 1975: 89–91; Wissowa 1971: 240), there exists a goddess called Genita Mana. Pliny (*HN* 29.58) writes that she receives the sacrifice of puppies; Plutarch, in one of his *Roman Questions* (*Quaest. Rom.* 52), provides additional insight:

> Διὰ τί τῇ καλουμένῃ Γενείτῃ Μάνῃ κύνα θύουσι καὶ κατεύχονται μηδένα χρηστὸν ἀποβῆναι τῶν οἰκογενῶν;
>
> Ἢ ὅτι δαίμων ἐστὶν ἡ Γενείτα περὶ τὰς γενέσεις καὶ τὰς λοχείας τῶν φθαρτῶν; ῥύσιν γάρ τινα σημαίνει τοὔνομα καὶ γένεσιν ἢ ῥέουσαν γένεσιν. ὥσπερ οὖν οἱ Ἕλληνες τῇ Ἑκάτῃ, καὶ τῇ Γενείτῃ κύνα Ῥωμαῖοι θύουσιν ὑπὲρ τῶν οἰκογενῶν. Ἀργείους δὲ Σωκράτης φησὶ τῇ Εἰλιονείᾳ κύνα θύειν διὰ τὴν ῥᾳστώνην τῆς λοχείας. τὸ δὲ τῆς εὐχῆς πότερον οὐκ ἐπ' ἀνθρώπων ἐστὶν οἰκογενῶν, μηδένα χρηστὸν γενέσθαι ἀλλὰ κυνῶν; χαλεποὺς γὰρ εἶναι δεῖ καὶ φοβεροὺς τοὺς κύνας.

> Ἢ διὰ τὸ χρηστοὺς κομψῶς λέγεσθαι τοὺς τελευτῶντας αἰνιττόμενοι διὰ τῆς εὐχῆς αἰτοῦνται μηδένα τῶν συνοίκων ἀποθανεῖν; οὐ δεῖ δὲ τοῦτο θαυμάζειν· καὶ γὰρ Ἀριστοτέλης ἐν ταῖς Ἀρκάδων πρὸς Λακεδαιμονίους συνθήκαις γεγράφθαι φησὶ μηδένα χρηστὸν ποιεῖν βοηθείας χάριν τοῖς λακωνίζουσι τῶν Τεγεατῶν, ὅπερ εἶναι μηδένα ἀποκτιννύναι.
>
> Why do they sacrifice a bitch to the goddess known as Genita Mana? And why do they pray that no one born in the house will turn out good?
>
> Is it because Genita is a *daemon* concerned with the origin and birthing of the perishable? For her name means something like 'flow' and 'birth', or 'flowing birth'. Therefore, just as the Greeks sacrifice a bitch to Hecate, so the Romans do likewise to Genita for the sake of those home-born. Socrates says that the Argives sacrifice a bitch to Eilioneia (Eileithyia) because of the ease with which it births. But does the prayer that 'no one born in the house be good' refer not to people but to dogs? For dogs ought to be dangerous and terrible.
>
> Or, because the dead are euphemistically called 'the good,' are they tacitly, through this prayer, asking that no one of the household may die? This should come as no surprise. Aristotle says that in the treaty of the Arcadians with the Spartans, it is written that "no one will be made good on account of giving aid to the Spartanizers at Tegea"—that is to say, no one will be killed.

While Plutarch's etymologizing may be slightly askew, the second of his conjectures regarding the sense of the prayer offered to the goddess is likely right on target—a prayer that those born within the house will not (soon) join the ranks of the Manes (the 'good'). In any event, Genita Mana, like her alloform Mania, Mother of the Lares,[21] plainly appears to be an infernal deity, and one affiliated with fecundity, the bringing forth of the fruit of the womb.

Is not the Manius who is addressed at the outset of the archaic lustral formulae preserved by Cato simply the male "counterpart" of the chthonic goddess Mania, the Mater Larum? The pattern is a productive one, as we have seen, within the ranks of the deities of the soil and fertility (Dumézil's third function), though the historical and cultic processes through which such "couplings" arose may have been manifold: Libera has her Liber, Ceres her Cerus, Consiva her Consivius, and Tellus her Tellumo/Tellurus. In the very same way, feminine Mania is matched by masculine Manius. His name is a part of the same linguistic stock as that of Mania, Mana, and the Manes,

[21]With the sacrifice of a dog to Mana, compare the representation of the Lares Praestites as accompanied by a dog (Ovid, *Fast.* 5.129–146; see Boyle and Woodard 2000: 259–260) and the tradition that they were clothed in dog skin (Plutarch, *Quaest. Rom.* 51).

placing him in the realm of the infernal. Moreover, the god is undoubtedly that same chthonic deity, *deus Manius*, who, as Varro (*Ling.* 5.148) records, caused *terra* to gape wide in the Forum Romanum and required the bravest Roman citizen to be plunged down into the earth. We saw that Manus Cerus is invoked in the lines of the Carmen Saliorum (Festus p. 122M)—the song of the priests of Mars; and in verses from the obscure and poorly understood Carmen preserved by Varro (*Ling.* 7.26), a deity of procreation can be addressed as both *duonus Cerus* and *duonus Ianus*, god of beginnings. In an intriguingly parallel fashion, at the beginning of Cato's lustral rite, prior to the offer of the prayer to Mars, the deity with whom the rite is centrally concerned, Manius is first entreated, after which Janus himself, as well as Jupiter, is invoked.

And what role does chthonic Manius play in Cato's lustration rite? This god of the earth is bidden to control the movements of the trio of victims, to direct them through *fundus*, *ager*, and *terra*, and to do so for the efficacy of the lustration:

> Undertake the preparations for the *suovitaurilia* to be driven about: "So that each [victim] may be allotted propitiously to the good-willed gods, I bid you, Manius, that you determine in which part that *suovitaurilia* is to be driven or carried around my farm, land and earth—that you take care to purify . . . ."

It is not a slave, or a soothsayer, or a land manager, or a John Doe, but a god of the earth who plays a key role in a purificatory ritual played out within a bounded space of earth—a ritual directed first and foremost at the warrior deity, Mars. The role of Manius in this ritual, as well as the relationship of the worshipper to him, however, is fundamentally different from that of the other deities involved.[22] He is not invoked with offerings of wine as are Janus and Jupiter; he is not humbly implored to show kindness and endow the worshipper with health, protection, and abundance as is Mars. The relationship is one of dependence, but not one of worshipful adoration. The god is directed to guide the victims along the proper path as they

[22] And the role of Manius is obscured in various English translations of the passage: for example, Hooper and Ash 1993: 121: "Bidding the *suovetaurilia* to be led around, use the words: 'That with the good help of the gods success may crown our work, I bid thee, Manius, to take care to purify my farm, my land, my ground with this *suovetaurilia*, in whatever part thou thinkest best for them to be driven or carried around' "; and *BNP*, vol. 2: 152: "Order the *suovetaurilia* to be driven round the land, using these words: 'With the good will of the gods, and so that the result may be favourable, I bid you, Manius, to take care to purify my farm, my land, my ground with this *suovetaurilia*, over whatever area you judge that they should be driven or carried around.' "

move through the agrarian space turned ritual space, in such a way as to ensure an efficacious lustration.

Mando tibi, Mani—"I bid you, Manius." How can the worshiper use such direct language with a deity? Such directness with a chthonic deity appears to be a feature of prehistoric Indo-European theology, no less primitive than the ritual that Cato has passed on to us in this, the "oldest Latin text preserved." Hittite religious practice provides the cognate tradition. Almost without exception, the Hittites invoke and worship their deities with reverence. Reichardt (1998: 66–68) has shown, however, that the Sun goddess of earth—like Manius, a chthonic deity—can be threatened with the "oath of the ritual" if she should fail to provide certain blessings; otherwise such coarse address is used only with a group of foreign deities, the gods of Gasga. In Reichardt's words (p. 68), "These deities, then, are being treated like human vassals."[23] Cato's worshipper treats the chthonic Manius in a similar way and, accordingly, as we have seen, many had supposed Manius to be merely human.

3.3.4 Virgil

In his *Georgics*, Virgil offers a poetic account of an agrarian rite involving circumambulation with sacrificial victims—one not uncommonly identified with the Ambarvalia. After describing the destruction and fury of wind- and rain-storms in autumn and spring, Virgil writes (*Georg.* 1.335–350):

> hoc metuens caeli mensis et sidera serva,
> frigida Saturni sese quo stella receptet,
> quos ignis caelo Cyllenius erret in orbis.
> in primis venerare deos, atque annua magnae
> sacra refer Cereri laetis operatus in herbis
> extremae sub casum hiemis, iam vere sereno.
> tum pingues agni et tum mollissima vina,
> tum somni dulces densaeque in montibus umbrae.
> cuncta tibi Cererem pubes agrestis adoret:
> cui tu lacte favos et miti dilue Baccho,
> terque novas circum felix eat hostia fruges,
> omnis quam chorus et socii comitentur ovantes,
> et Cererem clamore vocent in tecta; neque ante
> falcem maturis quisquam supponat aristis,

[23] The present author wishes to express his appreciation to Professor H. Craig Melchert for bringing the Hittite parallel and Reichardt's work to his attention.

quam Cereri torta redimitus tempora quercu
det motus incompositos et carmina dicat.

Fearing this, watch the months and constellations of heaven,
to which the cold star of Saturn withdraws itself,
into what heavenly orbits fiery Mercury wanders.
Especially worship the gods, and to great Ceres
her yearly sacrifices pay, worshipping on lush lawns
beyond the eclipse of winter's end, now in fair spring.
Then lambs are fat, then wine most mellow,
then sleep is sweet, then shadows deep upon the hills.
Let all your country folk worship Ceres:
for her bathe honeycomb in milk and mellow wine;
and around the young crops thrice let the auspicious victim pass,
which the whole band of revelers and friends accompany rejoicing,
and who with shouts summon Ceres into their homes; and
the scythe let no one apply to the ripe grain crop, before
having crowned his temples with a twining oaken garland,
he makes the clumsy gestures and chants the hymns for Ceres.

With a setting in spring and such attention paid to Ceres, one immediately suspects reference to a private observance of the Cerialia. This festival of Ceres was celebrated with games annually from April 12–19; the Cerialia proper are marked in the calendars as falling on the last of these days. In his *Fasti* entry for April 12, Ovid writes (ll. 393–416):

Hinc Cereris ludi: non est opus indice causae;
  sponte deae munus promeritumque patet.
panis erat primis virides mortalibus herbae,
  quas tellus nullo sollicitante dabat;
et modo carpebant vivax e caespite gramen,
  nunc epulae tenera fronde cacumen erant.
postmodo glans nota est: bene erat iam glande reperta,
  duraque magnificas quercus habebat opes.
prima Ceres homine ad meliora alimenta vocato
  mutavit glandes utiliore cibo.
illa iugo tauros collum praebere coegit:
  tum primum soles eruta vidit humus.
aes erat in pretio, Chalybeia massa latebat:
  eheu, perpetuo debuit illa tegi.
pace Ceres laeta est; et vos orate, coloni,
  perpetuam pacem pacificumque ducem.
farra deae micaeque licet salientis honorem
  detis et in veteres turea grana focos;

et, si tura aberunt, unctas accendite taedas:
parva bonae Cereri, sint modo casta, placent.
a bove succincti cultros removete ministri:
bos aret; ignavam sacrificate suem.
apta iugo cervix non est ferienda securi:
vivat et in dura saepe laboret humo.

Next the Ceres Shows. Their cause requires no telling.
The goddess' gift and service are clear.
The bread of primal man consisted of green plants,
Which the earth created unprovoked.
At times he plucked the living grass from the turf
Or feasted on a treetop's juicy leaves.
Later acorns were found. The acorn made life good;
Hardy oak trees held sumptuous wealth.
Ceres was the first to improve man's nutrition
By replacing acorns with better food.
She forced the bull to offer its neck to the yoke;
Uprooted soil then first glimpsed the sun.
Copper was prized, and iron ingots lurked concealed—
Ah! they should have been hidden for ever.
Ceres rejoices in peace; you should beg, farmers,
Perpetual peace and pacific leader.
You may honor the goddess with spelt and dancing salt
And grains of incense on ancient hearths.
If incense is missing, light some pitchy torches;
Little things, if pure, please good Ceres.
Remove your knives from the oxen, cassocked priests.
The ox should plough; sacrifice idle sows.
The neck suited to the yoke should not be pole-axed;
Let him live and often work the hard ground.

As the boar, or suckling pig, and other members of the *suovetaurilia* are offered corporately to Mars, so the sow, a female pig, is the characteristic victim of the goddess Ceres (see also *Fast.* 1.349–353).

Cato (*Agr.* 134) describes the sacrifice of yet another sow to Ceres, the *porca praecidanea* (and also to Tellus, on whom see immediately below; Varro in Nonius p. 163L). Unlike the springtime rite described in the above passage, the sacrifice of the *porca praecidanea* precedes a harvest: the sow is offered prior to gathering in spelt, wheat, barley, beans, and rape seed, by Cato's account. Along with the sacrifice of a sow to Ceres, the harvest ritual is marked by the offering of prayers, incense, and wine to Janus, Jupiter, and Juno; the two first-named also receive cakes—*strues* to Janus and *fertum* to Jupiter, the same cakes specified in Cato's field lustration (see §3.3.3). According to Aulus Gellius (*NA* 4.6.7–8), the *porca praecidanea* was offered to Ceres prior to harvest as an expiation (*piaculum*)—a precautionary measure in case someone had failed to perform the proper rite of purification for a household contaminated by a death.[24] Festus (p. 250M) tells us that a sacrifice of a sow, the *porca praesentanea*, is made to Ceres close by the body of one who has died for the sake of purifying the family.

Yet, as we have already seen, porcine sacrifices are not unique to Mars (nominally so—as one element of the *suovetaurilia*) and Ceres. Recall that in Iguvium, three suckling pigs are sacrificed to Fisus Sancius (see §1.5.4), and that Ovid, in his description of the celebration of the Terminalia in the private cult (*Fast.* 2.639–658), tells us that pigs are offered to Terminus (see §2.8.5).

The list of recipients can be expanded. According to Macrobius (*Sat.* 1.12.18–20), a pregnant sow is sacrificed to the Roman goddess Maia, which, he continues, some view as evidence that she is to be regarded as Earth, since this is the victim proper to Earth (in fact, Macrobius, *Sat.* 1.12.21 cites Cornelius Labeo as reporting that in the *Books of the Pontifices*, Maia is also invoked as Bona Dea, Fauna, Ops, and Fatua). Arnobius (*Adv. Nat.* 7.22), in agreement, states that a pregnant sow is sacrificed to Tellus, goddess of the earth. Similarly, Ovid, in his verses on the moveable festival called the *Feriae Sementivae* 'Festival of Sowing', writes that spelt and a pregnant sow are offered to Ceres and Tellus (*Fast.* 1.671–672), two deities closely linked by their fields of operation (see Boyle and Woodard 2000: 246–246; Wagenvoort 1956: 162–166). According to Macrobius (*Sat.* 3.11.10), a pregnant sow is sacrificed to Ceres and Hercules twelve days before the Kalends of January (December 21), along with bread and oenomel (*mulsum*).[25] Horace (*Odes* 3.23.1–8) advises the *rustica* Phidyle that if she should offer incense, grain, and a pig to the Lares, then vine, crop, and flock will be kept safe

[24]As Warde Fowler (1911: 121) puts it: "In case a man has wittingly or unwittingly omitted to pay the proper rites (*iusta facere*) to his own dead, it was his duty to make this offering, lest as a result of the neglect the earth-power should not yield him a good harvest." His ensuing remark is of interest, though the opening speculation should be taken with some caution, as "originally" may refer to some far more archaic moment than Warde Fowler envisioned: "Originally, we need hardly doubt, Tellus was alone concerned in this; but Ceres, who at all times represented rather the ripening and ripened corn than the seed in the bosom of the earth, gradually took her place beside her, and the idea gained ground that the offering was more immediately concerned with the harvest than with the Manes."

[25]A rite about which nothing else is known (see Scullard 1981: 210). Might it be connected with the Larentalia which is celebrated two days later?

and sound; so in *Satires* 2.3.164–165: *immolet aequis hic porcum Laribus*. The Fratres Arvales offer pigs in their sacred grove to effect expiation (*porcae piaculares*; see Scheid 1990: 553–571). Cato (*Agr.* 139), along the same lines, says that before any grove is thinned, a pig (*porcus piaculum*) should be sacrificed to the deity of the grove with a prayer that the deity might thereby be "gracious and propitious" to the sacrificer, his house, household, and children (*uti sies volens propitius mihi domo familiaeque meae liberisque meis*; compare the prayer to Mars which accompanies the *suovetaurilia*). Long ago, Frazer (1929, 2: 157, 297) pointed out that cross-culturally pigs are commonly sacrificed for the good of crops and that the blood of pigs is widely considered of great potency for returning fecundity to the soil.

Even a quick perusal of the preceding enumerations clearly reveals that the sacrifice of pigs is intimately bound up with deities of the earth and agriculture, with purification of the earth for the sake of fertility and agrarian well-being, and even with purification of the agrarian household.[26] The offering of pigs is, in fact, even more broadly associated with the realm of fertility (Dumézil's third function), as can be seen by their sacrifice to Juno, goddess of childbirth, among her other attributes.[27] Thus, the Regina Sacrorum (wife of the priest called the Rex Sacrorum; see §1.5.1) sacrifices either a female lamb or a sow to Juno in the Regia on the Kalends of each month (Macrobius, *Sat.* 1.15.19). According to Cicero (*Div.* 1.101) during an earthquake an admonition was reported to have been heard coming from the temple of Juno Moneta, instructing that a pregnant sow be offered to her as an expiatory sacrifice (*procuratio*). Ovid (*Am.* 3.13) records how Juno receives from priestesses of Falerii a sacrificial threesome: in addition to a pig, they offer to the goddess white cows, as well as calves, and a ram. The assemblage of victims appears to be simply a variant of the *suovetaurilia*, with which the priestesses annually process within a grove sacred to their goddess.[28]

Returning to our earlier point, the springtime festival of Ceres to which Virgil refers is most likely the Cerialia of mid-April. Le Bonniec, in his study of Ceres (1958: 136; drawing on Bayet 1955, and others), makes the

[26]Compare the Greek custom of purifying one who has committed homicide by cutting the throat of a young pig so that the blood flows down on the hands of the one being cleansed; see Aeschylus, *Eum.* 276–286; 443–452; Apollonius Rhodius, *Argon.* 4: 700–717.

[27]On Dumézil's interpretation of Juno as being trifunctional in origin, see Boyle and Woodard 2000: 186–187 with references.

[28]There is also a sort of scapegoat involved in the ritual, though apparently not as a sacrifice to Juno. A female goat is pelted with missiles by boys; the boy who wounds the goat receives a prize. Ovid considers the entire ritual to be of Greek (Argive) origin.

same observation,[29] though he thinks that more than one festival is being described in the lines of *Georgics* 1.335–350—aside from the harvest scene to which the poet makes a forward-looking allusion in the lines 348–350. Beginning with line 343 (*cuncta tibi Cererem pubes agrestis adoret*), Le Bonniec (p. 139) sees a straightforward description of the Ambarvalia; in this he seems to be in fundamental agreement with Warde Fowler (1899: 126), whom he cites:

> It is not clear to what festival or festivals Virgil is alluding in the first few of these lines. . . . But from line 343 onwards the reference is certainly to Ambarvalia *of some kind* [emphasis is mine], perhaps to the private *lustratio* of the farmer before harvest began, of which the Roman festival was a magnified copy.

Certain more recent works have followed suit: for example, Scullard (1981: 125) cites the passage in his description of the Ambarvalia; the *Oxford Classical Dictionary* (p. 70) cites the text as evidence for the private rite in its entry for "Ambarvalia"; Turcan (2001: 40) casually defers to this hypothesis; and so forth.

There are dissenting opinions, however. As Le Bonniec points out, both Hunziker (1877–1919a) and Grimal (1949) read lines 343 and following as a continued description of the Cerialia. In his careful analysis of the Ambarvalia, Kilgour (1938: 226) identifies Virgil's rite in its entirety as what he terms a *lustratio agri*, a ritual of lustration celebrated by an individual farmer "for the protection of his steading against such physical or spiritual enemies as might dare to cross its boundary." Also included under Kilgour's rubric of *lustratio agri* is Cato's rite of *De Agricultura* 141 (see §3.3.3), and these two he opposes to the state Ambarvalia described by Strabo (see §3.3.1). Scheid (1990) follows in large measure the analysis of Kilgour.

The disagreement which we see here is, unfortunately, symptomatic of the dearth of evidence which has survived for the Roman rite or rites under consideration. Definitive resolution may remain an elusive goal, but in an attempt to bring some clarity to these matters vis-à-vis their Indo-European background, let us consider a few mutually related points. First of all, as other investigators have noted, both Macrobius and Servius comment on Virgil's text. According to Macrobius (*Sat.* 3.5.7), the victim (*hostia*) of *Georgics* 1.345 is denoted *ambarvalis*, citing Festus for the iden-

[29]See also Warde Fowler 1899: 126, n. 1. The description is not generally that of a harvest festival, as in Spaeth (1996: 63), though there is reference to a rite conducted prior to harvest, on which see below.

tification of the term. In his commentary on the passage, Servius notes that the victim is "auspicious" (*felix hostia*) in that it is "fertile," as sows characteristically are, he adds, and that the rite is an *ambarvale sacrum*. The ritual is undeniably *ambarvalic*, to coin a term: Virgil, as well as Macrobius and Servius, makes it plain that the victim—a *porca* says Servius, as we would surely expect—is led around the new growth of the field. By definition, then, the victim and rite are to be denoted as *ambarvalis* (from *ambi-* 'round' + *arvum* 'field'; we will return to the etymology below—see §4.6); the use of the adjective probably tells us nothing more than this. In other words, we likely need to make a distinction between some rite that can be characterized as ambarvalic, on the one hand, and a specific ritual, the Ambarvalia, on the other hand, as identified by Strabo. This is in effect the above noted distinction made by Kilgour (1938: 225–235). It echoes the sentiment captured by Warde Fowler (1911: 80), who writes this about the *Georgics* passage:

> Like the descriptions of Ovid [*Fast.* 1.663ff.; Warde Fowler refers to Feriae Sementivae] and Tibullus [see below], it is more valuable to us for the idea it gives us of the spirit of old Italian agricultural religion than for exact knowledge about dates and details. There was, of course, endless variety in Italy in both these; and it is waste of time to try and make the descriptions of the rural poets fit in with the fixed festivals of the Roman city calendar.

Note that Warde Fowler veers from his earlier musings (1899: 126) cited by Le Bonniec and mentioned above—that two different festivals hide within these lines. In his 1911 work he sees the *Georgics* verses as referring to a single rite, which he calls a *lustratio pagi* (p. 213):

> . . . we have in the later poets several charming allusions to a *lustratio pagi*, and it is of a rite of this kind that Virgil must have been thinking when he wrote the beautiful passage in the first Georgic beginning "In primis venerare deos"; and the lines
>
> terque novas circum felix eat hostia fruges,
> omnis quam chorus et socii comitentur ovantes, etc.,

This leads us to the second point. As we have just reminded ourselves, Le Bonniec argues that in *Georgics* 1.335–350, Virgil must be referring to both the Cerialia and the Ambarvalia, rather than solely to the former, for the following reason. The Ambarvalia, or we might say an ambarvalic rite, is a lustration; that is, it is conducted for the sake of ritual purification. This is certain. However, Le Bonniec (1958: 139, 145 n. 1) contends that the Cerialia do not involve a lustration; had they, he writes, Ovid would certainly have mentioned such in his description of the festival (see above). Since Ovid does not mention *lustratio* in conjunction with the Cerialia, and since an ambarvalic rite is a *lustratio*, lines 343 and following cannot, ergo, describe the Cerialia.

The argument seems to me to be a fragile one, constructed *ex silentio* (and we plainly see how hampered we are by a deficiency of data). Ovid waxes poetic about the Cerialia, but he transmits precious little information to us regarding the specifics of the private ritual. Lustrations, whether of fields or of arms (the Armilustrium) or of trumpets (the Tubilustria) or of animals (the Parilia) are ritual purifications. Ceres receives the sacrifice of pigs; if the shedding of pigs' blood is supposed to have any efficacy, it is the efficacy of purification, particularly purification of the earth, as we have seen quite clearly. The Cerialia could hardly be divorced from the notion of *lustratio*; to attempt to do so would amount to little more than semantic quibbling. It would come as no surprise at all if a lustral circumambulation formed a component of the rite, and that is precisely what we see attested if we read the lines beginning with *Georgics* 1.343 as continuing Virgil's description of the Cerealia, as seems most natural.

Third, while Virgil writes of a lustral circumambulation, there is no mention of the *suovetaurilia* commonly associated with such a lustration. To the contrary, Servius identifies the auspicious victim (*felix hostia*) conducted around the new growth as Ceres' favorite, the sow. We have already seen evidence, provided by Ovid (*Am.* 3.13), that outside of Rome, in the Faliscan city of Falerii, Juno is worshipped in her sacred grove with a procession and the sacrifice of a pig, cows with calves, and a ram—transparently a variant of the *suovetaurilia*. What are we to make of these things? It seems that we have unmistakable evidence that the victims involved in lustral circumambulation exhibit ritual, and perhaps regional, variation. Such variation is precisely what we found in the case of the Greek counterpart, the τριττύς (see §3.3.3.1).

As we have seen from our study of Terminus, the extensive ritual records of ancient India often shine an illuminating light on the more meager testimony of Roman rite. If we look to India for enlightenment in this case, we find that alongside the Sautrāmaṇī, preserving the Vedic homologue of the *suovetaurilia* discussed above (§3.3.3.1), ritual circumambulation is also attested there. However, circumambulation in Vedic India is a matter quite distinct from that of the Sautrāmaṇī. We encounter circumambulation in the animal sacrifice of the great Soma ritual discussed above (see §2.6.1). According to *Śatapatha Brāhmaṇa* 3.8.1.6, prior to the sacrifice of the victim, an Agnīdh, the fire-carrying priest, takes a firebrand and carries it around the victim (three times; *AB* 2.5). He does so to put a protective perimeter about the victim to protect it from evil spirits. As the rite is described in the *Kātyāyana Śrauta Sūtra* (6.5.2.3), the priest carries the fire three times around the space in which are situated the victim, the sacrificial butter (*ghee*), the *yūpa* (the post to which the victim is tied, marking the boundary of the sacrificial space), the place of immolation, the Cātvāla (the pit outside of the sacrificial ground), and the Āhavanīya. Alternatively, it is carried around a more limited space, containing the victim, the sacrificial butter, and the place of immolation.

While the circumambulation of the animal sacrifice is probably of most significance for our purposes (as we shall see), other instances of the practice are attested. Thus, in the sacrifice called the Aśvamedha, the horse sacrifice in which Dumézil discerned a common Indo-European origin with the Equus October of Rome (see *ARR*: 224–227), the wives of that king on whose behalf the sacrifice is made walk three times around the body of the victim, and then three times again (*ŚB* 13.2.8.4). In the Śatarudriya ceremony, dedicated to the god Rudra, terrifying and wild member of the warrior element of divine society who can be both friend and foe,[30] an Agnīdh sprinkles the great fire altar. After doing so he must circumambulate the altar three times, as a kind of apology to the altar for the sprinkling, and so protecting himself and regaining vital energy (*ŚB* 9.1.2.1–8). Dumézil (*ARR*: 230, n. 41) notes that *Atharva Veda* 6.28 (a hymn against birds of ill omen; see Whitney and Lanman 1996, 1: 300–301) was recited in association with the leading of a cow and fire three times around a house.

Circumambulation and the triple victims of the Sautrāmaṇī are discrete components of Vedic rite. This is an important observation vis-à-vis certain assumptions that have been made about the prominence of Ceres in the above ambarvalic text and rite. As we shall see immediately below, Tibullus also records a lustral circumambulation in which Ceres plays a dominant role. Some investigators have proposed that these poetic records indicate a diachronic shift, with Ceres gaining ground in the agricultural realm at the expense of Mars. Thus, Warde Fowler (1899: 126) wrote of Virgil and his *Georgics* lines:

[30] In the present context, Warde Fowler's (1911: 134) characterization of Mars is interesting: "I do not see in him only a deity of agriculture, or only a god of war; in my view he is a spirit of the wilder regions, where dwell the wolf and the woodpecker which are connected with him in legend: a spirit who dwells on the outskirts of civilisation, and can with profit be propitiated both for help against the enemies beyond, and for the protection of the crops and cattle within, the boundaries of human activity."

> His description answers closely to the well-known directions of Cato; and if it is Ceres who appears in Virgil's lines, and not Mars, the deity most prominent in Cato's account, this may be explained by the undoubted extension of the worship of Ceres, and the corresponding contraction of that of Mars, as the latter became more and more converted into a god of war.

Warde Fowler's analysis is of course based on the view that Mars is fundamentally ("originally") an agrarian deity. This idea was popular when Warde Fowler wrote, and later as well—an idea which Dumézil confronted head-on ("the great debate"; see *ARR*: 213–241) and which has now lost much of its appeal and following. Kilgour (1938: 236), in his study of the Ambarvalia, expresses a similar sentiment about Ceres and Mars, but with a somewhat different twist:

> Some notice ought to be taken here of the Virgil and Tibullus references. The Ambarvalia, as has been said, is generally considered to have been celebrated, originally at least, in honor of Mars. The private "lustratio agri" was still a piece of Mars-worship in the time of Cato, but when Virgil and Tibullus describe these festivals, the leading deity is clearly Ceres. This is fairly intelligible, since during the latter end of the Republic and the early days of the Empire, Ceres seems to have come more and more into the forefront of the deities of agriculture, which was, of course, her place. Mars, on the other hand, became more and more what he probably was originally, a fierce war-god. Their line of thought may have been that Mars (being now under the influence of the Greek Ares) was not in his proper place in an agricultural festival, failing to observe that the deity was being propitiated for the protection of the crops, not to cause them to grow. They therefore substituted Ceres, whom they knew as an agricultural deity, thus unwittingly causing her to take over a task which could not have been altogether congenial.

The personality and worship of Ceres undeniably underwent changes as she came under Greek influence, experiencing assimilation to Demeter.[31] That, however, is a separate matter. What the Vedic evidence reveals to us is that the Ambarvalia or, more precisely, the ambarvalic rite of circumambulation, is not "celebrated . . . in honor of Mars" (and certainly not "originally"). If there were a one-to-one correspondence here—a sort of *if and only if* relationship—the proper association would be that of Mars with the canonical *suovetaurilia*, corresponding to Indra's association with the

[31] See Le Bonniec 1958: 379–455; Spaeth 1996, especially pp. 8–9, 127–134; Boyle and Woodard 2000: 223–224.

Sautrāmaṇī—not of Mars with lustral circumambulation. Yet even here, the correspondence is not strictly one-to-one in India; as we saw above (§3.3.3.1), the Aśvins and Sarasvatī, deities of fertility and fecundity, also have a part of the threefold animal sacrifice. So it is in Rome as well—Mars is only nominally the recipient of the triple offering; the *suovetaurilia* has its own set of constituent recipients.

Circumambulation within a sacred plot of earth is one component of Vedic and Roman rite, inherited from common Indo-European ancestors—a component which could be mixed and matched with other elements to create various ritual permutations. Circumambulation is paired with the *suovetaurilia* when Mars is the central deity of the rite; it is paired with a *porca* when that deity is Ceres. There is no reason why the affiliation of Ceres—a goddess of the earth—with lustral circumambulation must be considered a secondary development of the late Republic.[32] And yet other considerations militate against this view, as we shall see.

3.3.5 Tibullus

As alluded to directly above, Tibullus records in his second book (2.1.1–24) a rite of lustration in which Ceres plays a central role:

> Quisquis adest, faveat: fruges lustramus et agros,
> ritus ut a prisco traditus extat avo.
> Bacche, veni, dulcisque tuis e cornibus uva
> pendeat, et spicis tempora cinge, Ceres.
> luce sacra requiescat humus, requiescat arator,
> et grave suspenso vomere cesset opus.
> solvite vincla iugis; nunc ad praesepia debent
> plena coronato stare boves capite.
> omnia sint operata deo; non audeat ulla
> lanificam pensis imposuisse manum.
> vos quoque abesse procul iubeo, discedat ab aris,
> cui tulit hesterna gaudia nocte Venus.
> casta placent superis: pura cum veste venite
> et manibus puris sumite fontis aquam.
> cernite, fulgentes ut eat sacer agnus ad aras
> vinctaque post olea candida turba comas.
> di patrii, purgamus agros, purgamus agrestes:
> vos mala de nostris pellite limitibus,

[32]Le Bonniec (1958: 147–148) and Dumézil (1944: 44–45) likewise argue, on the basis of functional differences in the deities, that Ceres has not supplanted Mars in agrarian rites.

neu seges eludat messem fallacibus herbis,
    neu timeat celeres tardior agna lupos.
tunc nitidus plenis confisus rusticus agris
    ingeret ardenti grandia ligna foco,
turbaque vernarum, saturi bona signa coloni,
    ludet et ex virgis extruet ante casas.

Whoever is present, keep silent: we lustrate crops and lands,
    with a rite passed down from ancient fathers.
Bacchus, come, and let the sweet cluster hang from your
    horns; Ceres, ring your temples with bristling grain.
This sacred day let the earth find rest, let the ploughman find rest;
    the ploughshare's hung up, let hard labor cease.
Loosen the bonds from the yokes; now at filled troughs ought
    the oxen stand with garland-crowned heads.
Let all efforts be devoted to the god; be sure that no wool
    spinner intends to put her hand to working the wool.
You also I bid to keep your distance, stay away from the altar
    if Venus visited her pleasures upon you last night.
Chastity pleases the gods above: in unsoiled clothing come
    and with unsoiled hands lift water from the fount.
Perceive how the sacred lamb goes to the shining altar and
    the white-clad throng comes after with olive encircled locks.
Gods of our fathers, we purify the fields, we purify the country folk:
    You, drive away evil beyond our boundaries.
Neither let the grain field cheat the harvest with stunted shafts,
    nor the dawdling lamb fear the swift wolves.
Then the beaming country-man confident in fields of plenty
    will heap great wood upon the blazing hearth,
And a host of slaves born at home, good signs of a palled farmer,
    will make merry before it and heap up hovels of twigs.
My prayers will be answered: don't you see in the auspicious entrails
    that the liver omen reveals the gods to be indulgent.

An ambarvalic sort of lustration appears to be suggested, though there is no specific reference to circumambulation, unless *lustrare* is used in its secondary sense, which denotes such a procession. This is clearly a bit different from the texts examined earlier, and Kilgour separates it from his *lustratio agri* and his Ambarvalia proper (see §3.3.4). For Kilgour (1938: 227–228) it is a *lustratio pagi*—a lustration which involved a procession around the boundaries of a rural community, a *pagus*. Similarly, Warde Fowler (1911: 80) was inclined to view the passage as describing "a *lustratio* of the *ager paganus*." Some investigators have argued for similarities to the Feriae

Sementivae (the moveable 'Festival of Sowing') at which a pregnant sow and spelt are offered to Ceres and Tellus (see Boyle and Woodard 2000: 182–183), and the Paganalia (yet another moveable festival, celebrated in the *pagi*; see Varro, *Ling.* 6.24, 26), against which view see Le Bonniec 1958: 144–146.

Lines 17–20 are particularly interesting in light of our observations about Cato's chthonic Manius (see §3.3.3.2):

> di patrii, purgamus agros, purgamus agrestes:
> vos mala de nostris pellite limitibus,
> neu seges eludat messem fallacibus herbis,
> neu timeat celeres tardior agna lupos.

> Gods of our fathers, we purify the fields, we purify the country folk:
> You, drive away evil beyond our boundaries.
> Neither let the grain field cheat the harvest with stunted shafts,
> nor the dawdling lamb fear the swift wolves.

The Di Patrii who are invoked to drive away evil beyond the boundaries of the purified space and to protect vegetation and flocks are very probably the Lares. In 1.10.15, Tibullus calls on the Lares Patrii to protect him in war, offering them a pig, a *rustica hostia*. We saw that in Tibullus 1.1.19–24 (§3.3.3.2) the poet calls on the Lares for abundance of crops and wine, promising a lamb in return.

3.3.6 The Fratres Arvales

Is the public Ambarvalia as described by Strabo (see §3.3.1) to be equated with the rites conducted by the priesthood of the Fratres Arvales in honor of their goddess Dea Dia, as preserved in their ritual records, the *Acta Fratrum Arvalium* (see §3.3.3.2)?[33] If within the history of the study of Roman land lustration rituals there has been a tempest in a teacup, this is it. Writing at the close of the century before last, Warde Fowler (1899: 125) could rehearse the controversy, citing Mommsen, Henzen, and Jordan as authorities on the pro side of the issue, Marquardt on the con side, and circumspectly conclude: "The question is, however, for us of no great importance, as the *acta* do not add to our knowledge of what was done at the Ambarvalia." The advent of the twentieth century, the century of the great

[33]For over a century, the standard edition of the Arval *Acta* has been Henzen 1874, with additional inscriptions appearing in a supplemental volume, Pasoli 1950; for a bibliography of the publication of additional fragments, see Scheid 1990: 8 and Beard 1985: 114, n. 1. For the corpus of the *Acta*, see now Scheid 1998.

global conflicts, ushered in no peaceful resolution of this controversy. By the final decade of that century, Scheid (1990: 99, n. 13; 446, n. 11; 447, n. 12, drawing on Kilgour 1938: 225) could enumerate a list of scholars favoring the *identity* of the Arval rites and those of Strabo (or generally the Ambarvalia) which includes: Mommsen (1859: 70, n. 99a); Henzen (1874: 46ff.); de Rossi (1877, 3: 690ff.); Jordan (1879: 200ff.); Beloch (1880: 43–44); Boehm (*RE* 8: 2029); Marbach (*RE* 14: 1919); Wissowa (*RE* 2: 1478); Gatti (1895: 690, 695); Warde Fowler (1899: 124–125; 1911: 213); Usener (1911: 298); Pais (1913: 605, n.2); Frazer (1929, vol. 2: 497); Birt (1937: 969); Norden (1939: 162, 175); Latte (1960: 65); Lugli (1966: 647); Chirasi (1968: 199); Scholz (1970: 64–66). Scheid's list of those who *distinguish* the two rituals includes: Desjardins (1854: 235–236); Schwegler (1856, vol. 1: 434); Marquardt (1878: 418); Preller (1858, vol. 1: 301, 371, 406, 424–425); Huschke (1869: 63); Hirschfeld (1869: 1501–1502); Oldenberg (1875: 20–30); Hunziker (1877–1919b); Kilgour (1938: 225–240); Alföldi (1965: 296–304); Lasserre (1967: 206); Gjerstadt (1967: 277–278); Schilling (1970: 256–257); and Scheid himself (1990: 442–451).

Dumézil, in the course of his discussion of Roman priests in *Archaic Roman Religion* (p. 592), places himself in the former camp—not in addressing the controversy directly but in operating with an assumed identity of the rites of the Fratres Arvales and the Ambarvalia:

> The twelve Fratres Arvales were charged with protecting the *arva*, the cultivated fields, against all dangers. In primitive times they did this, like Cato's peasant on his little property, by means of a circumambulation of the *ager*, followed by *suovetaurilia*. In this festival, the Ambarvalia, as in the ritual which Cato describes, Mars was honored not as an "agrarian god" but in his traditional role as a warrior god who puts his military prowess or his menacing strength in the service of the *arva*, against visible or invisible foes. Before the end of the Republic, the ritual had been replaced by sacrifices at various points on the former boundary of the ager, and the sodality itself had disappeared, leaving its cult to the Pontifices. Augustus renewed it, and the fortunate preservation of long fragments of the Acta of the new Arvales makes their rituals among the best known; unhappily, however, these are not the primitive rituals.

For Dumézil, the relationship which exists between the Arval rites and those described by Strabo is thus revealed to be of a chronological nature. The surviving Acta date from about 21 BC to AD 304, with the appearance of the earliest inscriptions usually held to evidence a reform or revitalization of the priesthood at the hands of Augustus (see Scheid 1990: 679–746). For his above analysis, Dumézil has clearly drawn on the fragments of the

Carmen Arvale, the hymn of the Arvals (see §3.3.3.2), and on Varro's (*Ling.* 5.85) etymologizing of the name of the priesthood:

> Fratres Arvales dicti qui sacra publica faciunt propterea ut fruges ferant arva: a ferendo et arvis Fratres Arvales dicti.
>
> The priests are named Fratres Arvales who perform public rites so that the fields might be fruitful: from *ferre* and from *arva* the Fratres Arvales are named.

That may have been so in the late Republic when Varro wrote, but by the time Augustus comes to power, suggests Dumézil, the public rite of land lustration—Ambarvalia—as Strabo records it, is a ceremony being conducted by the Pontifices at Φῆστοι and several other sites on the old Ager Romanus (see §3.3.1). Thus, Dumézil appears to reason, the role of the earlier Fratres Arvales in this affair has been supplanted diachronically by the Pontifices. When the priesthood is revitalized by Augustus, its province is something other than what it once was.

While exercising care not to put words in Dumézil's mouth, one might still abstract from the preceding the conclusion that for Dumézil the assumed Ambarvalia of the earlier Fratres Arvales and that of their successors in the rite, the Pontifices, are rightly related as variant forms of a rite of land lustration. ("Before the end of the Republic, the ritual had been replaced by sacrifices at various points on the former boundary of the ager. . . .") This very view is in fact expressed more overtly earlier in the same work (*ARR*: 230–231), when in his defense of Mars against the "agrarian" interpretation, Dumézil writes:

> The Ambarvalia belong to a class of lustrations which has several other varieties; for example, the great quinquennial lustration of the people (*lustrum conditum*) and the *amburbium* are also performed by the circumambulation of animals to be sacrificed . . . .[34] But these various rituals, like the Ambarvalia, do not make Mars a specialist in anything but "protection by force"; his whole function is on this periphery which the processions render perceptible; whatever may be the objects which he is charged with protecting, he is the sentinel who operates at the front, on the threshold as the *carmen Arvale* probably says, and who halts the enemy.

3.3.6.1 THE FESTIVAL OF DEA DIA The Fratres Arvales celebrated the rites of their goddess Dea Dia annually in the month of May. The exact dates

[34]This view is, of course, fundamentally that captured by Kilgour 1938 in his study of the Ambarvalia.

of the festival, as recorded in the Acta, differ from year to year, but the celebration always entails three days of ritual activity[35] over a span of four days, with a one-day interval separating festival days one and two. The rites of day one are conducted in Rome at the home of the Magister, the chief member of the Fratres Arvales, and were characterized by offerings of wine and incense, with feasting and the anointing of an image of Dea Dia.

After an intermission of one day, the rites of day two begin in the sacred grove of the Fratres Arvales, located at the fifth milestone from Rome along the Via Campana (at modern La Magliana). In the morning, the Magister sacrifices two pigs (*porcae piaculares*; see §3.3.4) to Dea Dia, followed by the offering of a cow (*vacca honoraria*). Before or about midday the Fratres Arvales dine on a meal which includes the sacrificed pigs and their blood. Afterward a third victim is sacrificed, a lamb (*agna opima*), a libation of wine and incense are offered, and various rituals are conducted such as the passing of grains (*fruges*) among the priests, who receive them with the left hand, passing them on with the right (see Scheid 1990: 601–612); the tossing down of clay vessels from the temple of Dea Dia (see §3.3.3.2); a ritual sharing of loaves of bread decorated with laurel; and the anointing of statues of goddesses with *lumemulia cum rapinis* (see Scheid 1990: 625–627). The Carmen Arvale is sung, invoking Mars, the Lares, and Semones (see §4.9.2.1), followed by a dinner banquet in the tetrastyle of the grove, into which plates along with *campanae* and beakers of sweet wine were brought in *more pompae*, "in processional style" (see Scheid 1990: 633–634). Afterward chariot races are held in the circus of the grove. With the games concluded, the Fratres return to the home of the Magister in Rome for the offering of libations and further banqueting.

The third day is a simpler affair, looking much like the first day. The setting is again the home of the Magister in Rome. The rites consist of banqueting; offerings of wine, incense, and grain; and the lighting of lamps. On the curious ritual elements denoted as *Tuscanicae* 'Etruscan' which are used in conjunction with lamp lighting, see the discussion below (§4.9.4.1).

3.3.6.2 THE AGER ROMANUS Is the Arval festival of Dea Dia identical to the state Ambarvalia described by Strabo (*Geography* 5.3.2)? Let us look again at what Strabo has to say:

[35]For a schematic overview of the rituals conducted during the course of the three days, see Scheid 1990: 478 and the accompanying discussion. In the paragraphs of this section we briefly rehearse the ritual structure of the three-day festival and return in §4.7 and §4.9 to a more detailed examination.

> μεταξὺ γοῦν τοῦ πέμπτου καὶ τοῦ ἕκτου λίθου τῶν τὰ μίλια διασημαινόντων τῆς Ῥώμης καλεῖται τόπος Φῆστοι. τοῦτον δ' ὅριον ἀποφαίνουσι τῆς τότε Ῥωμαίων γῆς, οἵ θ' ἱερομνήμονες θυσίαν ἐπιτελοῦσιν ἐνταῦθά τε καὶ ἐν ἄλλοις τόποις πλείοσιν ὡς ὁρίοις αὐθημερόν, ἣν καλοῦσιν Ἀμβαρουίαν.
>
> In any event, between the fifth and sixth stones marking the miles from Rome is a place called Festi. And this was then, they claim, the boundary of Roman territory; the Pontifices celebrate a sacred festival both there and, on the same day, at still other places—these being boundaries. They call the festival the Ambarvia.

If we limit our comparison by using only that evidence which Strabo provides—the only incontrovertible account of any annual public Ambarvalia which we seem to possess—a case for equivalence is difficult to support: we could say that we surmise that the two rituals are identical; we cannot say that the surviving evidence of the two rituals clearly reveals that they are identical. The only shared distinctive feature is that of locale, and this is only a subset relationship.

The grove of the Fratres Arvales is located on the Via Campana at the fifth milestone from Rome; Strabo writes that the public rites of the Ambarvalia are celebrated at the mysterious Festi (Φῆστοι) "between the fifth and sixth stones marking the miles from Rome" and *at several other sites which constitute boundaries*. On the basis of locale alone, could we not just as well argue that Strabo's so-called Ambarvalia at Festi, which the text actually names as *Ambarvia* (Ἀμβαρουία), is one instantiation of the boundary festival, the public Terminalia, a festival that, as we have seen (§3.2), Ovid reports (*Fast.* 2.679–684) was celebrated at the sixth milestone of the Via Laurentina—a festival that is on the same day celebrated as a private ritual at many boundaries (see §2.8.5)? Such an equation would even offer the prima facie advantage of not requiring us to rationalize the contradiction in the identity of the presiding priests—Strabo's priests are the Pontifices (οἱ ἱερομνήμονες), not the Fratres Arvales. There is of course the matter of Strabo's naming of his ritual—Ἀμβαρουία. But it would come as no surprise if the Terminalia were celebrated with an ambarvalic rite; which is after all a ritual tracing, declaration, and protecting of a boundary.

Regardless, the argument by locale is not persuasive for either of these equations: (i) Strabo's Ambarvia = the Arval festival of Dea Dia; or (ii) Strabo's Ambarvia = the Terminalia. As Alföldi (1965: 296–304) demonstrated, the approximate distance from Rome at which these festivals are held is not unique to these three, but is shared by several sites of ritual significance. Being located at approximately equidistant points from Rome in various directions from the city, these sites are situated along a circumference which at an early period in the history of Rome constituted the boundary of the Ager Romanus, to which Strabo alludes. In addition to (i) the Arval grove on the Via Campana; (ii) the place of the public Terminalia on the Via Laurentina; and (iii) the site of Strabo's public Ambarvia, these include the following:

(iv) *Fortuna Muliebris*: The sacred precinct and temple of Fortuna Muliebris ("Fortune of Women") stood on the Via Latina at the fourth milestone from Rome. According to Roman tradition, early in the fifth century BC, Marcius Coriolanus, a prominent Roman who had opposed providing grain to the plebeians during a famine, went into exile among the Volscians. Under the urgings and command of Coriolanus and the Volscian Attius Tullius, the Volscian peoples revolted and waged war against Rome. After capturing numerous cities under Roman control, Coriolanus turned to attack Rome itself. In repeated attempts to negotiate peace, Rome sent both envoys and priests to the camp of Coriolanus, but all to no avail. Finally, a large contingent of Roman women, which included Veturia, the mother of Coriolanus, and his wife Volumnia, marched to the Volscian camp. Berated and shamed by his mother, Coriolanus relented and peacefully withdrew the Volscian army, terminating the campaign (see Livy 2.34.1–40.12).

To celebrate this peaceful and uncanny victory of the women of Rome, the senate, at the request of the women, funded the establishment of a sacred precinct and annual rites of worship of Fortuna Muliebris, and the construction of a temple for the goddess at the site of the encounter with Coriolanus. The first celebration of the rites was held on the Kalends of December, one year to the day after the retreat of the Volscians. Valeria, a woman who had been prominent in organizing the delegation of women, was designated to serve as priestess (see Dionysius of Halicarnassus, *Ant. Rom.* 8.55.1–5). Two statues of the goddess were erected in her temple, one funded by the senate, the other by the Roman women. On two occasions the latter statue (as recorded in the *Books of the Pontifices*, according to Dionysius of Halicarnassus, *Ant. Rom.* 8.56.1) was reported to have spoken. The words of the statue are variously reported; according to Valerius Maximus (1.8.4), for instance, she announced: *Rite me, matronae, dedistis riteque dedicastis* ("Rightly, Matrons, you have given me and rightly you have dedicated me"); compare Dionysius of Halicarnassus, *Ant. Rom.* 8.56.2; Plutarch, *Cor.* 37.3; *De Fort. Rom.* 318. On the goddess Fortuna and her numerous specific forms, see Boyle and Woodard 2000: 235.

(v) *The Robigalia*: The festival of Robigus (or female Robigo), deity of grain rust, was annually celebrated on April 25. Verrius Flaccus (*CIL* I^2 pp. 236, 316) records that the place of celebration was a grove located at the fifth milestone from Rome along the Via Claudia. One of the archaic priests, the Flamen Quirinalis, presided and offered the sacrifice of sheep and a dog to Robigus for the protection of the new standing crop from fungus. The festival is ancient, Numa Pompilius having established it in the eleventh year of his kingship, according to Pliny (*HN* 18.285; compare Tertullian, *De Spect.* 5). Of the Robigalia, Ovid (*Fast.* 4.905–932) writes as an observer and participant:

hac mihi Nomento Romam cum luce redirem,
obstitit in media candida turba via:
flamen in antiquae lucum Robiginis ibat,
exta canis flammis, exta daturus ovis.
protinus accessi, ritus ne nescius essem;
edidit haec flamen verba, Quirine, tuus:
"aspera Robigo, parcas Cerialibus herbis,
et tremat in summa leve cacumen humo.
tu sata sideribus caeli nutrita secundi
crescere, dum fiant falcibus apta, sinas.
vis tua non levis est: quae tu frumenta notasti,
maestus in amissis illa colonus habet;
nec venti tantum Cereri nocuere nec imbres,
nec sic marmoreo pallet adusta gelu,
quantum si culmos Titan incalfacit udos:
tum locus est irae, diva timenda, tuae.
parce, precor, scabrasque manus a messibus aufer,
neve noce cultis; posse nocere sat est.
nec teneras segetes, sed durum amplectere ferrum,
quodque potest alios perdere perde prior.
utilius gladios et tela nocentia carpes:
nil opus est illis; otia mundus agit.
sarcula nunc durusque bidens et vomer aduncus,
ruris opes, niteant; inquinet arma situs,
conatusque aliquis vagina ducere ferrum
adstrictum longa sentiat esse mora.
at tu ne viola Cererem, semperque colonus
absenti possit solvere vota tibi."

On this day, as I returned to Rome from Nomentum,
A crowd in white obstructed me mid-street.

A Flamen marched to the grove of ancient Robigo
 To give dog guts and sheep guts to the flames.
I accosted him at once to learn of the rite.
 Your Flamen delivered these words, Quirinus:
"Scaly Robigo, god of rust, spare Ceres' grain;
 Let silky blades quiver on the soil's skin.
Let growing crops be nourished by a friendly sky
 And stars, until they ripen for the scythe.
Your power is not slight. The lachrymose farmer
 Counts as lost the corn which you have marked.
The damage done to Ceres from wind and rain,
 Or from the burning white of marble frost,
Is far less than when Titan sears the sodden stalks.
 That is the time of your anger, dread goddess.
Spare us, I pray, keep scabrous hands from the harvest.
 Harm no crops. The power to harm is enough.
Do not grip the delicate corn, but hard iron,
 And destroy what is destructive, first.
It is better to devour swords and lethal spears.
 They have no use; the world practices peace.
Now let the hoe, hard fork and arcing plough shimmer;
 They are the field's wealth. Let neglect rust arms;
And let any attempt to unsheathe the sword
 Feel the iron clogged from long disuse.
Do not violate Ceres: always let the farmer
 Fulfill his pledges for your absence."

(vi) *Ager Gabinus and the augural boundary:* Alföldi adds to the list of radial points a locus (or continuum) east of Rome on the augural boundary separating the Ager Romanus from the Ager Gabinus. As we have seen (§3.3.1), Varro (*Ling.* 5.33) lists five types of *agri*, of which the Ager Gabinus and the Ager Romanus are two, and that both of these regions have their own particular form of auspices, on which basis the Augures hold them distinct from the various other three types of *agri*. The designated point would lie on the Via Praenestina (running from Rome to Gabii) where the road is intersected by the augural boundary.

(vii) *Statue of Mars:* Finally, Alföldi draws into this set of ritual boundary-locales a certain statue of Mars and images of wolves located on the Via Appia. Livy (22.1.12), in a long list of prodigies reported to have occurred in 217 BC, writes that these statues were observed to sweat. Alföldi suggests that these must have been associated with the temple of Mars that stood along the Via Appia. From Rome to the town of Bovillae, a distance of about 10.5 miles, the Via Appia was stone-paved in two stages. The first round of paving covered the road from the Porta Capena,[36] where it exited the city, to the temple of Mars (295 BC; Livy 10.23.12–13; compare 38.28.3), the second from the temple to Bovillae (292 BC; Livy 10.47.4). Given this bisection, Alföldi (1965: 302–303) concludes: "so this Mars with the wolves stood just at the distance from Rome, where we must look for our old demarcation line."

The temple of Mars on the Via Appia , however, was located rather closer to Rome than to Bovillae. According to an inscription of the Collegium of Aesculapius and Hygia (*ILS* 7213), Mars' temple was situated between the first and second milestones on the Via Appia (see *LTUR*, vol. 5: 31; Richardson 1992: 244–245; Platner 1929: 327). The temple was vowed in 390 BC, during the Gallic war, and dedicated in 387 by one Titus Quinctius (see Livy 6.5.8), a Duumvir Sacris Faciendis, the priests in charge of the Sibylline Books (see Boyle and Woodard 2000: 239, 285). The deviation of this site on the Via Appia from the canonical four- to six-mile distance from Rome may or may not be of significance for including its locale in the list of cardinal ritual points surrounding the city along the ancient boundary of the Ager Romanus. In any event, an interesting feature of this temple does invite comparison to boundary marking.

Next to the temple of Mars on the Via Appia was positioned a stone, called the Lapis Manalis. During periods of drought the stone was dragged into the city, resulting in an immediate rainfall according to Festus (pp. 2, 128M). In this ceremony of *aquaelicium*, it is the Pontifices who transport the stone within the city walls (Servius, *Aen.* 3.175). For Festus (p. 128M) the name of the stone is derived from *manare* 'to flow', but the prospect of an affiliation with the Manes is tantalizing; Festus, in fact, identifies in the same passage another Lapis Manalis which he reports was believed to cover the opening to Orcus, the infernal abode of the Manes (and even here he makes an etymological link, not only with Manes, but again with *manare*, in its sense 'to pass'; for a similar etymological link of *manare* and *mane* 'morning', compare Varro, *Ling.* 6.4).

3.3.6.3 THE SAME OR DIFFERENT? We have seen that the evidence provided by locale is not in itself sufficient to establish the identity of Strabo's Ambarvia (Ambarvalia) and the Arval rites of Dea Dia. Is there anything

[36]For Dumézil's ideas concerning the Porta Capena, the temple of Mars, and archaic Roman tripartition, see Dumézil 1985: 47–54.

else? Those who have argued for, or assumed, the identity of the two rituals have, of course, done so by bringing to the problem the evidence provided by other attestations of ambarvalic rites and land lustration. The procedure is based on the tacit assumption that one such rite informs another and that one can extrapolate from the composite evidence an idealized Ambarvalia which can then be used to hypothesize the identity of Strabo's rite and that of the Fratres Arvales.[37]

Let us, however, look at it in a different way. On the basis of the evidence which has survived, no two of the various instantiations of field and crop lustration can be demonstrated to be identical. We have already seen that *suovetaurilia* and ambarvalic lustration appear to be separate ritual components of such rites, inherited from ancestral traditions and which can be used in various combinations with other ritual elements. If one tries to extrapolate an idealized form of the Ambarvalia, and compare it to the Arval ritual, then what immediately becomes clear in the process is that the Arval ritual itself departs from any sort of idealized norm. What are preserved in the evidentiary record are several variations on a theme. Such ritual variation is well known in the Indo-European world. This is precisely what we find in India in the case of the plethora of Soma rituals, all of which are variations on a single basic ritual, the Agniṣṭoma (see Keith 1988a: 326, 336). Vis-à-vis Vedic India, it is interesting that, impressionistically, among the various Roman lustration rites, the Arval ritual of Dea Dia is most reminiscent of Indian ritual with its detailed sequence of offerings punctuated by ritual meals. To this evocative matter we shall return in §4.3.5, examining the Arval ritual in greater detail.

Given such variation in ambarvalic rites, could we even begin to demonstrate that the two rituals—Strabo's Ambarvalia and the Arval rite of Dea Dia—are identical, are to be equated, on the basis of the evidence which attests them? The answer to *that* question is certainly "no." To the contrary, on that basis the two are seen to be complementary—they themselves look to be variations on a theme. One is celebrated at a single site (the grove of Dea Dia); the other at a multiplicity of sites (Festi and

[37]Calendrical data have at times been submitted as evidence for the identity of the state Ambarvalia and the Arval rites of May in the grove of Dea Dia, as in, for example, Scullard 1981: 124; Henzen 1874: 46–47. Specifically these data are provided by the *Menologia Rustica* (*CIL* I^2: 280) noting that Roman grain was lustrated in the month of May (*segetes lustrantur*) and by an entry in the *Acta Sanctorum* on the martyrdom of Sissenius on 28 May, AD 393 that makes reference to a lustration of the fields. The entries have little bearing on the date of the Ambarvalia; see Kilgour 1938: 229–230 and Scheid 1990: 448–451 for rebuttals of the claim.

other boundary places). One set of priests conducts one ritual (the Fratres Arvales); another set the other (the Pontifices). One is at least in name (and possibly only nominally) identified with an ambarvalic rite of circumambulation (Ambarvia/Ambarvalia), without the record specifying any victims; the other involves *suovetaurilia*—and not exactly the canonical type—without circumambulation. The *suovetaurilia* of Dea Dia takes the form of (i) two pigs (*porcae piaculares*), expiatory offerings, sacrificed in the morning; (ii) a cow (*vacca honoraria*) offered thereafter; and (iii) a lamb (*agna opima*) sacrificed following the midday meal. Rather than the bull, boar, and ram which are led around a boundary, and images of which depict the animals as queued up awaiting slaughter at the hands of *victimarii*, the Arval *suovetaurilia* brings to mind much more readily a comparison to Faliscan Juno's received offering of a pig, cows with calves, and a ram led through her grove (see §3.3.4).

3.4 CONCLUSION

From the summit of Jupiter's Capitoline temple, Terminus—god of boundaries—looks out on a world whose space is unboundedly Roman: "Rome's city and the world are the same space." Yet there are recognized sacred boundaries—the *pomerium* around urban Rome, and the more distant boundary of the Ager Romanus. These are boundaries encapsulating spaces of sacred activity. The sacred spaces are complementary. Thus, the urban auspices can only be taken within the space bounded by the *pomerium*. The assemblage of the three canonical sacred flames—ancient and Proto-Indo-European in origin—burn within and along the boundary of that smaller, urban sacred space.

The ritual activities conducted within the space bounded by the Ager Romanus are more varied—though within variety is similarity. Along the distal boundary of the Ager Romanus are celebrated the public rites of Terminus, as well as the Ambarvalia (at Strabo's mysterious *Festi*) and the Arval ritual of Dea Dia—and yet other rituals. A careful examination of the several known "ambarvalic" rites reveals that these are related to one another as variations on a theme (*allorituals*, to coin yet another term); Vedic India provides an instructive parallel in the variation exhibited among the several forms of the Soma sacrifice—all being variants modeled on the Agniṣṭoma, and all well documented, in contrast to the Roman rites. What is more, an investigation of Roman lustral rites vis-à-vis Vedic ritual shows that the ancient Indo-European cultic elements of the triple victim—the Roman *suovetaurilia*—and of circumambulation are independent constituents not uniquely bound to each other. They are utilized separately and in various ritual combinations.

Chthonic or infernal deities are conspicuously present in ambarvalic rites. The Lares and, especially, the Mater Larum, occupy a prominent position in the Arval celebration of Dea Dia. Tibullus invokes the Lares for abundance of crops and wine. In Cato's deeply ancient lustral prayer, Manius—certainly to be identified with Varro's chthonic *deus Manius*—is charged with leading the victims through the field in such a way as to produce a lustration of maximum efficacy. In the previous chapter we saw that the blood of a victim is to be poured into the hole dug for a *terminus*, and this must undoubtedly constitute an offering to the chthonic beings whose domain has been disturbed in the planting of the boundary stone, just as *ghee* and barley water are poured into the hole dug for the *yūpa* and the Sadas post—offerings for the earth-dwelling Pitaras—equivalent to the Manes—and for evil spirits that could rise from the earth through the hole.

CHAPTER 4

The Fourth Fire

4.1 INTRODUCTION

Chapter 4 brings us to the heart of the present work. We will begin by examining the large sacred space of Vedic cult, the Mahāvedi, its geometry and its use, and then turn to its homologous Roman space, the Ager Romanus. Around the periphery of that Roman space are positioned several sites of ritual importance, as we saw in chapter 3. We will investigate almost all of these in turn, focusing on that locale and ritual attested in greatest detail, the Arval festival of Dea Dia celebrated in the grove of the goddess along the Via Campana, as well as in Rome. Of particular importance is the "Carmen Arvale," the song which the Fratres Arvales sing invoking the Lares, the Semones, and Mars.

4.2 THE FOURTH FIRE

As we discussed in §2.8.1, three canonical fires play a vital role in Vedic ritual and serve as salient landmarks of the ritual space. Within this sacred space, the Gārhapatya (the round fire of the master of the house) and the Āhavanīya (the quadrangular fire of offering) lie along an east–west axis (see Figure 4.1). Situated to the south of this axis is the guardian fire, the Dakṣiṇāgni. Dumézil identified homologous Roman structures corresponding to these three flames—fires positioned within the sacred space of the city. Respectively, these are the flame of the round temple (*aedes*) of Vesta; the flames of the altars of Rome's numerous (quadrangular) temples; and the fire of Volcanus at the border of the *pomerium*.

The Vedic sacred space within which burn the three fires is characteristic of *śrauta* (public) rituals (see §2.8.1), as opposed to *gṛhya* (domestic) rituals, which utilize only one fire and at which the presence of priests is not required (see Keith 1998: 313–314; Renou 1957: 97–98, 101). This sacred space is sufficient for basic public rites, Iṣṭis, but not for the great ceremonies, the Soma sacrifices in their various forms. For these, a much larger sacred space is laid out to the east, namely the Mahāvedi, to which we have already made passing reference. Among the prominent landmarks of that space is yet a fourth fire, placed near the eastern boundary of the Mahāvedi, and positioned on that same east–west axis on which lie the Gārhapatya and Āhavanīya. This is the flame of the altar called the Uttaravedi; immediately to the east of the altar stands the sacrificial post, boundary marker of the large sacred ground, the *yūpa*.

4.3 THE MAHĀVEDI

To say that the fire which now lies at the eastern terminus of the axis formed by the Gārhapatya and Āhavanīya is a "fourth flame" is only partially accurate. While the flame is positionally distinct from the three canonical fires of the Devayajana (the small space of the Iṣṭi), it is in effect a new Āhavanīya, moved eastward from its original site (via the rite called the Agnipraṇayana, 'the carrying forth of fire'); correspondingly, the original Gārhapatya is chain-shifted to the place of the original Āhavanīya. In fact, the entirety of the ceremony celebrated in conjunction with the Mahāvedi can be viewed as a ritual progression from west to east: the first rites within the sacrificial area are performed to the west, where the three fires are housed; on the altar of the "fourth" flame, at the eastern boundary of the Mahāvedi, the final rites are performed; the time in between is marked by much ritual activity, traversing the sacred spaces from west to east with fire and Soma.

The Mahāvedi is a topographically complex space, measured out with ritual precision. Its western aspect is of greater length along the north–south axis than its eastern aspect, so that the entire area is trapezoidal in

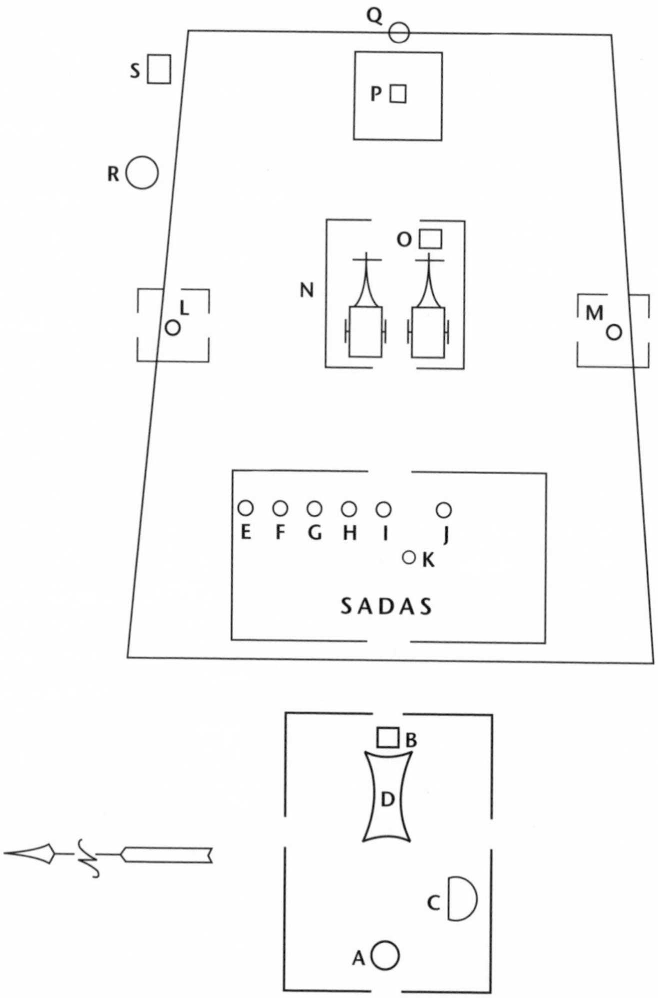

A	Gārhapatya	M	Mārjāliya
B	Āhavanīya	N	Havirdhāna
C	Dakṣiṇāgni	O	earthen mound (khara) for Soma cups
D	excavated altar (vedi)	P	Uttaravedi
E-J	the six Dhiṣṇyas within the Sadas	Q	Yūpa
K	Sadas post	R	Utkara
L	Āgnīdhrīya	S	Cātvāla

FIGURE 4.1. *The Vedic sacrificial ground: the Devayajana to the west and the Mahāvedi to the east. Used by permission of Roland D. Woodard.*

shape.[1] At the western end of the Mahāvedi, immediately east of the (original) Āhavanīya, there is constructed the shed called the Sadas, already encountered in our discussion of the Sadas post (see §2.6.3.4). Being the height of the sacrificer at its midpoint (at the central east–west axis), and slanting to the height of his navel at the north and south ends, the Sadas houses six of the hearths called Dhiṣṇyas, each constructed for a different priest (the Hotar, the Brāhmaṇācchaṃsin, the Potar, the Neṣṭar, the Acchāvāka, and the Maitrāvaruṇa). The Sadas is said to belong to Indra (*ŚB* 3.6.1.1, while being identified as "Viṣṇu's stomach").

Two other hearths are set up in the Mahāvedi, one at about the midpoint of the northern boundary of the space, the other due south of it, on the southern boundary. Each is covered by a square hut. The former is the Āgnīdhrīya, the Dhiṣṇya-hearth for the fire-carrying priest, the Agnīdh (or Āgnīdhra); and the latter hearth is that of the Mārjāliya. The hearth of the Agnīdh is said to be sacred to all the gods (*ŚB* 3.6.1.26–29); it is the first of the Dhiṣṇyas to be built (*ŚB* 9.4.3.5) and is lit from the fire of the Gārhapatya (*ŚB* 6.6.4.15). The Mārjāliya hearth is used for the cleansing of the ritual utensils (*ŚB* 14.2.2.43); in *Śatapatha Brāhmaṇa* 9.4.3.8 (a part of the description of the building of the great fire altar) we read that six bricks are placed on the Mārjāliya for the Pitaras (the Manes), being in the south, the region of the Pitaras.

Between the two latter hearths, in the middle of the Mahāvedi, is built another shed, the Havirdhāna. After being anointed by the sacrificer's wife (on which see Jamison 1996: 124–127), two Soma carts are moved eastward from the small sacred space of the Devayajana into the great sacrificial arena of the Mahāvedi. It is for the sheltering of these carts, following their journey from the west, that the Havirdhāna is built. The carts are parked side by side, facing east. Beneath the front portion of the cart parked to the south, four sound-holes are dug, the Uparavas, using formulas and a ritual akin to those used at the digging of holes for the *yūpa* and Sadas-post (see *ŚB* 3.5.4.1–24). The dirt from the Uparavas will be used for constructing the six Dhiṣṇya-hearths set up within the Sadas (see above). Over these holes boards are placed which will be used for pressing the Soma, the holes

[1] As described in *Śatapatha Brāhmaṇa* 3.5.1.1–11, the western border of the Mahāvedi stretches 30 steps—15 "steps" north and south of a benchmark peg driven into the ground on that border, along the east–west axis passing through the *Gārhapatya* and *Āhavanīya*. The eastern boundary falls 36 steps from this peg and extends for 24 steps—12 steps north and south of the east–west axis (cf. *ŚB* 10.2.3.1–18, where dimensions of the ground of the Iṣṭi are also given). A 'step', *prakrama*, is about 3 feet.

amplifying the sound of the pressing. This shed, like the Soma carts it shelters, is sacred to Viṣṇu (*ŚB* 3.5.3.2).

Following the construction of the various sheds comes the ritual of "leading forth of Agni and Soma" into the Mahāvedi. The sacrificial post, the *yūpa*, is then prepared and erected as described in §2.6.1.

4.3.1 The conquest

At least two aspects of worship within this enlarged ritual space, the Mahāvedi, are of particular interest and significance for our investigation. First, the movement of fire, Soma, cultic implements, priests, and the sacrificer from the smaller sacred ground of the Devayajana to the much enlarged space of the Mahāvedi is clearly presented as a journey, or more precisely, a migratory conquest. In her study of the sacrificer's wife, Jamison (1996: 125) notes:

> Just as the journey to the new Āhavanīya has its ritual procession, so the driving of the Soma-carts to their garage in the middle of the Mahāvedi is accompanied with some fanfare. The wife's anointing of the linchpins and the oblation in the wheel-tracks immediately precede the start of their eastern progress.[2] Despite the brevity of the journey, it is treated in some ways as if it were a pioneering expedition to the unknown east—as is dramatized by the wife's anointing the pins in only one direction, toward the east, thus giving the wheels a preliminary warm-up spin.

Heesterman (1993) directly addresses the fundamentally itinerant and questing nature of the Agniṣṭoma—the model Soma sacrifice—with its ritual trek into the Mahāvedi (p. 126):

> But it is significant that carrying the fire and Soma to their place on the Mahāvedi (Agnīṣomapraṇayana) is pictured as a wide-ranging, conquering progress. . . . The Mahāvedi is a temporary encampment that will be left again after completing the Soma sacrifice. And indeed, at the end of the Soma ritual proper, a cow dedicated to Mitra and Varuṇa is sacrificed, and finally the fires are taken up in the fire drill to settle elsewhere for, again, another sacrifice, the "breaking-up" Iṣṭi.

In offering these observations, Heesterman alludes to the mantra of *Taittirīya Saṃhitā* 1.3.4.c, spoken as the priests make their way toward the altar of the Agnīdh within the Mahāvedi (Keith 1967: 39, with modification):

[2] See *Śatapatha Brāhmaṇa* 3.5.3.13–17 for the ritual of the wife anointing the cart.

May Agni here make room for us;
May he go before us cleaving the foe;
Joyously may he conquer our foes;
May he win spoils in the contest for spoils.

The priestly procession into the great sacred space is an invasion, divinely led and bent on acquisition of space and spoils. Addressing the elaborate landscape of the Mahāvedi of the Soma sacrifice, Heesterman (1993: 128) continues:

> Apart from the shed where the two carts are put . . . at the back of the oblational hearth, there are the Āgnīdhrīya and the Mārjāliya or cleansing huts on the northern and southern boundaries, each with its own fire hearth, and, in between these two huts, the Sadas where the Dhiṣṇya hearths are located, and where the Soma is drunk. . . . The Soma Mahāvedi would seem to continue the tradition of an independent temporary emplacement at a considerable distance, somewhere out in the wilderness. Otherwise it would be hard to explain the presence of the two Soma carts solemnly driven to their shed on the Mahāvedi—an act that, given the limited space, looks distinctly odd if not somewhat comical.

Among other evidence which Heesterman (1993: 128–129) cites for the conceptualization of the sacrifice as an expedition is that provided by the ritual called the Yātsattra, the various Sattras ('sessions') being rituals having more than twelve Soma-pressing days (see Keith 1998a: 349–352; Renou 1957: 107).[3] The Yātsattra is dedicated to the goddess Sarasvatī (*KŚS* 24.5.25) and takes the form of an eastward journey along the Sarasvatī river; the trek begins in the desert regions where the river disappears and continues on to the river's source at Plakṣa Prāsravaṇa (a distance of forty days by horseback; *PB* 25.10.16). Each day of the ritual the hearth of the Gārhapatya is moved progressively farther to the east, the distance moved being determined by the throw of a *śamyā*, a wooden yoke-pin. In the usual case, what is being advanced each day, however, is the Mahāvedi, the relocated Gārhapatya no longer being identified with the original fire of the ritual

[3]Consider Keith's (1998a: 349–350) encapsulating summary: "The Sattras all differ from other forms of the Soma sacrifice, because all the performers must be consecrated and must be Brahmans: there is therefore no separate sacrificer: all share in the benefits of the offering: each bears the burdens of his own errors, whereas at the ordinary sacrifice the sacrificer receives the benefit and the evil results of errors alike. . . . The aims of the Sattras are most various: the obtaining of wealth, of cattle, of offspring, of prosperous marriage, and many other things. Much as they are, it is clear, elaborated by the priest, they reflect here and there primitive conceptions of sacrifice."

ground of the Devayajana. Like so many sacral mobile-units, the Sadas, the Āgnīdhrīya shed, and the shed for the Soma carts, the Havirdhāna, are all built on wheels so they can be easily advanced to the next day's location. Similarly, the base of the *yūpa* is given a shape which will facilitate its being dragged to a new, extended boundary (on all of which, see *PB* 25.10.4–5). The Brahmans who advance into this self-perpetuating sacred space take with them a herd of one hundred cows and one bull and the hopeful expectation that the herd will have grown to one thousand head by the end of the sacrificial journey. If the herd should increase to that number before Plakṣa Prāsravaṇa is reached, the sacrificial session is terminated. Cessation of the rite likewise occurs if the cattle should all die or if the sacrificer should die before the ritual "land's end" is reached (*PB* 25.10.19–22; *KŚS* 24.6.16). At the union of the Sarasvatī and the river Dṛṣadvatī, an offering is made to the fire god who burns within the waters, Apām Napāt.[4] Upon arrival in the region of Plakṣa Prāsravaṇa, an Iṣṭi is performed for the fire god in the form of Agni Kāma 'erotic desire'. In addition, a female slave and a mare who have recently given birth are presented as a gift, along with their offspring, to someone in that place (*PB* 25.10.22; *KŚS* 24.6.5).

In this sacred expedition and cattle drive, Heesterman (1993: 129) sees a reflection of more mundane nomadic activities:

> In reality the Yātsattra reflects the transhumance circuit with fire and cattle. Its sacral aspect has been lifted out of its natural context and ritualistically translated into a daily moving sacrificial ritual that completely fills out the intervals between encampments.

Indeed such nomadic behavior and its age-old antecedents may inform the structure of the rite; but there is more here than just a rote transference of cyclic migration to a sacred realm (and Heesterman undoubtedly does not mean to suggest otherwise). The Yātsattra is not only a pageant but a metaphor. As in the basic Agniṣṭoma and its more typical variants, the ritual is accomplished toward the realization of specific advantage for the sacrificer. Perpetual eastward movement through sacred space, measured out by one *śamyā* toss after another, brings the sacrificer to the heavenly world. According to the *Pañcaviṃśa Brāhmaṇa* (25.10.16), the distance from the ritual's starting point in the desert to its end point at Plakṣa Prāsravaṇa is equivalent to the distance from earth to heaven: "they go to the world of heaven by a journey commensurate with the Sarasvatī" (Caland's translation). It was by this ritual that one Namin Sāpya, king of Videha, passed

[4] A similar Sattra is conducted along the course of the Dṛṣadvatī; see *PB* 25.13.

immediately into the heavenly world (*PB* 25.10.17). The journey by the Sarasvatī is the path to the gods (*TS* 7.2.1.3).

Reminiscent of the stepwise Soma ritual conducted eastward along the Sarasvatī is the legend of Māthava Videgha (noted by Heesterman, 1993: 129), which perhaps embodies a collective memory of Indo-European advances into India. The tale is preserved in *Śatapatha Brāhmaṇa* 1.4.1.10–19. Māthava Videgha carried the fire god Agni Vaiśvānara (Agni 'for all the people') within his mouth. His family priest, Gotama Rāhūgaṇa, addressed Māthava but received no response, Māthava Videgha fearing that Agni would slip through his lips if he should speak. The priest thereupon recited various verses to Agni, and at the mention of "ghee" in one verse (*RV* 5.26.2), Agni bolted from Māthava's mouth. The fire fell to the ground and swept eastward along the Sarasvatī, by (or in) which Māthava had been standing. The fire continued cascading eastward, pursued by Māthava Videgha and his priest, as far as the Sadānīrā river. This river—flowing cold from the Himalayas—the fire did not devour as it had all other rivers in its path. For that reason the Brahmans did not pass beyond that river in olden days, this *Brāhmaṇa* reports, though they had done so by that period which the work recognizes as the "present day."

One could well imagine that the tradition of an ancient eastward advance of Agni along the Sarasvatī provided a certain historical and theological legitimization for situating the ritual journey of the Yātsattra in that geographical space. As we have seen, however, the notion of Soma ritual as a journey is not unique to the sessions along the Sarasvatī. In Heesterman's words (1993: 129):

> The Yātsattras cannot be viewed as a special or exceptional case. . . . It is this mobile pattern that is preserved, in telescoped form and drawn together within the confines of the single *devayajana*, by the basic paradigm of the soma ritual, the Agniṣṭoma.

4.3.2 Sanskrit Dhiṣṇyaḥ

The second feature of the enlarged ritual ground of the Mahāvedi of which we should take note is that of the various hearths raised along the northern and western boundary of that great ritual space, the Dhiṣṇya-hearths. As pointed out above (§4.3), the Āgnīdhrīya (the Dhiṣṇya-hearth located along the northern boundary of the Mahāvedi) and the six fires of the Sadas each belong to a different priest. These seven hearths along with the (new) Āhavanīya on the eastern boundary, standing next to the *yūpa*, and the Mārjāliya on the southern border are said to be raised for the protection of the Soma (*ŚB* 3.6.2.22); the Dhiṣṇyas once guarded Soma in the world beyond, before it was taken by the gods (*TS* 6.3.1.2).

The Sanskrit name for these priestly hearths is an ancient one, descended from Proto-Indo-European cultic terminology. Beyond its nominal use, *Dhiṣṇyaḥ* occurs adjectivally with the meaning 'devout, pious, holy'. Its origins can be traced to the Proto-Indo-European root *$d^{h}eh_{1}s$-. This root provides Armenian *dik'* 'gods' and may well be the source of the Greek word for 'god', θεός. Italic reflexes are well attested and widespread. The suffixed form *$d^{h}eh_{1}s$-yeh_{2}- gives Latin *fēriae* (Early Latin *fēsia*; see Festus, pp. 86, 264M), 'a religious festival, holy day'. Formed with a *to-* suffix, the stem *$d^{h}eh_{1}s$-*to-* develops into Latin *fēstus* 'festive', commonly occurring in the phrase *diēs fēstus* 'holy day'—which certainly preserves in a frozen context an archaic sense of the adjective. The zero-grade *no-* stem, *$d^{h}h_{1}s$-*no-*, gives rise to Latin *fānum* 'plot of consecrated ground' (as in Livy 10.37.15), from which develops the senses 'shrine, temple'; compare Italic cognates with similar meanings, Oscan *fíísnú* (nominative), Umbrian *fesnaf-e* (accusative plural + enclitic postposition), Paelignian *fesn.*

Though earlier investigators seem to have neglected it, there is certainly one other Latin reflex of Proto-Indo-European *$d^{h}eh_{1}s$-. More precisely, this reflex is a variant of one of the above; and this reflex is, of course, Strabo's *fēstī* (φῆστοι), < *$d^{h}eh_{1}s$-*to-*, the sacred "place" (τόπος) where the priests celebrate the Ambarvalia on behalf of the Roman people. The "place" is undoubtedly not a geographic locale, as has been widely assumed, but an element of cultic topography. It is not a town or a village, but an altar or a fire or some similar sacrificial "spot." Strabo's term, τόπος, is commonly used to denote some kind of "place" other than a geographic one. Given the plural morphology of the term, at least in origin it must have denoted a set of such cultic items; and we are reminded immediately of its Sanskrit counterpart and the multiple number of Dhiṣṇya-hearths set up in the Soma sacrifice, each belonging to a priest. One might wonder if such a multiplicity is reflected in Strabo's report that the priests (ἱερομνήμονες) "celebrate the sacred festival both there and, on the same day, at still other places (ἐν ἄλλοις τόποις)—these being boundaries."

Or perhaps by Strabo's day the term *fēstī* had come to denote, by a metonymic shift, the site(s) of the sacred ground consecrated for the celebration of the rite. In this case *fēstī* is semantically equivalent to *fānum* in its earlier sense, which itself undergoes an eventual shift in meaning from 'consecrated ground' to 'temple, shrine'. One would then suspect that the two forms participate in a semantic chain shift, a common enough phenomenon in the history of language. In other words, one advancing meaning displaces the next:

fēstī	⇒	fēstī		
SACRED IMPLEMENTS		SACRED GROUND		
		fānum	⇒	fānum
				SHRINE

Particularly instructive for the development of *fēstī* is the semantic evolution evidenced in Latin singular *aedēs* 'temple, sanctuary, shrine', plural *aedēs* 'house, household' from the Proto-Indo-European root **h_2ei-* 'to burn'. This root, in the extended form **h_2ei-d^h-*, is also the source of Greek αἴθος 'fire, burning heat'; Sanskrit *édhaḥ* 'firewood'; Old Irish *aed* 'fire'; Welsh *aidd* 'heat'; Old Icelandic *eisa* 'fire'. In this instance the denotation of the Latin reflex of **h_2ei-d^h-* clearly shifts from a sense 'fire' to 'place of the fire'.

An additional and partially overlapping consideration is this. Semantic variation between the singular and plural forms of a noun—even as in *aedēs* (singular) 'temple, sanctuary, shrine' beside *aedēs* (plural) 'house, household'—is well known in Latin. Examples include the following, to name but a few: *castrum* 'fortified post', *castra* 'camp'; *fīnis* 'boundary', *fīnēs* 'territory'; *littera* 'letter' (that is, 'alphabetic symbol'), *litterae* 'letter' (that is, 'document', 'scholarship'). In most of the preceding instances, and in other similar examples, the denotative shift moves from particular instance to a broader expression of which the particular instance is a part.[5] In the present case we may be dealing with a variation of the sort *fēstus* 'sacred X', *fēstī* 'sacred ground' (that is, 'ground/space of the sacred X'), where X is a hearth or some similar cultic apparatus.

Notice also that given the interpretation of *fēstus*, *fēstī* proposed here, the Latin term matches the semantics of the Sanskrit exactly. The Proto-Indo-European thematic suffixes **-to-* and **-no-* are both used to derive adjectives from verb roots; their use is essentially equivalent (though presumably at some very early period of Proto-Indo-European linguistic history there was some distinction in that use). Sanskrit *Dhiṣṇyaḥ* preserves the *no-* stem form of the adjective derived from **d^heh_1s-*, Latin *fēstus* the *to-* stem. Both have the same meaning, 'sacred, holy', and both are pressed into service as nouns to name a topographic feature of the cultic ground of sacrifice.

Like Sanskrit, Latin also shows a *no-* stem form—the *fānum* of our chain-

[5] Also, in Latin pluralization is used to derive concrete nouns from abstracts.

shifting model presented above—preserving the archaic zero-grade of such derivatives, *$d^h h_1 s$-no-*. In its earliest attested use, it has been already nominalized to denote the sacred ground; the adjective survives in the prefixed form *profānus* 'profane, secular, polluted'. Beside *profānus*, compare *profēstus*, used of days which are not sacred (on *profānus* and *profēstus*, see Benveniste 1960).

Regardless of semantic specifics, what is most significant is the cognate relationship which exists between a Latin and a Sanskrit term denoting cultic elements associated with religious rites of bounded, bordered sacred spaces. Undoubtedly we must look for a common origin in the vocabulary and practice of Proto-Indo-European ritual.

4.4 THE ROMAN MAHĀVEDI

Like the ritual space of the Vedic Devayajana—the smaller, more confined sacred ground containing the three fundamental fires, the Gārhapatya, Āhavanīya, and Dakṣiṇāgni—so for the Romans there is a more limited arena of the sacred—Rome itself. This is the space within which are positioned the flames of the hearth of Vesta (= the Gārhapatya), burning within her round shrine (*aedēs*) in the Forum Romanum, and the fires of the offering-consuming altars (= the Āhavanīya) of Rome's many temples (*templa*). This is the space at the boundary of which burns the flame of Volcanus (= the Dakṣiṇāgni; see §2.8.1). While for Vitruvius (1.7.1) the placement of Volcanus' temple may be described vis-à-vis the city wall (*extra urbem, extra murum, extra moenia*; compare Plutarch *Quaest. Rom.* 47; for Plutarch the temple is ἔξω πόλεως 'outside the city'), it is certainly the *pomerium* which marks the critical boundary.

The *pomerium* is that sacred boundary of the city beyond which the *auspicia urbana*, the urban auspices, cannot be conducted. Varro (*Ling.* 5.143; *Rust.* 2.1.9–10) describes how at the foundation of a town, the *pomerium* is traced out by ploughing a furrow around the place. A white cow and bull are yoked side by side, pulling a bronze ploughshare, the bull on the right (outside), the cow on the left (inside), animals which are sacrificed following the ploughing, according to Dionysius of Halicarnassus (*Ant. Rom.* 1.88.2; see also Ovid, *Fast.* 4.825–826); the movement is thus counterclockwise. The ploughman wears Sabine ritual dress (Servius, *Aen.* 5.755). In tracing the perimeter of the *pomerium*, when the plough reaches a place where a gate will be installed in the city walls, the ploughshare is lifted off of the ground and carried across that expanse. Plutarch (*Quaest. Rom.* 27) says this is because the gates cannot be consecrated since the bodies of the dead and other such unclean things must necessarily pass through the gates. The trench so furrowed out is called the *fossa* (and is designated the *primigenius sulcus* 'firstborn furrow'; Festus, pp. 236–237M); the displaced dirt, which is thrown to the inside of the furrow (any falling to the outside is tossed to the inside by people following the ploughman; Plutarch, *Rom.* 11.2), is called the *murus*, and within that the city proper will lie. The sacred urban boundary, writes Varro, is thus called the *postmoerium* (*quod erat post murum*), later *pomerium*. For Varro (*Ling.* 5.143) the custom is of Etruscan origin.[6]

Even for Vitruvius, the requirement that certain temples be placed outside the city wall—shrines belonging not only to Volcanus, but to Venus, Mars, and Ceres as well—is mandated in conjunction with augural practice. It is by the direction of the Etruscan Haruspices, those priests responsible

[6]One can hardly read the descriptions of the ploughing of the *pomerium* without being reminded of the ploughing of the sacrificial ground of the fire altar in the Vedic rite of the Agnicayana. In this variant form of the Soma ritual, a large brick fire altar is constructed within the Mahāvedi. Prior to laying the bricks, the ground of the altar is prepared by ritual ploughing. As described in *Śatapatha Brāhmaṇa* 7.2.2.1–21, the plough is made of *udumbara* wood; to it are yoked oxen (a team of six, twelve, or twenty-four)—first the ox on the right, then the one to its left. The furrow is said to be a womb, into which seed is cast. The body of the altar is square in shape (bisected by an east-west and a north-south axis), with appended portions to the north and south (the "left" and "right wing" respectively) and to the west (the "tail"). Ploughing marks out only the body of the altar. Beginning at the southwest corner, a furrow is ploughed along the southern border, the plough being drawn from west to east. Then returning to the same starting point, a furrow is ploughed along the western border, from south to north. The northern border is next ploughed, from west to east; and finally the eastern border, from north to south. Each of these four furrows is ploughed while reciting prayer; the succeeding ploughings will be made in silence. The plough is then pulled northward, bisecting the space along the north-south axis; next it is drawn diagonally through the space from the southwest corner to the northeast, then through the center from east to west, and finally from the northwest to the southeast corner. In each of these four directions, three furrows are ploughed. The oxen are then released to the northeast and presented to the Adhvaryu; the plough is placed on the Utkara, a refuse mound located just beyond the northern boundary of the Mahāvedi. Frazer (1929, vol. 3: 383–384) cites numerous examples of eastern European folk traditions which involve ploughing an encompassing furrow in order to keep away illness or some other misfortune. Adhering to his typological method, Frazer (p. 384) thus sees in the Roman tradition a similar purpose: ". . . we may conjecture that the furrow drawn round the site of the future Rome was intended to guard its inhabitants against the incursions of those invisible foes whom stone walls were powerless to exclude."

for examining the liver and other entrails of sacrificed animals (see §1.8), that these temples (*fana*) are positioned without the city (Vitruvius 1.7.1).[7] In the case of Volcanus, the rationale is one which invokes a combination of theological and pragmatic elements:

> uti . . . , Volcanique vi e moenibus religionibus et sacrificiis evocata ab timore incendiorum aedificia videantur liberari
>
> And so that . . . , the power of Volcanus having been called forth with rites and sacrifices outside of the walled city, the buildings might seem to be free from the fear of fires.

In regard to inherited Indo-European ritual at Rome, Volcanus has another flame which may be of even greater significance. As we noted above, in Dumézil's comparison of the Vedic and Roman doctrines of the three fires, he draws attention not only to the extramural temple of Volcanus, but also to the Volcanal (see §2.8.1). The latter is an ancient shrine of the fire god that stood in the Area Volcani, at the base of the Capitoline hill. It now appears that the Volcanal is to be identified with the sanctuary of the *Lapis Niger*, constructed perhaps in the early sixth century.[8] As Dumézil pointed out, in an early period it likely stood outside or very near the sacred boundary. Again, the crucial line of demarcation is not the city wall but, in this instance, the ancient *pomerium* around the Palatine (on which, see Holloway 1994: 101–102; Richardson 1992: 293–296). The Volcanal's liminal situation with regard to the sacred boundaries even in the sixth century is supported by the apparent prolonged exclusion of the neighboring Capitoline from within the perimeter of the *pomerium* (see Richardson 1992: 70, 330). The inscribed cippus found within the sanctuary bears one of the earliest-known Latin texts—continuing to resist secure interpretation. Richardson's comments regarding the stone are of interest in the context of the present study:

> In view of its unusual material, obviously foreign and unsuitable for inscribing, it is more likely to be a boundary stone than anything else,

[7]While the positioning of the flame of Volcanus beyond or at the cultic border of Rome follows, by our analysis, from deeply archaic ritual practice, the requirement that Mars, Venus, and Ceres must likewise be worshipped at temples beyond the city walls, whatever the nature of Etruscan involvement in the matter, must certainly be seen as a secondary (or set of secondary) developments; see the comments of Capdeville 1995: 340, n. 3.

[8]See Cornell 1995: 94–95, 162–163; Coarelli 1992: 161–178; *LTUR*, vol. 5: 209–211; Richardson 1992: 432); on the evidence for a possible cult presence at the site predating the sixth century, see Holloway 1994: 86. On the Volcanal, see also the several comments in Capdeville 1995: 86–87 and passim.

and the inscription on it is then likely to be a curse on anyone who moved it. The appearance of the name Jupiter and words such as *sakros* and *iouxmenta* also supports this notion. The alphabet is close to the version of the Greek alphabet in use in southern Etruria and the Faliscan territory in the late seventh and sixth centuries, with certain additions.[9]

In Vedic India the restricted sacred ground of the three fires, the space of the Devayajana, has adjacent to it a much larger sacred space, the Mahāvedi. In Rome a homologous spatial and cultic juxtaposition exists. The smaller sacred space of the Roman city, defined by the boundary of the *pomerium*, is contiguous with a great sacred ground, the Ager Romanus. In India, the sacred spaces, small and large, are temporary structures—in effect, encampments established, then broken up to be established again, preserving in ritual the pastoral nomadism of those early Indo-Europeans who made their way into south Asia, and of yet even more remote Proto-Indo-European ancestors. Contiguous temporary spaces have given way in the landed society of the Romans to a sacred geometry of a permanent nature. The unmoving Devayajana-space of urban Rome lies at all points adjacent to the encircling Mahāvedi of the Ager Romanus. Whether by design or by a process of accretion as distant altars came to be perceived as so many cultic orbitals lying along a continuous ring, the great sacrificial arena has become all encompassing.

Several of these distant altars—consuming fires set up at the far end of the great sacrificial space, each a distal "fourth fire" separated from the proximal canonical three by cultic space—we have already identified. Perhaps there were others. Each of the identified sites lies along a Roman road, the path of entry leading into and through the great sacred space, permanent in nature, but fully corresponding to the routes by which priests, sacrificers, and cultic accoutrements advance from the temporary ground of the Vedic Devayajana into the Mahāvedi and on to its eastern border where burns the "fourth fire." Let us consider several of these again in turn.

4.5 THE PUBLIC TERMINALIA

As we saw, on February 23, the public rites of the god Terminus are celebrated at the sixth milestone from Rome along the Via Laurentina. As the *yūpa*, the Vedic sacrificial post, stands on the far boundary of the Mahāvedi, so Terminus stands on the distal boundary of the Ager Romanus, and there

[9]Richardson 1992: 268. See Richardson for references. See also Dumézil 1979: 259–293.

he is venerated. From Ovid's description of the rite (see *Fast.* 2.679–684) one might wonder whether the milestone itself is the celebrated *terminus*:

> Illa lanigeri pecoris tibi, Termine, fibris
> sacra videt fieri sextus ab Urbe lapis.
>
> Its sixth stone from the city sees a woolly sheep's guts
> Being sacrificed, Terminus, to you.

Perhaps this is so; or, in light of the reports of the *gromatici*, we might suspect that an affiliated *terminus sacrificalis* stood close by (see §2.8.2). In any event, some *terminus* stands at this site, the palpable expression of the boundary god, and the positional equivalent and evolutionary homologue of the Vedic *yūpa*.

We noted, in passing, Ovid's curious and antithetical remark: within the context of the state celebration of the boundary god, observed at what we have now identified as the boundary of the Ager Romanus—the great sacred space—the poet asserts that Rome has no boundary, and does so while recognizing that other nations are so bounded.

> Gentibus est aliis tellus data limite certo:
> Romanae spatium est Urbis et orbis idem.
>
> For other nations the earth has fixed boundaries;
> Rome's city and the world are the same space.

If the earth is segmented by state boundaries (defining those states), how then can Rome have none? Ovid's words are tantalizing—at the same time oxymoronic and revealing. Are these lines drawn from the liturgy of the occasion, as are his prayerful verses on the celebration of the Robigalia? While one may be inclined to brush aside Ovid's sentiment as so much nationalistic rhetoric (whatever his purpose for invoking such sentiment), they likely have theological content, rooted in a Proto-Indo-European doctrine that equally finds expression in the Vedic view of the Mahāvedi as conquered space and the interpretation of the *yūpa* which stands at its farthest point. Thus, for example, at *Śatapatha Brāhmaṇa* 3.7.2.1 we read (after Eggeling 1995, pt. 2: 175):

> Verily as large as the *vedi* is, so large is the earth. The *yūpas* are thunderbolts; and by means of these thunderbolts he obtains possession of this earth, and excludes his enemies from sharing therein.

And, at 3.7.1.14, we find (after Eggeling 1995, pt. 2: 171):

> He raises the *yūpa* with, "With your crest you have touched the sky; with your middle you have filled the air; with your foot you have steadied the earth;"—the *yūpa* being a thunderbolt, [he raises it] for the conquering of these worlds; with that thunderbolt he gains these worlds, and deprives his enemies of their share in these worlds.

Through the journey into the great sacred space—Mahāvedi or Ager Romanus—bounded by *yūpa* or *terminus*, an unbounded possession of earth is claimed.[10]

4.6 THE PUBLIC AMBARVALIA

Between the fifth and sixth milestones from Rome along a road of, unfortunately, undisclosed identity, the priests that Strabo calls ἱερομνήμονες celebrate the state festival of the Ambarvalia, or Ambarvia by Strabo's record (see §3.3.1). The festival, as we have seen, is celebrated not only here, at this boundary place, but at several other boundary locales as well and on the same day. These places being boundaries, *termini* are certainly involved. Moreover, as we have argued (see §4.3.2), other cultic implements having homologous structures found within the Vedic Mahāvedi are also present: *fēstī*, quite probably hearths, cognate in name and likely in function to the Dhiṣṇya-hearths of the several priests of the Soma rituals.

Viewed within the context of the Ager Romanus as the great sacred space—ritually comparable and evolutionarily homologous to the Vedic Mahāvedi—the name of the festival takes on new significance. An idea that one commonly encounters in the scholarly literature on the Ambarvalia is that the state ritual essentially replicates the private rites of field lustration, but on a much larger geographic scale, with the result that a circumambulation using the *suovetaurilia*, of the sort described by Cato (see §3.3.3), must necessarily be omitted from or in some way modified in the public observance. For example, Kilgour (1938: 228) writes:

> . . . there is the practical difficulty of conducting such a procession round the boundary of the Ager Romanus once, much less three times. Even in the earliest days, when Rome had just become a city, this must have caused a rite so elaborate, if it were ever conceived, to be very early abandoned.

[10]There is of course no mention of a flame in Ovid's few lines on the public Terminalia, but given general sacrificial practice and Ovid's lengthier description of the private rites in the preceding lines, a flame is undeniably present.

And then, commenting on Strabo's account of the public Ambarvalia (p. 229):

> There, it is not suggested that any circumambulation of the Ager Romanus took place, but rather, as we should expect, that sacrifices were made at a particular spot or spots on the boundary, the whole ceremony being intended as a symbolical lustration of the Ager.

Quite similarly, Scullard (1981: 125) observes:

> When Rome was a group of Iron Age villages, victims could easily be driven round the bounds of each settlement and later around the united town. But as Rome grew, it would become physically impossible to follow her expanding boundaries beyond a few miles: instead sacrifices were apparently made at certain fixed points.

Warde Fowler (1899: 125), speaking of the Fratres Arvales and the Ambarvalia in the same breath, remarks:

> . . . it is almost certain that, as the Roman territory continued to increase, the brethren must have dropped the duty of driving victims round it, for obvious reasons.

The reader gets the picture.

It is indeed most improbable that the *suovetaurilia* were ever driven around the perimeter of the Ager Romanus. Anyone familiar with handling the modern domesticated boar, presumably bred to be somewhat more docile than his ancient ancestor, can hardly imagine getting such a creature around even a single field. The Vedic rites which we are using for comparison suggest something very different, and this something different is probably preserved in the Latin name of the event, Ambarvalia. The morphology of the term is straightforward, being a derivative of *amb(i)-* + *arvum*; the semantics of the term may, however, be somewhat less obvious.

Latin *arvum* denotes 'field', 'ploughed land' as well as simply 'ground, territory, countryside'. An Umbrian cognate survives in **arvam-en**, accusative singular plus the postposition **-en**, meaning 'to the field', as well as locative **arven** 'in the field'. The Umbrian forms are preserved in the rites of the priests called the Atiedian Brothers—recorded in the Iguvine Tables—and occur in the following context (table III 7–14; text and translation from Poultney 1959: 202–204):

> **iinuk : uhtur : vapeře : / kumnakle : sistu : sakre : uvem : uhtur : / teitu : puntes : terkantur : inumek : sakre : / uvem : urtas : puntes : fratrum :**

upetuta : / inumek : via : mersuva : arvamen : etuta : / erak : pir : persklu : uřetu : sakre : uvem : / kletra : fertuta : aituta : arven : kletram : / amparitu : eruk : esunu : futu :

Then the *auctor* shall sit on the stone seat in the meeting-place. The *auctor* shall designate a young pig and a sheep, the groups of five shall inspect them, then the groups of five rising shall accept the young pig and the sheep. Then they shall go by the accustomed way to the field. On the way load the fire [with incense] with a prayer. They shall lift and carry the young pig and the sheep on a litter. Set up the litter in the field. Then the sacrifice shall take place.

The "field" is clearly a place of ritual significance, though of uncertain location; following Rosenzweig (1937: 18–19), Poultney (1959: 203) suggests it may be "the level plain near the Roman theatre where the [Iguvine] Tables were discovered." After the victims are taken to this field, they are then sacrificed, but not in the field, rather in a grove (or temple, **vukum**). The **sakre** ('young pig'; compare Untermann 2000: 650–651) is offered to Jupiter (**Iuvepatre**) and the sheep to the god Pomonus Poplicus.

The Latin preverb *amb(i)-* means 'round, about'; its sense is less fundamentally 'around': "Le sens est plutôt «de chaque côté de» que «autour» (*circum* et gr. περί) proprement dit" (*DELL*: 26). Both senses characterize the Proto-Indo-European etymon *$^*amb^hi$, $^*m̥b^hi$* (*WP*, vol. 1: 54). In Latin words made with *amb(i)*, the meaning is commonly that of (indirect) movement within and through some sphere of activity—sometimes this is the sole sense, sometimes it co-occurs with the sense of movement around the periphery. Let us consider a few examples (in all instances, see *OLD*):

1 *Ambages* (from *amb(i)-* + *ago*) denotes chiefly 'a meandering', 'a wandering about', also some sort of evasive movement or discourse; similarly, *ambiguus* is 'wavering, having uncertain direction'.
2 *Ambio* (from *amb(i)-* + *eo*) is 'to visit (in rotation)', 'to go round', or 'to bypass'; also 'to encircle, surround'; similarly, *ambitiosus* means 'winding, twisting, embracing'.
3 *Ambulo* (from *amb(i)-* + the Latin reflex of Proto-Indo-European *$^*h_2elh_2$-* 'to wander, go aimlessly' (*LIV* 264), not surviving as a simplex form in Latin) means 'to walk, go about, walk abroad, to march'; it does not mean *'to go around a perimeter'.
4 *Amfractus* (from *amb(i)-* + *frango*) denotes 'a bend', 'a winding course, a turn in the road'; also 'the circular course of a heavenly body'.
5 *Anquiro* (from *amb(i)-* + *quaero*) is 'to seek, search for'.

If we are correct in identifying the functional equivalence and common historical origin of the great sacred spaces of Vedic India and of Rome, ritual movements within the sacred space of the Vedic Mahāvedi suggest that *ambarvalis* originally denotes the movements of priests (and sacrificer?) within the great sacred ground of the Ager Romanus—movement not around its periphery, but movement across the space from the proximal boundary of the *pomerium* to the distal boundary of the Ager Romanus. The recurring Latin use of *amb(i)-* in the sense of 'meandering', 'twisting'—that is, 'from side to side'—suggests that the archaic ambarvalic journey is not a straight passage through the sacred space, but involves priestly trips here and there, just as in India, perhaps visits to several *fēstī* and/or other features of cultic topography within the great sacred ground. And perhaps the sense of Strabo's claim that the public Ambarvalia are celebrated at various places that are boundaries is this—that the priests in their ambarvalic journeying move from one *terminus* to another within the great sacred space, or that the Ambarvalia in toto involves priests or teams of priests wandering through the Ager Romanus, individually concluding their sacred journeys at one of several *termini* marking the distal boundary of this space, as many as are required for properly observing this public festival.

There is yet another consideration, and possibly one of even greater significance for the Latin semantics. In Vedic ritual the very journey of priests from the small space of the Devayajana into the great space of the Mahāvedi is itself not one which traverses the shortest possible distance. When fire from the Āhavanīya is placed in a pan of gravel and conducted eastward to the Uttaravedi at the distal end of the Mahāvedi (the Agnipraṇayana; see §4.3), the route which is followed is an indirect one which leads from the conjunction of the two contiguous spaces, up along the northern edge of the Mahāvedi, and over and down to the Uttaravedi (see Eggeling 1995: pt. 2: 122, n. 3; for the circuitous route followed by the priests in the Agniṣṭoma which Martin Haug witnessed in the mid-nineteenth century, see the end map in Haug 1922).[11]

Similar is the route of the priests and sacrificer as they pass from

[11]In 1863, Haug (1922: iv–v) wrote: ". . . I made the greatest efforts to obtain oral information from some of those few Brāhmaṇs who are known by the name Śrotriyas, or Śrautis, and who alone are the preservers of the sacrificial mysteries as they descended from the remotest times. The task was no easy one, and no European scholar in this country before me even succeeded in it. This is not to be wondered at; for the proper knowledge of the ritual is everywhere in India now rapidly dying out, and in many parts, chiefly in those under British rule, it has already died out. Besides, the communication of these mysteries to foreigners is regarded by old devout Brāhmaṇs (and they alone have the knowledge) as such a monstrous profanation of their sacred creed, and fraught with the most serious consequences to their position, that they can only, after long efforts, and under payment of very handsome sums, be prevailed upon to give information. Not-

the space of the Devayajana into and through the Mahāvedi in the rite of Agnīṣomapraṇayana, "the carrying forth of fire and Soma"—that rite which we have seen, in Heesterman's words (1993: 126), to be "pictured as a wide-ranging, conquering progress" (see §4.3.1). Following the construction of the various sheds and hearths within the Mahāvedi and the eastward journey of the Soma carts, and prior to the erection of the *yūpa* and the offering of the animal sacrifice, fire, Soma, and various movable cultic implements[12] are transported from the small space into the large. With Agni 'fire' leading the way—warding off evil spirits, striking down those who hate, gaining riches and conquering the enemy (*ŚB* 3.6.3.11–12)—the procession of fire and Soma moves into the Mahāvedi, heading first to the northern-most Dhiṣṇya-hearth, the Āgnīdhrīya (see §4.3). After the Adhvaryu lays fire on that hearth, the procession continues to the north side of the Uttaravedi at the eastern boundary of the Mahāvedi, and then west and south to the Soma-cart shed (the Havirdhāna; *ŚB* 3.6.3.12–21).

The use of Latin *ambarvalis* to denote ritual movement through the great sacred space of the Ager Romanus linguistically replicates the attested circuitous movements of priests and sacrificers within the corresponding Vedic ritual space. Both point back to a common Proto-Indo-European practice of a journey made around and about a sacred ground delimited for sacrifice. Each is evidence of an internalization of a single ancestral tradition.

The deeply archaic prayer preserved for us by Cato (*Agr.* 141), recited at a rite of land lustration (see §3.3.3), appears clearly to support this interpretation of a wandering journey within the sacred arena:

> Cum divis volentibus quodque bene eveniat, mando tibi, Mani, uti illace suovitaurilia fundum agrum terramque meam quota ex parte sive circumagi sive circumferenda censeas, uti cures lustrare.
>
> So that each [victim] may be allotted propitiously to the good-willed gods, I bid you, Manius, that you determine in which part that *suovitaurilia* is be driven or carried around my farm, land (*ager*) and earth—that you take care to purify.

This movement of the *suovitaurilia* within the sacred space of this pri-

---

withstanding, at length I succeeded in procuring the assistance of a Śrauti, who not only had performed the small sacrifices, such as the Darśapūrnamāsa Iṣṭi, but who had even officiated as one of the Hotars, or Udgātars, at several Soma sacrifices, which are now very rarely brought. In order to obtain a thorough understanding of the whole course of an Iṣṭi and a Soma sacrifice, I induced him (about 18 months ago) to show me in some secluded place in my premises, the principal ceremonies."

[12]See, for example, the set of items enumerated in *Śatapatha Brāhmaṇa* 3.6.3.10.

vate rite is not simply a driving around the periphery. The journey of the threefold sacrifice is not predetermined. A god of the ground, Manius, is invoked to lead the victims in the proper path though the sacred space of the farm—whatever path that might be—in order to ensure or maximize the efficacy of the purificatory rite.

Cato's rite of land lustration is certainly part and parcel of a set of Roman ambarvalic rites. This is widely recognized. As we proposed above, the members of this set are synchronic variants of the same sort as the many variants of the Soma ritual in Vedic India. Both sets, Roman and Vedic, have a common origin in the cultic life of their common ancestors, the Proto-Indo-Europeans. There is, however, a fundamental difference in the internal composition of the two sets; and this difference follows from the nature of the Roman and Vedic societies. The Vedic rites preserve basic features characteristic of a pastoral society and its nomadism. The site of the Gārhapatya must be swept of animal dung before the flame is established. The sacred spaces, both the small space of the Devayajana and the great space of the Mahāvedi, are temporary structures, put down and taken up like the encampments of a people on the move. The various forms of the Soma rite all involve the same kinds of spaces, however. All are variations on the theme of the Agniṣṭoma with an Iṣṭi and subsequent rites conducted within the Mahāvedi.

Things are different at Rome. In the landed society of the Romans, not nomadic but sessile, it is the constant and unmoving temple of Vesta, where no animals are kept, that must be annually cleansed of "dung" (*stercus*; a fossilized remnant of the archaic Indo-European procedure survives and is observed annually; see §4.12). The small sacred space, that within the *pomerium*, and the great space, that lying between the *pomerium* and the far boundary of the Ager Romanus, are of permanence; though the boundary of the *pomerium* and that of the Ager Romanus certainly shifted at times. Variation among related rites is more complex in Rome; it is probably not so in terms of casuistic complexity, but it is so to the extent that variation involves not only formal permutations of ritual elements, but the use of different planes and regions of the total sacred space of Roman society. One might say that Roman ritual variation is more complex geometrically.

The various rites and ceremonies which involve some sacred locale on the distal boundary of the Ager Romanus geographically constitute so many ritual wedges of that great sacred space. However, similar rites are celebrated in both the private and public domain, within more confined areas which are superimposed on the small and great sacred grounds. Such rites are celebrated on the many plots of privately owned land and in public subdivisions of urban space—many of those same spaces with which one normally associates a presence of Lares. The early Indo-European rites of the sacred movable spaces of a pastoralist people, ceremonies which involve a ritual questing journey into a sacred ground as revealed in Vedic tradition, have given rise to Roman rites of fixed space, already subdued and possessed.

In the case of Roman rites celebrated on privately owned property—ambarvalic rites of field lustration—the role of the sacred ground has undergone a theological shift. No longer is it only the medium of the sacred journey and sacrifice; instead, it has become the object of the sacrificial ritual as well. No longer is it the space invaded so as to facilitate a metaphysical possession of the earth; it is now actually possessed ground in need of protection and purification. The space of ambarvalic lustration remains the arena of the sacred, but it is now possessed space. As a consequence, the boundary marker of the sacred ritual ground is no longer a temporary, even movable, cultic implement—as the Vedic *yūpa* remains. In Rome it has become the fixed *terminus*, permanent in nature, protected by the law of Numa, tampered with on pain of death. Yet the longed-for result of the ritual conducted within the space so bounded remains in essence unchanged. Just as the Vedic sacrificer journeys into the Mahāvedi, all the way to the *yūpa*, touching it, even mounting it, in order to obtain blessings of increase and prosperity, so for the same blessing does the Roman landowner lustrate his fields. What is more, annually the landowner and his neighbor honor Terminus at the *terminus* erected on their shared boundary. And at the public festival celebrated on the same day, it would seem, the old doctrine of metaphysical possession of the earth, accomplished by a journey to the limits of the great sacred space, is dusted off and trotted out (see §4.5).

Let us return briefly to the matter of the presence of sacrificial victims at the public Ambarvalia. As we noted in §3.3.6.3, Strabo provides no indication that his public ritual is one that entails the use of the *suovetaurilia*; though, as we have witnessed, this is commonly assumed. Such an assumption may or may not be warranted; we observed in §3.3.5 that the *suovetaurilia* and circumambulatory rites are separate ritual components inherited in Rome and Vedic India from Proto-Indo-European tradition, and we examined variation in these features among the several "ambarvalia-type" rituals. Regardless of whether or not Strabo's priests are offering the set of victims which consists of a boar, ram, and bull, his use of θυσία to denote the rite celebrated (οἵ θ' ἱερομνήμονες θυσίαν ἐπιτελοῦσιν) certainly reveals that sacrifice is being made at these various boundary locales, as we would expect.

4.7 THE ARVAL RITES OF DEA DIA (I)

The next of the sacred altar-sites on the distal boundary of the great sacred space, the Ager Romanus, is that of the grove of the Fratres Arvales, found at the fifth milestone from Rome on the Via Campana. The uncharacteristically richly detailed record which has survived of this festival reveals to us a spatial progression remarkably reminiscent of that found in the Vedic Agniṣṭoma and related rites.

Just as the Vedic rites commence within the space of the Devayajana, so the Roman festival of the Arvales begins within Rome, that is within the small sacred ground bounded by the *pomerium*, the space of the three canonical fires. Recall that the first day's rites are celebrated at the home of the Magister of the Fratres Arvales (*domi ad magistrum, in domo apud magistrum*, and so on; see Scheid 1990: 173). Or, in the case of a few exceptions, elsewhere in urban Rome. For example, in AD 38, the location is the *domus quae fuit Ti. Caesaris aui* (likely the palace of Caligula; Scheid 1990: 174); on three occasions, the site is on the Palatine, *in aede divorum.*[13] Addressing the typical case, Scheid (1990: 176) sees the Roman locale as essentially an urban extension of the grove of the goddess:

> La similitude entre les banquets consommés au *lucus* et ceux qui se déroulaient dans la résidence du président nous permettent par ailleurs de considérer celle-ci comme une extension urbaine du sanctuaire de La Magliana, bref comme un lieu cultuel. De la même façon que la maison du flamine de Jupiter était sacrée, les maisons des arvales revêtaient de par la fonction du maître de maison un statut particulier.

On this first day of the annual Arval rites, the priests make offerings to the goddess—incense and wine, along with green and parched grains[14] and loaves of bread decorated with laurel. They anoint an image of the goddess; they sit down in chairs (*cathedrae*) and receive gifts (*sportulae*) of one hundred denarii. After midday, the Fratres, having bathed, are again seated, whereupon they retire to couches and feast at the home of the Magister.

[13]For a list of those years in which some other Roman site was used, see Scheid 1990: 175, n. 14.

[14]The priests are said to have touched the grains (*fruges virides et aridas contigerunt et panes laureatos*); on the ritual significance of which, see Scheid 1990: 522–525.

After the banquet they offer libations of incense and wine, which are carried to the altar by acolytes—boys whose parents are both still alive, sons of senators—and by public slaves (*publici*). The priests receive gifts (*sportulae*), distribute rose petals, and speak words of good fortune.

When the sun rises on the second day of the festival of Dea Dia, we find the Magister and the other Fratres not in Rome but in the grove of the goddess five miles away, preparing to sacrifice two pigs to the deity. Recall that a day has elapsed between the first and second days of ritual observance. Between the time of the completion of the ceremonies at the home of the Magister in Rome and the beginning of those in the goddess' grove, not only has time progressed by more than twenty-four hours, but the priests of the goddess have processed into and through the sacred ground of the Ager Romanus. Whatever the form and nature of this procession, it is a journey beyond the *pomerium* to a cultic point on the distal boundary of that great sacred space. Within the context of inherited common Indo-European cultic practice, the parallel which this pilgrimage presents to the ritual activity of Vedic priests and sacrificers within the Devayajana and their subsequent journey from that place into and across the Mahāvedi is clear.

Beyond this passage through the great sacred space—however it was accomplished—there is, as noted earlier (see §3.3.6.1), a processional act conspicuously recorded in the Acta of the Fratres Arvales. After singing the Carmen Arvale, the priests of Dea Dia withdraw to the tetrastyle of the grove for a sacrificial banquet. The dishes of the first course of the banquet are carried to the tetrastyle in *more pompae*, 'in processional style' ("pour souligner le caractère rituel de ce banquet"; Scheid 1990: 633). With them are brought beakers (*urnalia*) of sweet wine (*mulsum*)—one of these 13-liter vessels for each priest (!)—and *campanae*, items of uncertain identification but probably Campanian vessels. The measure of wine provided for each priest is so great that it could hardly have been consumed in one sitting. Thus surmises Scheid (1990: 633):

> Or cette quantité de vin dépassait nettement les capacités d'un convive—même s'il en cédait une partie à son *kalator* —, et il faut conclure soit que les *urnalia* des arvales contenaient moins de treize litres, soit que le vin distribué représentait un don qui n'avait pas à être consommé entièrement au cours du banquet.

Regardless, the fruit of Liber can be said to be present in this ritual moment in a conspicuous fashion. In addition, at the conclusion of the banquet, each of those present receives a gift of one hundred denarii. Afterward come the *ludi*—the Magister ascends above the starting gate and gives the signal for the chariots (two- and four-horse) and "jumpers" (*desultores*; see §4.9.2). Following the *ludi*, the Fratres make a return trip across the Ager Romanus to Rome and the home of the Magister for offerings of incense and wine, more banqueting (notably with desserts), and again each of the Fratres receives a gift of one hundred denarii.

The locale for the rites of the third day is again that of the small sacred space of urban Rome. The priests gather once more at the residence of the Magister for a banquet, one which in large measure replicates that of the first day of the ritual. ("À quelques nuances près, la structure du banquet de la troisième journée est identique à celle de *l'eplum* du premier jour"; Scheid 1990: 647.) During the meal, libations are made with incense and wine. The Fratres Arvales then make an offering of grains with the help of *kalatores*, priestly assistants, and these offerings are carried to the altar by, again, boys whose parents are both still alive, sons of senators, and attendant public slaves (see Scheid 1990: 648). Following is a curious ritual of fire: lamps are lit and implements identified as *Tuscanicae* are seemingly "touched" with the lamps; the Fratres then have their *kalatores* deliver these *Tuscanicae* to their individual homes. A dessert course then follows; and garlands, ointments, and yet another gift of one hundred denarii are distributed.

In the instance of the Arval rites of Dea Dia we are in the fortunate and unusual position of possessing a somewhat detailed record of the ancient procedures—detailed, that is, in the face of the sort of documentation typically available for Roman rituals, but certainly paling in comparison to the level of extraordinary detail preserved in the records of the Vedic sacred ceremonies. We have in the Acta of the Fratres Arvales the chronicle of a ritual that begins in the small sacred space, moves into the great ground of the Ager Romanus, and then returns for its completion to the small space in which it began. Similar procedures of beginning and ending, oscillating between small and great space in continuous ritual, may have characterized other rites also celebrated at the distal boundary of the Ager Romanus—the public Terminalia and Ambarvalia, to name two obvious candidates—but no description of comparable detail has survived in the case of these other rites.

We will return to the Arval rites and examine them in yet greater detail (see §4.9). First, however, we must turn again to Vedic India and the Agniṣṭoma.

4.8 THE SOMA-PRESSING DAY

The priests have journeyed into the great sacred space of the Mahāvedi. Completed are the days of preparation and the three Upasad days (the days of, inter alia, acquisition of the Soma, preparation of the altars, erection of the various sheds and the *yūpa*, celebration of the rites described above). It is now the day of the Soma feast, when Soma plants will be pressed and the Soma beverage consumed and offered. The centerpiece of this day of myriad ritual is the midday pressing of Soma (Mādhyandinasavana; *ŚB* 4.3.3.1–4.3.4.33), bracketed by a morning pressing (Prātahsavana) and an evening pressing (Tṛtīyasavana; *ŚB* 4.3.5.1–4.5.2.18). Each of these three events is described below; the descriptions are summary rather then exhaustive in the presentation of ritual detail.[15] To provide the reader with a guidepost, some seminal elements of the pressing day which will prove to be of particular interest to us are outlined in figure 4.2.

- Soma-pressing day
  - Morning pressing
    - sacrifice of two goats (Ṣoḍaśin)
  - Midday pressing
    - sacrifice of ram (Ṣoḍaśin)
    - offering of gold at old Āhavanīya
    - Indra and the Maruts
    - Soma and *surā* (Vājapeya)
    - chariot race (Vājapeya)
  - Evening pressing
    - sacrifice of sterile cow
    - movement out of the Mahāvedi
    - offering of cow's embryo to Maruts
    - consumption of goat

FIGURE 4.2. *Selected elements of the pressing day of the Vedic Agniṣṭoma*

[15]In addition to the sources cited below, on the Soma pressings, and the *Agniṣṭoma* generally, see especially Caland and Henry 1906–1907.

4.8.1 The morning pressing

The day begins with prayers to Agni, god of fire, Uṣas, the dawn goddess (cognate and equivalent to Latin *Aurora*, Greek 'Hώς), and her twins sons, the Aśvins. Next follows the morning pressing of Soma in two parts—a preliminary pressing followed by the Mahābhiṣava, 'great pressing' (which itself consists of three rounds of pressing).[16] Subsequent to the pressing of the Soma, there occurs a procession of priests and sacrificer; while the Hotar remains seated at the Soma-cart shed, a column led by the Adhvaryu, followed by five other priests and the sacrificer, each holding the clothing of the preceding person, moves northward within the Mahāvedi toward the altar. Then positioning themselves close to the Cātvāla, the pit just beyond the northern boundary of the Mahāvedi (at the northeastern corner), the Adhvaryu throws a stalk of grass toward the pit and the *Bahiṣpavamāna stotra* is chanted (*ŚB* 4.2.5.1–7; Caland and Henry 1906: 171–172).

A goat is sacrificed to Agni, as a part of the rites of the morning pressing, and it will be cooked throughout the day.[17] If the particular variant of the Agniṣṭoma celebrated is that called the Ukthya (characterized by the chanting and recitation of five, rather than three, sets of *stotras* (hymns) and *śastras* (praise songs) during the evening pressing, and so having the same number of such sets as the two earlier pressings), then *two* goats are sacrificed. In this instance, the second victim is offered both to Agni and to Indra (see *ŚB* 4.2.5.14).

In addition to the above rites, the morning pressing includes various cake offerings and offerings of other grain products as well as, of course, the numerous priestly libations and draughts of Soma. An element common to the three pressings of the day is the ritual movement called *sarpaṇa* (a 'creeping'; compare Latin *serpo* 'to crawl, to wind, twist, to creep'; Greek ἕρπω 'to creep, to crawl'). The term connotes the movement of priests to and from the Dhiṣṇya-hearths in the Sadas. According to the *Kātyāyana Śrauta Sūtra* (9.6.33), at the time of the morning pressing, the movement is to be made in a sitting position; during the midday pressing the priests proceed while assuming a bent-over posture; and for the evening pressing they are to walk erect. While sitting by the several fires in the Sadas, to which they have crept, the priests consume their cups of Soma.

[16]For the rites associated with the morning pressing, see *ŚB* 3.9.3.1–4.3.2.13; Keith 1998a: 328–329; Renou 1957: 105.

[17]On the previous day, the final of the Upasad days of the *Agniṣṭoma*; a goat was sacrificed to both Agni and Soma.

4.8.2 The midday pressing

The midday pressing belongs almost exclusively (*niṣkevalya*) to the warrior god Indra (*ŚB* 4.3.3.6). In conjunction with Indra, ritual attention is also paid to the Maruts—thus Indra Marutvat is invoked, Marutvatīya cups of Soma are drawn, and so on. The Maruts[18] are a band of warrior deities, sons of Rudra (later Śiva), who are especially closely linked to Indra as comrades-in-arms, but are at times also associated with Viṣṇu, and also with Parjanya, god of rain and thundering storm, or Trita Āptya, another warrior deity affiliated with and showing similarities to Indra. Their mother is said to be a cow, identified with the goddess Pṛśni. In *Rig Veda* 1.133.6 their number is said to be "thrice-seven," while in the *Rig Veda* 8.85.8 they are "thrice-sixty." They are known for their singing, which brings strength to Indra, and they play the pipe. In domestic ritual, offerings are made to the Maruts on the thresholds.[19]

The Maruts are connected with rain and storm. They are described as bright, wearing ornaments and helmets of shining gold, cloaked in rain, riding in golden chariots, drawn by the winds or bay steeds; lightening is their weapon—their spear—as well as a golden ax. They bring rain, accompanied by lightning and thunder. They are commonly identified as the winds, and their name comes to provide a common noun denoting 'wind', *maruta-*. According to the *Atharva Veda* (18.2.21–22), the Maruts carry the dead on pleasant winds into the presence of the Pitaras (the Manes), sprinkling the dead one with rain.

The general form of the midday pressing is much like that of the morning pressing. There again occur the chanting of verses and numerous libations and draughts of Soma. The midday pressing is also the occasion for the Dadhigharma, a libation of hot milk combined with sour milk. It is during this pressing that the priests receive gifts, *dakṣiṇās* (their fees), from the sacrificer; an offering of gold is made at the Gārhapatya fire (the old Āhavanīya) and the gifts are distributed to the officiating priests. According to the *Śatapatha Brāhmaṇa* (see 4.3.4.2–7), no fewer than one hundred cattle ought be given for a Soma sacrifice. Other sources specify that one hundred and twelve cattle are to be presented, some identify smaller numbers— sixty, twenty-one, or seven—and some call for a gift of one thousand cattle or all of the wealth of the sacrificer, except for his eldest son (for these and still other gift possibilities, see Caland and Henry 1907: 290).

[18]On the Maruts, see especially Keith 1998a: 150–153. On their connection to the gods called the Ṛbhus (who have an affiliation with the evening pressing), see p. 176.

[19]As well as to Dhātṛ, Vidhātṛ, and Puṣan; see Keith 1998a: 360.

4.8.3 The evening pressing

The evening pressing is again marked by various Soma libations and draughts, though it is a less spectacular affair, at least to the extent that Soma plants from the earlier pressings are now re-pressed. The victim which was offered in the morning pressing and which has cooked throughout the day is now used in making oblations and is eaten—in conjunction with which bits of rice cake are thrown into the *camasa* cups (cups of the various priests) for the departed ancestors of the sacrificer (see Caland and Henry 1907: 344, 350–352; Eggeling 1995, pt. 2: 356–357, n. 3). A rice pap offering is made to Soma, unique to the third pressing, and in the account of the *Śatapatha Brāhmaṇa* (4.4.2.1–5) its presence here is explicated in terms of Soma's sacredness to the Pitaras.[20] Conspicuous among the Soma libations of the evening is that of the *Hāriyojana graha* (*ŚB* 4.4.3.2–15; an "additional" libation). The cup takes its name from the hariyojana, the team of bay steeds yoked to Indra's chariot. For the libation, the *Taittirīya Saṃhitā* (1.4.28) preserves the mantra:

> You are the bay who yokes the bay steeds, driver of bay steeds, bearer of the thunderbolt, lover of Pṛśni. To you, god Soma, for whom the sacrificial formulas are uttered, the songs sung, the verses recited, I draw the libation associated with the bay steeds.

(For several close variants of the mantra, see Caland and Henry 1907: 383–384.) Parched grain (the grain of the steeds) is added to the Soma.[21] The libation is called the "horse-winning" and "cow-winning" draught.

There then follows the rite of the Avabhṛtha, an expiatory bath (*ŚB* 4.4.5.1–23). Priests, sacrificer, and sacrificer's wife walk northward across the boundary of the Mahāvedi en route to a designated water source, standing or flowing. Various ritual implements that have been used in the Soma sacrifice are tossed into the water, and the sacrificer and his wife descend for a bath. After bathing they put on a change of clothing, retracing their steps back into the Mahāvedi.

At the conclusion of the evening ceremony, yet another victim is sacri-

[20] Coming a bit later in the ceremony is the offering of the Pātnīvata cup with the curious rite of the Neṣṭar sitting on the lap of the Agnīdh, at which point the wife of the sacrificer (the Patnī) is led up. On the rite and the prominent position of the sacrificer's wife in the evening pressing, see Jamison 1996: 127–146.

[21] A libation of grain to the Pitaras is recorded in *BŚS* 8.17, and only there. See Caland and Henry 1907: 387.

ficed. A sterile cow is offered to the gods Mitra and Varuṇa.[22] If no sterile cow is available, however, a bullock may be substituted (*ŚB* 4.5.1.9).[23]

In addition to the goat and sterile cow offered on the pressing day, certain variants of the Agniṣṭoma require the sacrifice of yet other victims. Thus, the Ṣoḍaśin ceremony, having sixteen *stotras* and *śastras* (rather than twelve) includes the sacrifice of a second goat, like the Ukthya described above, as well as the offering of a ram to Indra (for a total of four victims on the pressing day—two goats, a ram, and a cow). The variant called the Atirātra adds one more victim, a he-goat offered to Sarasvatī, and extends the Soma ceremony beyond the evening pressing through the night, with twenty-nine *stotras* and *śastras.*[24]

4.8.4 The concluding Iṣṭi

The completion of the Soma-sacrifice is marked by the performance of an Iṣṭi, the Udavasānīyā Iṣṭi. It is not, however, performed within that small sacred space located west of the Mahāvedi, that place of the three canonical flames which is set up for the performance of an Iṣṭi. Instead, the ceremony takes place north or east of the Mahāvedi (Caland and Henry 1907: 411). The Udavasānīyā Iṣṭi entails the use of the "churning sticks," the *araṇis*, (that is, a fire drill), to kindle a flame, and the presentation of a cake offering to the fire god Agni. The kindling is required because the sacrifice at this late hour in the ritual is perceived as having lost its strength, as being exhausted. The flame which is generated is "lifted" from the various hearths of the officiating priests; that is to say, the churning sticks are placed close to those hearths and heated, or actually lit by their flames, and in this way the priests "lift" fire from those hearths and set it down at the site of the Udavasānīyā Iṣṭi (*ŚB* 4.5.1.13–16).

The Soma-sacrifice has been completed. The priests take their leave and the sacrificer returns home. Before him goes the sacrificial fire—either in the form of an actual flame, or symbolically contained within the churning sticks (Caland and Henry 1907: 413).

[22] If, however, postmortem inspection of the uterus reveals that the cow was not barren but carried a fetal calf, special measures must be taken, which include offering the fetus to the Maruts (see *ŚB* 4.5.2.1–18).

[23] Or even an offering of milk curds, according to *Kātyāyana Śrauta Sūtra* 10.9.15.

[24] On the *Ukthya*, *Ṣoḍaśin*, and *Atirātra*, see Keith 1998a: 334–336; 1998b: 53–54. See also *ĀpŚS* 14.1; the author wishes to express his appreciation to Prof. Stephanie Jamison for bringing this text to his attention.

This concluding Iṣṭi serves as a counterpart, structurally and functionally, to that rite which occurs at the very beginning of the Agniṣṭoma, called the Adhyavasāna (Caland and Henry 1907: 411). The Adhyavasāna marks the solemn entry of the sacrificer into the newly constructed prācīnavaṃśa, the shelter which is built to cover the Devayajana, the small sacred ground of the Iṣṭi. In his processional entry into that covered space, the sacrificer is accompanied by his wife and various cultic officiants. The processors carry cultic implements required for the now unfolding Agniṣṭoma, the sacrificer bringing Soma and the fire drill (Caland and Henry 1906: 9–10).

The Udavasānīyā Iṣṭi and the Adhyavasāna not only bracket the Agniṣṭoma as coda and onset, but the Udavasānīyā Iṣṭi, in a similar fashion, formally parallels the ritual of the Paunarādheyikī Iṣṭi (see Eggeling 1995, pt. 2: 389, n. 2). The latter is the Iṣṭi which is undertaken when it is deemed necessary for the sacrificer to reestablish his sacrificial fires, and so, again, serves as an initiatory ritual in contradistinction to the concluding function of the Udavasānīyā Iṣṭi. The Paunarādheyikī Iṣṭi is performed if the sacrificial fires do not bring prosperity to the sacrificer; the old flames are permitted to die down, and new fires are generated by means of the fire drill (see Keith 1998a: 316–318; Renou 1957: 101–102).

4.9 THE ARVAL RITES OF DEA DIA (II)

When the Arval rites of the goddess Dea Dia are examined within the context of an archaic Indo-European doctrine of dual sacred spaces (urban Rome and Ager Romanus; Vedic Devayajana and Mahāvedi) certain structural parallels and similarities between these Roman rites and those of the Agniṣṭoma, particularly those observed on the Soma-pressing day, unexpectedly present themselves. Obviously suggestive is the parallel triadic structure[25] of the pressing day rituals and the central day of the Arval ritual, both in terms of a gross three-way division of the day and of features replicated within the divisions. Thus, the second day of Arval rites is punctuated by three episodes of banqueting: (i) the meal made from the pigs sacrificed in the morning; (ii) the dinner banquet in the tetrastyle of the grove; and (iii) the evening banquet at the home of the Magister back in Rome. The pressing day of the Agniṣṭoma is similarly segmented by three episodes of Soma libation and ingestion—morning, midday, and evening.

[25]Or should we say "tripartite structure"? According to *Śatapatha Brāhmaṇa* 4.3.5.1, the morning pressing belongs to the Vasus (third function), the midday pressing to the Rudras (second function; the conspicuous position of Indra in this pressing has already

We shall consider in turn each of these culinary episodes and the activities which cluster with them. Again, to provide the reader with a guide through the coming discussion, elements of the second day of the Arval ritual which will prove especially important from a comparative perspective are outlined in figure 4.3.

Second Arval festival day

- Morning culinary event
  - sacrifice of two piglets
  - sacrifice of cow
  - offering of the cow's *exta* in circus
  - consumption of piglets
- Midday culinary event
  - sacrifice of lamb
  - monetary offering at the altar
  - Mars and the Semones
  - wine
  - chariot race
- Evening culinary event
  - movement out of the Ager Romanus

FIGURE 4.3. *Selected elements of day two of the Arval festival of Dea Dia*

4.9.1 The morning culinary episode

Recall that the Arval rites of the second day—the core day of the festival of Dea Dia—commence with the priests present in the grove of their goddess, along the distal periphery of the Ager Romanus.[26] The day's rites begin with the Magister sacrificing two piglets (*porcae piaculares*) to the goddess; next a cow (*vacca honoraria*) is offered. The Magister removes himself to the tetrastyle; there he takes a seat, and subsequently returns to the

been noted), and the evening pressing to the Ādityas (first function), along with the other gods.

[26]The descriptions which follow are based chiefly on the *Acta* of AD 218, 219, 237 and 240. See Scheid 1998: 293–304, 319–320, 331–337; Scheid 1990: 490–503.

altar (*ara*), where he offers the entrails of the sacrificed pigs. In the *circus* of the grove he then offers the entrails of the cow on a silver brazier arranged with sod (or simply grass? *c(a)espes*). He returns again to the tetrastyle and makes a written record of his priestly activities. He then removes the *toga praetexta* (and bathes) and retires to his *papilio*—a tent or hut, or some similar temporary shelter (see Scheid 1990: 134–136). Before midday, the other Fratres join the Magister in the tetrastyle, again documenting their activities. These then share a small meal—a preliminary *gustatio* (see Scheid 1990: 566–567)—of the sacrificed pigs and a dish made from pigs' blood (*sanguniculus*).

Like earlier investigators, we observed that the sacrifices offered within the grove of Dea Dia on this day constitute a form of the *suovetaurilia*, if not of the canonical sort (see §3.3.6.3). Bearing that in mind, perhaps the most immediately noticeable similarity of the morning culinary episode to the morning pressing of Soma is the offering of victims. Recall that the Vedic form of this threefold sacrifice—that of the Sautrāmaṇī—consists of a goat alongside ovine and bovine victims, pigs not being used for sacrifice in Vedic India (see §3.3.3.1). As pigs are offered in the morning culinary episode of the Arvals, so a goat, the homologous Vedic victim, is offered during the morning pressing of Soma. That goat is cooked throughout the day and eaten by the priests at the time of the evening pressing; in Rome the victims are likewise consumed, but such consumption takes place during the climax of the morning culinary episode, the *gustatio* shared by the Arval priests. Note further that there is also agreement in the number of such victims in the instance of the Ukthya variant of the Agniṣṭoma, with two goats being offered.

The second victim of the Arval *suovetaurilia*, a cow (*vacca honoraria*), is likewise offered during the morning culinary episode. There is again a comparable victim present on the day of Soma pressing, the sterile cow (or a bullock) sacrificed to Mitra and Varuṇa. In the Vedic rite, however, the bovine sacrifice forms part of the evening pressing ceremonies. With regard to this variance, we might offer two considerations. First, though both the pigs and cow are sacrificed as a part of the morning culinary episode of the Arvals, the Acta record only the pigs as being consumed during the ensuing *gustatio*. Scheid (1990: 571) notes that the flesh of the cow is evidently reserved for a later dining event; he suggests the final banquet of the three-day festival. Thus both rites likely agree to the extent that consumption of the bovine sacrifice by the priests occurs in later rather than earlier stages of the ritual. The second consideration concerns the peculiar rite of the offering of the cow's *exta*. These entrails, unlike those of the pigs, are not offered on the Arval altar (*ara*) but on a silver brazier, a *foculus*, arranged with sod and situated within the *circus* of the grove. This second consideration requires further examination.

That the Arval Magister should offer the *exta* of the piacular piglets (*porcae piaculares*) and those of the freely given cow (*vacca honoraria*), *both* in different locales *and* on different altars, is almost certainly noteworthy. Given that the *foculus* is a portable hearth, one variable does not of necessity follow from the other: place and altar are separate issues to the extent that both altars could have been used in the same locale, or the same portable altar could have been used in different locales. Scheid (1990: 326–330), making reference to Dumézil's analysis of the quadrangular and round flames of Rome, cultural cognates of the Vedic Āhavanīya and Gārhapatya respectively (see §2.8.1), reminds us that while the flames of a quadrangular *ara* are regularly used for conveying animal offerings to the gods (like the Āhavanīya), those of the round *foculus* are used instead for initial rites, for offerings of wine, incense, and cake.[27] For Scheid (1990: 562), the silver *foculus* is essentially transformed into an altar for the offering of flesh by the addition to it of the piece of turf (*caespes*).[28] Perhaps Scheid is correct in seeing the presence of the grass as effectively transforming the *foculus* into an *ara*—from a synchronic perspective. Diachronically, this detail is quite intriguing because of the uncommon use of grass in Roman ritual and its very common use in Vedic ritual. Scheid further suggests that the altar must have been situated right on the racetrack, hence the need for the portable *foculus* rather than a permanent structure.

Just possibly, the Vedic sacrifice of the sterile cow provides some insight regarding this marked arrangement of the offering of the bovine *exta*. In Vedic India how can one be certain beforehand that the cow to be offered to Mitra and Varuṇa is, in fact, sterile? Seemingly, one cannot be. After the victim is immolated, its carcass is inspected for the presence of an embryonic calf, and a ritual is provided to accommodate such a discovery. Succinctly—the embryo is removed and is offered to the Maruts, warrior companions of Indra, divine charioteers (see §4.2.5). The embryo is not offered on the (relocated) Āhavanīya, the principal altar of the Mahāvedi,

[27]Scheid (1990: 561–562) calls attention to Macrobius, *Sat.* 3.2.3, in which passage Veranius is cited for his comment on the word *porricere*: *exta porriciunto, dis danto, in altaria aramue focumue eove quo exta dari debebunt* ('let the entrails be offered, be given to the gods, on an altar, or on an *ara*, or on a *focus*, or on whatever thing they should be given'). *Focus* normally denotes the household hearth, though apparently is at times used synonymously with its derivative *foculus* (see *OLD*: 718).

[28]On Umbrian *perso* as a turf-altar, see Poultney 1959: 263.

but is buried beneath the coals of the cooking fire of the animal sacrifice, the Śāmitra (on the ritual see *ŚB* 4.5.2.1–18).

Much as the Vedic offering of a cow to Mitra and Varuṇa includes as a component the rite of presenting an embryo to the warrior companions of Indra, so the Arval offering of a cow's internal organs to Dea Dia is set in the arena of the chariot, the marked vehicle of the warrior. That we may perhaps be on the right track in forging this connection is suggested by the further appearance of Roman comparanda of the Maruts a bit further along in the Arval rite, as we shall see below.

4.9.2 The midday culinary episode

After finishing their *gustatio* of pork, the priests don the *toga praetexta*, and with heads covered and garlanded with grain they return to the grove, where the Promagister sacrifices the third member of the *suovetaurilia*, a lamb (*agna opima*), and examines the entrails for omens. After a libation of wine and incense, the priests proceed to the temple, in and around which numerous rites are performed. Beginning with the libations, these rites, in the view of Scheid (1990: 577–578), themselves constitute a sacrificial banquet, one celebrated for the Arval goddess Dea Dia. The elements of this complex of sacrificial events include the following: within the temple, sacrifices are made with the *ollae* (the clay vessels that will be offered to the Mater Larum); the Promagister and Flamen sacrifice on grass (*caespite*) before the temple; then going out to the altar they make a monetary offering (see Scheid 1990: 613–615); the Promagister and Flamen offer libations of incense and wine with vessels of silver; two Arval priests go down with the public slaves to obtain grains (while others remain before the temple door); returning with the grains, the priests pass them from one to another (giving with the right hand and receiving with the left) and then give them to the public slaves; they go into the temple and pray to the *ollae*, and then throw the clay vessels down the hill (the offering to the Mater Larum; see §3.3.3.2); the priests then sit on benches of marble and share bread decorated with laurel; they take *lumemulia cum rapinis* 'soap (?) with turnips' and anoint images of the goddess; the temple is then closed and all leave but the priests, who, shut up within the temple, dance and sing the Carmen Arvale (the translation is based on that of Schilling 1991: 604):

> Enos Lases iuvate, | [e]nos Lases iuvate, enos Lases iuvate!
> Neve Luae Rue Marma sins incurrere in pleores, neve Luae Rue Marmar | [si]ns incurrere in pleoris, neve Lue Rue Marmar sers incurrere in pleores!

Satur fu, fere Mars, limen | [sal]i, sta berber, satur fu, fere Mars, limen sali sta berber, satur fu, fere Mars, limen sa[l]i s[t]a berber!
[Sem]unis alternei advocapit conctos, Semunis alternei advocapit conctos, Simunis altern[ei] advocapit | [conct]tos!
Enos Marmor iuvato, enos Marmor iuvato, enos Marmor iuvato!
Triumpe, triumpe, triumpe, trium[pe, tri]umpe!

Help us, O Lares; help us, O Lares; help us, O Lares!
Mars, O Mars, don't let Dissolution, Destruction pounce upon the people (?)! Mars, O Mars, don't let Dissolution, Destruction pounce upon the people (?)! Mars, O Mars, don't let Dissolution, Destruction pounce upon the people (?)!
Be surfeited, savage Mars; leap to the border, take your position! Be surfeited, savage Mars; leap to the border, take your position! Be surfeited, savage Mars; leap to the border, take your position!
You will invoke the Semones one by one, all together! You will invoke the Semones one by one, all together! You will invoke the Semones one by one, all together!
Help us Mars, O Mars! Help us Mars, O Mars! Help us Mars, O Mars!
Victory, victory, victory, victory, victory!

When the dancing and hymning are finished, the public slaves enter and collect the books (*libelli*) which had been used by the Arvals in the rite of the Carmen. The priests stand before the door of the temple (now reopened; see Scheid 1990: 629–630); garlands are offered and carried within the interior of the temple by the *kalatores* (the priestly assistants) to crown the statues, the name of each priest is called out, and each touches the altars. The Arvals elect their Magister for the coming year and propose a new Flamen. After speaking felicitations to one another (for Scheid [1990: 631], bringing to a close the sacrificial "banquet" of the goddess) the priests descend from the grove for their meal in the tetrastyle.

This feast in the tetrastyle, the capstone event of the midday culinary episode, is that banquet which we examined earlier (see §4.2.5). The priests exchange the *toga praetexta* for white dinner attire. Dishes arrive *more pompae*, 'in processional style', accompanied by *campanae* (likely 'Campanian vessels') and great quantities of sweet wine (*mulsum*). Those present obtain a gift of one hundred denarii, and there is a distribution of rose petals as well.

The midday culinary episode, appearing to be the centerpiece of this the second day of the Arval festival for Dea Dia, bears unmistakable similarities to the climax of the Agniṣṭoma pressing day, the midday Soma pressing. Generally, the various and repeated movements of the Arval priests and their several assistants through the sacrificial arena of the goddess, especially those ambulations concerned with activities in and around her temple, the monetary offering at the altar, the ritual seating of the priests and their reciprocal sharing of cultic elements, the return to the tetrastyle, the processional delivery of the dishes and wine within the tetrastyle, the distribution of gifts—all are reminiscent of the activities and movements of the Vedic priests and their own assistants within the Mahāvedi, their "creeping" back to the Sadas where, seated by their various Dhiṣṇya-hearths, the priests drink Soma; their passing of cultic implements to one another; the offering of gold at the altar of the old Āhavanīya and the distribution of the sacrificer's gifts.

Particularly intriguing is the profuse quantity of sweet wine which is provided for the Arval priests during the tetrastyle banquet—thirteen liters for each. The inebriating product of the grape provides for Rome the functional, cultic equivalent of the intoxicating substance of Vedic ritual. In the present context, we think immediately of pressings of the Soma plant (see Dumézil 1975: 87–97; Woodard 2002: 93–94). Soma "provokes in the men (and gods) who drink it a kind of euphoric exaltation that the texts take great pains to distinguish from ordinary intoxication and that in certain ways suggests the effects of hallucinogenic substances . . ." (Malamoud 1991: 803). The Soma drinker is carried away in a state of ecstasy, imagining himself to be capable of superhuman feats (*RV* 10.119). The priest who presses Soma finds joy; a sense of greatness is acquired through use of the substance; and the Soma drinker achieves immortality (*RV* 9.113). The ritual use of this material (eluding definitive identification)[29] is at least of Proto-Indo-Iranian origin, as revealed by the equivalent use in Iranian rites of *Haoma*, cognate in name to Sanskrit *Soma*. Of the Iranian material, Boyce (1996: 158) writes:

> When crushed it yielded a drink which exhilarated and gave heightened powers; and this was the only intoxicant (*madha*) which produced no harmful effects. "All other *madha* are accompanied by Wrath with the bloody club; but the *madha* of Haoma makes one nimble" [*Yasna* 10.8]. "The *madha* of Haoma is accompanied by its own rightfulness (*aša-*)" [*Yašt* 17.5].

It has long been suggested that the Indo-Iranian ritual use of the intoxicant **sauma* continues a Proto-Indo-European use of **med^{h}u-* 'mead' (see Keith 1998a: 172, Renou 1957: 71).

[29] For an attempt at its identification, see especially Wasson 1972, 1971.

There is, however, another intoxicating substance which receives ritual use in Vedic India—the fermented beverage called *surā*. This is the material which we encountered earlier in our discussion of the rites of the Vājapeya (see §2.6.1.1) and of the rites preserving the *suovetaurilia* homologue, the Sautrāmaṇī (see §3.3.3.1). Its sacred use is restricted to these primitive rituals—undoubtedly a testimony to the great antiquity of their heritage.

Might the Arval use of excessive quantities of wine at the banquet of the midday culinary event—conducted into the tetrastyle *more pompae*—be a fossilized reflex of an early Indo-European custom of ritual intoxication? If so, a homologous structure may survive generally in the Vedic ritual use of Soma (and the corresponding Zoroastrian Haoma rites). Perhaps a more likely and specific homologue of the Arval practice, however, is provided by the use of *surā* and its processional conveyance (along with honey) out of the Soma-cart shed which appears in the midday pressing of the Vājapeya (as described in §2.6.1.1).

That we are on the right track in identifying a particularly close relationship of ritual homology between the Arval rites celebrated on the second day of the May festival and the rites of the Soma-pressing day of the primitive Vājapeya is suggested by what happens next in the grove of Dea Dia. Following the meal in the tetrastyle, the Magister puts on his *laticlave* and *ricinium* and a garland of roses. He ascends above the starting gates in the *circus* of the grove and signals for the *ludi* to begin—chariot races, with both four-horse and two-horse chariots running, as well as events involving *desultores* (riders jumping between horses). Other priests position themselves by the finish line. The victors receive palms and crowns of silver.

The significance of the races for this day is signaled by their prominent mention in the more skeletal versions of the Acta. Thus, in the records of AD 38, the entire second day of the festival is very succinctly summarized by reference to three seminal rites only—the sacrifice of the cow, that of the lamb, and the running of the races. Scheid (1990: 636) draws attention to the prominent position accorded the *ludi*, stating: "Par conséquent, les jeux doivent être considérés comme l'un des temps forts de l'office de la deuxième journée."

We have seen that a seminal event of the Vājapeya—one which takes place as a part of the midday Soma-pressing and one which serves as a distinctive feature of this primitive rite—is likewise the running of a chariot race (see §2.6.1.1). The sacrificer in a three-horse chariot races against sixteen opponents in four-horse chariots. The victor of the race is predetermined—the sacrificer takes the honors.

The Vājapeya is a ritual in which are conjoined the acquisition of victory and the gaining of fertility. Keith (1998a: 340) draws attention to this concatenation, as we noted in our discussion of the Vājapeya. The combination is one which renders the primordial nature of the ritual obscure for Keith: "It is accordingly impossible to lay down precisely the original character of the rite: it was not merely the feast of victory of the winner in a chariot race, such as might be paralleled in Greek ritual, nor was it solely an agricultural rite. . . ."

Whatever its "original" value—one which must surely be situated in yet more archaic Indo-European cult—the peculiar conjunction of fertility and victory that characterizes the Vedic Vājapeya is exactly replicated in the rites of the second day of the Arval festival of Dea Dia. The Fratres Arvales are those priests whose ritual activities are conducted to imbue the fields with fertility, as Varro tells us and as their name transparently reveals. Yet there is more to the ritual. The "attainment of victory" lies at its very core—not only prominently evidenced by the seminal position of the chariot race, but by the imploring of Mars in the hymn of the Arvales to bring "Victory, victory, victory, victory, victory!" (*Triumpe, triumpe, triumpe, triumpe, triumpe!*).

The Vājapeya also intersects with the second day of the Arval festival in yet another way. The victims offered in the grove of Dea Dia, as we have seen (§3.3.6.3), represent a variant form of the canonical *suovetaurilia*: two pigs (*porcae piaculares*), a cow (*vacca honoraria*), and a lamb (*agna opima*). In our discussion of the Agniṣṭoma, we noted that the victims offered on the Soma-pressing day show some variation, depending on whether the ceremony is of the type called Ukthya, Ṣoḍaśin, or Atirātra (§4.8.3). The Vājapeya is a Ṣoḍaśin rite, meaning that the pressing-day victims are these: two goats, a ram offered to Indra, and a sterile cow offered to the Mitra and Varuṇa (*ŚB* 5.1.3.1–3)—mutatis mutandis, a replica of the Arval *suovetaurilia*. While the Arval set matches the Ṣoḍaśin set one-to-one, the Vājapeya departs from the norm of the Ṣoḍaśin by the offering of yet additional victims: a goat is offered to the goddess Sarasvatī (*ŚB* 5.1.3.2; compare *ŚB* 5.1.3.11) and, in keeping with the characteristic number of the Vājapeya, seventeen goats (hornless, male) are sacrificed to Prajāpati (*ŚB* 5.1.3.7–10), a creator god bestowing fertility and, in the Brāhmaṇas and Saṃhitās, the creator god *par excellence* (see Keith 1998a: 207). Here we certainly see at work the Vedic propensity for ritual proliferation.

It will be readily apparent to the reader that a number of the Arval practices mentioned in the preceding paragraphs do not uniquely link the *midday culinary episode* to the *midday Soma pressing*. That is to say, many of the corresponding events of the Agniṣṭoma are not specific to the midday pressing but are shared by the morning and evening pressings as well. Conversely, at least one element of the midday Soma pressing, the distribution of gifts, characterizes not only the midday culinary episode of the second day of the Arval rites but also the evening episode as well as the banquets of days one and three (see §4.2.5). Apart from the *mulsum-surā* and chariot-racing homologues linking the Vājapeya with the Arval ritual, this, in effect, leaves only—among those shared midday elements *specified thus far*—a single uniquely similar feature: the Arval monetary offering which the Promagister and the Flamen make upon returning to the altar from the temple of the goddess, alongside the offering of gold which the Adhvaryu makes upon returning temporarily from the Mahāvedi to the old Āhavanīya in the Devayajana, the space of the Iṣṭi (see Caland and Henry 1907: 289).

The several similarities which do not share temporal specificity—coupled with those that do share such specific agreement—provide, however, a general context of agreement between the Arval and Vedic midday events within which a single overriding point of idiosyncratic correspondence firmly joins the two. The crescendo of the midday culinary episode seems plainly to be reached at the moment of the performance of the Carmen Arvale. As discussed above, the midday Soma pressing belongs almost exclusively to Indra, the chief warrior god. The Carmen Arvale of the midday culinary event is a hymn sung first and foremost to Indra's Roman counterpart, Mars. Scheid (1990: 622) surmises:

> L'association du banquet de Dia et de l'invocation de Mars avec ses compagnons nous engage à conclure que, dans les rituels qui se déroulent *in luco*, on s'adresse à deux divinités avant tout, à dea Dia, patronne des lieux, et à Mars, dont l'assistance est requise pour que Dia puisse déployer son activité bénéfique; . . .

As in the Agniṣṭoma, the midday Soma pressing is the special domain of the warrior Indra, so in the Arval festival celebrated within the precinct of Dea Dia, it is the midday culinary event that is bound up with the warrior Mars—the second of the two deities with which the Arval rites of May are principally concerned.

4.9.2.1 THE SEMONES Indra is, however, not the only deity who leaves his stamp on the midday Soma pressing. Particular ritual attention is also paid to his companions, that band of warriors called the Maruts. Just so, beside Mars, the Carmen Arvale entreats two bands of deities, the Lares, beings of a clearly chthonic nature within the context of the Arval ritual, and the somewhat more mysterious—but certainly of greater significance for our comparative analysis—Semones. The identity of the Semones is commonly intuited from their name's supposed etymon, *semina* 'seeds'. Given the dearth of information which the hymn provides about these beings and the affiliation of the Arval rites with the fertility of Roman fields, the linkage of Semones and *semina* is a natural one. The interpretation is seemingly reinforced by the opening of the hymn, verses invoking the Lares, deities of the ground. Thus, Scheid (1990: 621) writes:

> Mars est à prendre dans ce contexte comme le dieu guerrier qui se dresse «sur le seuil» de Rome et défend le territoire; les Lares et les *Semones* lui sont adjoints, les uns en tant que dieux du sol et du terroir, les seconds vraisemblablement comme dieux des *semina*, des semences. . . .

Here Scheid, in envisioning the Semones to be gods of the seeds, is following, as he acknowledges, the interpretations laid down by Norden (1939: 204–222) and subsequently developed by Dumézil (*ARR*: 228–231). For the latter, the Semones "preside over the life of the *semina*."[30]

Two observations should be made at this point. First, there is an asymmetry in the invocation of the two divine groups named in the Carmen Arvale. The priests call on the help of the Lares directly—not so with the Semones. It is "savage Mars" who must invoke these gods; the war god in effect serves as an intermediary through whom the band of the Semones are individually and collectively summoned for their assistance.

Secondly, while seeds are undeniably necessary for plant growth, vis-à-vis field fertility, they are obviously of a fundamentally quite different nature from the material of that other band of deities who are invoked in the *carmen*—namely, soil. Seeds are the raw stuff of plant growth, the germ of plant life; soil is the medium which makes possible that life, a part of the support mechanism. As every gardener knows, however, a rich soil only provides half of the equation for a fertile field; there is an additional support mechanism required. One also needs rain. If the Fratres Arvales are responsible for bringing fertility to the Roman fields, as Varro tells us and as is commonly accepted, one would expect—practically automatically—that their great hymn would invoke not only gods who reside in the

[30]On the unpersuasive etymology which Martianus Capella proposed in antiquity, deriving *Semo* from *se homo*, from *semihomo* (as though the name reflected the Semones' status as demigods), see Norden 1939: 204; Wissowa 1971: 130, n. 2; Frazer 1929, vol. 4: 165.

soil, but those who send the rains. What the Vedic rites almost certainly reveal to us is that Mars' companions (whom Mars himself must invoke) the Semones, like Indra's companions the Maruts, are deities of the rain.

Latin *sēmen, sēminis* 'seed' is a derivative of *serere* 'to sow', evolved from the Proto-Indo-European verb root **seh₁*-, of the same meaning.[31] The name of our Roman rain deities, *Sēmonēs*, however, probably shares a common origin with forms such as Lithuanian *séilė* 'saliva, drool' from Proto-Indo-European **seh₁(i)*-, which itself is probably etymologically linked to the roots **seikʷ*- 'to flow out' and **seib*- 'to pour out, let flow'. The former serves as etymon of, inter alia, Old High German *seihhen* and Serbian Church Slavic sъčǫ, both meaning 'to urinate'; Tocharian A *sikaṃtär* 'they are flooded'; and Sanskrit *siñcáti* and Young Avestan *hiṇcaiti* 'he pours out'. The two last named are nasal-infix presents from **si-né/n-kʷ*-, which appears also to have a Sabellian reflex **simpe*- 'to pour out, to ladle', as reflected in the Latin loan word *simpulum*, the name of a cultic vessel used for pouring or ladling (see *LIV*: 523; *WP*, vol. 2: 464, 466–467). The related root **seib*- gives, inter alia, Epic Greek εἴβω 'to drop, to let fall in drops', in the passive 'to trickle down' (*LSJG*: 482), Middle Dutch *sīpen* 'to drop' (*LIV*: 521); compare Latin *sēbum* (*sēvum*) 'tallow' and the associated verb *sēbāre* 'to dip in tallow', denoting candle making,[32] perhaps from **seh₁(i)b*- (*WP*, vol. 2: 467–468). Proto-Indo-European **seh₁(i)*-, our proposed source of *Sēmonēs*, is probably, at least originally, that same root **seh₁(i)*- which provides one group of widely attested reflexes meaning 'sieve, strainer' and 'to sift, to strain', and another group meaning fundamentally 'to let loose': examples include Greek ἠθέω 'to sift, strain, let trickle out'; Old Norse *sáld* 'sieve'; and Vedic *-syati* 'to make loose' (*LIV*: 518–519; *WP*, vol. 2: 459–463).

As in the Carmen Arvale, sung at the midday culinary episode, it is the warrior Mars who invokes the Semones, those who pour down the waters, so in the midday Soma pressing, the warrior Indra calls on the Maruts to come and join him in his fight against the monstrous Vṛtra, the drought-bringing serpent who holds back the rains and the streams. According to the *Śatapatha Brāhmaṇa* (4.3.3.6–18), the three Marutvatīya cups are drawn so that Indra may press the Maruts into service against Vṛtra. The slaying of this monster is Indra's great heroic deed, for which his praises are rehearsed again and again in the Vedas—a slaying which causes the waters to flow down "like lowing cattle" (*RV* 1.32.2; see §4.9.2.4).

[31]The Latin verb comes from a reduplicated zero-grade **si-sh₁*-.

[32]Which activity Columella (*Rust.* 2.21.3) says to be among those permitted by the religious rites of the ancients.

4.9.2.2 SEMO SANCUS Aside from their presence in the hymn of the Arvals, the Semones corporately receive vague mention in a Sabellian inscription from Corfinium, and individually through references to a goddess Semonia (see Wissowa 1971: 130–132) and the somewhat-better-documented—but still rather mysterious—god Semo Sancus. The last-named is commonly identified as a god of Sabine origin and is equated with the deity called Dius Fidius, being at times denoted by the quadranomial Semo Sancus Dius Fidius. The great antiquity of the notion that Semo Sancus and Dius Fidius are one and the same is revealed by the presence in Umbrian ritual of the god called Fisus Sancius (see Poultney 1959: 252–254).

Identifying the Semones of the Fratres Arvales as gods who send rains, and drawing them into the sphere of Indra's warrior companions, the Maruts, is harmonious with—and brings a certain unexpected clarity to—what precious little is known of Semo Sancus (Dius Fidius). Much of this knowledge is succinctly summarized by Varro (*Ling.* 5.66), who attributes its source to the emminent Roman scholar Lucius Aelius (Stilo). Having cited the name Dius Fidius in an etymologizing disquisition, Varro writes of the god:

> Itaque inde eius perforatum tectum, ut ea videatur divum, id est caelum. Quidam negant sub tecto per hunc deierare oportere. Aelius Dium Fidium dicebat Diovis filium, ut Graeci Διόσκορον Castorem, et putabat hunc esse Sancum ab Sabina lingua et Herculem a Graeca.

> And so, his [temple] roof is pierced with a hole so that the *divum*, that is, the sky, may thus be seen. Some say that one ought not swear an oath by the god's name while under a roof. Aelius used to say that Dius Fidius is a son of *Diovis*, just as the Greeks call Castor a *Dioskoros* ['boy of Zeus'], and he always thought this god to be Sancus in the Sabine language and Hercules in the Greek.

Let us consider in turn the elements of Varro's description of this god.

First, Semo Sancus Dius Fidius is a deity whose province is the sky. According to Lydus (*Mens.* 4.90), sancus is the Sabine word meaning 'sky'. The roof of the temple of Dius Fidius is open to the heavens, like that of the Capitoline shrine of Terminus. Oaths are commonly sworn by this deity—*me Dius Fidius* (see Plautus, *Asin.* 23; Festus, p. 147M; Aulus Gellius, *NA* 10.14.3–4; and so on)—and as Varro notes in the above passage, such oaths must be sworn beneath the open sky. Elsewhere Varro (in Nonius, p. 793L) reports, concerning domestic ritual, that when one swears by this god it is necessary to leave the roofed areas of the house and to step into the *com-*

pluvium beneath open sky. Similarly, the solemn oaths sworn *per Iovem lapidem*, by Jupiter and his stone, the *lapis silex* housed in the temple of Jupiter Feretrius, must be made outside of the god's temple (see Warde Fowler 1899: 138). By Varro's testimony, Aelius reckoned Dius Fidius to be son of Jupiter (*Diovis*; compare Festus, p. 147M). Whatever popular synchronic relationship the two gods may have had in Aelius' day, the divine names *Dius* and *Jupiter* and the divine personalities that they denote are almost certainly related diachronically. Latin *Jupiter* (**Diove Pater*) is descended from Proto-Indo-European **Dyeus Ph₂tēr*, name of the sky god, which also provides Greek Ζεύς Πατήρ, Vedic *Dyaus Pitar*, and Luvian (*Tatis*) *Tiwaz* (see §1.7). Varro is thus etymologically on target when he draws Διόσκορος into the equation.[33] Proto-Indo-European **Dyeus* is itself derived from the root **deiw-* 'to shine', and this etymon is very likely also the ultimate source of Latin *Dius*.

Beyond this general affiliation with the sky, Semo Sancus Dius Fidius shows a clear link to one specific atmospheric phenomenon, the hallmark of the storm—lightning. The god possessed a temple on the Quirinal hill (see *LTUR*: 4: 263–264; Richardson 1992: 347), said to have been built by Tarquinius Superbus but dedicated only in 466 BC on the Nones of June (Dionysius of Halicarnassus, *Ant. Rom.* 9.60.8; Ovid, *Fast.* 6.213–218). It appears that on the Quirinal the god was served by the priesthood called the *Decuria Sacerdotum Bidentalium*. Evidence of their service is provided by votive inscriptions left by the priests to this god on the Quirinal as well as on the Tiber Isle.[34] An inscription from the Tiber Isle was found in conjunction with a statue of the deity that appears to have held a thunderbolt in its left hand.[35] The Sacerdotes Bidentales are priests whose name reveals them to be affiliated with the lightning strike, a place so struck being denoted

[33]And he perhaps would have remained so had he added Διόνυσος 'Dionysus' (Pamphylian Διϝονύσεις, Mycenaean di-wo-nu-so). Plutarch (*Quaest. Rom.* 28) writes that the Roman children were not permitted to swear by Hercules under a roof, but were required to go outdoors to do so. By "Hercules" he is most probably referring to Semo Sancus Dius Fidius; as Varro notes the latter is commonly equated with Hercules, and to this association we return below. But Plutarch goes on to record that the Romans also do not swear by Dionysus beneath a roof. Might the ancient savant here be bifurcating Semo Sancus Dius Fidius into Hercules (= Semo Sancus) and Dionysus (= Dius Fidius)?

[34]*CIL* 6.567 (*Semoni Sanco deo Fidio*); *CIL* 6.568 (*Sanco sancto Semon(i) deo Fidio*); *CIL* 6.30994 (*Semoni Sanco sancto deo Fidio*).

[35]Early Christians commonly identified the inscription and statue with Simon Magus; see Eusebius, *Hist. Eccl.* 2.13.3; Tertullian, *Apol.* 13.9. See also *LTUR*, vol. 4: 264; Richardson 1992: 347–348.

bidental; and the sacrificial victims, commonly sheep, offered in expiation for the strike, *bidentes*. The evidence of the strike was buried, which, together with the sacrifice, purified the ground.

The term *bidentes* is curious. In antiquity it caught the attention of Aulus Gellius (*NA* 16.6), who tells us that in his own study of documents of Pontifical law he discovered that the word had earlier been *bidennes*, used of animals 'two-years' old (that is, derived from *annus* 'year'), and speculates that by sound change it had evolved into *bidentes*. Iulius Hyginus, he allows, has a different understanding of the sense of the term, claiming that *bidentes* are animals with two teeth larger than the remainder (having eight in all), marking the age of the animals as appropriate for sacrificial use (compare Festus, p. 33M). Given that the fulgural science was well developed among the Etruscans, the term may conceivably be an Etruscan word which the Romans folk-etymologized.[36]

There are yet other indications of the fulgural affiliation of Semo Sancus. A bird of augury bears the god's name, the *avis Sanqualis* (see Festus, p. 317M; compare the name of the god's gate at the southwest end of the Quirinal, the *porta Sanqualis*, located near his temple, Festus, p. 345M). Festus (p. 317M) and Pliny (*HN* 10.20) identify the bird as an *ossifraga* ('bone- breaker', probably a lammergeier), of a sort not spotted in Rome since the days of the augur Mucius, adds Pliny (anchoring his observations in his own time). Livy records consecutively two sets of prodigies which occurred in 177 BC; the *avis Sanqualis* plays a role in the second, and the two sets are probably linked. The *first* set (41.9.4–7) consists of those prodigies reported *before* the consuls Gaius Claudius Pulcher and Tiberius Sempronius Gracchus drew lots in preparation for war against Sardinia and Histria. Livy records the *second* set (41.13.1–3) immediately *following* his account of the outcome of those conflicts—Sempronius' victory in Sardinia and Claudius' defeat of both the Histrians and the Ligurians. The first-named of those prodigies of the former set concerns a stone that had fallen from the sky, landing in a grove sacred to Mars in Crustumerium, a Sabine town north and slightly east of Rome. The first-named prodigy of the second set likewise concerns a sacred stone of Crustumerium; while Livy does not explicitly equate the two stones, given the shared context of the prodigies, their identity may well be rightly construed as self-evident (see Warde Fowler 1899: 140, n. 2). Concerning this stone, Livy reports that an *avis Sanqualis* (a 'bonebreaker')

[36]For Roman accounts of fulgural doctrine and its place in Etruria, see especially Seneca, *Q. Nat.* 2.32–59; Pliny, *HN* 2.138–144. For modern treatments and interpretations of the Roman accounts, see *ARR*: 637–649; Thulin 1968.

had struck it with his beak and cleaved it. The account of this prodigy is doubly interesting in that it presents the god Semo Sancus, through his augural bird, not only displaying his fulgural nature, striking and breaking apart a stone which had rained down from heaven, but sets him in conjunction with Mars, into whose grove the meteor had fallen. Here, much as in the Carmen Arvale, Mars and Semones—one rather than all—are united.

Semo Sancus Dius Fidius, god affiliated with the heavens and lightning, deity by whom oaths are sworn, also operates within the domain of the warrior. These various affiliations are intertwined within an episode of great antiquity in Rome's history, the conquest of Gabii by Tarquinius Superbus. Through intrigue and subterfuge, Sextus, son of the Tarquin king of Rome, had placed himself in a position of power within Gabii, so that the city was in time delivered to Rome with almost no opposition from the Gabini (see Livy 1.53.4–54.10; Dionysius of Halicarnassus, *Ant. Rom.* 4.53.1–58.4). According to Dionysius of Halicarnassus, Tarquinius, thinking it would strengthen his own position in Rome, treated the inhabitants of the captured city with beneficence and made certain concessions to them, taking oaths and certifying these arrangements with a treaty (*Ant. Rom.* 4.58.4):

> καὶ ἵνα μηδὲν αὐτοῖς ἔτι δεῖμα περὶ τοῦ μέλλοντος ὑπάρχῃ χρόνου μηδ' ἐνδοιάζωσιν εἰ βέβαια ταῦτα σφίσι διαμενεῖ, γράψας ἐφ' οἷς ἔσονται δικαίοις φίλοι, τὰ περὶ τούτων ὅρκια συνετέλεσεν ἐπὶ τῆς ἐκκλησίας παραχρῆμα καὶ διωμόσατο κατὰ τῶν σφαγίων. τούτων ἐστὶ τῶν ὁρκίων μνημεῖον ἐν Ῥώμῃ κείμενον ἐν ἱερῷ Διὸς Πιστίου, ὃν Ῥωμαῖοι Σάγκον καλοῦσιν, ἀσπὶς ξυλίνη βύρσῃ βοείᾳ περίτονος τοῦ σφαγιασθέντος ἐπὶ τῶν ὁρκίων τότε βοός, γράμμασιν ἀρχαϊκοῖς ἐπιγεγραμμένη τὰς γενομένας αὐτοῖς ὁμολογίας.

> And in order that [the Gabini] should neither be in fear regarding the future nor in doubt whether the promises made to them would be preserved intact, after specifying in writing the terms by which they would be considered friends, [Tarquinius] immediately sanctioned a treaty concerning these matters in the assembly [of the Gabini] and he swore an oath over the victims. There is a copy of this treaty in Rome, installed within a temple of Dius Fidius, whom the Romans call Sancus—a wooden shield covered with ox-hide, that of the ox sacrificed at the time of the treaty, with the terms thereof inscribed in archaic letters.[37]

[37]Compare the decrees which Servius Tullius had engraved on a bronze stele and displayed at the Aventine temple of Diana. According to Dionysius of Halicarnassus (*Ant. Rom.* 4.26.5), the decrees were written with a script that had been used in Greece in the remote past.

Thus Rome's first treaty—an archaic document marking the terms for cessation of war—finds refuge in the temple of Semo Sancus.[38]

We should note as an aside that a bronze statue of a woman called Gaia Caecilia was also displayed in the temple of Semo Sancus. Plutarch (*Quaest. Rom.* 30) identifies her as the female companion of one of the sons of Tarquinius. For Festus (p. 241M), Gaia Caecilia is wife to Tarquinius Priscus; similarly, Pliny (*HN* 8.194) reports that Gaia Caecilia is an alternative denotation for Tanaquil, wife of the elder Tarquin. Gaia's statue in Semo Sancus' temple, continues Festus, is girded by a belt in which certain prophylactic devices (*remedia*) of her invention, called *praebia*, had been laced. Those in danger would come and scrape off shavings of these *praebia*[39] for protection. Pliny further records that the wool on the distaff and spindle of this woman was kept in the temple of Semo Sancus. Plutarch (*Quaest. Rom.* 30) writes that the sandals and spindle of Gaia Caecilia had been kept there in the old days. The temple also housed, according to Livy (8.20.8–9), certain bronze *orbes* provided by the sale of the property of Vitruvius Vaccus, the Fundanian general defeated by Rome in 329 BC.

Semo Sancus Dius Fidius is drawn yet more fully into the realm of the warrior. As Varro tells us, he is identified with the warrior par excellence, Hercules. Festus (pp. 147, 229M) attests to the same identification (*id est Hercules*). In his poem on the setting up of the Ara Maxima, the altar said to have been built by Hercules at his defeat of the cattle-thieving monster Cacus, Propertius (4.9.71–74) can invoke Hercules as Sancus, the *sanctus pater*.[40] Semo Sancus and Hercules share an immediate affiliation in that the Romans swear oaths by both: *me Dius Fidius* stands alongside *me Hercule*[41] (as does *me Castor* [see Festus, p. 125M], the first typically used by men, the second by women). The source of the Roman oath by Hercules is obviously Greek, Heracles being one of those deities by whom the Greeks commonly swear. The ready Roman acquisition of the oath *me Hercule* must, however, betray a fundamental similarity between Roman Semo Sancus

[38]Compare Virgil, *Aen.* 12.200: *audiat haec genitor qui foedera fulmine sancit* ('May the *genitor* hear these [words] who ratifies treaties by [his] lightning').

[39]By the same name, *praebia*, Varro (*Ling.* 7.107) identifies such devices (*remedia*) as being worn by boys for protection.

[40]With Propertius' *sanctus pater*, compare the dedications of the Sacerdotes Bidentales: *CIL* 6.568 (*Sanco sancto Semon(i) deo Fidio*); *CIL* 6.30994 (*Semoni Sanco sancto deo Fidio*). *Sancus* is by editorial revision; Propertius actually names the god *Sanctus*, as is otherwise attested (by, among others, St. Augustine, *De Civ. D.* 18.19), undoubtedly by folk etymology based on *sanctus*, 'sacred'.

[41]See the above note on Plutarch, *Quaest. Rom.* 28.

Dius Fidius and Greek Heracles. Over a century ago, Warde Fowler aptly gave expression to this observation, though his own interpretation of the Roman god was assuredly quite different from our own:

> Again, the Roman oaths *me Dius Fidius* and *me Hercule* are synonymous; that the former was the older can hardly be doubted, and the latter must have come into vogue when the Greek oath by Heracles became familiar. Thus the origin of *me Hercule* must be found in a union of the characteristics of Hercules with those of the native Dius Fidius.

4.9.2.3 HERCULES AND CACUS A significant feature of Hercules' affiliation with the oath in Rome is his above-mentioned altar, the Ara Maxima (the 'Greatest Altar'). Standing in the Forum Boarium, opposite the entrance to the Circus Maximus, the Ara Maxima was an altar at which oaths were taken, agreements made, and tithes offered (Dionysius of Halicarnassus, *Ant. Rom.* 1.40.6; Diodorus Siculus 4.21.3–4). Hercules himself was said to have offered a tithe of cattle at the altar (Festus, p. 237M; *Ant. Rom.* 1.40.3). Rituals conducted at the Ara Maxima were said in antiquity to be Greek in form rather than Roman.[42]

It was during Hercules' visit with Evander and other Arcadian Greek settlers of the pre-Romulean Palatine, that the Greek hero is said to have established the Ara Maxima. At the time, Hercules was en route back to Greece with the trophies of the tenth labor assigned to him by his master Eurystheus—the cattle of Geryon. After crossing the Tiber in the vicinity of the Palatine, Hercules rested, and as he slept some of his cattle were stolen by the monstrous Cacus. Ovid tells the tale (*Fast.* 1.543–582; compare Virgil, *Aen.* 8.184–305; Propertius 4.9.1–20):

> Ecce boves illuc Erytheidas adplicat heros
> emensus longi claviger orbis iter,
> dumque huic hospitium domus est Tegeaea, vagantur
> incustoditae lata per arva boves.
> mane erat: excussus somno Tirynthius actor
> de numero tauros sentit abesse duos.
> nulla videt quaerens taciti vestigia furti:
> traxerat aversos Cacus in antra ferox,
> Cacus, Aventinae timor atque infamia silvae,
> non leve finitimis hospitibusque malum.

[42] *Ant. Rom.* 1.39.4; Servius, *Aen.* 8.276; Macrobius, *Sat.* 3.6.17; see the discussion in *ARR*: 436.

dira viro facies, vires pro corpore, corpus
grande (pater monstri Mulciber huius erat),
proque domo longis spelunca recessibus ingens,
abdita, vix ipsis invenienda feris;
ora super postes adfixaque bracchia pendent,
squalidaque humanis ossibus albet humus.
servata male parte boum Iove natus abibat:
mugitum rauco furta dedere sono.
"accipio revocamen" ait, vocemque secutus
impia per silvas ultor ad antra venit.
ille aditum fracti praestruxerat obice montis;
vix iuga movissent quinque bis illud opus.
nititur hic umeris (caelum quoque sederat illis),
et vastum motu conlabefactat onus.
quod simul eversum est, fragor aethera terruit ipsum,
ictaque subsedit pondere molis humus.
prima movet Cacus conlata proelia dextra
remque ferox saxis stipitibusque gerit.
quis ubi nil agitur, patrias male fortis ad artes
confugit, et flammas ore sonante vomit;
quas quotiens proflat, spirare Typhoea credas
et rapidum Aetnaeo fulgur ab igne iaci.
occupat Alcides, adductaque clava trinodis
ter quater adverso sedit in ore viri.
ille cadit mixtosque vomit cum sanguine fumos
et lato moriens pectore plangit humum.
immolat ex illis taurum tibi, Iuppiter, unum
victor et Evandrum ruricolasque vocat,
constituitque sibi, quae Maxima dicitur, aram,
hic ubi pars Urbis de bove nomen habet.

Look, here comes the club-carrying hero driving
Erythea's cows on his long world journey.
And while he is hosted in the Tegean house,
Cattle roam unguarded through broad acres.
It was morning: the acting herder from Tiryns
Jolts from sleep and counts two bulls as missing.
He searches, but sees no tracks from the silent theft;
Cacus had dragged them backward to his cave,
Savage Cacus, the Aventine wood's terror and shame,
No light problem for neighbors and guests.
His face was grim, his strength matched his body, his body
Huge: this monster's father was Mulciber.

A vast labyrinthine cavern served as his house,
  Remote: even beasts could barely find it.
Faces and limbs hang nailed above the doorposts;
  The filthy ground blanches with men's bones.
Jupiter's son was leaving with part of the herd
  Lost; the plunder bellowed raucously.
"I welcome the recall," he shouts. The avenger tracks
  The sound through the woods to the impious lair.
Cacus had blocked the entrance with a barricade of rock;
  Scarcely ten ox-teams could have shifted it.
Heaving with his shoulders (heaven once rested there),
  Hercules moves and topples the huge mass.
The crash of its dislodgment dismayed heaven itself;
  The battered earth sank beneath the bulk's weight.
Cacus at first fights hand to hand and skirmishes
  Ferociously with boulders and trees.
When this does nothing, he resorts unbravely
  To his father's arts, and retches roaring flame.
You would think every blast was Typhoeus' breath,
  A bolt of lightning hurled from Etna's fire.
Alcides grabs him, and sinks the tri-knotted club
  Three or four times in his opponent's face.
He collapses and vomits smoke mingled with blood,
  And hits the ground, dying, with his broad chest.
The victor sacrifices one bull to you, Jove,
  And calls Evander and the country folk.
He set up an altar to himself called 'Maxima'
  In the city district named from cattle.

For Virgil (*Aen.* 8.193–199), Cacus is a huge creature, half-human (*semihomo*) and fire-bellowing, a son of Volcanus (equivalent to Ovid's *Mulciber*, a name which may be derived from *mulcere*, 'to soothe, appease'; see *DELL*: 418.). Propertius (4.9.10) knows the monster to have three heads.

4.9.2.4 INDRA AND VṚTRA One familiar with the Vedas can hardly read the story of Cacus, his theft of cattle, and his destruction at the hands of the hero Hercules without being immediately reminded of the tale of Indra's great heroic deed, the destruction of the cattle-thieving, drought-bringing monster, Vṛtra. The resemblance is unmistakable and did not escape the attention of earlier investigators. While there are still earlier mentionings of the similarity (for example, in Kuhn 1848), in 1863 Michel Bréal, the French philologist and pioneering linguist, published a book-length analysis of Hercules and Cacus (republished in Bréal 1877), in which he invoked the comparison of Indra and Vṛtra.[43]

The significance of the comparison and the common Indo-European origin which it entails was slipping into the background, however, by the second decade of the twentieth century, chiefly under the influence, it would seem, of Wissowa (1971: 282–283) and subsequently Bayet (1926). For both scholars, the story was introduced to the Romans by Greeks of Magna Graecia. Wissowa (1971: 283) sees in the legend a Roman adaptation of a blending of three different Greek traditions—those of Heracles' fights with Geryon, owner of the cattle, and with the giant Alcyoneus, and the tale of Hermes' theft of Apollo's cattle. The Roman account, Wissowa conjectures, does not predate Virgil by much. The same sentiment is offered, almost verbatim, by Dumézil himself (*ARR*: 433): ". . . the legend of the rather unfriendly meeting of Hercules and Cacus was certainly not very old when Virgil reinforced it by his art."

Drawing on Bayet's study, which seems to have exerted an appreciable influence on him, Dumézil points out that the Roman tradition looks to be only one particular form of a Herculean tale which must have been popular in Magna Graecia. Thus at the site of Crotona in the south of Italy, a certain Lacinius tried to steal Heracles' cattle as he was driving them through that region; the strong man killed Lacinius and, accidentally, Croton as well, who had welcomed Heracles. In expiation, Heracles built a great tomb for Croton and prophesied that a city (Crotona) would one day be named for him. A similar story is told of Lacinius and one Locrus, who, slain by Heracles, becomes the namesake of Locri. To be sure, the Cacus described by Livy (1.7.5–7) and Dionysius of Halicarnassus (*Ant. Rom.* 1.39.2–4) is no fire-breathing monster, but a cave-dwelling shepherd. The second-century BC annalist Gnaeus Gellius knows Cacus as a man who comes to Italy with the Phrygian king Marsyas; this Cacus leads an attack against Campania and is there killed by Hercules (see Alföldi 1965: 228–229; note his discussion of an Etruscan Cacus, a prophet captured by the Etruscan heroic pair, the

[43] Various subsequent investigators followed Bréal's lead: inter alia, Schwegler 1853: 371; Peter 1937, vol. 1: 2279; Oldenberg 1917: 143–144; cf. Frazer 1929, vol. 2: 209–210. Bréal's work is a gem from the very infancy of the comparative analysis of Indo-European myth and religion, probably of greatest value for a study of the history of the discipline; indeed, in the preface to Bréal 1877, the author writes: "Mon souhait, en finissant, est que ce livre contribue à répandre de plus en plus le goût des recherches historiques appliquées à la religion et au langage, et qu'il leur attire de nouveaux disciples" (p. vi). Dumézil writes (*ARR*: 433): "'Hercules and Cacus'—these names call to mind the fine book by Michel Bréal—now out of date, but how intelligent (1863)!—written in the heroic, enthusiastic period of Indo-European studies."

brothers Vibenna). For Diodorus Siculus (4.21.1–3) he is Cacius, a prominent member of the Palatine community who welcomes Hercules hospitably. Some authorities report that Cacus has a sister, Caca, a fire goddess with a shrine in which a perpetual flame burns, and who is worshipped in a manner similar to the worship of Vesta; she was promoted to such divine status as a reward for betraying her brother to Hercules.[44]

The story of Hercules and Cacus could well be a Roman expression of a tale commonly told among Greeks of Italy as they nurtured memories of their homeland, a story of their beloved hero Heracles and a cattle thief whom he encounters and kills as he drives Geryon's cows homeward to Eurystheus. The whole affair smacks of the sort of local legends about folk heroes such as Paul Bunyan that sprang up as new settlers arrived in and moved across the frontier of America. The fact remains, however, that the Roman "variant" of this story is remarkably similar to the single most prominent achievement in the dossier of Indra, his destruction of Vṛtra, and appears particularly so when viewed in the light of the character of Semo Sancus and the Semones which we see emerging. The Indic account itself exists in several variant forms, for more than one of which there is good evidence of an antiquity that antedates Vedic India. More than that, we would contend, the Roman account of Hercules and the monstrous Cacus is indeed descended from the same Indo-European tradition that gives rise to the Vedic stories.

> Indrasya nu vīriyāṇi pra vocaṃ yāni cakāra prathamāni vajrī
> ahann ahim anu apas tatarda pra vakṣaṇā abhinat parvatānām
>
> Now I proclaim the bold deeds of Indra,
> the first done by the thunderbolt-wielder.
> He killed the dragon and opened the waters;
> he cleaved the belly of the mountains.

So begins *Rig Veda* 1.32, telling the deed to which allusion is made again and again in the Vedas (see especially Watkins 1995: 297–320 and passim; Benveniste and Renou 1934). The dragon (*ahi-*) is named Vṛtra 'resistance'. In his mountain cave he has held back the waters—commonly likened to cattle—and so he brings drought. Indra slays the dragon and the waters stream down "like lowing cattle" (*RV* 1.32.2). The great warrior god does not accomplish this deed alone, however. He is assisted by Viṣṇu and by his

[44]Lactantius, *Div. Inst.* 1.20; Servius, *Aen.* 8.190. On Caca, see Wissowa 1971: 161, n. 6. Of Caca's existence as a goddess, Dumézil is suspicious; see *ARR*: 43, n. 10. The variant of this story preserved by Aurelius Victor (*Orig. Gent. Rom.* 6.8) identifies the owner of the cattle as a Greek of Herculean strength named Recaranus; cf. Servius, *Aen.* 8.203.

comrades-in-arms, the storming Maruts.[45] At times, the Maruts alone are said to have defeated the monster. The deed is also credited to Trita Āptya, to whom we shall return shortly.

Indra is commonly called Vṛtrahan, 'slayer of Vṛtra', an epithet which can also be applied to other conquering deities, but which first and foremost belongs to Indra. The figure of the Vṛtrahan is at least of common Indo-Iranian origin, being matched by Avestan Vərəθraγna (both descending from Proto-Indo-Iranian **vr̥tra-ǰʰan-* 'smiting resistance', though the latter is quite distinct from Avestan Indra, who has been demonized through the religious reforms of Zaraθuštra. Dumézil (1970: 111–138), looking further afield, draws attention to a related warrior figure, the Armenian Vahagn, acquired from the Iranian Parthians. Comparing the birth narrative of Vahagn, preserved by the Armenian historian Moses of Chorene, with the Brahmanic account of the rebirth of Indra following his defeat of Vṛtra, Dumézil can argue that the common linguistic antecedent of Vedic Vṛtrahan and Avestan Vərəθraγna was a denotation applied already to Proto-Indo-Iranian Indra (see especially pp. 117, 128–129). Even so, there is good reason to suspect that the monster Vṛtra has acquired his name derivatively from the epithet of his slayer (see Watkins 1995: 298, 304, with references to Benveniste and Renou 1934).

4.9.2.5 TRITA ĀPTYA AND THE TRICEPHAL As already noted, the Vedic tale of the destruction of the worm exists in varied forms. The variant which is richest in mythic detail, and so provides the most valuable diagnostic for detecting homologous traditions among other Indo-European peoples, is the tale identifying the slayer of the dragon—one with three heads—as Trita Āptya, operating in league with Indra (who sometimes acts alone, who sometimes seems to be identical to Trita Āptya). Because of the similarities demonstrably shared with other Indo-European traditions, this account ipso facto leaves the impression of being of a more primitive, a more primary sort than the variety "Indra Vṛtrahan slays Vṛtra," for which there is a dearth of specifics.[46]

The dragon slayer Trita Āptya is a deity affiliated with water (compare Sanskrit *ap* 'water', *āpaḥ* 'waters'), the 'third' (*trita*) of the Āptya broth-

[45]The slaying of the monster is at times associated with Soma and Agni. In one tradition, the Maruts are said to have retreated from the fray, as in *RV* 1.165.6.

[46]Compare Watkins' (1995: 299, n. 4) citation and translation of remarks penned in Benveniste and Renou 1934 (p. 108): "The myth of Vṛtra can be subsumed essentially in the formula 'Indra slew Vṛtra': the brute fact is repeated a hundred times with different variations which most of the time bring no additional information. But one feature predominates, namely that this act is considered important. . . ."

ers (the other two being, naturally, Ekata 'first' and Dvita 'second' Āptya). The fire deity, Agni, had hidden in the waters, from which he was unwillingly extracted by the gods. The *Śatapatha Brāhmaṇa* tells it thus: Agni spat on those waters, from which then emerged Trita Āptya and his brothers (compare *MS* 4.1.9; *TB* 3.2.8.9–12).[47] These three then attached themselves to the retinue of Indra, following him in his wanderings. Consonant with their name, the Āptya are affiliated with a ritual of purification which is conducted while pouring water for each of the three brothers in turn (see *ŚB* 1.2.3.1–5). Trita Āptya has a dwelling in the heavens. In *Rig Veda* 2.34, a hymn to the Maruts—who are praised as lovers of rain, glowing like fire, gleaming in their armor, bringing food to those who praise them—Trita Āptya is said to convey the Maruts to their worshippers in his chariot (v. 14). The Maruts, conversely, are said to have reinforced the strength of Trita as he aided Indra in his fight against the dragon in *Rig Veda* 8.7.24, in which hymn the Maruts are also praised for hacking away the limbs of Vṛtra and cleaving the mountain in which the waters were held.

In the default tradition, the dragon who is killed by Trita Āptya bears the name Viśvarūpa 'having many shapes'. He is a son of Tvaṣṭṛ, the smith-god who made the thunderbolt for Indra. Viśvarūpa, also called Triśiras 'tricephalic', is characteristically and redundantly described not only as three-headed but as six-eyed as well. As in Indra's slaying of Vṛtra, the cattle motif is again prominent: Viśvarūpa possesses cattle which are driven away by the one who slays him. The Indic tradition of Trita Āptya slaying Viśvarūpa is exactly matched by an Iranian account; the *Avesta* preserves a record of the warrior Thraētaona (= Trita Āptya) and his destruction of the dragon Aži Dahāka—three-headed, six-eyed, three-mouthed. The motif is not only common Indo-Iranian but early Indo-European, as we have seen, being matched by the Greek tradition of Heracles' murder of the three-headed (three-bodied) Geryon and the theft of his cattle.[48]

Other variant forms of the Indic tradition should be mentioned. First, there are the Paṇis, demonic creatures who pen up stolen cattle in a cave. Indra (or some other deity, such as Agni or Soma) attacks them and releases the cattle. Similarly, Trita Āptya or Indra shatters the creature called Vala 'enclosure' and releases cattle he has corralled.

4.9.2.6 SEMO SANCUS AND THE TRICEPHAL To return to the point made prior to the recent digression on the slaying of monsters—three-headed,

[47]On the two last-named texts, see Bloomfield 1896 and Dumont 1956.

[48]See Benveniste and Renou 1934; Dumézil 1970: 12–28; Watkins 1995: 313–320, 464–468.

cattle-thieving, and otherwise—the Roman tradition about Cacus and his theft of the cattle of Hercules might very well preserve a folk legend common among Greeks of the south of Italy—one that recounts how a human thief had tried to rob Heracles as he drove Geryon's cattle toward Greece. At the same time, in view of the secure Indo-European motif of the hero who slays a three-headed monster, attested by parallel Indic, Iranian, and Greek accounts, coupled with the Roman predilection for preserving ancient Indo-European religious ideas, structures, and vocabulary, there is a strong a priori case for identifying Hercules' destruction of Cacus as yet another inherited form of this ancient Indo-European myth. The two formative phenomena here at work—one of borrowing, one of inheritance—are certainly not of necessity mutually exclusive processes. There is, one might deduce, an a posteriori suggestion of this dual operation in the striking dichotomy that characterizes the differing accounts of this event. Cacus is a man for the historians, Livy, Dionysius of Halicarnassus, Gnaeus Gellius, Diodorus Siculus—there is no suggestion to the contrary. Cacus is a terrifying monster for the poets, Ovid, Virgil, Propertius—there is no suggestion to the contrary.

Given the Roman assimilation of Greek Heracles to native Semo Sancus, underlying the story of Hercules and Cacus is almost certainly an inherited Italic myth of Semo Sancus and his slaying of a three-headed, cattle-holding fiend. Like Trita Āptya, Semo Sancus is one member of a larger set of deities, and these, in both instances, are deities whose essential affiliation is with water—rainwater in the case of the fulgural Semo Sancus, and in a naturalistically parallel manner, the waters from which fire emerged in the case of Trita Āptya. The same affiliation equally characterizes the stormy Maruts, who themselves are credited with assisting in or performing the execution of Vṛtra and Viśvarūpa. Each band of deities—Italic Semones and Indic Āptyas and Maruts—forms part of the retinue of the great warrior god, Roman Mars and Indic Indra: the Indic relationship is amply attested; the Roman is revealed by Mars and the Semones conspiring in the Carmen Arvale, with Mars invoked to call this band into action.

The cattle-holding villains similarly match. Like Viśvarūpa, the Roman thief Cacus is three-headed. This we learn from Propertius, who writes not only of three temples struck by the hero (*tria tempora*; 4.9.15) but describes the monster as producing noises emanating from three mouths (*per tria ora*; 4.9.10); compare Avestan descriptions of Aži Dahāka as "three-mouthed, three-headed, six-eyed" (as in *Yašt* 9.8: . . . Azīm Dahākəm θrizafanəm θrikamərəδəm xšuuaš.ašīm . . .). Propertius' description likely rests on an archaic Indo-European "poetic and mythographic formula" of the sort identified by Watkins ("THREE-HEADED and SIX-EYED") on the basis of Indo-

Iranian and Greek evidence (see Watkins 1995: 464–468). The Roman evidence taken in tandem with the Avestan likely suggests a fuller form of the formula (THREE-MOUTHED and THREE-HEADED and SIX-EYED).

Also like Viśvarūpa (and Vṛtra by some accounts), Cacus is the son of the smith-god. Virgil, describing the half-human monster, terrible in form (*semihominis*[49] *Caci facies dira*; *Aen.* 8.194), tells us that his father was Volcanus (*huic monstro Volcanus erat pater*; 8.198). In the same way, Ovid identifies Cacus' father as Mulciber (*pater monstri Mulciber huius erat*; *Fast.* 1.554). The agreement between the Indic and Italic myths at this point involves an element so idiosyncratic as to provide a compelling diagnostic of the ultimate common source of the two traditions. An equivalent paternity is absent from the Greek traditions of Heracles and Geryon, in which the latter is held to be son of Chrysaor, offspring of Medusa and Poseidon (see Hesiod, *Theog.* 280–288; Apollodorus, *Bibl.* 2.4.2–3). Greece and its Heraclean traditions, hence, do not provide the Romans with a pedigree for the monster Cacus; the origin of that element of the Italic tradition is of far greater antiquity.

The Latin poetic descriptions of the struggle between Hercules / Semo Sancus and Cacus are likewise impressively similar to Vedic accounts of Indra's battle with Vṛtra. No other two Indo-European strains of the myth are so similar in this regard. In India, Vṛtra is holed up in his mountain lair:

- Indra splits open the mountain where Vṛtra has penned up the cattle (*RV* 1.32.1–2).
- With his thunderbolt of a thousand points, Indra strikes the dragon, who is situated down within his lair (*RV* 6.17.9–10).
- The dragon enshrouds himself in fog and fights with lightening (*RV* 1.32.13).
- Vṛtra cannot withstand the attack of Indra; the hero shatters him and crushes his nose (*RV* 1.32.6). He smashes Vṛtra's jaws (*AV* 1.21.3).
- Indra strikes Vṛtra on the neck with his thunderbolt, or cudgel (*RV* 1.32.7; for the meaning 'cudgel' of Sanskrit *vájra-* and its significance, see Watkins 1995: 332, 410–411, 430–431).
- Indra fells the dragon like a tree laid low by an ax (*RV* 1.32.5).

In Rome, Cacus blocks the entrance to his cave:

- Hercules heaves and topples the great obstructive mass with an

[49] Has Virgil in his description of the monster as *semihomo* inadvertently left a trace of the ancient Italic tradition in which the slayer of the monster was named as Semo or the Semones? Compare the Roman folk etymology that derives Semo from *semihomo* to which Martianus Capella gives voice (see note above).

enormous heaven-shaking crash (Ovid, *Fast.* 1.563–568); or he wrenches the top from the mount, gutting the cavern of Cacus.

- Hercules rains down missiles on the monster (Virgil, *Aen.* 8.236–250).
- Cacus enshrouds himself in a fog of smoke (Virgil, *Aen.* 8.251–255) and belches flames (Ovid, *Fast.* 1.573–574).
- Hercules throttles Cacus (Virgil, *Aen.* 8.259–261); he seizes him and strikes the monster in the face (*os*) "three times, and four times" (*ter quater*) with his "three-knotted" club (*clava trinodis*; Ovid. *Fast.* 1.575–576).
- The hero strikes the monster on each of its three temples with his club (*ramus*) and lays him out dead (Propertius 4.9.15–16).

A word about Ovid's lexical choices: as cited above, Boyle and Woodard (2000: 20) translate *Fasti* 1.575–576, *occupat Alcides, adductaque clava trinodis ter quater adverso sedit in ore viri*, as "Alcides grabs him, and sinks the tri-knotted club three or four times in his opponent's face." The rendering of *os* as English "face," rather than by its primary sense of "mouth," is typical of translations of the verse (compare Frazer 1989: 43; Nagle 1995: 52) and is perhaps informed by Propertius' corresponding use of *tempus* (*iacuit pulsus tria tempora ramo Cacus*; 4.9.15–16). A literary depiction of the tri-notted club being repeatedly slammed on the monster's *face*—as opposed to slammed on his *mouth*—probably has a somewhat more heroic flavor and makes for a more dramatically pleasing translation.

Even so, examination of the lines within their immediate context gives one cause to reconsider. Lines 569–578 are repeated below together with the Boyle and Woodard translation, slightly modified:

> prima movet Cacus conlata proelia dextra
> remque ferox saxis stipitibusque gerit.
> quis ubi nil agitur, patrias male fortis ad artes
> confugit, et flammas *ore* sonante vomit;
> quas quotiens proflat, spirare Typhoea credas
> et rapidum Aetnaeo fulgur ab igne iaci.
> occupat Alcides, adductaque clava trinodis
> *ter* quater adverso sedit in *ore* viri.
> ille cadit mixtosque vomit cum sanguine fumos
> et lato moriens pectore plangit humum.

> Cacus at first fights hand to hand and skirmishes
> Ferociously with boulders and trees.
> When this does nothing, he resorts unbravely
> To his father's arts, and retches flames from his roaring *mouth*.

You would think every blast was Typhoeus' breath,
  A bolt of lightning hurled from Etna's fire.
Alcides grabs him, and sinks the tri-knotted club
  Three or four times in his opponent's *mouth*.
He collapses and vomits smoke mingled with blood,
  And hits the ground, dying, with his broad chest.

The monster has abandoned his hand-to-hand tactics; it is Cacus' fire-belching mouth (l. 572) which has become the immediate source of danger to the hero. That the hero's cudgel-blows are being described as delivered directly to the monster's mouth, serving now as the creature's chief weapon, appears probable and is reinforced by the significant textual variant *in ora* 'against the lips', 'against the mouth'. This line of inquiry is made yet more intriguing by the poet's declaration that these blows to the mouth are made three times (or four times): *ter quater adverso sedit in ore viri*. It would involve taking but a small interpretative step to posit that lying behind Ovid's line is a tradition of a strike being delivered to each of three mouths (whether the account is intentionally altered by Ovid or the poet simply uses a modified version circulating in his day—or to which he otherwise had access). So interpreted, Ovid's description of the hero's fight with the monster transparently points back to an archaic Italic mythic theme (and ultimately Proto-Indo-European formula) of the hero's destruction of a three-mouthed, three-headed monster, one which is preserved more fully and explicitly by Propertius. Indeed, the sense of the variant reading *in ora* could be "against the mouths," reflecting the ancient tricephalic tradition of the monster.

4.9.2.7 HERCULES AND BONA DEA A marked feature of rituals conducted at Hercules' altar in the Forum Boarium, the Ara Maxima, is the exclusion of women. Not so very far from this altar, situated on the slopes of the eastern prominence of the Aventine (*Aventinus Minor*), stood the temple of the 'good goddess', Bona Dea. The cult of Bona Dea was characterized by an equal but opposite form of discrimination, males being prohibited from entering the temple of the goddess (Ovid, *Fast.* 5.153–154; Macrobius, *Sat.* 1.12.26–27). Men were similarly excluded from a secret nocturnal rite of Bona Dea held each December at the home of a Roman magistrate—the setting of the scandalous affair of 62 BC when Clodius, disguised as a lute girl, slipped into the rites as they were being celebrated at the home of Julius Caesar (see Plutarch, *Caes.* 9.3–10.7 and the discussion of Brouwer 1989: 363–370).

The rationale proffered for excluding women from rites observed at the Ara Maxima is linked to the neighboring goddess Bona Dea. Propertius preserves the tradition (4.9.21–74). Following Hercules' defeat of Cacus and release of the pent-up cattle (and prophesying the future Forum Boarium), the hero is exhausted and parched with thirst (4.9.21–26):

> Dixerat, et sicco torquet sitis ora palato,
> terraque non ullas feta ministrat aquas.
> sed procul inclusas audit ridere puellas,
> lucus ubi umbroso fecerat orbe nemus,
> femineae loca clausa deae fontesque piandos,
> impune et nullis sacra retecta viris.

> He spoke, and his palate dry, thirst torments his lips,
> and water-rich earth offers him not a drop.
> But from afar he hears secreted maidens laughing,
> where a wood had made a grove of shadowy orb,
> Place enclosed for women's goddess and springs for cleansing,
> and rites unveiled to no man with impunity.

Captivated by the lilting, watery sounds, the spent hero hurries to the grove, desperately in search of relief. It is a place of deep shade and song birds, with suspended red headbands veiling its entrance (4.9.31–36):

> huc ruit in siccam congesta pulvere barbam,
> et iacit ante fores verba minora deo:
> "Vos precor, o luci sacro quae luditis antro,
> pandite defessis hospita fana viris.
> fontis egens erro circum antra sonantia lymphis;
> et cava succepto flumine palma sat est. . . ."

> Here he rushes with dust clumped in his dry beard,
> and before the gates he speaks words too small for a god:
> "I beg you, who play within the sacred hollow of this grove,
> make your sacred spaces hospitably open to exhausted men.
> In need of a spring, I wander around dells that sing with waters;
> a cupped hand of scooped-up water is enough. . . ."

The hero identifies himself, rehearses his warrior fame, especially his descent into the realm of Dis (an anachronistic reference to Heracles' twelfth labor, not yet accomplished at the time he acquires Geryon's cattle), and continues to bemoan his present anguish (4.9.65–66):[50]

[50] Here we have followed Goold's transposition of lines 65–66; see Goold 1999: 374.

"Angulus hic mundi nunc me mea fata trahentem
accipit: haec fesso vix mihi tecta patent. . . ."

"This corner of the world now has me—dragging out
my fate: exhausted, these shelters hardly take me in. . . ."

Hercules tries to persuade the priestess of the goddess to admit him to the grove, recounting his service to Omphale in women's clothing (an event lying beyond Heracles' service to Eurystheus; 4.9.51–60):

talibus Alcides; at talibus alma sacerdos,
puniceo canas stamine vincta comas:
"Parce oculis, hospes, lucoque abscede verendo;
cede agedum et tuta limina linque fuga
interdicta viris metuenda lege piatur
quae se summota vindicat ara casa.
magno Tiresias aspexit Pallada vates,
fortia dum posita Gorgone membra lavat.
di tibi dent alios fontes: haec lympha puellis
avia secreti limitis unda fluit."

Thus spoke Alcides; but said the kindly priestess,
her hoary locks tethered by a red band:
"Avert your eyes, stranger, and depart this holy grove,
withdraw now and leave its thresholds in safe retreat.
Prohibited to men, it is avenged by a law to be feared,
by which the altar in this secluded hut takes its revenge.
At a great price Teresias the prophet gazed upon Pallas,
while she bathed her strong limbs, her Aegis laid aside.
May the gods give you other springs: these waters for maidens
flow, remote spring of hidden course."

The "great price" paid by the Greek prophet Teresias is the blindness which struck him as he gazed at Athena, naked in her stream-bath (see Apollodorus, *Bibl.* 3.6.7; Callimachus, *Hymn* 5.57–130). Clearly, the message of the old priestess is that the hero would see the women within the grove naked, should he enter, and suffer a similar fate.[51] Hercules is not, however,

[51]This is not to suggest that the poet's words betray a practice of ritual nudity in the cult of Bona Dea. Regarding that consideration, however, certain observations made by Brouwer in his study of the goddess (1989: 331) are of interest: "Descriptions of the festivities of the goddess, too, make it clear that the wine is an important element and certainly not an offering only. In his picture of the perverse celebration of the Bona Dea mysteries by men, Juvenal warns the degenerate that he will be received by those

to be dissuaded from obtaining relief from his anguish—naked women or no (4.9.61–70):

> sic anus: ille umeris postis concussit opacos,
> nec tulit iratam ianua clausa sitim.
> at postquam exhausto iam flumine vicerat aestum,
> ponit vix siccis tristia iura labris:
> "Maxima quae gregibus devotast Ara repertis,
> ara per has" inquit "maxima facta manus,
> haec nullis umquam pateat veneranda puellis,
> Herculis externi ne sit inulta sitis."

> Thus spoke the hag: he rammed in the shady door-posts with his shoulders,
> and the closed gate did not withstand his furious thirst.
> But after he had subdued his raging heat, the stream now drained,
> with lips barely dried he ordains a solemn law:
> "The Ara Maxima, which was vowed with my cattle recovered,
> altar made greatest," said he, "by these hands,
> Let this venerable site never be open to any woman,
> lest the thirst of the foreigner Hercules be unavenged."

Propertius than concludes this etiological story with a remarkable postscript (4.9.71–74; the order of the couplets is that of Goold 1999):

> hunc, quoniam manibus purgatum sanxerat orbem,
> sic Sancum Tatiae composuere Cures.
> Sancte pater, salve, cui iam favet aspera Iuno:
> Sance, velis libro dexter inesse meo.

> This one, since by his hands he consecrated the orb made pure,
> Cures of Tatius thus established as Sancus.
> Blessed Father, hail, whom now harsh Juno kindly favors:
> Sancus, may you, propitious, be pleased to have a place in my book.

Cures is the city of the Sabine Titus Tatius, and, as noted above, it is with

---

who, at home, wear long ribbons round their foreheads and hide their necks under necklaces 'trying to mollify Bona Dea with the belly of a young sow and a larger crater' (with wine). Juvenal's diatribe against immoral women gives a description of the feast in honour of Bona Dea as an opportunity for sexual dissipations, stimulated, among other things, by wine-drinking: 'The mysteries of Bona Dea are known when the flute stirs the loins and Priapus' maenads delirious with music and wine whirl round with flying hair and uttering loud shrieks. Oh, how strong is then the desire for the pleasures of the bed that sways their senses, what cries now passion is roused, how abundantly streams that old wine down their wet legs.'"

the Sabines that Semo Sancus Dius Fidius is commonly affiliated.[52] Compare the remarks of St. Augustine (*De Civ. D.* 18.19):

> Sed Aenean, quoniam quando mortuus est non conparuit, deum sibi fecerunt Latini. Sabini etiam regem suum primum Sancum sive, ut aliqui appellant, Sanctum, rettulerunt in deos.
>
> But Aeneas—since he disappeared when he died, the Latins made him their god. The Sabines also assigned to the gods their first king, Sancus, or, as others call him, Sanctus.

Lactantius (*Div. Inst.* 1.15) agrees with St. Augustine.

The two final couplets of Propertius 4.9 are remarkable for several reasons. For one, with these lines Propertius not only links Semo Sancus directly to the personage of Hercules but also brings the Italic god explicitly into the context of the myth of the triple-mouthed, triple-headed monster and the hero who slays him. Moreover, it is clear that Propertius is thereby tying together the tale of the tricephalic monster, the ensuing exhaustion of the hero, and the establishment or legitimization of Sancus as a deity among the Sabines. To see why this concatenation of events, and specific elements thereof, is of such significance, we must examine some of Dumézil's own findings about the hero who slays the tricephal—but, first, an aside.

4.9.2.7.1 Propertius the poet Before moving ahead—a word on Propertius. The author is all too aware that some classicists will object to his use of Propertius and other poets as providers of data for deeply ancient Indo-European traditions and the reflexes of those traditions in Rome, crying that "the poets have their own agendas, literary and political"; "the poets possess personal creativity and are not just conduits for the transmission of archaic motifs"; and similar such things. Unquestionably these are not completely irrelevant matters. However, to reject out of hand cross-culturally recurring structure because of the mantle in which it is cloaked in Rome would be abjectly nonsensical and a pitiable squandering of precious data. That complex Roman data preserved by the poets closely match equally complex data from other and widely distributed Indo-European traditions—Indic, Scythian, Celtic—self-evidently demonstrates the value

[52]As noted earlier, *Sancus* in lines 72 and 74 is an editorial revision of *Sanctus*, a modified form of the god's name that certainly owes its shape to folk etymology; see St. Augustine's remarks that follow in the main text. Obviously, Propertius is here making precisely such an etymological connection, linking *Sancus* (*Sanctus*) with *sanctus*, in *Sanctus Pater*, 'blessed father'.

of a comparative investigation using the core traditions preserved by Roman poets. In the case immediately at hand, the poet is Propertius—who, by the time he has penned his fourth book of elegy has become the self-styled Roman Callimachus (4.1.61–64):

> Ennius hirsuta cingat sua dicta corona:
>   mi folia ex hedera porrige, Bacche, tua,
> ut nostris tumefacta superbiat Umbria libris,
>   Umbria Romani patria Callimachi!

> Ennius may crown his lines with a shaggy garland:
>   Hold out to me leaves of your ivy, Bacchus,
> So that Umbria may burst with pride at my books,
>   Umbria, homeland of the Roman Callimachus!

Propertius is Umbrian—in the hills and valleys of which place the ancient Italic rites and gods were preserved down to the century of Propertius, as revealed by the bronze *tabulae Iguvinae* of the Atiedian priesthood of Umbria (see §§1.5.4; 3.3.3.2.3)—traditions making their presence felt even to the present day (see §1.7.1.4.5). He is an Umbrian come to Rome with the death of his father and the confiscation and parceling out of his family's property by Octavian following the Perusine War. In Rome he would put on the *toga virilis* in the presence of "his mother's gods" (*matris et ante deos libera sumpta toga*; 4.1.132). And now, in his fourth book of elegy, he instructs his readers in ancient gods and rites; the Umbrian continues (4.1.67–70):

> Roma, fave, tibi surgit opus; date candida, cives,
>   omina; et inceptis dextera cantet avis!
> sacra deosque canam et cognomina prisca locorum:
>   has meus ad metas sudet oportet equus.

> Rome, show me favor—for you my work arises; give favorable omens,
>   Citizens, and let an auspicious bird proclaim its start!
> Rites and gods I shall sing, and the ancient names of places:
>   To that goal my sweating steed must strive.

Though he puts behind him much of the erotic emphasis of his earlier work, Propertius remains politically irreverent to the end; consider his Callimachean account of Actium (4.6). And one wonders whether that irreverence might find subtle expression in aetiological recounting of ancient Italic tradition on which he was weaned in Umbria; we have noted already the conspicuous presence of Fisus Sancius (recall Semo Sancus in Propertius 4.9) in the Umbrian ritual of the Atiedian priests (see §1.5.4; and §4.9.2.2 on Semo Sancus Dius Fidius). In any event, Augustus must have given the nod to the poet's new venture—all to the benefit of the comparativist.

By the rationale of my critics, the historical linguist would reject the value of, for example, Tocharian for providing data relevant to the study of the parent Indo-European language. Tocharian is first attested only in the sixth century AD. Its speakers had been settled in the deserts of China for centuries prior to the earliest attestation of the language. The documents preserving the Tocharian languages are largely Buddhist materials, culturally far removed from the speakers of the parent language. Yet the structures of the language are unequivocally Indo-European and provide important data for comparative Indo-European analysis and the reconstruction of Proto-Indo-European.

By that same rationale, the comparative ichthyologist would reject the value of the cartilaginous skeletal structure of chimaeras for studying the developmental history of cartilaginous fish. Chimaeras have only a single external gill opening, possess an erectile dorsal spine, a tentaculum in front of the pelvic fins and another on the forehead, and teeth fused into plates. In spite of their specialized developmental features, however, they remain relevant to the comparative study of Chondrichthyes, whether a member of the class, together with sharks, skates, and rays, or constituting a separate class.

Moreover, though the process is fundamentally different (one of borrowing rather than shared inheritance), by the same token Hellenists would reject the value of looking to the Near East for literary sources of Homeric and Hesiodic traditions. Homer and Hesiod, no one would deny, are personally creative and have their own literary designs grounded in archaic Greece. Nevertheless, they can incorporate in their epics Near Eastern motifs found, for example, in the Anatolian and Mesopotamian traditions of a king in heaven and his struggle for the throne, and in the Babylonian *Atrahasis* with its account of the division of the cosmos among three gods by the casting of lots. And the poets of those Near Eastern traditions are themselves no less creative and no less culturally contextualized.

The reader gets the picture. The movement from the known to the unknown, reminding ourselves again of Bernard's dictum, the crux of all scientific investigation and discovery, only occurs by the careful, informed analysis of the data with which the investigator is presented. To ignore that data is to choose not to move, not to discover.

4.9.2.8 THE HERO BEYOND THE BOUNDARY An item in Indra's dragon-slaying dossier has been carefully studied by Dumézil vis-à-vis Ossetic (Iranian) and Irish heroic traditions. This episode proves to be of great importance, we will argue, in understanding the Roman tradition of the dragon-slayer Semo Sancus, a.k.a. Hercules, and reflects fundamental elements of Roman cult, inherited from much earlier Indo-European religious practice. Dumézil's own interpretative analysis focuses on the canonical Indo-European "threeness" of the several accounts and on the calming or cooling of the hero which follows his destruction of the monstrous tricephalic foe. These are undeniably central and crucial elements of the traditions; however, I would claim that equal, if not greater, significance lies in events acted out within the spatial domain—the hero's withdrawal to a place beyond "the boundary," his eventual return, and the benefit that society accrues upon his return.

4.9.2.8.1 The Indic hero Indra has defeated the cattle-thieving serpent Vṛtra. With the monster destroyed, however, a loss of strength and vitality, a sense of foreboding ironically overwhelm the warrior god. He flees and takes refuge in a remote, watery corner of the earth.

The trauma is mentioned only once in the *Rig Veda*, in hymn 1.32, one of the principal texts praising Indra's incomparable deed (noted above). This hymn succinctly touches on numerous aspects of Indra's fight with the monster—so many teasingly compact building blocks of the episode. Recitation of these heroic deeds comes to a crescendo in the thirteenth verse:

> nāsmai vidyun na tanyatuḥ siṣedha na yām miham akirad dhrādunim̩ ca
> Indraś ca yad yuyudhāte ahiś ca utāparībhyo Maghavā vi jigye.

> Neither lightning nor thunder helped him,
> nor the hail and fog he spread about.
> When Indra and the dragon struggled,
> Maghavan gained the victory for all time.

The description is familiar. Ovid (*Fast.* 1.573–574) has told us how the monster struggling with Hercules resorts at the end to flames, belched forth like lightning from Etna. Virgil (*Aen.* 8.251–255) describes how in desperation—the hero having split open the monster's cavernous enclosure—Cacus cloaks himself in a fog of smoke:

> Ille autem, neque enim fuga iam super ulla pericli,
> faucibus ingentem fumum (mirabile dictu)
> evomit involvitque domum caligine caeca

prospectum eripiens oculis, glomeratque sub antro
fumiferam noctem commixitis igne tenebris.

But he, since now there can be no flight from danger,
from his jaws heavy smoke (marvelous to tell)
he belches forth, and shrouds his den in blinding fog
snatching away sight from eyes, and he gathers deep in the cave
smoke-borne night, darkness mixed with flame.

It is all to no avail in the end. Hercules charges through the smoke (8.259–261):

Hic Cacum in tenebris incendia vana vomentem
corripit in nodum complexus, et angit inhaerens
elisos oculos et siccum sanguine guttur.

Here in darkness Cacus retching useless flames,
the hero seized him in a knot-tight hold, and with a viselike grip
he throttles him, his eyes bulging and throat choked of blood.

Back to *Rig Veda* 1.32—after the great victory of Maghavan (epithet of Indra) something happens, ever so briefly described in verse fourteen:

aher yātāraṃ kam apaśya indra hṛdi yat te jaghnuṣo bhīr agachat
nava ca yan navatiṃ ca sravantīḥ śyeno na bhīto ataro rajāṃsi

What dragon-avenger did you see, Indra,
  that terror grabbed your heart when you had slain him [the dragon],
and that you crossed the ninety-nine streams
  like a frightened eagle crosses the skies?

These are strange lines that one would not expect to find appended to the praises of Indra's great victory—coming immediately after the laudatory verse thirteen. In Dumézil's words (1970: 124): "they constitute the surfacing, unique in the entire hymnal, of a mythical theme that was perplexing rather than useful."

The tradition is preserved more fully in various other sources, most importantly in book 5 of the *Mahābhārata*. There the tale is much embellished, in the fashion typical of this epic of myriad verse, and the two major variants of Indra's fight with the dragon are presented as sequential events. The core account runs as follows (*MBh.* 5.9–18).

Indra slays tricephalic Viśvarūpa, whereupon the hero burns with a fever as he looks on the glory of the fallen monster. He persuades a woodcutter to cut off Viśvarūpa's three heads. The notion of "three-mouthed" (see §4.9.2.6) again presents itself as seminal, this time in an Indic context: each of the tricephal's three mouths had served its own purpose; with one he had spoken the Vedas and drunk Soma; with one he had swallowed up space; with one he drank the ancient alcoholic beverage *surā*. Now, from the mouth of each decapitated head, birds fly out—heathcocks, partridges, and sparrows, respectively. With the decapitation, Indra is cooled of his fever.

Furious at the death of his son, Tvaṣṭṛ (the Indic Volcanus) creates the monster Vṛtra for the purpose of killing Indra. Vṛtra and Indra fight. The dragon swallows Indra; but the gods, coming to the rescue, create "the yawn," and through Vṛtra's yawning mouth Indra makes his escape. Indra retreats from the fray, but with the assistance of Viṣṇu kills the monster by stealth. The gods and all manner of creatures heap praises on the monster-slayer, Indra.

Then comes the depression. Indra flees—"The Indra of the Gods went to the end of the worlds and, bereft of consciousness and wits, was no longer aware of anything, being pressed down by his guilt. He dwelled concealed in the Waters, writhing like a snake" (van Buitenen 1978: 207). With Indra's withdrawal, desolation and drought seize the earth: "the earth looked ravaged, her trees gone, her wilderness dried up. The streams of the rivers dwindled and the ponds stood empty. Panic seized all creatures because of the drought, and the gods and all great seers trembled sorely." (van Buitenen 1978: 207).

The gods, desperate for the restoration of order, choose one Nahuṣa to be their king. Upon gaining kingship, Nahuṣa becomes consumed with lust; chief among the objects on which falls his lustful gaze is Indra's wife, Śacī (also called Indrāṇī). She finds his advances repulsive and in her despair devotes herself to the worship of the goddess Rātri 'Night'.

As a consequence of Śacī's devotion to Indra and to truth, a female spirit of divination, Upaśruti, presents herself to the goddess. Upaśruti leads Śacī, and together the two pass beyond the Himalayas to an island lush in trees and plants, in the midst of a great sea. On the island is a pond, a place of birds, filled with thousands of colorful lotuses. Upaśruti conducts Śacī into the stalk of a large white lotus, and there within a fiber of the lotus is Indra, reduced to a tiny form. Śacī and her oracular guide likewise assume miniature size. The goddess tells Indra of Nahuṣa's lustful intentions, pleading with her husband to return to his former greatness and reclaim his position as king among gods. Indra responds that he is too weak to challenge Nahuṣa but proposes a plan which will lead to Nahuṣa's downfall through his own arrogance. Śacī departs from Indra's hideaway.

In what appears to be a variant form of the discovery episode, the god Bṛhaspati sends Agni in the shape of a woman to search for Indra. At first unsuccessful, having searched all places except within the waters of the world, the unwilling fire god is compelled by Bṛhaspati's praise to search even the waters. He finds mini-Indra within the lotus fiber at the remote watery locale described above.

Next, Bṛhaspati and others gods, along with seers and gandharvas (centaurlike creatures), journey to the place of Indra's withdrawal. Coaxed by their praises, Indra begins to grow and recovers his size and strength. Indra's plan proves to be effective, and Nahuṣa falls from power. Śacī is reunited with her husband and he, Indra, again is enthroned as king of gods.

4.9.2.8.2 The Irish hero Dumézil recognized that we are here confronted with a mythic theme that is not unique to Indic or even Indo-Iranian tradition. It is an early Indo-European theme of (i) the tricephal-slayer (the monster-slayer) experiencing a traumatic crisis following his heroic deed—a crisis that threatens to disrupt society; (ii) the tale of his recovery and restoration; and (iii) the consequent benefit to society. This archaic tradition, he argued, is one which surfaces among the Celts, preserved in Irish traditions about CúChulainn, the great warrior of Ulster (see Dumézil 1970: 133–137; 1942: 37–38, 41–44, 58–59). The story is preserved in various manuscripts, notably the *Lebor na hUidre* ("The Book of the Dun Cow"), the *Lebor Buide Lecáin* ("The Yellow Book of Lecan"), and the *Lebor Laighnech* ("The Book of Leinster").

When CúChulainn is still a boy, he learns from the Druid Cathbad that whoever should mount a chariot for the first time on that very day would acquire never-ending fame. Taking possession of the chariot and driver that belong to Conchobor, king of Ulster, CúChulainn travels from the royal village of Emain Macha to the frontier of Ulster. On this day, the frontier boundary is being guarded by the celebrated warrior Conall Cernach. CúChulainn smashes the shaft of Conall's chariot, tells him to return to Emain Macha, and continues on his own journey farther into the borderlands. He comes at last in this remote region to the place inhabited by the three sons of Nechta Scéne, terrible beings who have killed half of the warriors of Ulster. They are Foill, Fannall, and Tuachell, each possessing a fabulous battle advantage. One of the brothers is undefeatable unless killed by the first blow struck against him; one is able to move across the surface of water with the ease of a swan or a swallow; one has never before been injured by any weapon. Using the spear called Del Chliss, the young CúChulainn slays all three of these preternatural foes. He decapitates them each and, with their heads stowed in his chariot, hurries back toward Emain Macha, possessed by a maniacal warrior-fury.

What next follows in this tale is a remarkable account of the cooling of CúChulainn's fevered rage. His approach to Emain Macha is seen by the woman Leborcham, wise and clairvoyant, who warns that if he is not stopped, his fury will be turned against the warriors of Ulster and they will perish. Conchobor, the king, is keenly aware of the danger at hand and orders that the appropriate measures be taken to protect the Ulster warriors and the people of Emain Macha. He sends out one hundred and fifty nude women to show themselves lewdly to CúChulainn. According to the *Lebor Laighnech*, they are led by the woman named Scandlach; in the version of the *Lebor na hUidre* and the *Lebor Buide Lecáin*, they are led by Mugain, wife of Conchobor, who verbally confronts CúChulainn and, flaunting her breasts, says, "these are the warriors you must fight." Upon gazing at this exhibitionistic horde, CúChulainn averts his face, is seized, and is doused in three vats of cold water successively. His heat causes the first vat to explode; it causes the water in the second to boil; it makes the cold water of the third sufficiently hot as to be of a temperature that some would find unbearable. When he emerges from the third vat, his raging heat has been cooled so that he no longer poses a danger to the people of Ulster. The queen Mugain presents CúChulainn with a blue cloak having a silver brooch and he then takes a seat at the king's feet, which will henceforth be his place.

4.9.2.8.3 The Ossetic hero This Irish tale of the warrior who must be cooled of his fevered rage, Dumézil perceived, shares certain elements with a tradition of Iranian origin. Among the mythic lore of the Ossetes, an enclave of Indo-European peoples in the Caucasus, descended from the Iranian Scythians and Sarmatians of antiquity, are the epic accounts of those heroes called the Narts (see Dumézil 1930a; 1978; *ME* 1: 440–603).

One of the greatest Nart warriors is Batraz, son of Xæmyc (whose mythology in part appears to continue that of the Scythian "Ares," identified by Herodotus (4.62); (see Dumézil 1970: 137; *ME* 1: 570–575). Batraz will be born from an abscess on his father's back, created when his pregnant mother spits on Xæmyc, implanting between his shoulders the embryo she was carrying. When the time comes for Batraz to be born, he is delivered by Satana, the sagacious sister of Xæmyc. Satana takes her pregnant brother to the top of a tower seven stories high; at the base of this tower seven cauldrons of water have been positioned. With a steel blade she lances the abscess, and from it neophyte Batraz falls flaming into the cauldrons of water below. He is a child of steel, and so great is the heat with which he burns that the water does not cool him. The fiery child calls out for water to quench the flame that burns within him (or to temper his steel). Satana rushes to a spring for more cooling water. There, however, she is confronted by a seven-headed dragon (or the devil) who will only allow her to collect water on condition of first having intercourse with him; this she does. Following his childhood, which shows certain similarities to that of Hercules (Charachidzé 1991: 317–318), Batraz will ascend into the heavens to make his home. Periodically he will streak down to earth in a fulgural form to protect his people, or sometimes to harm them.[53]

4.9.2.8.4 The Italic hero While it might be fair to claim (as we have allowed) that the legend of Hercules and Cacus (that is, the tale of Hercules' visit to Evander and the Arcadian Greeks who settled the pre-Romulean Palatine, the theft of the Greek hero's cattle by Cacus, and Hercules' consequent destruction of the thief) may not be much older than Virgil, beneath the veneer of the Roman story of Hercules and Cacus, we must certainly discern a deeply archaic Italic myth of Semo Sancus and the monster that he slays, *three-headed*, and *three-mouthed* (and *six-eyed*), cattle-corralling, son of the smith-god. Both these attributes and the very struggle itself between monster and monster-slayer we have already seen to be identical to Indo-Iranian, especially Indic, expressions of a common Indo-European tradition. The similarities, however, go even further.

Crisis and flight. First is the matter of the trauma of the hero. After Indra's victorious acts of monster-slaying, he is laid low by a crisis; he flees into a remote place and takes refuge within the waters. After the young CúChulainn's initial combat and triumph over the triple adversary, the three terrible sons of Nechta Scéne, in remote lands beyond the Ulster border, he also enters a traumatized state. His is not a debilitating depression and anxiety but a debilitating pathological rage—a warrior-fury that burns within him and must be relieved by a double remedy which involves

[53]On the birth narrative, see *ME* 1: 571–572; Dumézil 1970: 137–138; 1978: 22–24. Dumézil (1970: 138) notes that the story of Batraz and the cooling of his fire is obviously different from the tale told of CúChulainn's similar experience in that the former is a birth narrative. For Batraz the thermal condition is innate; for CúChulainn it is acquired. Dumézil finds a parallel to the Indic account of mini-Indra emerging from the Lotus stalk fiber in the birth narrative of the Armenian warrior Vahagn (of Iranian origin), born flaming from a reed in the sea (see Dumézil 1970: 127–132). To this extent, he observes, there is an analogous relationship between these traditions concerning Batraz and CúChulainn, on the one hand, and those concerning Vahagn and Indra, on the other.

a spectacle of parading female nudity and successive applications of cooling water. In each case, Indic and Celtic, the well-being of society has been jeopardized by the hero's trauma.

Hercules has vanquished his triple-headed opponent Cacus. The aftereffect of his great victory, however, is a debilitating trauma of thirst and exhaustion, revealed in the ancient tradition preciously preserved by Propertius—a dryness consumes Hercules like the drought that grips the earth in the midst of Indra's trauma. In his crisis, Hercules, like Indra, flees to a place of waters, and like Indra, king of gods, his demeaning, panicked response stands in stark contrast to his divine greatness. Consider again Propertius 4.9.31–36:

> huc ruit in siccam congesta pulvere barbam,
> et iacit ante fores verba minora deo:
> "Vos precor, o luci sacro quae luditis antro,
> pandite defessis hospita fana viris.
> fontis egens erro circum antra sonantia lymphis;
> et cava succepto flumine palma sat est. . . ."

> Here he rushes with dust clumped in his dry beard,
> and before the gates he speaks words too small for a god:
> "I beg you, who play within the sacred hollow of this grove,
> make your sacred spaces hospitably open to exhausted men.
> In need of a spring, I wander around dells that sing with waters;
> a cupped hand of scooped-up water is enough. . . ."

The society of the Indic gods is plunged into turmoil with Indra's flight; the lecherous and villainous Nahuṣa becomes king, menacing even Indra's wife. The hero of the Italic form of the myth, going about in the guise of Hercules in the surviving sources, is portrayed as disrupting the ordered calmness of Bona Dea's rites and the society of her followers gathered within her sacred grove.

Female nudity. The Italic tradition shows a particular closeness to the Celtic, an alignment which we might not have anticipated but one which in retrospect should come as no surprise. Whatever its "original" significance, the curious episode of massive female nudity invoked in conjunction with the restoration of the dysfunctional hero is certainly as much a part of the Italic tradition as it is the Celtic. That Hercules will see the women within Bona Dea's grove in a nude state should he enter is clearly the envisioned event upon which the old priestess' warning is predicated:

> "Parce oculis, hospes, lucoque abscede verendo;
> cede agedum et tuta limina linque fuga

. . . .
magno Tiresias aspexit Pallada vates,
    fortia dum posita Gorgone membra lavat.
di tibi dent alios fontes: haec lympha puellis
    avia secreti limitis unda fluit."

"Avert your eyes, stranger, and depart this holy grove,
    withdraw now and leave its thresholds in safe retreat.
. . . .
At a great price Teresias the prophet gazed on Pallas,
    while she bathed her strong limbs, her Aegis laid aside.
May the gods give you other springs: these waters for maidens
    flow, remote spring of hidden course."

Hercules certainly does not depart from the place, but forces his way into the grove and heads straight for the maidens' springs. Since he does not share the fate of Teresias—though Propertius has the priestess declare he will, should he gaze upon the women—perhaps in the underlying Italic tradition the raging warrior, like CúChulainn, does in fact avert his gaze. Is this peculiar element of the myth of Indo-European origin, or is it specifically Italo-Celtic (or western Indo-European)? No unambiguous hint of it appears to be preserved in the Indo-Iranian traditions.[54]

Cooling waters. The second element involved in cooling the fevered rage of CúChulainn—an immersion in successive cold water baths—likewise surfaces in Propertius' poem. In the Italic tradition as preserved, there is a sort of reversal evidenced, in that Hercules takes the entire stream into himself, rather than having his body thoroughly immersed within the waters; though one could imagine that the motif of swallowing the waters is a natural extrapolation from a tradition of lying in them, given that Hercules' hero-crisis is presented as one of extreme thirst. That the notion of the hero's thirst may have been less pronounced—and his "heat" more so—in an antecedent form of the Italic tradition is suggested by the choice of words preserved in line 63, almost surprising in the present context: *at postquam exhausto iam flumine vicerat aestum . . .* ("But after he had subdued his raging heat, the stream now drained . . ."). While thirst and exhaustion drove the hero to the "remote spring of hidden course" (*avia secreti limitis unda*), the relief that the waters bring is said to have subdued (*vicerat*) not his thirst, but his *aestus.* The word means 'heat, feverishness, rage, fury', of common origin with *aestās* 'summer' and *aedēs* 'temple' (the place of

[54]Unless it might have common origin with the sexual advances that Nahuṣa makes toward Indra's wife and the intercourse with the seven-headed monster to which Satana must consent before she can bring water from the spring to cool flaming Batraz.

the hearth), and its use places Hercules and CúChulainn squarely within a common domain of post-combat trauma. That the motif of cooling the warrior's flaming rage by immersion in cold water is common Indo-European is suggested by the recurrence of this element in the birth account of Batraz, the "Nart Hercules." Beyond which, it is within the waters that the warrior Indra hides in his traumatized state.

Remote space. There is an additional feature common to the Indic and Celtic traditions—namely, a notion of liminal space figures saliently. In each tradition the hero crosses the boundaries of society and journeys into some remote locale. In his crisis state, Indra flees to the "end of the worlds." Young CúChulainn passes beyond the frontier boundary of Ulster, and in this remote space he confronts his tricephalic foe and is possessed by a fevered rage.

Is this seminal notion of remote space also present in the Italic tradition as evidenced in Propertius' poetic tale of Hercules? There is an indication of this. The old hag who confronts the hero refers to the waters of the women as *avia secreti limitis unda*, "a remote spring of hidden course"—a somewhat curious designation for a stream lying within a grove of the Aventine. Upon the lips of the hero in crisis, the poet places the words (4.9.65–66):

> Angulus hic mundi nunc me mea fata trahentem
> accipit: haec fesso vix mihi tecta patent. . . .

> This corner of the world now has me—dragging out
> my fate: exhausted, these shelters hardly take me in. . . .

To be sure, Greek *Heracles* is in a foreign and remote place, a "corner of the world" far from his home in Greece, but this is of course a tradition different from that one with which we are here centrally concerned. The remoteness of Heracles at this moment in the "distant labor" of Geryon's cattle readily assimilates to the remoteness of the Italic hero, Semo Sancus, who has fled in crisis following his destruction of the three-headed monster.

Clairvoyant woman. Another element bound up with this motif of remote space is again shared by the Indic and Irish traditions. In each instance, there is a female figure—wise, clairvoyant—who serves as a bridge between that liminal space and the space of the dysfunctional hero's own society. In India she is the spirit of divination, Upaśruti, who knows the whereabouts of the hero's remote, watery hiding place—space filled with birds and colorful lotuses—and who leads Śacī there to him. In Ireland she is Leborcham, a sorceress of Ulster, who perceives and announces the approach of the raging CúChulainn and the peril he brings as he returns from his destruction of the triple foe in the remoteness of the frontier, headed toward Emain Macha, where, as with Indra, waters will cover him.

Structurally and functionally, this is the very position occupied by the silver-haired hag (*anus*) who confronts Hercules at the gated threshold of Bona Dea's grove. She is physically located at the boundary that separates the waterless space in which the hero languishes (*terraque non ullas feta ministrat aquas*, "and water-rich earth offers him not a drop") from the watery shadeland of the grove. She is a priestess of the goddess, proclaiming that the "remote spring" lies within the lush, songbird-filled space of the grove blossoming with the priestesses' red headbands, and foretelling the hero's fate should he gaze upon the bathing maidens.

Order and inauguration. Following the hero's recovery in both the Celtic and Indic traditions, order is restored and the hero undergoes an inauguration. The warriors of Ulster are preserved, and CúChulainn is elegantly cloaked and takes the place he will thereafter occupy at the knee of King Conchobor. The despotic Nahuṣa is toppled, and Indra takes up his position as king of gods.

It is the same in the Italic tradition—a remarkable parallel of Indo-European antiquity preserved for us only in the poetic account of Hercules and Cacus told by Propertius. And at this moment in the story, the Italic myth slips out of its Greek disguise: Hercules establishes the Ara Maxima, place of oaths, agreements, and tithes—all planks in the structured order of Roman society; and he "becomes" Sancus (Propertius 4.9.73–74):

> hunc, quoniam manibus purgatum sanxerat orbem,
> sic Sancum Tatiae composuere Cures.

> This one, since by his hands he consecrated the orb made pure,
> Cures of Tatius thus established as Sancus.

The tricephal-slaying hero, recovered from his trauma, is inaugurated as the Sabine deity Semo Sancus. To judge from the record of St. Augustine and Lactantius (see above), Semo Sancus enjoyed a position of sovereignty: the similarity to Indra is patent; CúChulainn—at the knee of king Conchobor—is not far removed. In the Italic version of the myth did the warrior Semo Sancus become a divine king or regain the throne he held *before* his trauma? We can see this final, inaugural element of the tradition in its Italic form only dimly, but clearly enough to recognize that, as in the Celtic and Indic versions, it completes the myth.

4.9.2.9 THE ITALIC REFLEX The Roman account of Hercules and Cacus may indeed present the local instantiation of a folk tradition common among the Greek colonists of Magna Graecia. If so, however, it exists only as a thin veneer spread across an Italic reflex of a deeply archaic Indo-European myth. Semo Sancus faces a dreadful monster, *three-headed, three-mouthed* (and *six-eyed*). The creature is a son of the smith-god, corralling cattle in his cavernous lair. Semo Sancus splits open the lair, struggles desperately with the monster cloaked in fog and hurling flame; he slays the creature and releases the pent-up cattle. Yet after his great victory, Semo Sancus is overwhelmed by a crisis. Fleeing like one vanquished rather than a victor, he moves through space to a lush place of cooling waters; a female figure of clairvoyance plays some intermediary role in locating the space. There, being exposed to a great show of feminine nudity, he finds recovery through the ministrations of the cooling waters. Order thereby returns to society and Semo Sancus is inaugurated in a position of, or proximate to, sovereignty.

Such is the minimalistic form of our recovered Italic myth of the tricephal slayer. That we should find well-preserved forms of a Proto-Indo-European tradition along *both* the Indo-Iranian and the Italo-Celtic rims of the ancient Indo-European world comes as no surprise. These are places of peoples noted for their religious and mythic conservatism. The striking thing here is that the Italic reflex of the myth is so very closely aligned to the Indic but at the same time preserves in common with the Celtic tradition at least one major component of the ancestral myth absent from its Indic form—the exhibition of female nudity. The intermediate status of the Italic tradition and its particular similarity to the Indic is made readily evident by a schematic summary of the structural elements of this Indo-European myth as presented in figure 4.4, where the "Indo(-Iranian)" features entail both the slaying of the serpent Vṛtra and the three-headed Viśvarūpa.

Clearly a fair amount of restructuring has occurred in the Celtic tradition by the time of its medieval Irish attestation. The three-headed opponent has been teased apart into a preternatural triple foe, each member of which is decapitated by the tricephal-slayer. The remote space is now not that to which the hero in crisis flees, but the space in which the tricephal is killed, the dysfunctional warrior then "fleeing" back to the space of society. Drought—that is, the absence of water—plays a conspicuous role in both the Indic and Italic traditions. Vṛtra holds back the waters, released when Indra slays him; later drought comes when traumatized Indra has fled. In parallel fashion, Hercules experiences agonizing thirst, the earth offering him no water, after he has killed Cacus and released the cattle. In

	Indo(-Iranian)	*Italic*	*Celtic*
Son of the smith god	+	+	
Theft of cattle	+	+	
Drought	+	+	
Breach of the cave	+	+	
Struggle in fog/smoke and flame/lightning	+	+	
Slaying of the tricephalic foe	+	+	+
Crisis of the hero	+	+	+
Flight to distant locale	+	+	+
Clairvoyant woman	+	+	+
Exhibition of female nudity		+	+
Submersion in /Application of waters	+	+	+
Order and inauguration	+	+	+

FIGURE 4.4. *Structural elements of the slaying of the tricephalic foe*

all three traditions, the warrior fleeing in crisis then passes into a place of copious water.

Just as the folktale of Hercules and Cacus is an accretion deposited on the foundation provided by the ancient Italic myth of Semo Sancus and the three-headed monster that he slays, so Bona Dea certainly has nothing to do with this tale in origin.[55] Her presence here is the consequence of a gender-charged topographic juxtaposition of sacred spaces that both required and provided an interpretative scheme. Women are excluded from worship at Hercules' Ara Maxima; men are excluded from the rites celebrated at Bona Dea's Aventine temple. The two sites effectively bookend the Circus Maximus, the Ara Maxima being directly opposite the open end of the chariot arena and the temple of Bona Dea lying almost due south of the opposite (turning) end. While the remains of the temple have yet to be

[55]Note that the cause of the exclusion of women from the rites of Hercules' great altar is not uniquely bound to this archaic Italic myth of the slaying of the tricephal. Plutarch (*Quaest. Rom.* 60) records a separate tradition, according to which women were not allowed because Carmenta (goddess of the *carmen*, identified with Evander's mother) had arrived late at the inaugural rites (cf. Aurelius Victor, *Orig. Gent. Rom.* 6.7). The Bona Dea opposition is a sufficient but not necessary etiological feature of the Ara Maxima's discriminatory rites.

identified, its location is securely described as situated on the slopes of the Aventine (Aventinus Minor) just beneath the Saxum, where Remus had stood as he scanned the skies for a sighting of augural birds (see Richardson 1992: 59–60l; *LTUR*, vol. 1: 149). The altar and temple were no more than about 900 meters apart. Once Hercules and Cacus were assimilated to Semo Sancus and his three-headed foe, the gravity generated by this +/- opposition of space and gender pulled Bona Dea and her temple spaces inextricably into the tale.

Additional factors may have contributed to Bona Dea's eventual integration into the archaic Italic myth, the most likely being the position of these two sites vis-à-vis the ancient *pomerium*. This sacred urban boundary, writes Tacitus (*Ann.* 12.24), was ploughed from the Forum Boarium so as to include the Ara Maxima, which seemingly stood very close to the boundary and marked the southwest cardinal point of its circuit. The Aventine, in sharp contrast, remained conspicuously outside the *pomerium* up until the time of Claudius. Not only that, but "it appears that the Aventinus was originally *ager publicus*, as the settling there of people from the various towns conquered by Rome shows" (Richardson 1992: 47; see also *LTUR*, vol. 1: 147–148).[56]

The spatial contrast characterizing the position of the Ara Maxima and the temple of Bona Dea is an exact mirror of the contrast between the two alternating spaces in the episode of the traumatized warrior. One is the space of society, the other the remote space beyond the boundary of society. The first is Vedic India (land of the seven streams) and Emain Macha. The latter is the watery space beyond the Himalayas at the worlds' end, and the distant fortress of the three sons of Nechta Scéne beyond the frontier boundary of Ulster. The spatial contrast of the ancient Italic tradition of the hero in crisis translates locally in Rome as near and remote by reference to the sacred boundary of the *pomerium*. The near, native space of ordered Roman society is that of the Palatine, the Forum Boarium, the Ara Maxima. The remote, foreign space is that of the Aventine (peopled by outsiders), the temple precinct of Bona Dea, envisioned as a lush, secreted grove and place of waters. The alternating spaces of the ancient Indo-European myth find an object lesson in the hills of Rome.

We have come to the myth of the tricephal-slaying Semo Sancus by way of the Fratres Arvales. One might be tempted at this point to interpret the Arval ritual as having spiraled in on itself. The May ritual of the Fratres

[56]On the latter point Richardson cites Livy 1.33.2 and Dionysius of Halicarnassus, *Ant. Rom.* 3.43.

Arvales is one which uses the two alternating Roman sacred spaces corresponding to those of the Vedic Devayajana and Mahāvedi—the space of urban Rome and that of the Ager Romanus. On the second day of the ritual the Arvals move across the *pomerium* from the former, proximal space into the latter, distal space. At the zenith of the midday culinary episode within the grove of Dea Dia the priests chant their Carmen Arvale to Mars, calling on him to invoke the Semones. One—and most probably chief—of the Semones is Semo Sancus, the slayer of the three-headed monster, who in his hour of trauma flees from the space of Roman society into the foreign space of remoteness, respectively expressed in Roman *myth* as the proximal space of the *pomerium* and the distal space of the Aventine beyond the *pomerium*. A similar spatial interpretation finds expression in *ritual*—in the Arval ritual, juxtaposing the proximal space of urban Rome and the distal space of the Ager Romanus, separated by the *pomerium*. A ritual requiring movement through two spaces invokes a myth which tells of movement through two spaces. The ritual undergoes an involution. Carnival fun-houses and childhood fascinations with pairs of mirrors readily come to mind. It is as though the Arval ritual were one mirror, while the Carmen Arvale, with its invocation of the Semones, were a second that is held before the first. Gazing at the one, we see the other reflected in it, and within that reflection we see again the counterreflection of the first mirror, and so on ad infinitum.

There is, however, an alternative interpretation of the myth-ritual spatial relationship which presents itself—a slight variant of the preceding and one which most likely cuts to the heart of the matter. The space into which the hero in crisis flees is a remote wilderness space beyond the boundary of order. This is not the space of the Mahāvedi; this is not the space of the Ager Romanus. In other words—in a Roman context—the *ritual* counterpart of the border beyond which the traumatized hero of the *myth* flees is not the boundary between the small sacred space of urban Rome and the great sacred space of the Ager Romanus—but the distal boundary of the Ager Romanus itself. It is a space beyond the realm of Roman religious order. The ritual significance of so identifying the mythic boundary crossed by the tricephal-slayer will present itself in the next section.

4.9.2.10 MARS AND SEMO SANCUS Before concluding our discussion of Semo Sancus and the myth of the tricephal-slayer, there is one question left to consider, an obvious one snatched into the foreground by the preceding observations: "Where is Mars in all of this?" Or to rephrase it a bit:

"If Mars is the great warrior god, why isn't he the tricephal-slayer?" The question is, mutatis mutandis, not so different from questions which might be, and have been, asked about Indra and Trita Āptya.

Long ago, the Johns Hopkins Sanskritist Maurice Bloomfield cogently summarized the relationship of Indra and Trita Āptya in the *Rig Veda*, observing that "Trita is in general the double of Indra in his struggles with the demons" (Bloomfield 1896: 434). In *Rig Veda* 1.187.1, 6, for example, Trita is credited with having slain and dismembered the dragon Vṛtra. *Rig Veda* 1.52 rehearses Indra's slaying of Vṛtra, and in the context of lines identifying his helpers in the deed, the Maruts (v. 5), likens the deed to Trita's smiting of Vala ('enclosure'; see §4.9.2.5). The word *Vala* is from the same root as *Vṛtra* and is used "of the cave where the (rain-)cows are pent up and of the demon who holds them prisoner" (Watkins 1995: 298); Indra is commonly identified as his slayer (see Keith 1998a: 128, 223, 235). Bloomfield sees that here (*RV* 1.52.5) Trita is presented as "Indra's predecessor and model in the fights against the dragons" (1896: 434); the idea that Trita Āptya is historically the predecessor of Indra in the role of dragon-slayer is one commonly encountered.

The familiar alternative interpretation is that Trita Āptya is Indra's assisting and assisted dragon-slayer. Thus, in *Rig Veda* 8.7.24 he is credited with fighting alongside Indra and assisting him in the killing of Vṛtra. In *Rig Veda* 10.48.2 Indra is said to have obtained cows from the dragon for Trita Āptya; in *Rig Veda* 1.163.2 Trita is said to have harnessed the horse that Yama gave to Indra (the horse of the Vedic horse sacrifice, the Aśvamedha). *Rig Veda* 10.99.6 praises Indra for overcoming the loud-roaring, six-eyed, three-headed demon and Trita for killing the boar, being strengthened by Indra for the deed; here "the MONSTER is assimilated to a 'boar'" (see Watkins 1995: 316; the Iranian hero Vərəθraγna undergoes a similar assimilation—see Watkins, p. 320). In *Rig Veda* 2.11.18–19, Indra is said to have dismembered Vṛtra and to have given over Viśvarūpa to Trita. *Rig Veda* 10.8.8–9 lauds Trita, urged on by Indra, for killing the "seven-rayed, three-headed" Viśvarūpa and for freeing his cattle, and praises Indra for dismembering and decapitating the tricephal and seizing his cattle.

A remarkably similar uneasy and volatile functional equivalence of Mars (corresponding to Indra) and Semo Sancus (corresponding to Trita Āptya) survives in Rome. Hercules is Semo Sancus; this, as we have seen, is quite cleanly attested. The fullest surviving version of the Roman myth of the tricephal-slayer, that preserved by Propertius, interprets the inaugural experience of the recovered hero as Hercules "becoming" Sancus. Consider, however, some fascinating bits of information that Macrobius recapitulates in the dialogue of *Saturnalia* 3.12. He places on the lips of the religious antiquarian Vettius Praetextus a defense of Virgil's report (*Aen.* 8.285–305) that the Salii sang the mighty deeds of Hercules at the Ara Maxima, concluding their performance with the tale of his defeat of fire-breathing Cacus. The Salii are the dancing priests of Mars, and their songs the obscure Carmina Saliaria (see §1.5.5). According to Praetextus, Virgil is right on target here, for among the Pontifices, Hercules is considered to be equivalent to Mars (*Sat.* 3.12.5). Moreover, he continues, Varro has demonstrated the same equivalence in his work Ἄλλος οὗτος Ἡρακλῆς. Praetextus' presentation of evidence continues to role. The Chaldeans give the name "star of Hercules" to that star which all others call the "star of Mars" (*Sat.* 3.12.6). In Octavius Hersennius' book *De Sacris Saliaribus Tiburtium*, that author shows that the Salii were established for Hercules, and that on certain days they perform rites for him after they take auspices (*Sat.* 3.12.7). The learned scholar Antonius Gnipho demonstrated that the Salii were assigned to Hercules (*Sat.* 3.12.8).

The distinction between Mars and Semo Sancus blurs. One is tempted to co-opt Bloomfield's observation about Indra and Trita Āptya and pronounce that "Mars and Semo Sancus are doubles" in a particular sphere of activity, for which monster slaying would be the probable candidate. Yet they are different—as are Indra and Trita Āptya. In the Carmen Arvale, Mars is implored to "invoke the Semones one by one, all together."[57]

The ground becomes soggier still. On the one hand, Semo Sancus is certainly the Italic comparandum of the Vedic watery third brother, Trita Āptya, monster-slayer operating alone or in tandem with Indra. On the other hand, as we argued, the Semones, "all together" are deities associated with rain who are called into the fray by savage Mars—a concatenation which places them on a par with the storming warrior companions of Indra who aid him, or desert him, in his fight with the dragon, or who accomplish the deed on their own—the Maruts.[58]

[57]And note the reference to a priest of the Cerfi and the Semunes in a dialect inscription from Corfinium; compare Çerfus Martius of the Umbrian ritual. On the inscription, see Norden 1939: 217, 220.

[58]In terms of the archaic tripartition of Indo-European society, the Maruts and Semo Sancus share in common a peculiar (and, hence, perhaps significant) feature. The Maruts belong to the warrior class (second function) of divine society, the Rudras. However, in Vedic tradition they are sometimes presented as being the common people (third function) among the gods. They are so depicted in, for example, *ŚB* 4.5.2.16, in the ceremony of offering the embryo of the "sterile" cow who turned out not to be. We noted above a possible connection of this Vedic rite with the midday culinary event of the Arvals; see §3.3.5.1. In a fully parallel fashion, Italic Semo Sancus has an undeniable

Latin *Mars* is of course a phonetically reduced form of earlier *Māvors*, descended from a still earlier **Māwort-*. Both Latin *Mars* and Vedic *Marút* denote beings that belong to the same ideological sphere—that of the warrior—and both are conspicuously celebrated as part of the midday rite within their own respective ritual cultures, Arval and Vedic. Beyond these ideological and cultic similarities, they perhaps show also a common linguistic origin: the great Italic warrior god may well share a common denotation with the dragon-slaying cohorts of the great Vedic warrior god. The etymological equation of **Māwort-* and *Marút* is old and well known and is a sensible one which may prove to be sound; uncertainty hinges on the difference of vowel quantity in the initial syllable—Italic long [a:] versus Sanskrit short [a] (see Leumann 1963: 115, with n. 1 and references).[59]

The above observations concerning relationships and fluctuations within the Italic and Indic mythic traditions are graphically summarized in figure 4.5. The use of symbols is as follows: ≈ represents a relationship of partial functional equivalence; ⇐ and ⇒ indicate a relationship of assistance; ⊂ indicates membership in a subset; the vertical connecting lines encode cross-cultural correspondences; the curved lines denote an etymological relationship.

In sum, the fluidity in the identity of the Vedic monster-slayer, mutatis mutandis, shows itself in Italy. Recurring variability at the eastern and western edges of the ancient Indo-European world suggests some synchronic heterogeneity in the antecedent mythic tradition of the common Indo-European ancestors of the Italic and Indic peoples. If the names of Mars and the Maruts are of common linguistic descent, the picture of heterogeneity is enhanced. As we have seen, in India the ambiguous function of Trita Āptya is commonly resolved into that of tricephal-slayer assisted by Indra. Exactly the same relationship recurs in the corresponding Iranian tradition, in which the hero Thraētaona (equivalent to Trita Āptya) slays the triple-headed dragon Aži Dahāka with the support of Vərəθrayna (compare Indra Vṛtrahan). Watkins notes that a black-figure amphora from the British Museum, which depicts Heracles facing a three-headed Geryon, places a likeness of Athena behind the hero—a source of divine support:

warrior affiliation (second function); yet he is said to have been a god of the Sabines, and we have seen that in Roman tradition, the Sabine gods are commonly deities associated with the realm of the third function (i.e. "the gods of Titus Tatius").

[59]There is a slightly different, somewhat more symmetrical interpretative scheme which will be considered only briefly in the present work: namely that the Indic threesome Indra-Āptyas-Maruts finds an Italic correspondent in the divine threesome hymned in the Carmen Arvale, Mars-Semones-Lares.

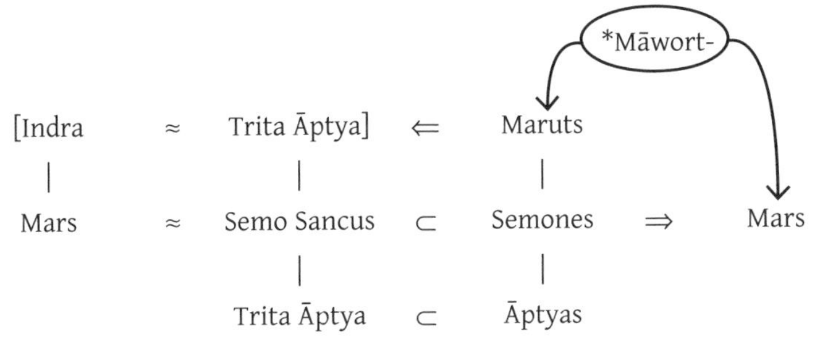

FIGURE 4.5. *Indic and Italic interrelationships in the myth of the monster-slaying hero*

"Athena thus has the same functional role toward Heracles in the myth as Vərəθraɣna toward Thraētaona and Indra toward Trita" (Watkins 1995: 467). This resolution is perhaps then common to the Indo-European ancestors of the Greeks and Indo-Iranians.

These latter considerations lead us to the final point to be made concerning the myth of the tricephal-slayer. There is one quite obvious difference between the Indic and Italic versions of the tale of the hero in crisis, which we have thus far neglected to address. In India, it is Indra himself who is overwhelmed and flees, not Trita Āptya. Conversely, in Rome it is not Mars, the chief warrior god (Indra's counterpart), who despairs and withdraws, but Semo Sancus, principal member of the body of the Semones. This is the configuration to which Propertius' poetic account points.

What do we make of this? Perhaps the Roman tradition keeps alive a strain of a Proto-Indo-European mythic tradition in which the dysfunctional hero is not the chief warrior god but another member of this class, functional ancestor of the homologous pair Trita Āptya and Semo Sancus. We have noted already that some Indologists have regarded Trita Āptya as Indra's historical predecessor in monster slaying. Given the meager nature of the Italic evidence, however, Propertius' account obviously does not obviate the possibility that there also existed an Italic version of the myth in which Semo Sancus slays the tricephal, strengthened by Mars, who himself is then overwhelmed by crisis. To be sure there is no internal evidence of a compelling nature to suggest this possibility—only a comparative analysis buttressed by the reported equivalence of Mars and Semo Sancus discussed above. One might wonder whether certain of those obscure lines of the Carmen Arvale addressed to Mars may have had as their "original" context such a tale of the traumatized Mars. Let us consider this possibility further.

When Indra has fled beyond the ends of the worlds and lies hidden within the waters in a lotus fiber, tiny in form, a host of gods, Brahmans and gandharvas come lauding his great deeds, calling on him to come forth and be strong. Their words of *Mahābhārata* 5.16 effect his growth and recovery (the translation is that of van Buitenen 1978: 214):

> Thou wert the killer of the grisly Asura Namuci, and of the Śambara and Vala, both of dreadful prowess. Grow, thou of the Hundred Sacrifices, destroy all foes! Rise up, Thunderbolt-Wielder, behold the Gods and seers assembled! Great Indra, by killing the Danavas thou hast rescued the worlds, O lord. Resorting to the foam of the waters that was strengthened by the splendor of Viṣṇu, thou hast slain Vṛtra of yore, king of the gods, lord of the world!
>
> By all creatures, desirable one, thou art
> To be worshipped, none in the world is your equal.
> Thou, Śakra, supportest the creatures all,
> Great feats hast thou wrought in the cause of the gods.
>
> Protect the gods and the worlds, great Indra, gain strength!

Consider again the verses that the Arvals sing to Mars during the midday culinary episode (after Schilling 1991: 604):

> Neve Luae Rue Marma sins incurrere in pleores!
> Satur fu, fere Mars, limen sali sta berber!
> Semunis alternei advocapit conctos!
> Enos Marmor iuvato!
> Triumpe, triumpe, triumpe, trium[pe, tri]umpe!
>
> Mars, O Mars, don't let Dissolution, Destruction pounce upon the people (?)!
> Be surfeited, savage Mars; leap to the border, take your position!
> You will invoke the Semones one by one, all together!
> Help us Mars, O Mars!
> Victory, victory, victory, victory, victory!

Is Mars the traumatized warrior who is implored to quit his retreat and return to action? Rather than "be surfeited!" is the meaning of *satur fu* "be sufficiently strong!"—that is, "regain strength!" (compare *satis* in the sense of 'one having sufficient strength, power')? Is the border to which savage Mars is adjured to leap that one which he had crossed in fleeing from society into the remote space? In other words, is the leap to the border a return from the place of withdrawal beyond ordered society to the boundary of the great sacred space of the Ager Romanus—the same boundary at which the Arvals sing their *carmen* to Mars?

On that note, let us return to our examination of the Arval festival.

4.9.3 The evening culinary episode

After the victors of the chariot races have been honored and the games concluded, the Fratres move back across the space of the Ager Romanus and the boundary of the *pomerium* to Rome and the home of the Magister. There, they put on their white dinner attire; offerings of incense and wine are made; and they banquet, served by boys, sons of senators, whose mother and father are still alive. Ointment and garlands are distributed along with a gift of one hundred denarii for each. Dessert is brought out, rose petals are distributed, and felicitations exchanged.

Paralleling the structure of the three pressing-events of the Soma-pressing day, the evening culinary episode of the Arvals is a ritually simpler affair than the two which preceded. Beyond this similarity—noteworthy in itself—there is a shared feature of the evening events which, following the interpretation of spatial salience developed herein, must be seen as significant. In both Rome and India, the celebrants move out of and beyond the boundary of the great sacred space. The Arval priests return to Rome, moving out of the Ager Romanus. The Vedic priests, sacrificer, and sacrificer's wife move northward out of the Mahāvedi to a water source for a ritual bath, a cleansing of their ritual implements, and a change of dress.

4.9.4 Bracketing rites of beginning and ending

We should recall that the three culinary events of the Fratres Arvales take up only the middle day of the May festival of Dea Dia; they are the meat in the sandwich. The events of the first day all occur within the small sacred space of urban Rome, as do those of the third day. Moreover, as we saw, the celebration of the third day consists of a banquet at the home of the Magister which by in large replicates that one of the afternoon of the first day of the festival (see Scheid 1990: 647). The great festival day with its three culinary events is thus bracketed by ritual banquets of basically identical structure. The banquet of the opening day is preceded by offerings made to the goddess and an anointing of her image (see §4.2.5). Within the course of the banquet of the closing day, a complex grain offering is made to the goddess (on the complexity, see Scheid 1990: 648); and the curious ritual of the *Tuscanicae* is conducted, a ritual mentioned earlier and about which we now need to say more.

4.9.4.1 THE TUSCANICAE The implements called *Tuscanicae* are commonly identified as "Tuscan vessels," these being some type of cultic containers having particular significance. Scheid (1990: 651–652) compares the reference made to *Tuscum fictile* in Persius' second satire (2.59–60):

aurum vasa Numae Saturniaque impulit aera
Vestalesque urnas et Tuscum fictile mutat.

Gold has unthroned Numa's vessels and Saturnian bronzes
and the Vestals' urns and Tuscan pottery.

To this he adds the observation that bronze vessels called κρατῆρες τυρρηνικοί 'Etruscan mixing bowls' were archived among the ritual ware of the Delian *hieropoioi* and the Delphic amphictiony. These are disparate references which he gauges to be a measure of the ritual weight of such objects: "il suffit pour notre propos que les deux seules attestations concernant des «*tuscanicae*» renvoient toutes deux à des vases sacrés de dimension relativement importante."

Building on Oldenberg (1875: 20), Scheid hypothesizes that the purpose of these Arval "vessels," the *Tuscanicae*, was to hold grain. Note that the mention of the *Tuscanicae* in the Acta follows the record of the grain offering made to the goddess during the meal. For Oldenberg this is green grain, a portion of which is being set aside for use in the following year ("Cette interprétation me paraît exacte dans son principe"; Scheid 1990: 652). The use of grain, dried and green, recurs throughout the three-day ritual of Dea Dia, and not unexpectedly so given the association of the Arval rites with the fertility of Roman fields. Scheid sees the grains as symbolic: dried grain represents the preceding harvest, green grain the one which is yet to come.

The *Tuscanicae* are touched with the lamps that have just been lit (Schilling 1979: 368) and the *kalatores*, priestly assistants of the Fratres Arvales, deliver the *Tuscanicae* to the individual homes of the Fratres.[60] Thus, by Scheid's interpretation, the sacred vessels are used to transport grain to the various priestly homes, green grain which symbolizes a harvest anticipated. For what purpose? Perhaps the grain is a sacrificial remuneration obtained from the goddess by the priests, or perhaps it is a portion of the coming harvest which she has given already to them—so conjectures Scheid (1990: 652–653).

The *Tuscanicae* may or may not be vessels. The adjective is not unique-

[60]*Deinde lampadibus incensis pariter tuscanicas contigerunt quas per kalatores suos domos suas miserunt* (*CFA* 99a.14–15 etc.). In keeping with the syntax of the Acta, the ablative *lampadibus incensis* is most naturally read as an instrumental ablative. Scheid (1990: 649) allows this and points to a similar act performed early in day one of the festival, when the priests touch dry and green grains with laurel-decorated loaves (*CFA* 114.I.31–32 etc.). Scheid, however, prefers to interpret the inscription to read that the priests touch the *tuscanicae* themselves.

ly used of containers (and note that it is not strictly the term of Persius) but is employed to denote various items deemed to be *of Etruscan style*. Varro (*Ling.* 5.161) writes of a type of *cavum aedium* (the inner court of a house) which is *Tuscanicum*. Vitruvius describes in detail (4.7.1–5) the architectural style of the *aedes* 'temple' which is called *Tuscanica* (4.6.6). Pliny knows not only of statues, *signa Tuscanica*, made in Etruria and widely dispersed (*HN* 34.34), but of four types of columns: Doric, Ionic, Corinthian, and *Tuscanicae* (*HN* 36.178). Quintilian (*Inst.* 12.10.1) likewise writes of *Tuscanicae statuae*, and so on. In short, the adjective *Tuscanicus* can be used, as one would expect, of any number of items of Etruscan style. Whatever the *Tuscanicae* of the Arvales are, they are clearly implements of considerable ritual import, the significance of which cannot be severed from the ritual act performed with them before the *kalatores* deliver the *Tuscanicae* to the homes of the Fratres (*CFA* 99a.14–15 etc.):

> Deinde lampadibus incensis pariter tuscanicas contigerunt quas per kalatores suos domos suas miserunt.
>
> And then together they touched the *Tuscanicae* with the lamps that had been lit, which they sent to their own homes by their *kalatores*.

To this we shall return shortly.

The meal at the end of the first day's rituals and the final banquet on the third day of the festival of Dea Dia bracket the several rites of the all-important second day—a day divided into a tripartite structure. Such an arrangement we have encountered before. Recall that in India, an Iṣṭi, the Udavasānīyā Iṣṭi, is celebrated at the conclusion of the Soma sacrifice. Functionally it is the terminating counterpart of the initiatory Iṣṭi of the Agniṣṭoma called the Adhyavasāna Iṣṭi, marking the solemn entry of the sacrificer into the Devayajana, the small sacrificial space of the Iṣṭi. Beyond that, as we saw, the Udavasānīyā Iṣṭi, being concerned with the establishment of a new fire, closely matches the form of the Paunarādheyikī Iṣṭi, an initiatory ritual which is conducted when the sacrificer must reestablish his sacrificial fires. While both are conducted outside of the great sacrificial space of the Mahāvedi, the Udavasānīyā (coda) and Adhyavasāna (onset) display an asymmetry, however, to the extent that the latter takes place within the small sacrificial space established for the Iṣṭi, and the former occurs in a space set up for this rite north or east of the Mahāvedi.

The middle day of the Arval rites of May and the Vedic Soma-pressing day show remarkable structural similarities, suggesting a shared Indo-European heritage. If we interpret the Arval bracketing rites of the first and third days of Dea Dia's three-day festival and the Vedic bracketing Iṣṭis of the Agniṣṭoma as likewise having a common origin in Proto-Indo-European cultic practice, an important clarification presents itself. Whatever synchronic theological interpretation had been assigned to the *Tuscanicae* by the time of their earliest attestation in the Arval Acta, the Vedic rite filling the comparable ritual slot suggests that in origin these implements—more properly, their ancestral forms—were used in the "lifting up" and "putting down" of sacrificial fire. As the Vedic churning sticks, the *araṇis*, were used to conduct flame from the priestly hearths to the fire of the concluding rite, and then to the home of the sacrificer (see §4.8.4), so the *Tuscanicae*, touched by flaming torches, must have been used to conduct a ritual fire from the site of the concluding rite of the Arval festival to the homes of the Arval priests (who were themselves the sacrificers, on behalf of the Roman state). This is not to say that the *Tuscanicae* were of necessity actually ignited or even that by the first century AD they contained or were made of combustible material; the transfer may have been simply symbolic, as it could be in Vedic procedure when the *araṇis* are placed close to the flame and heated. On the other hand, ritual lighting of portable light sources is well enough attested.

Particularly interesting is the Roman use of wax torches for ritual as well as for quite utilitarian purposes. Compare the custom, attested by Plutarch (*Quaest. Rom.* 1), of Roman brides touching fire (and water). In the succeeding question (*Quaest. Rom.* 2), Plutarch further notes that in the Roman marriage ritual they light five torches (λαμπάδες) called *cereones* (accusative κηρίωνας), clearly a kind of wax (*cēra*) light.[61] Among his several possible answers to the question of why they use *five* such torches, Plutarch makes recourse to Varro's statement that the praetors were allowed to have three of these lights, but that the aediles could have more, and it is the aediles, notes Plutarch, from whom the bride and groom light their fire. Compare *CIL* 1².594.1.3.22, recording that colonial duumviri and aediles have the right and power (*ius potestasque*) to possess the wax lights called *cerei.*[62] Varro elsewhere (*Ling.* 5.64) writes that *cerei* are presented to *superiores* at the Saturnalia (compare Martial 5.18.2). It was with flaming wax torches of this type (*ardentibus cereis*) that *duo quidam* suddenly appeared and set Julius Caesar's funeral pyre ablaze (Suetonius, *Iul.* 84.3).

[61]For the Roman wedding procession a torch is lit at the hearth of the bride's parents. The torch (*fax*) is made of white thorn (*spina*) and is carried by a boy having both father and mother living (Festus, pp. 244, 245M; Nonius p. 161L). Pliny (*NH* 16.75) writes that *spina* is the preferred wood for wedding torches, but others are used as well.

[62]As well as the *toga praetexta* and the waxed-rope torch called a *funale*.

Cicero (*Sen.* 44) and Valerius Maximus (3.6.4) record how Gaius Duilius (consul 260 BC; censor 258 BC), the celebrated recipient of Rome's first naval triumph, would return home after a banquet at night by the light of a *cereus*, his way led by a flautist and lyrist. In the opening scene of the *Curculio* (l. 9), Plautus presents Phaedromus making his way through the dark streets of Epidauros by the light of a *cereus*. Apuleius' procession of Isis is illuminated by *cerei*, among several light sources: *lucernis, taedis, cereis et alio genere facticii luminis* (*Met.* 11.9).

Such wax lights clearly have particular religio-symbolic and ritual value. Latin *cēra*, source of the name of the torches, undoubtedly matches Greek κηρός 'wax', neither of which appears to have a convincing etymology and which are almost certainly not of Indo-European origin. The gender variation (Latin feminine beside Greek masculine) may cast suspicion on a direct Latin borrowing from Greek; Ernout and Meillet (1959: 114) speculate that both may have been acquired from some third language. Within the same broad semantic range, we find a demonstrable Latin acquisition from Greek, one which does indeed show morphological alteration and gender vacillation, namely Latin feminine *lanterna, -ae* 'lantern' from Greek masculine λαμπτήρ, -ῆρος. The reason for the variation is in this case, however, quite clear: the Latin form was acquired from Greek through an Etruscan intermediary, Latin *lanterna* preserving well-known Etruscan morphology (*-erna*). Compare Latin *cisterna* 'underground tank' beside Greek κίστη 'basket, chest'.

Plutarch's unusual accusative form κηρίωνας, which editors have not been shy about correcting to something that transcribes better Latin, has quite possibly suffered from morphological misanalysis. Rather than a masculine accusative plural of κηρίων, -ωνος (see *LSJG*: 948), the Latin form may well be *cēreōnas*, accusative plural of feminine ***cēreōna, **cēreōnae*. Such a form would again show Etruscan morphology; compare Latin *persōna* 'mask' from Etruscan **φersu-na*, from *φersu* '[demon with] mask' (itself probably from Greek πρόσωπα 'mask'; see Rix 2004). The proposed Etruscan etymon denoting a light source made of wax would almost certainly be built on Greek κηρός. Latin *cēra* we would then analyze as a probable backformation from the Etruscan loanword ***cēreōna*, with the more common *cereus* derived from *cēra* (as it would be in any case).

Pieces of a puzzle look to join. Plutarch identifies a wax torch with ritual and symbolic value, used in the transfer of a ritual flame, the name of which appears to preserve Etruscan morphology. The Fratres Arvales record the rite of holding ritual implements to a torch which are subsequently transferred to the home (place of the hearth) of the priests—implements with an alleged Etruscan connection. It would be to take but a small step to posit that the *Tuscanicae* of the closing rite of the Arval festival of Dea Dia are *Tuscanicae* ***cēreōnae*, and if not, then some other *Tuscanicae* X, where X names a type of Etruscan ritual lamp or torch. The importance of Etruscan ritual implements to the Romans is well known; the use of such items serves the function of legitimating the antiquity of the rite, no doubt, though the ultimate origin of the Arval custom is to be traced to Proto-Indo-European, rather than Etruscan, religion, as evidenced by the Vedic parallel. The arrangement is a common enough one; as Dumézil writes (*ARR*: 625): "When the Romans and the other Latins settled in Italy, they were in possession of a well-structured system of beliefs and rites inherited from their Indo-European past. The Etruscan combination, no matter how early, important and repeated, if not continuous, it may have been, only enriched this structure without dislocating it."

We will bring this discussion to a close with a schematic summary (figure 4.6) of some of the principal features shared by the Vedic Agniṣṭoma and the Arval festival of Dea Dia. The comparison is not exhaustive. Greek subscript letters are used to identify homologous sacrificial victims and similar acts involving those victims.

4.10 THE ROBIGALIA

Having examined at length the Arval Festival of Dea Dia vis-à-vis the Vedic Agniṣṭoma, let us return to our survey of ritual sites along the distal border of the Ager Romanus. Among the remaining landmarks lying on that boundary, two especially capture our attention because, as in the Arval rites performed in the grove of Dea Dia, the god Mars is present. These we now consider in turn—first the Robigalia and then Mars' temple on the Via Appia (§4.11).

The April ritual of the Robigalia, like the May rites of Dea Dia, is celebrated for the benefit of Roman fields. In this instance (see §3.3.6.2), the desired effect is quite specific: protection from fungus infestation is afforded by appeasing the deity of grain rust, Robigus or Robigo. The locale is a grove located along the Via Claudia at the fifth milestone from Rome. The Via Claudia runs north and slightly west out of Rome, taking a somewhat more westerly course at the Pontus Milvius, where it diverges from the Via Flaminia. The grove thus stands at a northwest coordinate along the boundary of the Ager Romanus, corresponding roughly to the southwest coordinate provided by the Arval grove on the Via Campana.

VEDIC AGNIṢṬOMA	*ARVAL FESTIVAL OF DEA DIA*
Adhyavasāna Iṣṭi	*Evening meal of first festival day*
Soma-pressing day	*Second festival day*
Morning pressing	Morning culinary event
sacrifice of two goats (Ṣoḍaśin)$_{\alpha}$	sacrifice of two piglets$_{\alpha}$
	sacrifice of cow$_{\beta}$
	offering of the cow's *exta* in circus$_{\gamma}$
	consumption of piglets$_{\delta}$
Midday pressing	Midday culinary event
sacrifice of ram (Ṣoḍaśin)$_{\varepsilon}$	sacrifice of lamb$_{\varepsilon}$
offering of gold at old Āhavanīya	monetary offering at the altar
Indra and the Maruts	Mars and the Semones
Soma and surā (Vājapeya)	wine
chariot race (Vājapeya)	chariot race
Evening pressing	Evening culinary event
sacrifice of sterile cow$_{\beta}$	
movement out of the Mahāvedi	movement out of the Ager Romanus
offering of cow's embryo to Maruts$_{\gamma}$	
consumption of goat$_{\delta}$	
Udavasānīyā Iṣṭi	*Evening meal of third festival day*
conduction of fire by *araṇis*	conduction of fire by Tuscanicae

FIGURE 4.6. *Partial comparison of the Vedic Agniṣṭoma and the Arval Festival of Dea Dia*

At the time of the Robigalia, not only are sacrifices made to the deity, but *ludi* are held in which runners compete (*Feriae Robigo Via Claudia ad milliarium V ne robigo frumentis noceat. Sacrificium et ludi cursoribus maioribus minoribusque fiunt*; *CIL* I^2 pp. 236, 316). According to Tertullian (*De Spect.* 5), Numa Pompilius established *ludi* in honor of Robigus and Mars, an apparent reference to the games of the Robigalia. As at the southwest locus of the Ager Romanus, so also at the northwest Mars again makes an appearance; at each locale the rites conducted look to the well-being of Roman fields. Just so, as we saw in §3.3.3, Mars figures prominently in Cato's prayer of field lustration.

4.10.1 Agrarian Mars

It is the conjoining of Mars to obvious agricultural exercises such as these which gave rise to the scholarly notion of an "agrarian Mars"—a Mars who is fundamentally a god of nature and plant growth. The idea is one which enjoyed considerable popularity in the late nineteenth and early twentieth centuries,[63] and which continued to exist long thereafter. Already in 1912, however, Wissowa had begun to dispel this notion (Wissowa 1971: 143):

> Mit Unrecht haben Neuere in diesen Flurumgängen einen Beweis dafür finden wollen, daß Mars von Haus aus ein Vegetations- und Ackergott sei: soweit die Überlieferung uns ein Urteil gestattet, ist Mars den Römern nie etwas anderes gewesen als Kriegsgott, und wenn man ihn um Schutz der Fluren anfleht, so geschieht das nicht, damit er das Wachstum der Saaten fördere, sondern damit er Kriegsnot und Verwüstung von den Feldern fernhalte.

Norden (1939: 216–222) took up the issue of the nature of Mars vis-à-vis his affiliation with the Semones in the Carmen Arvale. The picture emerges from Norden's study of a Mars who provides protection, who drives away evil (*Übelabwehrer*), allowing the deities of agriculture to perform their tasks.

This doctrine of a guardian Mars working in concert with agrarian deities is methodically developed by Dumézil in *Archaic Roman Religion* (pp. 213–241). He does so by responding point by point to the arguments which H. J. Rose adduced in favor of "agrarian Mars"—Rose being a leading exponent of that theory in the mid-twentieth century. Following in the steps of Wissowa and Norden, Dumézil argues in effect that the idea of an "agrarian Mars" results from a confusion of place of operation with the operation itself: when Mars appears in an agrarian capacity he does so acting as the protecting, vigilant god of war exerting his martial powers in an agricultural setting (*ARR*: 228–229):

[63]For references to several works of the period in which Mars is so presented, see Wissowa 1971: 143, n. 6.

> . . . Mars, in the invocations which the Fratres Arvales address to him, is at the same time this savage divinity and this watchful divinity, while in the lustration of the field which Cato describes he is only the watchful god, in no way involved in the mysterious processes which perpetuate vegetable life.

Dumézil interprets the various Ambarvalic rites of the Romans as establishing an unseen boundary which Mars, the divine protector, the god of battle, is called on to defend (*ARR*: 230–231):

> These ceremonies establish around the *ager*, the *urbs*, etc., an invisible barrier which, provided it is guarded, will be crossed neither by human enemies, whom the ramparts and the army are already prepared for, nor by malignant powers, themselves invisible, especially those which can cause sickness. . . . But these various rituals . . . do not make of Mars a specialist in anything but "protection by force"; his whole function is on their periphery which the processions render perceptible.

As for Norden, so for Dumézil, Mars' presence at this peripheral space allows the deities of plant growth to function unimpeded by hostile forces (*ARR*: 231):

> On occasion he allows specialist divinities—in the Ambarvalia themselves, according to the *Carmen* [*Arvale*], the Lares, gods of the soil, and those designated by the term *Semones*, the animate form of the inanimate *semina*; Ceres, according to Virgil (*Georg.* 1.338)—to perform a technical, creative task which varies according to circumstance.

Scheid (1990: 621–622) seconds Dumézil's view of Mars' role in the rites of the Arvals and takes the interpretation a logical step further. The guardian Mars not only allows the Lares and Semones to accomplish their agricultural tasks, but he equally facilitates the actions of Dea Dia.

> . . . comme l'écrit G. Dumézil, Mars permet, par sa garde, à ces divinités spécialisées de faire un travail technique et créateur. Sur un plan plus général, Mars rend le même service à Dea Dia, en lui garantissant l'absence de toute mauvaise influence venue de l'extérieur. Cette collaboration entre Mars et une divinité «agraire» cautionnant la bonne maturation des *fruges*, Dea Dia, n'est pas isolée, comme le prouve le culte implanté sur la même rive du Tibre, au cinquième mille de la via Claudia, c'est-à-dire aux confins de *l'Ager Romanus antiquus*, qui s'adresse à Robigo, déesse de la rouille des blés, *et* à Mars.

And so we arrive back at the Robigalia. Yet notice that given this interpretative model, the role which the guardian Mars plays vis-à-vis Dea Dia (and the Semones and Lares) must be quite different than that which he fulfills at the grove of Robigus. Dea Dia, object of worship in the Arval rites, is a beneficent divinity whom Mars assists by warding off the evil and malignancy that would short-circuit her beneficence. In contrast, Robigus, placated at the Robigalia, *is* the malignancy. Varro, who has told us that the Fratres Arvales perform their rites so that Roman fields might be fruitful (*Ling.* 5.85), also writes (*Ling.* 6.16):

> Robigalia dicta ab Robigo; secundum segetes huic deo sacrificatur, ne robigo occupet segetes.
>
> The Robigalia is named for Robigo; sacrifice is made to this deity along the grain fields so that rust (*robigo*) may not seize the fields.

The rites of Robigus are celebrated at the boundary of the Ager Romanus; and an implicit notion of field-boundary is present in Varro's words. The "invisible boundary" is there for Mars to protect, but what is he warding off so that the agrarian deity, Robigus, can function effectively? Nothing, of course; for it is Robigus himself (herself) who is being held at bay by the rites of April 25. Ovid states this plainly in the Robigalia prayer of the Flamen Quirinalis which he recites (see §3.3.6.2). Aulus Gellius (*NA* 5.12.14) makes it clear in his discussion of gods who have power more for harm than for help:

> In istis autem diis quos placari oportet, uti mala a nobis vel a frugibus natis amoliantur, Auruncus quoque habetur et Robigus.
>
> Moreover, among those gods whom one ought to placate so that evil might be warded off from us or from our growing crops are numbered also Auruncus and Robigus.

Columella (*Rust.* 10.337–343) makes it clearer, when after lamenting an infestation of the destructive *eruca* (a caterpillar) brought on by rains, he continues:

> Haec ne ruricolae paterentur monstra, salutis
> Ipsa novas artes varia experientia rerum
> Et labor ostendit miseris, ususque magister
> Tradidit agricolis, ventos sedare furentes,
> Et tempestatem Tuscis avertere sacris.
> Hinc mala Rubigo virides ne torreat herbas,
> Sanguine lactentis catuli placatur et extis.
> Hinc caput Arcadici nudum cute fertur aselli
> Tyrrhenus fixisse Tages in limite ruris.

That the tillers should not suffer with these beasts,
mixed trial-and-error and labor have revealed
to the unfortunates new skills of remedy, and customs
a master passed on to the farmers, to calm raging winds,
and to turn aside the storm by Etruscan rites.
Hence lest malefic Rubigo should scorch green plants,
She is placated with the blood and guts of a suckling pup.
Hence the skinned head of an Arcadian ass, they say,
the Etruscan Tages hung up at the rural boundary.

(Tages being the fabled Etruscan soothsayer who was credited with introducing haruspices to the Etruscans; see Festus p. 359M, Cicero, *Div.* 2.50).

The proposed relational model of guardian Mars present at the boundary, warding off menace, allowing invoked deities of plants and soil to function unharassed by ill, begins to break down at the Robigalia. The god there worshipped is a deity having a force that is *in laedendo magis quam in iuvando potentem*, who must be placated by canine sacrifice and implored in prayer "to keep scabrous hands from the harvest" (Ovid, *Fast.* 4.921). Yet Mars is there too.

Dumézil's refutations of Rose's arguments are reasoned and persuasive. Mars, at least in some "original" sense, was not an agrarian deity. His presence in the rites celebrated along the boundary of the Ager Romanus and in private Ambarvalic rituals with their own "invisible boundaries" is almost certainly a function of his fundamentally bellicose nature. As we shall see in chapter 5, however, my understanding of the motivation for Mars' presence in the bounded spaces of those rites is not that articulated by Dumézil, his predecessors, and his followers.

4.11 THE TEMPLE OF MARS ON THE VIA APPIA

Lying on a diagonal extending from the grove of Robigus and crossing urban Rome is the temple of Mars on the Via Appia, with which Alföldi would associate Livy's statuary group composed of Mars and wolves (see §3.3.6.2). Alföldi marks the location of the temple as a southeastern point on the Ager Romanus; though as we saw there is good evidence that the temple was closer to Rome than is typically the case with the boundary points. Yet the temple site is of particular interest, we further noted, because by it was positioned a stone (rendering the locale reminiscent of a liminal space with its characteristic *terminus* of stone)—the stone called the Lapis Manalis. The Pontifices would transport the stone within the walls of Rome during times of drought, so bringing rain to the city. The rain-making stone likely takes its name from the Manes.

What little we know of the Lapis Manalis is enough to reveal features already encountered along the boundary of the Ager Romanus. Not only does Mars again make an appearance, but he does so in conjunction with a bringer of rains. This is exactly the concatenation elicited by the Fratres Arvales when, hymning Mars, they urge him to call in the Semones, the bringers of rain—a combination paralleling that of Indra and the Maruts. Can the Roman set be extended to three recurring members? Not only do the Arvals sing of Mars and the Semones, but of the Lares as well, sons of the chthonic Mater Larum. Just so, the rain-bringing stone of Mars on the Via Appia bears the name of the earth-dwelling Manes. In Vedic India, the Maruts are no strangers to the extended set. As we saw (§4.2.5) the *Atharva Veda* (18.2.21–22) presents the Maruts as conveying the dead to the company of the Pitaras (the Manes) and refreshing them with falling rain. On the Via Campana and the Via Appia we are likely in the presence of a divine set of three which has a deeply archaic Indo-European origin.

4.12 THE AGER GABINUS AND THE AUGURAL BOUNDARY

The last of the Ager Romanus terminal points identified by Alföldi which we will consider is that one located due east of Rome on the Via Praenestina, the augural boundary separating the Ager Romanus and the Ager Gabinus. Varro's recognition of five types of *agri* (*Ling.* 5.33; see §3.3.1)—"the Ager Romanus, Gabinus, peregrinus, hosticus, and incertus"—is predicated on an augural pronouncement (*Ut nostri augures publici disserunt, agrorum sunt genera quinque . . .*). This is not simply a geopolitical apportioning of space. The cleaving of the Roman and surrounding spaces into these five constituent units is one of ritual, augural significance.[64] Varro has told us that *Ager Peregrinus* is the denotation of that space into which the Romans first advanced from the Ager Romanus. The Ager Gabinus technically constitutes something like a subset of the Ager Peregrinus, he explains, but the Augures hold the Ager Gabinus distinct because it has its own particular form of augury (like the Ager Romanus and unlike the Ager Peregrinus). Drawing in the testimony of Livy (1.53.4–54.10) and of Dionysius of Halicarnassus (*Ant. Rom.* 4.53.1–58.4; see §4.2.5.2) that Tarquinius Superbus subjugated the city of Gabii and with it made Rome's first treaty (a venerated object seen by Dionysius), we can infer that the Ager Gabinus has not only ritual priority among the *agri* of the Augures but is assigned a certain historicized priority in the tradition of Roman expansion. Gabii is not the

[64] For Dumézil's views on the five types of *agri* vis-à-vis Indo-European tripartition, see Dumézil 1983: 161–170.

first city of Latium against which the Roman kings advanced militarily, but it is the first with which a sacred treaty is ratified. The treaty is preserved on a shield of hide inscribed with ancient letters, enshrined in the Roman temple of the Semo Sancus, the monster-slayer, chief among the Semones, those deities invoked by Mars in the Carmen Arvale.

Urban Rome, bounded by the *pomerium*, continues the small sacred space of Proto-Indo-European ritual which survives in India as the Devayajana, the space of the Iṣṭi. Beyond that boundary and surrounded by it lies the great sacred space of the Ager Romanus, descended from the large space of the ancestral rites, "cognate" with the space of the Vedic Mahāvedi. To the east of the Ager Romanus lies the Ager Gabinus, marked in both Augural ritual and Roman expansionist tradition. Does this augural space, one place further removed from the small sacred space of urban Rome, likewise continue an archaic Indo-European cultic space? Does it also have a Vedic counterpart?

In the variant forms of the Agniṣṭoma, the motif of the Mahāvedi as "invaded space" is particularly pronounced, as we saw, in the Yātsattra ritual, constituting an ongoing "eastward march" (Heesterman 1993: 129; see §4.3.1). Each day, the Mahāvedi is moved progressively farther to the east. The various sheds are drawn in tow, and the *yūpa*—marker of the distal boundary of the great sacred space—is dragged to its new limit. A cattle herd is moved along with the worshippers, and the entire ritual process mirrors the movement of a nomadic people—though is no less a spiritual journey for that reflection (see §4.3.1).

The nomadic movements of the pastoralist Indo-European ancestors of the Romans had ceased long before the foundation of Rome. Elements of that migratory life of the remote past are, however, ritually preserved in Rome. Each year on June 15, the temple of Vesta undergoes a sweeping out. The day is marked in the Fasti Antiates Maiores and other calendars as Q.ST.D.F. Varro (*Ling.* 6.32) explains the abbreviation:

> Dies qui vocatur Quando Stercum Delatum Fas, ab eo appellatus, quod eo die ex Aede Vestae stercus everritur et per Capitolinum Clivium in locum defertur certum.
>
> The day which is marked "When the dung has been carried away [the day is] lawful," is so named for this, that on this day the dung is swept out of Vesta's temple and is carried away on the Clivus Capitolinus to a certain place.

Festus (p. 344M) agrees and identifies the place to which the *stercus* is taken:

> Stercus ex aede Vestae XVII. Kal. Iul. defertur in angiportum medium fere clivi Capitolini, qui locus clauditur porta stercoraria.
>
> Dung is carried away from Vesta's temple on June 15 into an alley about halfway up the Clivus Capitolinus, a place close to the Porta Stercoraria ['Dung Gate'].

It is most unlikely that there was any accumulation of dung in the temple of Vesta. Dumézil (see *ARR*: 318–319) realized that the sweeping out of June 15 is a Roman rite of great Indo-European antiquity, frozen in time and space, descended from an age when early Indo-European pastoralists ritually cleansed a temporary designated space of the dung of flocks and herds. The area so cleansed is that of the fire of the master of the house (the first of the three canonical fires). The rite is alive and well in Vedic tradition; in India the site of the Gārhapatya must be swept of animal dung before the flame is established (see §4.2.4). The Roman counterpart of the Gārhapatya is the sacred flame that burns in Vesta's temple (see §2.8.1), and that space likewise undergoes a ritual cleansing of "dung"—reduced in the fixed space of urban Rome from a procedure conducted each time the site of the flame is established to an annual symbolic event.

The Ager Gabinus, the invaded sacred space into which the Romans advanced eastward beyond the Ager Romanus, is the Roman metaphor of the progressive eastward movement of the Vedic Yātsattra ritual. Like the sweeping out of *stercus* from the temple of Vesta, the Ager Gabinus is a fossilized memory of the ritual life of the Romans' migratory ancestors, played out more transparently in Vedic India. The Roman advance into the Ager Gabinus, the acquisition of that great space, and its utilization for sacred rites is, as it were, a pageant reenacting the iterative putting down of the great sacred space in an earlier era of Indo-European religion. While the Romans have inevitably simplified the ritual process—a necessary consequence of the permanence of Roman spaces—one might well suspect that the Vedic Yātsattra ritual, with its day-after-day relocation of the structures of the Mahāvedi, is an amplification, in typical Vedic fashion, of the common ancestral Indo-European rite. That both reflexes of this ancestral rite, Italic and Vedic, entail a retention of the site of the small sacred space coupled with an eastward translocation of the great space suggests that the early Indo-European ritual was not simply a portable celebration of a constantly wandering people, but a ritual of established form, acting out the progressive conquest of contiguous spaces. In Rome the ancient rite of conquest manifests itself as the actual acquisition of a further great sacred space lying to the east and the imbuing of that space with sacred import.

4.13 CONCLUSION

We have examined various Roman rites within a context of cultic space and geometry vis-à-vis Vedic ritual. Through this exercise, numerous unexpected discoveries have presented themselves.

The Roman ground of ritual—like the Vedic—is divided into two distinct sacred spaces: the small space of urban Rome, surrounded by the *pomerium* (equivalent to the Vedic Devayajana); and the large space of the Ager Romanus, bounded by a distal encircling boundary, marked by *termini*, along which numerous sacred rites are conducted (equivalent to the Vedic Mahāvedi, on the far border of which stands the *yūpa*). Celebration of the Vedic Soma-sacrifice, in its many variations, takes the form of a ritual progression from the small space into and through the large. The records of the May festival of the Fratres Arvales—unmatched in the history of Roman religion for their ritual detail—reveal a similar journey through the sacred spaces; moreover, a close semantic examination of Latin *ambarvalis* leads us to conclude, in light of both Roman and Vedic evidence, that its original sense is one of 'movement through' a ritual space rather than 'movement around'. The Dhiṣṇya-hearths of the Vedic Mahāvedi find a homologous cultic structure and linguistic counterpart in the Roman *fēstī*.

Earth is gained unbounded by both Vedic and Roman celebrants—by the individual sacrificer in the private rites of the former, and by the state through the public rites of the latter. The Vedic sacrificer who has climbed the *yūpa* at the boundary of the great sacred space gains all the worlds, he possesses the earth (§4.5); on the day of the celebration of the boundary marker deified—*Terminus*, the Roman poet can proclaim that "Rome's city and the world are the same space."

The Soma-pressing day of the Agniṣṭoma replicates the structure of the second day of the Arval festival of Dea Dia—three Soma pressings matching three culinary events. Particularly close to the Arval ritual is the primitive Soma sacrifice called the Vājapeya, with its array of victims, its chariot race supervised by priests, and its ritual use of the alcoholic beverage *surā* (and the priestly procession with *surā* out of the Soma-cart shed) all finding homologous expression in the Arval observance.

The Fratres Arvales singing their *carmen* as a part of the midday culinary event call on Mars to invoke the Semones—deities of water and rain. Probably chief among the Semones (certainly the one about whom we possess the most information) is Semo Sancus. Behind the facade of the poetic account of Hercules' fight with the monstrous Cacus and his recovery of the stolen cattle (likely informed by a Greek folk tradition about Heracles which was widely circulated in the south of Italy) stands the Roman reflex of the ancient Indo-European myth of the heroic dragon-slayer and his triple-headed foe—cattle thief and drought bringer. This hero is overwhelmed by a personal crisis upon accomplishing the deed and flees uncontrollably to a distant watery locale where he is restored by the ministration of waters (and through the agency of prodigious female nudity).

The relationship between Mars and Semo Sancus may be one of diachronic ambiguity, mirroring that of Indra and Trita Āptya. The Arval prayer to Mars—in which Mars himself is adjured to summon the Semones to action—is perhaps a call for the war god to regain strength and return from his place of retreat to take a stand on the sacred boundary which he protects. Mars is recurringly present at the boundary of the Ager Romanus and in rituals of lustrations of agrarian space. This latter characteristic led to the scholarly postulation of an "agrarian Mars"—which idea Dumézil, inter alios, enthusiastically opposed. Yet Mars is there in the field, as well as at the boundaries of the great sacred space. In the final chapter, we shall turn to the warrior god's presence in these places.

CHAPTER 5

From the Inside Out

5.1 INTRODUCTION

In this the final chapter of our study we will more closely examine elements of the Indo-European sacred spaces. Particular attention will be given to the boundary markers of the great sacred space, especially to their instantiation in Roman cult and the significance of their use for, inter alia, revealing the character of the gods Terminus and Mars. Discussions in this chapter will also focus somewhat more directly on the ancient Indo-European cult which is parent to the Vedic and Roman ritual practices examined throughout. The empirical method employed for these discussions is one that projects original (that is, historically antecedent) structures on the basis of identified homologous structures; Dumézil called it *pensée extériorisée* 'exteriorized thinking', which was discussed in §1.7.1.4.2. As we saw in that discussion, Dumézil's method, similar to Benveniste's, is in effect the scientific comparative method which linguists use in reconstructing earlier, unattested forms of language by comparing descendent languages, but here applied to cultural and social reflexes rather than linguistic forms.

5.2 PROTO-INDO-EUROPEAN CULT

Vedic and Roman cult share a duality of sacred space—one small (Devayajana and urban Rome), one great (Mahāvedi and Ager Romanus). The common linguistic and cultural origin of the Indic and Italic peoples is beyond question. The religious preservationism of these two Indo-European societies ringing the eastern and western rims of the Indo-European expansion area in antiquity is well documented, revealed both by lexical evidence (see Benveniste 1969) and by cultic practice (see *ARR*). Ergo, the most economical and at the same time compelling interpretation of this shared structure of sacred space is one which appeals to inheritance: Vedic and Roman religious practice both continue a Proto-Indo-European doctrine and cultic use of dual sacred spaces. Extrapolating from the Vedic and Roman traditions, what conclusions can we draw about the ancestral Indo-European practices?

5.2.1 The small space

Several considerations point to the freestanding cultic use of the Indo-European small space without the large. Most obvious of these is the Vedic observance of the various Iṣṭis—rites that require only the small space. In Rome the small sacred space—that bounded by the *pomerium*—likewise has a distinctive use, being the space within which the urban auspices must be conducted. In both India and Rome, the small space is that which houses the three canonical flames—flames which fulfill discrete ritual functions not dependent on operations being conducted within the large space.

5.2.2 East

In Vedic practice, the great space is laid out to the east of the small. In Roman ritual, the great space has become an all encompassing expansion surrounding the small. The concentric geometry of the sacred spatial arrangement in Rome, we have proposed, is consequent to the immobile and permanent nature of Roman society—so many great-space extensions emanating from the boundary of the fixed small space, melding together by design or by inevitable necessity to form a continuous enclosure. Yet even in Rome there is clear evidence of the theological primacy of the eastward expansion. Like the Vedic Yātsattra with its iterative eastward expansion of the Mahāvedi along the course of the river Sarasvatī (see §4.3.1), so in Rome there is an iterated movement of the larger sacred space beyond the eastern boundary of the Ager Romanus—along the course, as it were, of the Via Praenestina. The Ager Gabinus with its own form of auspices, and so distinguished from the Ager Peregrinus, is a great sacred space that projects from the eastern boundary of the Ager Romanus, one step further removed from the small space of urban Rome (see §4.12).

East is also otherwise revealed to be the direction of theological preeminence. In Vedic India, the east is the region that belongs to the gods,[1] and offerings are made to the gods while facing east (*ŚB* 3.1.1.6–7; compare *ŚB* 14.2.2.28). East is the region of the fire god Agni (*ŚB* 3.2.3.16; 6.3.3.2) and is under his protection (*ŚB* 8.6.1.5). It is the region associated with the *brāhmaṇa*, the priestly class (*ŚB* 5.4.1.3).[2] Note also that the three canonical flames of the Devayajana, the ground of the Iṣṭi, and the relocated Āhavanīya, Sadas, Soma-cart shed, and *yūpa* of the Mahāvedi all lie along the west-to-east axis passing through those two spaces.

East is similarly critical in Rome. Temples are to be situated—to the extent possible, writes Vitruvius (4.5.1)—so that the temple (*aedes*) and the image of its deity are profiled against the eastern sky (facing west); the sacrificer thus looks to the east toward the image, and from the east the deity's gaze is returned (compare Clement of Alexandria, *Strom.* 7 7). Servius (*Aen.* 12.172) records that it is to the east that Romans face when they pray to the gods (compare Ovid, *Fast.* 4.777–778).[3] Reminiscent of the east–west axis of the Vedic sacred spaces is the axis which Livy's *lituus*-wielding Augur traces in the sky from east to west at the inauguration of Numa Pompilius (1.18.7–10). While Numa sits facing south, the Augur (at his left) is turned to the east—revealed by his designation of the regions to the south as "right" and those to the north as "left." Servius (*Aen.* 2.693) concurs with the augural designation of north as "left"; and Isidorus Hispalensis (*Etym.* 15.4.7) writes that an augural *templum* faces to the east (*ut qui consuleret atque precaretur rectum aspiceret orientem*). Dionysius of Halicarnassus (*Ant. Rom.* 2.5.1–5) describes the best orientation for augury as

[1] The region of the north belongs to men, the south to the Pitaras, and the west to snakes (*ŚB* 3.1.1.6–7).

[2] The south is associated with the Kṣatriya, the warriors and the west with the Vaiśya, the goods producers (*ŚB* 5.4.1.4–5). At the same time, within the context of the space of the Mahāvedi, the lords of the east are said to be the Vasus (the third function of divine society), those of the south are the Rudras (second function), those of the west are the Ādityas (first function), and the lords of the north are the Maruts (*ŚB* 8.6.1.5–8).

[3] According to Tertullian (*Apol.* 16.9–10), Christians likewise pray toward the east, a custom which brought the charge of sun worshipping from pagans.

eastward-facing, being the region from which the sun, moon, stars, and planetary bodies rise.

There is an alternative Roman tradition according to which the front of the augural space faces south. The notion is preserved by Varro (*Ling.* 7.7) who, writing of the four sections of the *templum*, identifies the eastern as "left" and the southern as "front" (*Eius templi partes quattuor dicuntur, sinistra ab oriente . . . antica ad meridiem*). This looks to be part and parcel of the same doctrine espoused by Festus (p. 220M) when he records that the southern part of the sky illuminated by the sun is called "front" and the northern part "back." When that famous Augur Attus Navius (whose confrontation with Tarquinius we earlier examined; see §1.9.1.1) first displayed his augural skills by divining the location of the largest bunch of grapes in his vineyard, he measured out his augural *templum* while facing south—such at any rate is Cicero's account (*Div.* 1.30–31); Dionysius of Halicarnassus (*Ant. Rom.* 3.70.2–5) fails to mention the southward orientation. Whatever historical processes might lie behind this augural bifurcation in Rome, it is worth noting that even if the Augur should face to the south, east still plays a prominent role: east is then "left," and in Roman augural tradition, auspicious omens are observed on the left.[4]

The eastward progression of the Vedic Soma-sacrifices and the Roman ritual expansion eastward into the Ager Gabinus, coupled with the Roman propensity for eastward orientation in augural rites, and the identification of the east with the domain of the gods in both cultures points to a parent Indo-European cult and theology in which the direction of the rising sun played comparable roles. In Proto-Indo-European cult, the small sacred space could be used independently—marked off, cleaned of animal dung, and otherwise prepared as necessary by the Indo-European pastoralist worshippers and their priests. Certain religious concerns, however, required that the small sacred space be augmented by the measuring out of a large space to its east—the direction of the gods—and that the ritual be expanded by movement of the celebrants into and through that space. Judging from the iterative nature of the eastward expansion evidenced independently by the Yātsattra rites and the Ager Gabinus, the Proto-Indo-European eastward expansion of sacred space could likewise be realized as a repeated ritual event.

[4]See Dionysius of Halicarnassus, *Ant. Rom.* 2.5.2–5; Virgil, *Aen.* 9.630–631; Plutarch, *Quaest. Rom.* 78. For the spatial orientation of the Roman *templum*, see *ARR*: 597; Frazer 1929, vol. 3: 365–367.

5.2.3 *The unboundary*

On the distal boundary of the great sacred space is erected an upright marker—the *yūpa* (sacrificial stake) in Vedic India; the *terminus sacrificalis* in Rome. Though it stands on the border of the sacred terrain, dividing the realm of sacrificial order from the world of disorder which lies beyond, for the sacrificer the *yūpa* is not a limiting device. It does not mark an end point beyond which the sacrificer cannot progress. To the contrary, the *yūpa* is a facilitating device; in a sense it marks an "unboundary" for the sacrificer. The *yūpa* opens the way to the acquisition of blessings: it brings rain (§2.6.1); it provides livestock, offspring, fertility to the fields, sustenance, long life, and prosperity (§2.6.2). Positioned at the eastern edge of the sacred arena—on the unboundary—it stands at the highest point on earth, brings immortality, and gives the sacrificer access to the world of the gods (§§2.6.1.1; 2.6.2). By means of the *yūpa* the sacrificer gains possession of the earth—an earth which in the symbolism of ritual is equated in expanse with the *vedi* at the edge of which the *yūpa* stands (§4.5).

5.2.3.1 THE UNBOUNDARY LOST The notion of the unboundary—the boundary which is not—is also to be found in Rome. On the one hand, within the historicized mythology of Rome's first two kings, Romulus and Numa—radically contrastive personalities—the unboundary is presented as meeting its demise. Thus, in Plutarch's *Life of Numa* and *Roman Questions*, as we have seen, the Greek sage writes of how it was Numa who first built temples to Fides and Terminus (§1.5.4), and appears to suggest that it was Numa who first established sacrifices for the boundary god, making them bloodless as befits a guardian of justice and peace (§2.8.4). His predecessor Romulus had placed no such boundary markers around Roman territory, we are told (*Quaest. Rom.* 15):

> . . . ὅπως ἐξῇ προϊέναι καὶ ἀποτέμνεσθαι καὶ νομίζειν πᾶσαν ἰδίαν . . .
>
> . . . so that it might be possible to move forward and to seize and regard all [land] to be his own . . . .

This is precisely the realization of the advantage held out by the *yūpa*. It is the same act ritualized in the iterative expansion of the Mahāvedi in the Yātsattra rituals.

The Sabine Numa, however, was of a different ilk. While Romulus had much enlarged the territory of Rome by the spear, Numa—possessed by a passion for justice—is portrayed as promoting agriculture and introducing the benefits of the georgic lifestyle to Romans, and thereby removing from Rome the propensity for war. As a part of his land reforms, Numa is credited with dividing Roman territory into the rural districts called *pagi* (Plutarch, *Numa* 16.1–4; Dionysius of Halicarnassus, *Ant. Rom.* 2.76.1–2) and requiring each landowner to delineate his own property-boundaries, marking them with *termini* (*Ant. Rom.* 2.74.2–5).

Numa's boundary and land reforms—to use the phenomenology of the historicized mythic tradition—are the consequence of the transformation of an archaic Indo-European pastoral society, with its rituals of symbolic and ever-advancing acquisitions of earth, into the landed society of Rome in which shared boundaries between fields must remain fixed and inviolate (§4.4). The temporary sacrificial space intended to bring blessings and advantage for the sacrificer has been replaced by permanent properties—fields—in which the old rituals of the sacred space continue to be acted out. The perceived benefit is purification of the field with the goal of bringing to the sacrificer (the owner/tiller) blessings and advantage. The structures have changed; the theology remains unchanged (see §4.6). The inherited marker of the osmotic *unboundary* which is ancestral to both the Vedic *yūpa* and the Roman *terminus sacrificalis* must then become in Rome a marker of the impermeable *boundary* as well. This is the evolutionary bifurcation discussed in §2.8.4—the ancient Indo-European cultic implement splitting into both the benchmark *termini* and the sacred *termini sacrificales*.

There is an additional consequence of the Roman monumentalization of the Indo-European cultic marker of the sacred space. It is not a necessary consequence but indeed a natural one, given the well-known Roman tendency for divinely animating inanimate objects and abstract notions. The *termini*—in origin part of the equipment of the cult—have been deified as Terminus, god of the boundary. The religion of Rome is rife with such deifications—providing much fuel for the fires of the Church Fathers. St. Augustine (*De Civ. D.* 4.8)—using Varro, again, as his source for the names—would taunt Roman paganism for its dependence on deities such as Cluacina, goddess of sewers; Volupia, goddess of pleasure; Lubentina, goddess of *libido*; Rusina, goddess of fields; Jugatinus, god of mountain tops; Collatina, goddess of hills; Vallonia, goddess of valleys; Seia, goddess of seeds; Nodutus, god of the joints of stems; Forculus, god of doors; Cardea, goddess of hinges; Limentinus, god of the threshold. The list goes on. Terminus is the most significant member of this set, attesting to the great antiquity and significance of the object which he animates.[5]

The Vedic *yūpa* brings to the sacrificer blessings of fecundity and increase. This must certainly be the functional essence of the *yūpa*'s Indo-European prototype, since the same fundamental notion survives in its Roman reflex. The continuity is most readily apparent in the character of Terminus, the deified descendent of the "proto-*yūpa*." Terminus is one member of that set of deities collectively named as "the gods of Titus Tatius" (see §1.4)—Roman deities of "prosperity and fertility" (*ARR*: 170) who continue, ideologically, the third function of early Indo-European society. The primitive *terminus*—standing on the unboundary, bringer of fecundity and increase—has become Terminus—god of the boundary, assimilated into the body of the gods of fecundity and increase.

5.2.3.2 THE UNBOUNDARY GAINED On the other hand—with a view to the remainder of the world—a Roman notion of the unboundary survives—alive and well. Numa may have set up *termini* around Rome (Dionysius of Halicarnassus, *Ant. Rom.* 2.74.4; Plutarch, *Quaest. Rom.* 15; *Numa* 16.2), but as Ovid has told us in words describing the Terminalia and sacrifices offered to Teminus along the boundary of the Ager Romanus (*Fast.* 2.683–684; see §§3.2; 4.5):

> Gentibus est aliis tellus data limite certo:
> Romanae spatium est Urbis et orbis idem.

> For other nations the earth has fixed boundaries;
> Rome's city and the world are the same space.

Rome's boundary—*unlike all others*—is an unboundary. These lines likely preserve a Latin pun on *urbs* 'city' and *orbis* 'world' which is otherwise

[5]Such divine animation is bound up with the problematic notion of *numina*. Surveying the concept, *BNP* (vol. 2: 3) states "The word *numen*, meaning 'nod' or 'divine power', is used by Roman poets of the early Empire, such as Ovid, to indicate the mysterious presence of godhead in natural or man-made objects, in this case the boundary stone—the *terminus*. According to animistic theories of Roman religion, Terminus was an example of the earliest form of Roman deity; it was never represented in human style, but always seen as the divine power residing in the boundary stone. And the word *numen* itself, following these theories, was the standard Latin term for the pre-anthropomorphic 'divinities' of the early period." For Dumézil's arguments against the ideas of animistic theories, such as that of H. J. Rose and his followers, see *ARR*: 18–31.

attested, beginning with Cicero (*Cat.* 4.11), argues Nicolet (1991: 110–111, 114; see also Edwards 1996: 87, 100). And as we noted earlier (see §3.2), the poet captures the same view in lines on the Kalends of January (*Fast.* 1.85–86):

> Iuppiter arce sua totum cum spectet in orbem,
> nil nisi Romanum quod tueatur habet.
>
> Jupiter, viewing all the world from his citadel,
> Observes nothing un-Roman to protect.

The same cosmology finds expression in Virgil (*Aen.* 1.278–279); foretelling the future founding of Rome—the "walls of Mars"—Jupiter proclaims:

> His ego nec metas rerum nec tempora pono;
> imperium sine fine dedi.
>
> To these [walls] I set no boundaries or duration of possessions;
> an empire without limit I have given.

Ovid hints at the doctrine again—in words reminiscent of the Vedic sacrificer's proclaimed access to the world of the gods *and* possession of the earth by means of the elevated *yūpa*, when in the miserable gray of Tomi the poet looks back to that city from which he has been exiled (*Tr.* 1.5.69–70)—no mean city it is:

> Sed quae de septem totum circumspicit orbem
> montibus, imperii Roma deumque locus.
>
> But which surveys the whole world from seven
> hills—Rome, place of gods and empire.

(Compare *Tr.* 3.7.51–52; *Pont.* 2.1.23–24; Propertius 3.11.57.)

In the charming, learned style of early-twentieth-century scholarly prose, Frazer (1929, vol. 2: 90), in commenting on *Fasti* 1.85–86, writes:

> Roman poets loved to boast of Rome as the capital of the whole earth, and to speak of the Roman empire as co-extensive with the globe. It is curious to reflect that to the Greeks and Romans, civilized and enlightened as they were, by far the greater part of the terrestrial globe, with all its teeming population, remained utterly unknown. They were like ants who mistake their ant-hill for the world.

Writing in the last decade of the same century, Edwards (1996: 99) draws attention to Pliny's descriptions of Rome in *Historia Naturalis* 3.66–67 and

36.101–124, and especially to his claim of 36.101 regarding the buildings of Rome:

> universitate vero acervata et in quendam unum cumulum coiecta non alia magnitudo exsurget quam si mundus alius quidam in uno loco narretur.
>
> With the whole lot of them brought together and stacked up in a kind of mound, an expanse would rise up as if some other world were being described in one space.

Edwards surmises, "The sum of Rome is equivalent to another world, *mundus alius*" (pp. 99–100) and draws Pliny's remarks into the sphere of the notion that *urbs* equals *orbis*, citing *Fasti* 2.684. For Edwards, this is a rhetorical stratagem: "Another strategy for conveying the city's unique status is to represent Rome as in itself equivalent to the entire world" (p. 99). Again, she writes of Rome functioning "as a metonymy of the world" (p. 87).

Both of these scholarly views express vital synchronic interpretations. Frazer undoubtedly captures a kind of anthropological tendency, or even a universal—indeed, people do not have to live in such cosmopolitan places as Rome and Athens to "mistake their ant-hill for the world." Equally certain is that, as Edwards (following Nicolet 1991) notes, the tenet of "*urbs* equals *orbis*" becomes a literary motif which suits well the rhetoric of Roman imperialism. Lying behind this tenet, however, is an ancient theological doctrine of the sacred space which, in conjunction with the marker of the unboundary, is symbolic of the "earth to be possessed"—a promise of blessing to the sacrificer. Mutatis mutandis, the acclamation of *Śatapatha Brāhmaṇa* 3.7.2.1, "Verily as large as the *vedi* is, so large is the earth" (after Eggeling 1995, pt. 2: 175; see §4.5), is remarkably well paraphrased by Edward's observation (p. 87) that "Rome can function as a metonymy of the world. . . ." Something like a purist version of this doctrine is preserved in Ovid's lines penned in the *Fasti* entries for the Terminalia (2.683–684) and the Kalends of January (1.85–86); Virgil has not moved far from it in *Aeneid* 1.278–279. The theological doctrine, however, lends itself to more mundane interpretations of the imperial city's hegemony over the peoples and lands that Rome has subjugated. Thus Pliny, writing of the grandeur of Rome's buildings, declares the world has also been conquered in the architectural realm (*HN* 36.101; see Edwards 1996: 100).

5.2.4 A theo-geometric shift

Bearing in mind that precious little remains of the theology of the rites celebrated along the boundary of the Ager Romanus, we note what clearly appears to be a spatial differential distinguishing the Roman and Vedic traditions of the unboundary. In Vedic cult it is at the distal boundary of the great sacred space—where the *yūpa* stands—that the unboundary and other blessings provided by that erected post are realized. There the sacrificer—touching and climbing the *yūpa*—gains access to the world of the gods; there he possesses the earth; that spot—where the *yūpa* stands—is claimed to be the highest point on earth. In contrast, in Roman cult it is on the summit of the Capitoline, a proximal locale, that a *terminus* stands—the Capitoline Terminus—and from this lofty perch Jupiter looks down on the world, seeing nothing un-Roman. It is here, on the Capitoline hill, that the theology of the unboundary is most conspicuously realized. Edwards, in her 1996 study of the "literary topography" of Rome, notes the preeminent position of the Capitoline (see, especially, pp. 69–95): "If Rome can function as a metonymy of the world . . . , then the Capitol functions as a metonymy of Rome itself" (p. 87). And again she writes: "The Capitol was the seat not of day-to-day political power in Rome (most meetings of the senate and of the people took place elsewhere), but rather of Rome's symbolic power" (see also Borgeaud 1987: 91, whom she cites).

Why does this differential exist? It seems that we are dealing with a spatial shift in Rome (positing that the Vedic condition continues the practice of the primitive Indo-European cult). Such a shift may well be consequent to the temporary sacred spaces of Indo-European cult being replaced by the immovable spaces of Rome, and the accompanying evolutionary bifurcation of the inherited sacred boundary markers into secular and sacred alloforms. The *unboundary* marker shifts from the *termini* rimming the Ager Romanus—perceived as not only a sacred boundary but also as a *fixed boundary* of the state—to *the* Terminus standing on Jupiter's Capitoline summit, the symbol of Roman power—to appropriate the words of the Vedic commentary, the "highest point on earth" (the *summa* are in the power of Jupiter; St. Augustine, *De Civ. D.* 7.9; see §2.7.1). By this Roman *yūpa*, Rome—like the Vedic sacrificer—gains possession of the earth.

On the other hand, there is clear evidence that this shifted configuration itself has an Indo-European prehistory. As we saw in §2.4, the stone marker Terminus, standing on the Capitoline summit, ensconced within the temple of the sovereign deity Jupiter, is a Roman expression of an Indo-European matrix which also survives among both the Celts and the Indo-Aryans. This configuration among the latter peoples—a *linga* resting on an elevated structure within the residence of the king—was in fact our entrée into an examination of the *yūpa* and the Vedic sacred spaces. That is to say, the Vedic antecedent of the *linga* of the god Śiva is identified as the *yūpa* (§2.6). We subsequently discovered, however, that the *yūpa*—a *columna mundi* (like the Śiva *linga*)—is matched by several closely related by-forms: the *skambha*; the flaming *liṅgodbhava*; the *Indradhvaja*; and the Sadas post (§2.6.3). The last of these shares a mirror-image geometry with the *yūpa*—the Sadas post standing at the western boundary of the Mahāvedi, the *yūpa* standing at the eastern, so that the two posts bracket that great sacrificial space. The ritual conducted at the erection of the Sadas post is nearly identical to the one which accompanies the raising of the *yūpa* (§2.6.3.4). Even more significantly, like the *yūpa* the Sadas post is a facilitator of blessings, strengthening the *brāhmaṇa* and the *kṣatriya* (priest and warrior classes) through the ritual of its erection. Much as with the *yūpa*, the blessings of the Sadas post are anchored particularly in the realm of production and fertility. It brings wealth and abundance (*ŚB* 3.6.1.17). It is made of *udumbara*—a kind of wood equated with "strength and food" (*ŚB* 3.6.1.2). The sacrificer touches it (as he touches the *yūpa*) and prays, and thereby he gains offspring and cattle, or whatever he might wish (*ŚB* 3.6.1.20).

The general similarity in the rituals of raising the Sadas post and the *yūpa*, the Sadas post's transparent status as a *columna mundi* (see §2.6.3.4), and its pronounced affiliation with fertility, give us cause to ponder whether it might be this truncated *yūpa*—the Sadas post, an alloform of the sacrificial stake—which is more immediately antecedent to the Śiva *linga*, and hence which is the Vedic "cognate" of the Irish stone of Fál and (of greatest importance for our present purpose) of the Roman *terminus*—the divine Terminus—which stands on the Capitoline summit. To some extent, admittedly, identifying that antecedent pillar as the Sadas post rather than the *yūpa* is to make a moot distinction. The two structures are clearly closely related (we have called them alloforms), standing at either end of the Mahāvedi, raised on or very close to the east-west axis that bisects the small and great sacred spaces, on which lie the several sacred fires. In other words, one might claim that lying behind these two structures is a common, monolithic conceptual notion which likewise finds expression in the various members of the Indo-European matrix of the sacred stone. Two pieces of evidence, however, suggest that we are justified in splitting this hair of *yūpa* versus Sadas post.

First, in our discussion of the Indo-European matrix of which Terminus is the Roman member (§2.4), we argued that two of the features comprising that matrix concern the realm of sovereignty. The sacred stone is both affiliated with a figure of sovereignty and occupies an elevated position in a sovereign space. Thus Terminus resides within the temple of Jupiter Optimus Maximus and stands on the summit of the Capitoline hill; the *linga* of Śiva resides within the king's residence and is there positioned atop a pyramid; the Irish stone of Fál announces the legitimate king of Ireland and is positioned on top of the hill of the royal village of Tara.

These features are exactly replicated by the Sadas post, which in Vedic ritual is likewise affiliated with and positionally linked to the sovereign realm. The Sadas post stands at the western border of the Mahāvedi; and according to the *Śatapatha Brāhmaṇa* (8.6.1.7), the western region of that space belongs to the gods called the Ādityas (§1.6.1), representatives of the first function (see §1.4) of divine society—the domain of sovereignty. Beyond that, the protector of the west is said to be Varuṇa, who along with Mitra, stands at the head of the gods of the first function; Varuṇa and Mitra, as we have seen already (§1.3), occupy a position in Vedic India equivalent to that of Jupiter in Rome. The Sadas post stands on the extremity of the Mahāvedi that belongs to the gods of the sovereign domain, and thus like the various members of our Indo-European matrix bears an affiliation with figures of sovereignty. The element of elevation is also present in the west to the extent that when the sacrificer is choosing a space for the Soma sacrifice, he is to select a place which "lies highest" (*ŚB* 3.1.1.1) and which slopes downward from west to east (or slopes down to the north; *ŚB* 3.1.1.2). At the same time, we should bear in mind that the *yūpa* is ritually proclaimed to occupy the highest place on earth.

The second bit of evidence for identifying the Sadas post and the *terminus* on the Capitoline as homologous structures is this. We noted that the Indo-European matrix of the sacred stone is trifunctional in nature. Each of the three stones which evidence the matrix—Indo-Aryan, Irish, and Roman—belongs to the realm of fertility and productivity (third function); at the same time each is associated with both the domain of sovereignty (first function) and the domain of the warrior (second function; see §2.4).

Here again, the Sadas post shows a remarkable parallel. The affiliation of this western boundary marker with the realm of fecundity (third function) is fundamental—it brings blessings of increase and fertility to the sacrificer (on whose behalf the Soma-sacrifice is being performed). At the same time, when the Sadas post is ritually planted, an invocation is made to Dyutāna, son of the Maruts (Indra's warrior companions; second function) and to Mitra and Varuṇa (chief of the Ādityas; first function; *ŚB* 3.6.1.16). Moreover, as the priest mounds up earth around the planted Sadas post, he prayerfully addresses the pillar as champion of the *brāhmaṇa* class (first function), of the *kṣatriya* class (second function), and of the increase of wealth and abundance (third function; *ŚB* 3.6.1.17). As he tamps down the earth around the post, he prays that it will sustain the *brāhmaṇa* class (first function), the *kṣatriya* class (second function), and life and offspring (third function; *ŚB* 3.6.1.18).

5.2.4.1 TWO COLUMNS Two posts mark the limits of the great sacred space in India and Rome. The Vedic and Roman cults show a nearly exact match in the geometry of those two posts. They show only a slightly less exact theological match.

One of those posts stands on the distal boundary of the great sacred space. In India it is the *yūpa* (often one of several) raised at the eastern edge of the Mahāvedi; in Rome it is the *terminus* erected at the boundary of the Ager Romanus (any one of numerous *termini* located along that encircling boundary).

The other of the posts stands at the proximal boundary of the great space. In India, it is the Sadas post set up on the western extremity of the Mahāvedi, close to the seam where that space adjoins the small sacred space of the Devayajana. In Rome, the proximal *terminus* stands on the summit of the Capitoline hill; its placement there must date to the earliest periods of the Indo-European habitation of Rome and so to a time when the ancient *pomerium* passed around the Palatine (see Holloway 1994: 101–102) and excluded the Capitoline.

The traits of the Indic columns can be summarized as follows:

1 The temporary movable space of the Vedic Mahāvedi is studded by two columns standing at the polar extremities of that space, lying on or close to the east-west axis which bisects the Mahāvedi.
2 Each column is a *columna mundi*.
3 Each post brings blessings of increase and fecundity for the sacrificer.
4 The proximal column stands in the quarter of the Ādityas (the west), manifestly trifunctional in its affiliations.
5 The space slopes from the proximal to the distal column, though the latter—the *yūpa*—is declared to occupy the "highest point on earth."
6 The distal column is a marker of the unboundary.

In Rome, these traits are replicated, mutatis mutandis:

1 The fixed space of the Ager Romanus is marked by *termini* ringing the far boundary of that great Roman sacred arena and by a single proximal *terminus* standing on the Capitoline heights just beyond the Palatine *pomerium* (§4.4). This Capitoline *terminus* early on became the permanent Roman Sadas post from which one radiating axis after another was extended, like so many spokes from a hub, across the Ager Romanus—the Roman Mahāvedi—toward distal *termini sacrificales* set up at sites of

periodic ritual activity along the rim of the far boundary of the great sacred space, partitioning the Ager Romanus into so many wedges of sacred space. The revolving wheel of perpetual sacred activity so created is in effect the fixed-place, steady-state equivalent of the ever-advancing *yūpa* and the ever-extending Mahāvedi of the Vedic Yātsattra ritual (§4.3.1). So viewed, the perpetually cycling rituals along the periphery of the Ager Romanus would constitute a synchronically productive variant of the historically circumscribed expansion into the Ager Gabinus (on which, see §4.12).

2 Like the homologous Vedic columns, the proximal as well as the distal *termini* of Roman cult represents a *columna mundi* (§2.7.1).

3 Also like their Vedic homologues, each *terminus* is fundamentally affiliated with the realm of fecundity, revealed by the inclusion of the deified Terminus in the third-function set of deities that Varro denotes as the "gods of Titus Tatius" (§1.4), and by comparative evidence supplied by the Indo-European feature-matrix of the sacred stone.

4 As in India, the proximal column resides in the region of the realm of divine sovereignty—standing on Jupiter's Capitoline. The Roman sovereign god must have been affiliated with the Capitoline hill long before the construction of the temple of Jupiter Optimus Maximus. This is certainly the condition reflected in the annalistic tradition of Rome's origins: after his defeat of Acron, king of the Caeninenses, at the outset of the Sabine war, Romulus—Rome's founding regent—offers the slain warrior's spoils to Jupiter Feretrius on the Capitoline (depositing them at a sacred oak), and there vows to Jupiter Rome's first temple (Livy 1.10.4–7; compare Plutarch, *Rom.* 16.3–7; Propertius 4.10.5–22).[6]

Also like the Sadas post standing in the quarter of the Ādityas, the *terminus* of Jupiter's Capitoline participates in a trifunctional assemblage, being also affiliated with the warrior's realm: this deified Terminus is there affiliated with Juventas—and even Mars has a continued, if inconspicuous, presence, writes St. Augustine (§1.11). This trifunctionality brings us back to the very heart of the problem with which we began this study: this same trifunctional assemblage of Terminus, Juventas, and Jupiter *is* the Minor Capitoline triad.

[6]Jupiter appears to have had an even wider affiliation with non-Palatine Roman hills—and with their trees—at an early period in Rome's history (see Warde Fowler 1899: 228–229). On the Esquiline was found the grove of Jupiter called the Lucus Fagutalis (from *fagus* 'beech'), where there was a shrine (*sacellum*) of Jupiter Fagutalis (see *LTUR*: vol. 3: 135; Richardson 1992: 148). Juppiter Viminus had an archaic altar on the Viminal, with perhaps the name of both hill and altar derived from *vimen*, denoting a flexible branch, commonly willow (*LTUR*: vol. 3: 162; Richardson 1992: 227–228, 431). Compare also the *sacellum* of the Capitoleum Vetus on the Quirinal, which perhaps in origin predates the Capitoline triad (Warde Fowler 1899: 228–229).

5 Consider the prescribed raised elevation of the western boundary of the Mahāvedi. Obviously the lay of the Capitoline is likewise elevated, yet the Capitoline is the smallest of the seven hills of Rome (Richardson 1992: 68). Paradoxical it is, then, that the hill of Jupiter—in whose power are the *summa* (St. Augustine, *De Civ. D.* 7.9, following Varro)—is not the greatest. When the god who possesses the *summa* looks down on the world and sees nothing un-Roman, it is not from the highest possible elevation in Rome. It reminds us of the paradox of the elevation of the *yūpa*, which is declared to occupy the highest spot on earth, though the elevation of the great sacred space is to slope down toward the eastern boundary at which the *yūpa* stands.

6 We have already seen that the claim that the *yūpa* occupies the highest spot on earth is a declaration made about the marker of the unboundary and that in Rome, with the evolutionary differentiation of the ancient sacred boundary marker into a marker of state and private boundaries as well, the essence of the unboundary is shifted from the *termini* of the periphery—from the Roman *yūpas*—to the *terminus* of the Capitoline—the Roman Sadas post. That this shift was not simply an unconscious process—an automatic theological knee jerk—is suggested by an observation made much earlier in this work and, at the moment of the observation, seemingly unconnected with the Capitoline hill, the notion of an unboundary, and any other such matter—but very much connected with the column of the distal boundary.

In his account of the Ambarvalia, or Ambarvia as he dubs it, the Greek geographer Strabo says that the festival is celebrated at a place called Festi on the boundary of the Roman territory—and at still other boundary places (see §3.3.1). We argued that Strabo's Festi (Φῆστοι) is not a geographic τόπος, but a worship "place" that shares a linguistic and cultic origin with Vedic *Dhiṣṇya*, from Proto-Indo-European $*d^{h}eh_{1}s$- (see §4.3.2). The Dhiṣṇya-hearths of the Mahāvedi are six fires located beneath the Sadas (plus a seventh, the Āgnīdhrīya, along the northern boundary of the great sacred space). They stand in a row (running north to south) immediately to the east of the Sadas post. In other words, the Dhiṣṇya-hearths (six of the seven) are part of the landscape of the proximal boundary of the great sacred space of the Mahāvedi. Strabo's Festi, however, is situated along the distal boundary of the great sacred space of Rome, the Ager Romanus.

We did not entertain this spatial distinction in our earlier discussion of Festi vis-à-vis the Dhiṣṇya-hearths. Perhaps it is of no consequence; one might claim that Latin *fēsti* and Sanskrit *Dhiṣṇyaḥ* are simply terms descended from the available nomenclature of Proto-Indo-European cult and came to be applied independently to functionally similar but spatially dissimilar cultic structures in the Roman and Vedic great sacred spaces. The mirror-image spatial relationship which *fēsti* and the Dhiṣṇya-hearths display makes this suggestion unlikely, however, when it is viewed in tandem with the co-occuring mirror-image relationship of the placement of the marker of the unboundary in Rome and in India. We have argued that the marker of the unboundary shifts in Rome from being embodied in the column on the distal boundary of the great sacred space to that of the proximal boundary of that space. There appears to have been a concomitant or responsive Roman shift of the cultic implements—*fēsti*—located next to the column of the proximal boundary. As the unboundary marker moves proximally, the *fēsti* move distally, preserving an ancient cultic geometry of the great sacred space that remains intact in the homologous Vedic space:

Vedic geometry—Mahāvedi

[[Sadas post$_{\alpha}$	Dhiṣṇya-hearths$_{\beta}$]	*yūpa*$_{\gamma}$] UNBOUNDARY

Roman geometry—Ager Romanus

[Capitoline terminus$_{\gamma}$ UNBOUNDARY	[fēsti$_{\beta}$	terminus$_{\alpha}$]]

FIGURE 5.1. *The Mirror-image Geometry of the Vedic and Roman Great Sacred Spaces*

That the marker of the unboundary must remain separated from the Dhiṣṇya-hearths/*fēsti* by the length of the great sacred space—even when that marker has shifted in Rome—clearly suggests that the Vedic Dhiṣṇya-hearths and the Roman *fēsti* have not only denotations that are of common Indo-European origin but that they are in fact homologous cultic structures (see §4.3.2). Antecedent to both is a great sacred space of Proto-Indo-European cult, studded at each end by posts; just interior to the post of the proximal end of that space is a set of priestly altars.

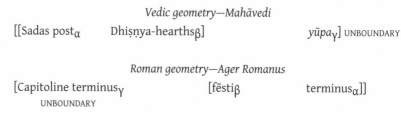

Like the architecture of the sacred edifices of many of the world's faiths, the geometry of the sacred spaces is ancient and resistant to change. When in Rome there is a realignment of the bracketing columns vis-à-vis the notion of the unboundary—consequent to the evolution of fixed boundaries in the landed society of Rome—the ancient geometry is preserved by a sliding of the altars to the far column. An intriguing typological parallel is provided by the rotation in sacred Christian architecture which occurred in the fourth century AD. In antiquity, churches were constructed along an approximate east–west axis. During the time of Constantine, the sanctuary was regularly located at the western end of a church. By the middle of the fourth century, however, church architecture had been reoriented 180 degrees, with the apse shifting to the eastern aspect (see Davies 1953: 81–83; the shift may actually represent a return to a still earlier east-west orientation).

5.2.4.2 TERMINUS What the preceding sections have made clear is just how central and fundamental Terminus was to the archaic Capitoline. Now it becomes clear why Terminus—in the mythic history of the Romans—could not possibly be compelled to leave his Capitoline locale to make room for the new triad. We see why Terminus was selected to continue the third-function presence among the members of the Minor Capitoline triad. The affiliation of a *terminus* with the place must have been every bit as old as Jupiter's presence there (compare Jupiter Terminus), born out of age-old cultic practices that the Italic peoples brought with them as they entered the Italian peninsula. In the ancient inherited Indo-European theology, Terminus could not be dissociated from the Capitoline, and the boundary god's presence there was requisite for the preservation of the unboundary of Rome. This is precisely the religious doctrine that is preserved—cloaked in garments of the state—in the accounts of his refusal to leave the Capitoline. These we encountered at the outset of our study (see §§1.2; 1.11); let us rehearse them once more as we come to the end. Dionysius of Halicarnassus (*Ant. Rom.* 3.69.6) writes of Terminus and Juventas:

> . . . ἐκ δὲ τούτου συνέβαλον οἱ μάντεις ὅτι τῆς Ῥωμαίων πόλεως οὔτε τοὺς ὅρους μετακινήσει καιρὸς οὐθεὶς οὔτε τὴν ἀκμὴν μεταβαλεῖ
>
> . . . and from this the Augures determined that nothing would ever bring about either the disruption of the boundaries of the Roman city or the loss of its vitality

Livy (1.55.4–5) records:

> idque omen auguriumque ita acceptum est, non motam Termini sedem unumque eum deorum non evocatum sacratis sibi finibus firma stabiliaque cuncta portendere
>
> And this omen and augury was so interpreted: that the seat of Terminus was not moved, and that he alone among the gods was not called out beyond the boundary made sacred to him, foreshadowed that all would be steadfast and unfailing

And St. Augustine (*De Civ. D.* 4.29), drawing on Varro, tells us:

> Sic enim, inquiunt, significatum est Martiam gentem, id est Romanam, nemini locum quem teneret daturam, Romanos quoque terminos propter deum Terminum neminem commoturum, iuventutem etiam Romanam propter deam Iuventatem nemini esse cessuram.
>
> Thus, they say, it was portended that the people of Mars—that is, the Roman people—would hand over to no one any place which they held; and that, on account of Terminus, no one would move the Roman boundaries; and again, on account of the goddess Juventas, that the Roman warrior manhood would surrender to no one.

As the Vedic evidence of the Sadas post also makes plain, Terminus—that is, the Capitoline *terminus*—is itself in its primitive cultic origins inextricably a part of a trifunctional assemblage. It is a member of a set no less trifunctional than the Pre-Capitoline triad itself (Jupiter, Mars, Quirinus), and no less ancient. One might wonder whether the Capitoline *terminus* belongs in a sense to an even more ancient trifunctional structure—a configuration of the archaic Indo-European cult preserved remarkably faithfully in Rome, while the Pre-Capitoline triad is a particular Roman—or early Italic—permutation of Indo-European tripartite theology. Regardless of relative antiquity, when Terminus is seen from the perspective of his cultic, trifunctional origin, it is little wonder that he—the Capitoline instantiation of the unboundary—must remain on the Capitoline as an element of a trifunctional set—what we have called the Minor Capitoline triad—at the seemingly Tarquin-inspired appearance of the temple of Jupiter Optimus Maximus.

5.2.5 Terminus and Mars

Terminus—or the *terminus*—and Mars have a particular closeness. St. Augustine, with Varro as his guide, has told us that in addition to Terminus and Juventas, Mars himself refused to vacate the Capitoline for the construction of the temple of Jupiter Optimus Maximus—a somewhat paradoxical state of affairs given that the raising of that edifice marks the replacement of an ancient Indo-European triad, of which Mars is a member, with a different triadic collection of deities. Mars is invoked along the distal boundary of the Ager Romanus, a place ringed by *termini*, by the Fratres Arvales, priests of the fields, as they hymn their *carmen* (see §4.9.2). Beyond that, we saw his presence recurring at various ritual sites along that ancient sacred boundary—homologous to the far boundary of the Mahāvedi (§§4.10–4.11). He is also notably present at ambarvalic rites celebrated in smaller bounded spaces, as in the lustration rite described by

Cato (§3.3.3). It is the centrality of Mars in such agrarian settings and ritual activities that led to the idea of an "agrarian Mars" (§4.10.1).

5.2.5.1 INDRA AND VIṢṆU To gain an understanding of why Mars is present in the fields and borderlands and why he is invoked in the rites of those places, we must once again look to Vedic India. The *yūpa*—standing on the distal boundary of the great sacred space, marker of the unboundary—is not only a *source* of blessing, fecundity, and wealth—it is also a *means*. The *yūpa* is a thunderbolt, and with it the sacrificer takes possession of the earth and—equally important—he prevents his enemies from having a part therein (*ŚB* 3.7.2.1; see §4.5). The *yūpa* is raised as a *columna mundi* transcending sky, air, and earth, and by that post—a thunderbolt—the sacrificer gains those worlds and prevents his enemies from doing likewise (*ŚB* 3.7.1.14; Eggeling 1995, pt. 2: 171). The post is described as an eight-edged weapon that protects the sacrificer and wards off demonic forces (*AB* 2.1.1–2). The thunderbolt is the weapon of Indra, warrior god, as we saw in our study of Semo Sancus (see especially §4.9.2.6), and Indra is himself associated with the *yūpa* (as in *AV* 4.24.4). We saw also that Indra is conspicuously present in the great sacred space on the Soma-pressing day; the midday pressing belongs almost exclusively to him (§4.8.2).

Of the various by-forms of the *yūpa* which we discussed in §2.6.3, one has particular relevance here, namely the *Indradhvaja*, 'Indra's banner'. It is set up "for the destruction of the king's enemies" and the top of the staff is pointed in the direction of the city of the enemy (see §2.6.3.3). Also conspicuously affiliated with the banner is Viṣṇu, which leads us to the next point.

Indra's affiliation with the *yūpa* itself is chiefly an indirect one. There is another warrior figure with whom the *yūpa* is more closely bound. He is the aforementioned Viṣṇu (see especially §§2.6.1; 2.6.3; 2.7), the three-stepping god who is companion to Indra, assisting him in the fight against the dragon (§§4.9.2.4; 4.9.2.8.1) and at times affiliated with Indra's warrior band, the Maruts (§4.8.2).[7] Indra's particular connection with the *yūpa*

[7]Consider Keith's summary remarks (1998a: 109) on the relationship of the two warrior gods: "Viṣṇu is closely associated with Indra: one hymn is devoted to the pair of gods, and, when Viṣṇu is celebrated by himself, Indra is the only other god who is given a place; when about to perform his supreme feat of slaying Vṛtra, Indra implores Viṣṇu to step out more widely. Through his association with Indra, Viṣṇu becomes a drinker of Soma, and he cooks for Indra 100 buffaloes and a brew of milk. Through his connexion with Indra Viṣṇu also is associated with the Maruts, with whom he shares honour in one hymn."

through Viṣṇu is made plain, for example, in *Śatapatha Brāhmaṇa* 3.7.1.17. The sacrificer touches the *yūpa* immediately after the priest hoists it into position, and he is made to address the post, reciting words from *Rig Veda* 1.22.19 (Eggeling 1995, pt. 2: 171–172, with modification):

> "See the deeds of Viṣṇu, whereby he beheld the sacred ordinances, Indra's allied friend!" For the one who has set up the sacrificial post has hurled the thunderbolt: "See Viṣṇu's conquest!" is what the sacrificer means to say when he says "See the deeds of Viṣṇu, whereby he beheld the sacred ordinances, Indra's allied friend!" Indra, for certain, is the deity of the sacrifice, and the sacrificial post belongs to Viṣṇu; he thereby connects it with Indra; therefore he says, "Indra's allied friend."

Viṣṇu, in taking his three steps, transcends and conquers the spaces of the universe (see Gonda 1993: 55 with references). He extends the spaces for the habitations of human kind. Thus he is praised in *Rig Veda* 7.100.4:

> vi cakrame pṛthivīm eṣa etāṃ kṣetrāya Viṣṇur manuṣe daśasyan
> dhruvāso asya kīrayo janāsa urukṣitiṃ sujanimā cakāra

> This Viṣṇu traversed the earth
>   for a habitable space for humankind, assisting.
> Itinerant people gained a fixed space;
>   the good creator made for them a broad habitation

Indra is at times drawn into Viṣṇu's conquering advance, creating space for humankind. In the Soma ceremony hymn of *Rig Veda* 6.69, for example, Indra and Viṣṇu (denoted by the dvandva *Indrāviṣṇū*) are invoked to come to the Soma feast on their "enemy-conquering horses" (stanza 4); are urged to lead the sacrificers forward on paths free from obstructions (stanza 1); are praised for stepping broadly and thereby increasing the space of the air and making broad the regions of space for humankind (stanza 5). The hymn ends (stanza 8) by addressing the two warrior deities as conquering but unconquered, as having brought about limitless threefold space when they had fought.

It can be no accident that the god to whom belongs the marker of the unboundary, Viṣṇu, is the god who conquers and creates space. In the carrying of fire and Soma from the small sacred space into the Mahāvedi, the rite of Agnīṣomapraṇayana—"pictured as a wide-ranging, conquering progress" (Heesterman 1993: 126; see §4.3.1)—Viṣṇu is addressed with lines from the *Sāma Veda* (5.38). The litany is rehearsed in *Śatapatha Brāhmaṇa* 3.6.3.15 (Eggeling 1995, pt. 2: 159–160, with modification):

> Stride widely, Viṣṇu, make wide room for our abode! Drink the *ghee*, you who are born of *ghee*, and speed the lord of the sacrifice ever onwards!

The Soma-carts that journey from the west into the Mahāvedi, as if setting out on "a pioneering expedition to the unknown east" (Jamison 1996: 125; see §4.3.1)—these Soma-carts belong to Viṣṇu (*ŚB* 3.5.3.15). Before the carts begin their journey, the sacrificer's wife anoints them with butter (*ghee*), and hymns to Viṣṇu are recited (*RV* 1.22.17; *RV* 7.99.3). When the carts are brought to rest at their journey's end in the Mahāvedi, both are propped in position; *Śatapatha Brāhmaṇa* 3.5.3.21–22 describes the act (Eggeling 1995, pt. 2: 133, with modification):

> The Adhvaryu, having gone round along the north side of the carts, props the southern cart, with "Now will I declare the heroic deeds of Viṣṇu, who measured out the regions of the earth; who propped the upper seat, striding three times, the wide-stepping!"
>
> The assistant then props the northern cart, with "Either from the heaven, Viṣṇu, or from the earth, or from the great wide airy region, Viṣṇu, fill both of your hands with wealth and bestow on us from the right and the left."

The Havirdhāna, the shed in which the Soma-carts are parked (§4.3), is likewise sacred to Viṣṇu (*ŚB* 3.5.3.2).

The *yūpa* belongs to wide-striding, space-extending, conquering Viṣṇu. At the other end of the great sacred space—the proximal end—stands the Sadas post, linked with fertility and blessings—like its taller counterpart, the *yūpa*—with its markedly trifunctional affiliations. The shelter beneath which it stands, the Sadas, is proclaimed to belong to Viṣṇu's warrior affiliate, Indra (*ŚB* 3.6.1.1).[8]

5.2.5.2 INVASION AND CONQUEST The questing journey of the sacrificer and priests into the great sacred space of the Mahāvedi, the staking out of that space with altars and huts, and the continued progress toward the column that stands on its distal, eastern border (a boundary which is not) constitute an odyssey in which gods of war play a fundamental role. Most notable in the event is Viṣṇu, the god who transcends, conquers, and expands space. Indra, most renowned of the warrior gods, accompanies him. In our initial discussion of this journey (§4.3.1), we saw that Agni,

[8]The Sadas is said to be Viṣṇu's belly (*ŚB* 3.6.1.1). Viṣṇu is equated with the sacrifice and various artifacts of the Mahāvedi are identified with parts of his body.

the god of fire, also plays an aggressive offensive role, serving as the point man, leading the way, as portrayed in the lines of *Taittirīya Saṃhitā* 1.3.4.c chanted by the priests moving into the Mahāvedi (Keith 1967: 39, with modification):[9]

> May Agni here make room for us;
> May he go before us cleaving the foe;
> Joyously may he conquer our foes;
> May he win spoils in the contest for spoils.

It is unmistakable that worshipful expansion into the Mahāvedi reflects and rehearses an event of invasion and conquest. In this questing journey the gods of war are conspicuously invoked; their presence is essential for gaining the space of expansion and crushing the opposition, mortal or demonic, which will inevitably present itself.

Homologous to the conspicuous presence of the warrior gods Indra and Viṣṇu in the space of the Mahāvedi is the presence of Mars in the space of the Ager Romanus. To phrase the matter somewhat differently: whatever it is that Indra and Viṣṇu are doing within the Mahāvedi, Mars is doing the same within the Ager Romanus. The procession of Vedic priests through the Mahāvedi and the ambarvalic movement of Roman priests through the Ager Romanus are both descended from a common ancestral rite of the questing journey from the small sacred space into the great. The journey is an invasion; the gods of war must be invoked to take the lead, to vanquish the opponent, to secure possession of the invaded space. As warrior Indra and, especially, Viṣṇu, the god who enlarges space, are bound to the Vedic *yūpa*, the marker of the unboundary, source and means of blessing, so Mars is linked to the Roman *terminus* (deified as Terminus). He is present and invoked around the distal rim of the Ager Romanus, at those terminal points of ritual salience. In the *carmen* of the Fratres Arvales he is called on to take up a position on that encircling boundary, to bring in the storming Semones, to drive away the forces of destruction. At the Robigalia he is present to protect against the demonic forces of crop destruction and ensure the blessing of fecundity. Doubtless he was similarly invoked, hymned, and celebrated at numerous other cardinal points at the far edge of the great Roman sacred space.

At some moment in the history of Roman religion, the ambarvalic move-

[9] Compare the sacrificer's prayer to Agni in *Śatapatha Brāhmaṇa* 3.6.3.11–12 (see §4.6) and the tale of Agni escaping from the mouth of Māthava Videgha and racing eastward along the Sarasvatī (*ŚB* 1.4.1.10–19; see §4.3.1).

ments into the Ager Romanus perhaps ceased to be assigned the synchronic interpretation of the conquering journey. Even beyond that moment, as certainly before it, Mars would remain at his old stations on the distal boundary, frozen there in form by a religious unwillingness to modify deeply ancient ancestral rites long removed from the context of migratory society. If he has been forgotten in the journey (and there seems to be no evidence which would compel us to believe that he has been), he is still remembered at the border—boundary between the ordered world of sacrifice and ritual within and the wilderness of disorder without, the place of the *termini* to which he bears an age-old linkage.

In the case of Cato's ambarvalic rites of field lustration, as we saw earlier (§4.6), a theological shift has occurred. The *medium* of the Indo-European sacred space has been transformed into the *object* of Roman ground which is to be made pure: the space which is invaded and conquered to bring blessing and afford possession of the earth has given way to space already possessed and in need of protection and purification in order that it may bring a blessing. An ambarvalic movement is preserved—a procession of the *suovetaurilia* about the space to be purified, the path of which is directed by the chthonic deity Manius; and the warrior god whose presence is crucial for victory likewise remains—Mars is invoked (Cato, *Agr.* 141):

> Ianum Iovemque vino praefamino, sic dicito: "Mars pater, te precor quaesoque uti sies volens propitius mihi domo familiaeque nostrae, quoius re ergo agrum terram fundumque meum suovitaurilia circumagi iussi, uti tu morbos visos invisosque, viduertatem vastitudinemque, calamitates intemperiasque prohibessis defendas averruncesque; utique tu fruges, frumenta, vineta virgultaque grandire beneque evenire siris, pastores pecuaque salva servassis duisque bonam salutem valetudinemque mihi domo familiaeque nostrae; harumce rerum ergo, fundi terrae agrique mei lustrandi lustrique faciendi ergo, sicuti dixi, macte hisce suovitaurilibus lactentibus inmolandis esto; Mars pater, eiusdem rei ergo macte hisce suovitaurilibus lactentibus esto."

> First invoke Janus and Jupiter with wine and recite this: "Mars Pater, I beseech and implore you, that you might be gracious and propitious to me, my house and my household, and on this account I have directed the *suovitaurilia* to be driven around my land, earth and farm; that you might avert, keep away, and ward off sickness, seen and unseen, scarcity and desolation, disaster and extremes of nature; and that you might allow crops, grains, vines and bushes to grow large and to bear well, that you might keep safe herders and herds and give well-being and good health to me, my house and my household. On account of these things, on account

> of purifying my farm, earth and land and performing a lustration, just as I have declared, be honored with these suckling victims, the *suovitaurilia*; Mars Pater, on account of this same thing, be honored with this suckling *suovitaurilia*."

The warrior god protects the sacrificer and the sacred ground of the sacrifice; he brings blessings of fecundity, wealth, and well-being. We are here not far removed theologically, mutatis mutandis, from the realm and actions of Indra and, especially, Viṣṇu within the great sacred space of the Mahāvedi. Only in Cato's prayer, blessings of fertility are sought from Mars rather than his *terminus* (Viṣṇu's *yūpa*)—which undoubtedly stood close by on the boundary of the field being lustrated. In the bounded space of the field with its boundaries held inviolate by the boundary marker (under the law of Numa), the focus has shifted from that marker—descended from the ancient fertility- and wealth-bringing sacred boundary post—to the warrior god inextricably bound to it.

5.2.5.3 AGRARIAN MARS Is Mars an agrarian deity? He is a warrior, descended from a great Indo-European class of warrior gods, representative of that class in the Pre-Capitoline triad. He is not a god of vegetable matter, not a deity who causes the plants to spring from the earth cyclically. His is not the vine; no patron of the budding tree is he. He is, however, quite at home in the fields.

The answer to the above question depends on how we frame the notion of "agrarian deity." If one is to define "agrarian deity" generally as 'a god associated with the fields', or even somewhat more narrowly as something like 'a god facilitating the growth of field crops', then the answer to the question is clearly, "Yes, Mars is an agrarian deity." He is addressed precisely as such a god in Cato's prayer. Mars is not simply the guardian deity who keeps a vigilant watch, allowing agricultural gods to accomplish their tasks unimpeded by threatening powers, as Dumézil claims (following Wissowa and Norden; see §4.10.1). He is implored by the landowner/worshipper to keep away disaster, to give a fecund harvest, to protect herds and family. These are the blessings of the *yūpa*; the warrior god has become the bestower of such advantages secondarily; they belonged originally to his column on the sacred boundary—the unboundary. Mars' integral involvement in the ritual journey into the great sacred space and his close affiliation with the marker of the unboundary—source of blessings and fertility—have led in Rome to a realignment of his role as the rites of the metaphysically unbounded sacred space are appropriated for use in the possessed space of the bounded field.

While this realignment occurs in Mars' personality, there is, nevertheless, a clear indication of a living Roman awareness or memory of Mars' special linkage to the *terminus*. As we saw early in our study (§1.11) and noted again in beginning this chapter, Varro records a tradition, passed on to us by St. Augustine, that not only Terminus and Juventas refused to vacate the Capitoline for the construction of the temple of Jupiter Optimus Maximus, but Mars himself could not be budged. The building of that temple is the visible expression of the radical shift that occurred when the old Indo-European Pre-Capitoline triad—Jupiter, Mars, Quirinus—was supplanted by the new Capitoline triad—Jupiter, Juno, Minerva—under (traditionally identified) Tarquin influence.

Mars is so closely bound to Terminus—the deified Roman "Sadas post" and Capitoline marker of the unboundary who cannot possibly leave the Capitoline—that even though the warrior god has been excised from the principal divine threesome of Rome, he still must remain in the space cleared out for the new triad. There is, we have argued, a continued Indo-European triad that remains in that space—the Minor Capitoline triad consisting of Jupiter, Juventas, and Terminus. The warrior Mars' ongoing presence on the Capitoline in the tradition preserved by Varro seems not only paradoxical but redundant. But Mars does not remain because he continues the warrior presence (Indo-European second function) in that space; he does not remain because he is still a member of a principal triad of deities served by the ancient Flamens; he remains because of his age-old bond to the boundary marker Terminus.

5.3 CONCLUSION

It is widely accepted that sometime in the third millennium BC, Indo-European societies began to abandon the familiar surroundings of their native regions and to spread themselves broadly across Europe and deeply into Asia. These migratory invasions[10] proved to be so successful that Indo-Europeans gained the upper hand throughout Europe, so that virtually all of the native languages of the pre-Indo-European peoples of that continent were annihilated. In the east the momentum generated by these move-

[10]For a different view of Indo-European expansion in antiquity, see Renfrew 1988.

ments would propel Indo-Europeans into the Indian subcontinent and central Asia, all the way to the deserts of China. What fueled this wanderlust? What drove the Indo-Europeans to be so intent on diffusion—and to be so effective in its realization?

The answers to these and related questions are undoubtedly complex and multifaceted. Far-flung population migration is not a phenomenon unique to ancient Indo-Europeans; one has only to look at the peopling of the Americas, for example, to find supporting evidence for this claim. Much of what drives a people to pick up their belongings and move (rapidly or incrementally) to a different place is clearly a function of human need, informed by particular social and cultural attitudes and practices. Broad considerations such as these, however, are far beyond the pale of the present investigation and would likely be readily claimed as the investigatory property of other disciplines.

In the case of the early Indo-Europeans, however, the present comparative study of Roman and Vedic cult and its operation within sacred spaces reveals at least one specific factor which almost certainly played a role in the Indo-European propensity to move and to establish dominance over "the other." Ancient Indo-European pastoralists practiced a religion in which sacred rites were observed within a temporarily demarcated sacred space. For certain more weighty rites, this space was enlarged by adjoining to its eastern border a larger sacred arena, each end of which was marked by the erection of a column. In the celebration of these rites, priests and worshippers advanced from the small space into and through the great space, journeying toward its eastern boundary, the region of the gods, and toward the column—a *columna mundi*—which stood there. That *columna mundi* makes the distal boundary of the great space in actuality no boundary at all, but a conduit for continued expansion. The trek into the great space is thus a metaphysical journey—a metaphor for an unending journey and a limitless acquisition of space. In making that journey, the Indo-European sacrificer gains a promise of land and the material blessings which it brings to the pastoralist; more than that, the sacrificer, by way of the *columna mundi*—the pole of blessing—gains access to the gods themselves and to their world—to the realm of divine space. This questing journey, like all journeys, is fraught with danger. The way is led by warrior gods who are invoked to vanquish any and all opposing powers, to remove obstructions that lie in the path of the journeying priests and worshippers, to lead them to spaces of blessing. The *columna mundi* which opens the way to those blessings is in the very possession of the warrior god(s).

The theology of the victorious journey though space, led by conquering warrior gods, translates into a divine imperative to advance across the spaces of the earth. It is the Biblical injunction of "be fruitful and multiply" raised to the nth power. Possessed of such a theology cum ideology and compelled by it, little wonder it is that early Indo-European peoples so doggedly pursued and achieved acquisition of the spaces of Europe and many of those of Asia.

Postscript

As promised in the preface, the discussions, analyses, and theories presented in the preceding pages mark only a beginning. There is much that remains to be done given the ideas developed herein. Three topics for study by application and further development of these ideas come readily to mind. First and foremost, an examination of the rites of the Umbrian city of Iguvium, preserved in the bronze tablets of the Frater Atiieřiur, the Atiedian Brothers, needs to be undertaken. The archaic Italic rites of this priesthood are celebrated as a journey through the spaces of the city of Iguvium. Second is the Roman college of priests called the Fetiales, who traversed space to a boundary in order to declare war for Rome, who conducted their rites with a sacred stone kept in the temple of Jupiter Feretrius, who tossed a spear across a column (Columna Bellica) standing near the temple of Bellona on the field of Mars (a later rite performed in lieu of throwing a spear across the boundary). Third, the Amburbium, lustration of the Roman city, about which little information has survived. There are probably others.

The author thanks his readers for their patience.

LIBRARY, UNIVERSITY OF CHESTER

ABBREVIATIONS

LATIN AND GREEK

Aeschylus,	
Eum.	*Eumenides*
Apollodorus	
Bibl.	*Bibliotheca*
Apollonius Rhodius	
Argon.	*Argonautica*
Apuleius	
Met.	*Metamorphoses*
Arnobius	
Adv. Nat.	*Adversus Nationes*
St. Augustine	
De Civ. D.	*De Civitate Dei*
Augustus	
RG	*Res Gestae*
Aulus Gellius	
NA	*Noctes Atticae*
Aurelius Victor	
Orig. Gent. Rom.	*Origo Gentis Romanae*
Ausonius	
Technop.	*Technopaegnion*
Callimachus	
Hymn 5	*Hymn to Athena*
Cato	
Agr.	*De Agricultura*
Cicero	
Acad.	*Academica*
Cat.	*In Catilinam*
Div.	*De Divinatione*
Nat. D.	*De Natura Deorum*
Sen.	*De Senectute*
Clement of Alexandria	
Strom.	*Stromateis*

Columella	
Rust.	*Rei Rusticae*
Diodorus Siculus	*Bibliotheca*
Dionysius of Halicarnassus	
Ant. Rom.	*Antiquitates Romanae*
Eusebius	
Hist. Eccl.	*Historia Ecclesiastica*
Festus	
M (= Lindsay 1913)	*De Verborum Significatu*
Florus	
Epit.	*Epitome*
Frontinus	
De Con. Agr.	*De Controversiis Agrorum*
The Gromatici	
Agrim.	*Corpus Agrimensorum (Blume, Lachmann, and Rudorff)*
Hesiod	
Theog.	*Theogonia*
Homer	
Od.	*Odyssey*
Horace	
Epist.	*Epistulae*
Isodorus Hispalensis	
Etym.	*Origines sive Etymologiae*
Lactantius	
Div. Inst.	*Divinae Institutiones*
Livy	*Ab urbe condita libri*
Lydus	
Mens.	*De Mensibus*
Lucan	*De Bello Civili*
Nonius	*De Compendiosa Doctrina*
Macrobius	
Sat.	*Saturnalia*
Ovid	
Am.	*Amores*
Fast.	*Fasti*
Met.	*Metamorphoses*
Pont.	*Epistulae ex Ponto*
Tr.	*Tristia*

Plautus	
Asin.	*Asinaria*
Pliny (the Elder)	
HN	*Historia Naturalis*
Plutarch	
Caes.	*Life of Caesar*
Cor.	*Life of Coriolanus*
De Fort. Rom.	*De Fortuna Romanorum*
Numa	*Life of Numa*
Pub.	*Life of Publocola*
Quaest. Rom.	*Quaestiones Romanae*
Rom.	*Life of Romulus*
Propertius	*Elegies*
Prudentius	
C. Symm.	*Contra Symmachum*
Quintilian	
Inst.	*Institutio Oratoria*
Servius	
Aen.	*Commentary on Virgil's Aeneid*
SHA	*Scriptores Historiae Augustae*
Aurel.	*Aurelian*
Seneca	
Q. Nat.	*Quaestiones Naturales*
Statius	
Silv.	*Silvae*
Suetonius	
Aug.	*Divus Augustus*
Iul.	*Divus Iulus*
Tacitus	
Ann.	*Annales*
Hist.	*Historiae*
Tertullian	
Apol.	*Apologeticus*
De Spect.	*De Spectaculis*
Varro	
Ling.	*De Lingua Latina*
Rust.	*De Re Rustica*
Sat. Men.	*Saturae Menippeae*
Valerius Maximus	*Facta et Dicta Memorabilia*

Virgil	
Aen.	*Aeneid*
Ecl.	*Eclogues*
Georg.	*Georgics*
Vitruvius	*De Architectura*

SANSKRIT

AB	*Aitareya Brāhmaṇa*
AGS	*Āśvalāyana Gṛhya Sūtra*
ĀpGS	*Āpastambha Gṛhya Sūtra*
ĀpŚS	*Āpastambha Śrauta Sūtra*
AV	*Atharva Veda*
BŚS	*Baudhāyana Śrauta Sūtra*
GS	*Gṛhya Sūtra*
HirGS	*Hiranyakeśin Gṛhya Sūtra*
KB	*Kauṣītaki Brāhmaṇa*
KŚS	*Kātyāyana Śrauta Sūtra*
MBh	*Mahābhārata*
MS	*Maitrāyaṇī Saṃhitā*
RV	*Rig Veda*
PB	*Pañcaviṃśa Brāhmaṇa*
ŚB	*Śatapatha Brāhmaṇa*
ŚŚS	*Śāṅkhāyana Śrauta Sūtra*
TB	*Taittirīya Brāhmaṇa*
TS	*Taittirīya Saṃhitā*
YV	*Yajur Veda*
VarāhBS	*Bṛhata Saṃhitā of Varāhamihira*
ViPur	*Viṣṇu Purāna*
VS	*Vājasaneyi Saṃhitā*

MODERN

ANRW	*Aufstieg und Niedergang der römischen Welt. 1972–.*
ARR	Dumézil 1996. *Archaic Roman Religion*
CFA	Scheid 1998. *Commentarii fratrum Arvalum qui supersunt*
CIL	*Corpus Inscriptionum Latinarum. 1863–.*
DA	Daremberg, et al. 1877–1919. *Dictionnaire des antiquités grecques et romaines*
DELL	Ernout and Meillet 1959. *Dictionnaire étymologique de la langue latine*
ILS	Dessau 1892–1916. *Inscriptiones Latinae selectae*
LIV	Rix 2001. *Lexicon der indogermanischen Verben*
LSJG	Liddell, Scott, and Jones 1996. *Greek-English Lexicon*
LTUR	Steinby 1993–1999. *Lexicon Topographicum Urbis Romae*

ME	Dumézil 1995. *Mythe et épopée*
OLD	Glare 1982. *Oxford Latin Dictionary*
RE	Pauly, Wissowa, and Kroll 1893–. *Real-Encyclopädie der klassichen Altertumswissenschaft*
BNP	Beard, North, and Price 1998. *Religions of Rome*
WP	Walde-Pokorny 1973. *Vergleichendes Wörterbuch der indogermanischen Sprachen*

BIBLIOGRAPHY

Alföldi, A. 1965. *Early Rome and the Latins.* Ann Arbor: University of Michigan Press.

Allen, N. 2003. "The Indra-Tullus Comparison." In *Indo-European Language and Culture: Essays in Memory of Edgar C. Polomé.* Pt. 1. Ed. B. Drinka and J. Salmons. *General Linguistics* 40: 148–171.

——. 1987. "The Ideology of the Indo-Europeans: Dumézil's Theory and the Idea of a Fourth Function." *International Journal of Moral and Social Studies* 2: 23–39.

Auboyer, J. 1949. *Le trône et son symbolisme dans l'Inde ancienne.* Paris: Presses Universitaires de France.

Bayet, J. 1955. "Un procédé virgilien; la description synthétique dans les «Géorgiques»." In *Studi in onore di Gino Funaioli,* 9–18. Rome: Signorelli.

——. 1926. *Les origines de l'Hercule romain.* Rome: École Française.

Beard, M. 1985. "Writing and Ritual: A Study of Diversity and Expansion in the Arval Acta." *Papers of the British School at Rome* 13: 114–162.

Beard, M., J. North, and S. Price. 1998. *Religions of Rome.* 2 vols. Cambridge: Cambridge University Press.

Beloch, J. 1880. *Der Italische Bund unter Roms Hegemonie.* Leipzig: Teubner.

Benveniste, E. 1969. *Le vocabulaire des institutions indo-européennes.* 2 vols. Paris: Minuit.

——. 1960. "Profanus et profanare." In *Hommages à G. Dumézil* (*Collection Latomus* 45), 46–53.

——. 1945a. "Symbolisme social dans les cultes gréco-italiques." *Revue de l'Histoire des Religions* 129: 5–16.

——. 1945b. "La doctrine médicale des Indo-Européens." *Revue de l'Histoire des Religions* 130: 5–12.

——. 1937. "Expression indo-européenne de l'éternité. *Bulletin de la Société de Linguistique de Paris* 38: 103–112.

——. 1932. "Les classes sociales dans la tradition avestique." *Journal Asiatique* 221: 117–134.

Benveniste, E., and L. Renou. 1934. *Vṛtra et Vṛθragna: Etude de mythologie indo-iranienne.* Cahiers de la Société Asiatique 3. Paris: Imprimerie Nationale.

Bernard, C. 1957. *An Introduction to the Study of Experimental Medicine.* Trans. H. Green. New York: Dover.

Bhat, R. 1993–1995. *Varāhamihira's Bṛhat Saṃitā.* 2 vols. Repr. Delhi: Motilal Banarsidass.

Biardeau, M. 1991a. "The Yūpa." In Bonnefoy and Doniger 1991: 811–813.

——. 1991b. "Devi." In Bonnefoy and Doniger 1991: 869–872.

Bietti Sestieri, A., and A. De Santis. 2000. *The Protohistory of the Latin Peoples*. Trans. E. De Sena. Rome: Electa.

Birt, T. 1937. "Dea Dia." In Roscher et al. 1937, 964–975.

Bloomfield, M. 1896. "Contributions to the Interpretation of the Veda." *American Journal of Philology* 17: 399–437.

Blume, F., K. Lachmann, and A. Rudorff. 1967. *Die Schriften der Römischen Feldmesser*. Hildesheim: Georg Olms.

Bonghi Jovino, M. 2000a. "Il complesso 'sacro-istituzionale.'" In Carandini and Cappelli 2000: 265–267.

——. 2000b. "Il deposito votivo." In Carandini and Cappelli 2000, 269–270.

Bonnefoy Y., and W. Doniger, eds. 1991. *Mythologies*. 2 vols. Chicago: University of Chicago Press.

Bonnet, J. 1981. Introd. to *Georges Dumézil: Cahiers pour un temps*. Paris: Centre Georges Pompidou / Pandora.

Borgeaud, P. 1987. "Du mythe à l'idéologie: la tête du Capitole." *Mus Helv* 44: 86–100.

Boyce, M. 1996. *A History of Zoroastrianism*. Vol. 1. Leiden: E. J. Brill.

Boyle, A., and R. Woodard. 2004. *Ovid: Fasti*. Revised ed. London: Penguin.

Bréal, M. 1877. *Mélanges de mythologie et de linguistique*. Paris: Hachette.

Brouwer, H. 1989. *Bona Dea*. Leiden: E. J. Brill.

Burkert, W. 1992. *The Orientalizing Revolution*. Cambridge, Mass.: Harvard University Press.

Caland, W. 1982. *Pañcaviṃśa Brāhmaṇa*. 2nd ed. Dehli: Sri Satguru Publications.

——. 1980. *Śāṅkhāyana-Śrautasūtra*. Repr. Dehli: Motilal Banarsidass.

Caland, W., and V. Henry. 1906–1907. *L'Agniṣṭoma*. 2 vols. Paris: La Société Asiatique.

Campbell, B. 2000. *The Writings of the Roman Land Surveyors*. London: Society for the Promotion of Roman Studies.

Capdeville, G. 1995. *Volcanus*. Rome: École Française.

Carandini, A., and R. Cappelli, eds. 2000. *Roma: Romolo, Remo e la fondazione della città*. Milan: Electa.

Charachidzé, G. 1991. "The Religion and Myths of the Ossets." In Bonnefoy and Doniger 1991: 316–319.

Chirassi, I. 1968. "Dea Dia e i fratres arvales." *Studi e materiali di storia delle religioni* 39: 191–291.

Clackson, J. 2004. "Latin." In Woodard 2004: 789–811.

Coarelli, F. 1992. *Il Foro Romano, 1: Periodo arcaico*. 3rd ed. Rome: Quaesar.

Cornell, T. 1995. *The Beginnings of Rome: Italy and Rome from the Bronze Age to the Punic Wars* (c. 1000–164 BC). London: Routledge.

Daremberg, C., et al. 1877–1919. *Dictionnaire des antiquités grecques et romaines*. Paris: Hachette.

Davies, J. 1953. *The Origin and Development of Early Christian Church Architecture*. New York: Philosophical Society.

De Rossi, G. 1877. *Roma Sotterranea cristiana*. Rome: Cromo-lithografia pontificia.

——. 1858. "Vicendi degli atti de' fratelli arvali ed un nuovo frammento di essi." *Annali del Istituto di Corrispondenza Archeologica* 30: 54–79.

De Ruggiero, E., et al. 1885–. *Dizionario epigrafico di antichità romane*. Rome: L. Pasqualucci.
Desjardins. 1854. *De tabulis alimentarii disputationem historicam facultati litterarum Parisiensi proponebat*. Paris: A. Durand.
Doniger O'Flaherty, W. 1981. *The Rig Veda*. London: Penguin.
Dumézil, G. 1999. *The Riddle of Nostradamus: A Critical Dialogue*. Trans. B. Wing. Foreword by G. Nagy. Baltimore: Johns Hopkins University Press.
———. 1996. *Archaic Roman Religion*. Trans. P. Krapp. Repr. Baltimore: Johns Hopkins University Press.
———. 1995. *Mythe et épopée*. 3 vols. Corrected ed. Paris: Gallimard.
———. 1992. *Mythes et dieux des Indo-Européens*. With editorial contributions by H. Coutau-Bégarie. Paris: Flammarion.
———. 1988. *Mitra-Varuṇa*. Trans. by D. Coltman. Repr. New York: Zone Books.
———. 1987. *Entretiens avec Didier Eribon*. Paris: Gallimard.
———. 1986. *Les dieux souverains des Indo-Européens*. 3rd, corrected ed. Paris: Gallimard.
———. 1985. *L'oubli de l'homme et l'honneur des dieux et autres essais: vingt-cinq esquisses de mythologie*. Paris: Gallimard.
———. 1983. *La courtisane et les seigneurs colores et autres essais: vingt-cinq esquisses de mythologie*. Paris: Gallimard.
———. 1982. *Apollon sonore et autres essais: vingt-cinq esquisses de mythologie*. Paris: Gallimard.
———. 1979. *Mariages indo-européens*. Paris: Payot.
———. 1978. *Romans de Scythie et d'alentour*. Paris: Payot.
———. 1975. *Fêtes romaines d'été et d'automne*. Paris: Gallimard.
———. 1973a. *Gods of the Ancient Northmen*. Berkeley and Los Angeles: University of California Press.
———. 1973b. *The Destiny of a King*. Trans. A. Hiltebeitel. Chicago: University of Chicago Press.
———. 1970. *The Destiny of the Warrior*. Trans. A. Hiltebeitel. Chicago: University of Chicago Press.
———. 1969. *Idées romaines*. Paris: Gallimard.
———. 1958. *L'Idéologie tripartie des Indo-Européens*. Brussels: Latomus.
———. 1954. *Rituels indo-européens à Rome*. Paris: Klincksieck.
———. 1949. *L'Héritage indo-européen à Rome*. Paris: Gallimard.
———. 1948. *Jupiter Mars Quirinus IV: Explication de textes indiens et latins*. Paris: Presses Universitaires de France.
———. 1947. *Tarpeia*. Paris: Gallimard.
———. 1944. *Naissance de Rome*. Paris: Gallimard.
———. 1942. *Horace et les Curiaces*. Paris: Gallimard.
———. 1941–1948. *Jupiter Mars Quirinus*. 4 volumes. Paris: Gallimard (vols. I-III), Presses Universitaires de France (vol. IV).
———. 1930a. *Légendes sur les Nartes, suivies de cinq notes mythologiques*. Paris: Honoré Champion.
———. 1930b. "La préhistoire indo-iranienne des castes." *Journal Asiatique* 216: 109–130.

Dumont, P.-E. 1956. "A note on *Taittirīya Brāhmaṇa* 3.2.8.9–12." *Journal of the American Oriental Society* 76: 187–188.

Edwards, C. 1996. *Writing Rome*. Cambridge: Cambridge University Press.

Eggeling, J. 1995. *The Śatapatha Brāhmaṇa*. 5 pts. Sacred Books of the East, vols. 12, 26, 41, 43, 44. Ed. M. Müller. Repr. Delhi: Low Price Publications.

Eitrem, S. 1910. "Hermes und die Toten." *Forhandlinger Videnskabs Selskabs in Christiania*, 37 ff.

Ernout, A., and A. Meillet. 1959. *Dictionnaire étymologique de la langue latine*. 4th ed. Paris: Klincksieck.

Filliozat, J. 1961. "Les images de Śiva dans l'Inde du sud." Pt. *Arts asiatiques* 8, fasc. 1: 43–56.

Frazer, J. 1989. *Ovid V: Fasti*. Second ed. Rev. G. Goold. Cambridge, Mass.: Harvard University Press.

——. 1929. *The Fasti of Ovid*. 5 vols. London: Macmillan and Company.

Gargola, D. 1995. *Lands, Laws and Gods*. Chapel Hill: University of North Carolina Press.

Gatti, G. 1895. "Arvales fratres." In De Ruggiero, et al. 1885–, vol. 1: 682–710.

Gjerstadt, E. 1967. "Discussions Concerning Early Rome 3." *Historia* 16: 257–278.

Glare, P., ed. 1982. *Oxford Latin Dictionary*. Oxford: Oxford University Press.

Gonda, J. 1996. *Viṣṇuism and Śivaism*. Repr. New Delhi: Munshiram Manoharlal.

——. 1993. *Aspects of Early Viṣṇuism*. Repr. Delhi: Motilal Banarsidass.

——. 1956. "Ancient Indian Kinship from the Religious Point of View." *Numen* 3: 122–159.

Goold, G., ed. 1999. *Propertius: Elegies*. Rev. ed. Cambridge, Mass.: Harvard University Press.

Griffith, R. 1990. *Yajurveda Saṃhitā*. Ed. S. Pratap. Delhi: Nag.

Grimal, P. 1949. "La Ve églogue et le culte de César." In *Mélanges Ch. Picard*. Vol. 1: 412–413. Paris: Presses Universitaires de France.

Harrak, A. 1997. "Mitanni." In Meyers 1997, vol. 4: 36–38.

Haug, M. 1922. *The Aitareya Brahmanam of the Rig Veda*. Repr. Bahadurganj, Allahbad: Subhindra Nath Vasu.

Heesterman, J. 1993. *The Broken World of Sacrifice*. Chicago: University of Chicago Press.

Henzen, W. 1874. *Acta Fratrum Arvalium quae supersunt*. Berlin: Georgii Reimeri.

Hirschfeld, O. 1869. "C. r. de henzen 1868." In *Göttingische gelehrte Anzeiger*, 1495–1517.

Hoenigswald, H., R. Woodard and J. Clackson. "Indo-European." In Woodard 2004: 534–550.

Holloway, R. 1994. *The Archaeology of Early Rome and Latium*. London: Routledge.

Hooper, W., and H. Ash. 1993. *Cato on Agriculture, Varro on Agriculture*. Repr. Loeb Classical Library. Cambridge, Mass.: Harvard University Press.

Hornblower, S., and A. Spawforth, eds. 1996. *The Oxford Classical Dictionary*. 3rd ed. Oxford: Oxford University Press.

Horsfall, N. 1982. "Prose and Mime." In *The Cambridge History of Classical Literature*, vol. 2.2: 112–120.

Hunziker. 1877–1919a. "Cerialia." In *DA*.
——. 1877–1919b. "Ambarvale sacrum." In *DA*.
Huschke, P. 1869. *Das alte römische Jahr und seine Tage: Eine chronologisch-rechtsgeschichtliche Untersuchung*. Breslau: F. Hirt.
Jamison, S. 1996. *Sacrificed Wife / Sacrificer's Wife*. Oxford: Oxford University Press.
Jordan, H. 1879. *Kritische Beiträge zur Geschichte der lateinischen Sprache*. Berlin: Weidmann.
Keith, A. 1998a. *The Religion and Philosophy of the Veda and Upanishads*. Repr. Delhi: Motilal Banarsidass.
——. 1998b. *Rigveda Brahmanas*. Repr. Delhi: Motilal Banarsidass.
——. 1967. *The Veda of the Black Yajus School entitled Taittiriya Sanhita*. 2 vols. Repr. Delhi: Motilal Banarsidass.
Kilgour, A. 1938. "The Ambarvalia and the Sacrificium Deae Diae." *Mnemosyne* 6: 225–240.
Kramrisch, S. 1947. "The Banner of Indra." In *Art and Thought (in Honor of Dr. A. K. Coomaraswamy)*, ed. K. Iyer, 197–201. London: Luzac and Company Ltd.
Krappe, A. 1942. "The Sovereignty of Erin." *American Journal of Philology* 63: 444–454.
Krause, M. 1931. "Hostia." In *RA*, supp. vol. 5: 236–282.
Kuhn, A. 1848. "Zur Mythologie." *Zeitschrift für Deutsches Alterthum* 2: 117–134.
Lasserre, F. 1967. *Strabon*. Vol. 3. Paris: Belles Lettres.
Latte, K. 1960. *Römische Religionsgeschichte* (Handbuch der Altertumswissenschaft, vol. 4). Munich: C. H. Beck.
Le Bonniec, H. 1958. *Le culte de Cérès à Rome*. Paris: Klincksieck.
Leumann, M. 1963. *Lateinische Laut- und Formen-Lehre*. 2nd ed. Munich: C. H. Beck.
Liddell, H., and R. Scott. 1996. *Greek-English Lexicon*. Revised by H. Jones. With a revised supplement by P. Glare. Oxford: Oxford University Press.
Littleton, S. 1982. *The New Comparative Mythology*. 3rd ed. Los Angeles and Berkeley: University of California Press.
Loraux, N., G. Nagy, and L. Slatkin. 2001. *Antiquities*. New York: The New Press.
Lugli, G. 1966. "I confini del pomerio suburbano di Roma primitiva." In *Mélanges J. Carcopino*, 641–650. Paris: Hachette.
MacKillop, J. 1998. *Dictionary of Celtic Mythology*. Oxford: Oxford University Press.
Malamoud, C. 1991. "Soma as Sacrificial Substance and Divine Figure in the Vedic Mythology of Exchange." In Bonnefoy and Doniger 1991: 803–805.
——. 1971. "The Work of Emile Benveniste: A Linguistic Analysis of Indo-European Institutions." In Loraux, Nagy, and Slatkin 2001: 428–438.
Mallory, J. 1989. *In Search of the Indo-Europeans*. London: Thames and Hudson.
Mallory, J., and D. Adams. 1997. *Encyclopedia of Indo-European Culture*. London and Chicago: Fitzroy Dearborn.
Marquardt, J. 1878. *Römische Staatsverwaltung: Die Kultusaltertümer*. Leipzig: Sittirzel.
Marshall, F. 1938. "Private Antiquities." In Sandys 1938.
Meier-Brügger, M. 2000. *Indogermanische Sprachwissenschaft*. Berlin: Walter de Gruyter.

Meyers, E. 1997. *The Oxford Encyclopedia of Archaeology in the Near East*. 5 vols. Oxford: Oxford University Press.

Mommsen, T. 1859. *Die römische Chronologie bis auf Caesar*. Berlin: Weidmann.

Moss, H. 1935. *The Birth of the Middle Ages*. Oxford: Oxford University Press.

Nagle, B. 1995. *Ovid's Fasti: Roman Holidays*. Bloomington: Indiana University Press.

Nicolet, C. 1991. *Space, Geography and Politics in the Early Roman Empire*. Trans. H. Leclerc. Ann Arbor: University of Michigan Press.

Norden, E. 1939. *Aus altrömischen Priesterbüchern*. Lund: C. W. K. Gleerup.

Oldenberg, H. 1917. *Die Religion des Veda*. 2nd ed. Stuttgart: J. G. Cotta.

——. 1875. *De sacris fratrum arvalium quaestiones*. Dissertation. Berlin.

Owst, G. 1933. *Literature and Pulpit in Medieval England*. Cambridge: Cambridge University Press.

Pais, E. 1913. *Storia critica di Roma durante i primi cinque secoli*. Vol. 1, pt. 2. Rome: E. Loescher.

Palmer, R. 1974. *Roman Religion and Roman Empire*. Philadelphia: University of Pennsylvania Press.

Pasoli, E. 1950. *Acta Fratrum Arvalium quae post annum MDCCCLXXIV reperta sunt*. Bologna: Cesar Zuffi.

Pauly, A., G. Wissowa, and W. Kroll. 1893–. *Real-Encyclopädie der klassichen Altertumswissenschaft*. Stuttgart: J. B. Metzler.

Peter, R. 1937. "Hercules." In Roscher 1937, vol. 1: 2135–2298.

Platner, S., and T. Ashby. 1929. *A Topographical Dictionary of Ancient Rome*. Oxford: Oxford University Press.

Poultney, J. 1959. *The Bronze Tables of Iguvium*. Baltimore: APA / Oxford: Blackwell.

Preller, L. 1858. *Römische Mythologie*. Berlin: Weidmann.

Puhvel, J. 1987. *Comparative Mythology*. Baltimore: Johns Hopkins University Press.

Radke, G. 1972. "Acca Larentia und die fratres arvales. Ein Stück römisch-sabinischer Frühgeschichte." *ANRW* 1.2: 421–441.

Ramat, A., and P. Ramat, eds. 1998. *The Indo-European Languages*. London: Routledge.

Ranade, H. 1978. *Kātyāyana Śrauta Sūtra: Rules for the Vedic Sacrifices*. Pune: Ranade and Ranade.

Rees, A., and B. Rees. 1989. *Celtic Heritage*. London: Thames and Hudson.

Reichardt, K. 1998. *Linguistic Structures of Hittite and Luvian Curse Formulae*. Dissertation. University of North Carolina at Chapel Hill.

Renfrew, C. 1988. *Archaeology and Language*. Cambridge: Cambridge University Press.

Renou, L. 1957. *Vedic India*. Trans. P. Spratt. Calcutta: Susil Gupta.

Richardson, L. 1992. *A New Topographical Dictionary of Ancient Rome*. Baltimore: Johns Hopkins University Press.

Ringe, D. 2004. "Reconstructed Ancient Languages." In Woodard 2004: 1112–1129.

Risch, E. 1979. "Zur altlateinischen Gebetssprache." *Incontri Linguistici* 5.43–53.

Rix, H. 2004. "Etruscan." In Woodard 2004: 943–966.

——. 2001. *Lexicon der indogermanischen Verben*. Wiesbaden: Dr. Ludwig Reichert.

Roscher, W., et al. 1937. *Ausführliches Lexicon der griechischen und römischen Mythologie*. Leipzig: Teubner.

Rosenzweig, I. 1937. *Ritual and Cults of Pre-Roman Iguvium.* London: Christophers.
Sandys, J. 1938. *A Companion to Latin Studies,* 3rd ed. Cambridge: Cambridge University Press.
Scheid, J. 2003. *An Introduction to Roman Religion.* Trans. J. Lloyd. Bloomington and Indianapolis: Indiana University Press.
———. 1998. *Commentarii fratrum Arvalum qui supersunt.* Rome: École Française.
———. 1990. *Romulus et ses frères.* Rome: École Française.
Schilling, R. 1991. "The Arval Brethren." In Bonnefoy and Doniger 1991: 603–605.
———. 1979. "Dea Dia dans la liturgie des frères Arvales." In *Rites, cultes, dieux de Rome,* 366–370. Paris: Klincksieck.
———. 1970. "La liturgie des Frères Arvales." *Annuaire de l'École des Hautes Études,* V[e] sect. 77: 256–258.
Scholz, U. 1970. *Studien zum altitalischen und römischen Marskult und Marsmythos.* Heidelberg: Carl Winter.
Schulze, W. 1904. *Zur Geschichte lateinischer Eigennamen.* Berlin: Weidmann.
Schwegler, A. 1856. *Römische Geschichte im Zeitalter des Kampfs der Stände.* Vol. 1. Tübingen: H. Laupp.
Scullard, H. 1981. *Festivals and Ceremonies of the Roman Republic.* London: Thames and Hudson.
Senner, W., ed. 1989. *The Origins of Writing.* Lincoln: University of Nebraska Press.
Spaeth, B. 1996. *The Roman Goddess Ceres.* Austin: University of Texas Press.
Steinby, M., ed. 1993–1999. *Lexicon Topographicum Urbis Romae.* 5 Vols. Rome: Edizioni Quasar.
Szemerényi, O. 1996. *Introduction to Indo-European Linguistics.* Oxford: Oxford University Press.
Tabeling, E. 1975. *Mater Larum.* Repr. New York: Arno Press.
Taylor, L. 1925. "The Mother of the Lares." *American Journal of Archaeology* 29: 299–313.
Thulin, C. 1968. *Die etruskische Disciplin.* 3 vols. Repr. Darmstadt: Wissenschaftliche Buchgesellschaft.
Turcan, R. 2001. *The Gods of Ancient Rome.* New York: Routledge.
Untermann, J. 2000. *Wörterbuch des Oskisch-Umbrischen.* Heidelberg: Carl Winter.
Usener, H. 1911. *Religionsgeschichtliche Untersuchungen.* Vol. 1. Bonn: F. Cohen.
van Buitenen, J. 1978. *The Mahābhārata.* Vol. 3. Chicago: University of Chicago Press.
van Nooten, B., and G. Holland. 1994. *Rig Veda.* Cambridge, Mass.: Harvard University Press.
Vian, F. 1960. "La triade des rois d'Orchomène." In *Hommages à G. Dumézil* (*Collection Latamus* 45), 216–224.
Wackernagel, J. 1923–24. "Dies ater." *Archiv für Religionswissenschaft* 22: 215–216.
Wagenvoort, H. 1956. *Studies in Roman Literature, Culture and Religion.* Leiden: E. J. Brill.
Walde, A., and J. Pokorny. 1973. *Vergleichendes Wörterbuch der indogermanischen Sprachen.* Repr. Berlin: Walter de Gruyter.
Wallace, R. 1989. "The Origins and Development of the Latin Alphabet." In Senner 1989: 121–135.

Warde Fowler, W. 1911. *The Religious Experience of the Roman People.* London: Macmillan.

——. 1899. *The Roman Festivals of the Period of the Republic.* London: Macmillan.

Wasson, G. 1972. *Soma and the Fly-Agaric.* Cambridge, Mass.: Botanical Museum of Harvard University.

——. 1971. *Soma, Divine Mushroom of Immortality.* New York: Harcourt Brace Jovanovich.

Watkins, C. 2004. "Hittite." In Woodard 2004: 551–575.

——. 2000. *The American Heritage Dictionary of Indo-European Roots.* 2nd ed. Boston: Houghton Mifflin.

——. 1998. "Proto-Indo-European: Comparison and Reconstruction." In Ramat and Ramat 1998: 25–73.

——. 1995a. *How to Kill a Dragon: Aspects of Indo-European Poetics.* Oxford: Oxford University Press.

——. 1995b. "Greece in Italy outside Rome." *Harvard Studies in Classical Philology* 97: 35–50.

Whitney, W., and C. Lanman. 1996. *Atharva Veda Samhita.* 2 vols. Repr. Delhi: Motilal Banarsidass.

Wissowa, G. 1971. *Religion und Kultus der Römer.* Repr. of 2nd ed. Münich: C. H. Beck.

——. 1917. "Zum Ritual der Arvalbrüder." *Hermes* 52: 321–347.

——. 1904. "Echte und falsche Sondergötter in der römischen Religion." In *Gesammelte Abhandlungen zur römischen Religions- und Stadtgeschichte,* 304–326. Munich: C. H. Beck.

Woodard, R., ed. 2004. *The Cambridge Encyclopedia of the World's Ancient Languages.* Cambridge: Cambridge University Press.

——. 2002. "The Disruption of Time in Myth and Epic." *Arethusa* 35: 83–98.

INDEX

TRADITIONS

Baby and Child Heroes in Ancient Greece
Corrine Ondine Pache

Assyrian and Babylonian Medicine:
Diagnostic Texts
Translated and with commentary by
Jo Ann Scurlock and Burton R. Anderson

Homer's Text and Language
Gregory Nagy

ROGER WOODARD is Andrew V. V. Raymond Professor of the Classics and Professor of Linguistics at The University of Buffalo (The State University of New York).

The University of Illinois Press
is a founding member of the
Association of American University Presses.

Composed in 10/12.5 Gentium
with ITC Stone Sans display
by Christopher Dadian
Manufactured by Thomson-Shore, Inc.

UNIVERSITY OF ILLINOIS PRESS
1325 South Oak Street Champaign, IL 61820-6903
www.press.uillinois.edu